Pro Android C++
with

Onur Cinar

Apress®

Pro Android C++ with the NDK

ISBN-13 (pbk): 978-1-4302-4827-9

ISBN-13 (electronic): 978-1-4302-4828-6

President and Publisher: Paul Manning
Lead Editor: Steve Anglin
Technical Reviewer: Grant Allen
Editorial Board: Steve Anglin, Mark Beckner, Ewan Buckingham, Gary Cornell, Louise Corrigan, Morgan Ertel, Jonathan Gennick, Jonathan Hassell, Robert Hutchinson, Michelle Lowman, James Markham, Matthew Moodie, Jeff Olson, Jeffrey Pepper, Douglas Pundick, Ben Renow-Clarke, Dominic Shakeshaft, Gwenan Spearing, Matt Wade, Tom Welsh
Coordinating Editor: Brigid Duffy
Copy Editor: Mary Behr
Compositor: SPi Global
Indexer: SPi Global
Artist: SPi Global
Cover Designer: Anna Ishchenko

Distributed to the book trade worldwide by Springer Science+Business Media New York, 233 Spring Street, 6th Floor, New York, NY 10013. Phone 1-800-SPRINGER, fax (201) 348-4505, e-mail orders-ny@springer-sbm.com, or visit www.springeronline.com. Apress Media, LLC is a California LLC and the sole member (owner) is Springer Science + Business Media Finance Inc (SSBM Finance Inc). SSBM Finance Inc is a Delaware corporation.

For information on translations, please e-mail rights@apress.com, or visit www.apress.com.

Apress and friends of ED books may be purchased in bulk for academic, corporate, or promotional use. eBook versions and licenses are also available for most titles. For more information, reference our Special Bulk Sales–eBook Licensing web page at www.apress.com/bulk-sales.

Any source code or other supplementary materials referenced by the author in this text is available to readers at www.apress.com. For detailed information about how to locate your book's source code, go to www.apress.com/source-code/.

Dedicated to my wife, Sema.

I could not have done this without you.

—Onur Cinar

Contents at a Glance

Contents

About the Author

Onur Cinar has over 17 years of experience in design, development, and management of large scale complex software projects, primarily in mobile and telecommunication space. His expertise spans VoIP, video communication, mobile applications, grid computing, and networking technologies on diverse platforms. He has been actively working with Android platform since its beginning. He is the author of the book Android Apps with Eclipse from Apress. He has a Bachelor of Science degree in Computer Science from Drexel University in Philadelphia, PA, United States. He is currently working at Skype division of Microsoft as the Sr. Product Engineering Manager for the Skype client on Android platform.

About the Technical Reviewer

Grant Allen has worked in the IT field for over 20 years as a CTO, enterprise architect, and database architect. Grant's roles have covered private enterprise, academia, and the government sector around the world, specializing in globalscale systems design, development, and performance. He is a frequent speaker at industry and academic conferences, on topics ranging from data mining to compliance, and technologies such as databases (DB2, Oracle, SQL Server, and MySQL), content management, collaboration, disruptive innovation, and mobile ecosystems like Android.

His first Android application was a task list to remind him to finish all his other unfinished Android projects.

Grant works for Google, and in his spare time is completing a PhD on building innovative high-technology environments.

Grant is the author of Beginning DB2: From Novice to Professional (Apress, 2008), and lead author of Oracle SQL Recipes: A Problem-Solution Approach (Apress, 2010) and The Definitive Guide to SQLite, 2nd Edition (Apress, 2010).

Preface

Android is one of the major players in mobile phone market, and continuously growing its market share. It is the first complete, open, and free mobile platform that is enabling endless opportunities for mobile application developers.

Althrough the official programming language for the Android platform is Java, the application developers are not limited to using only the Java techonology.

Android allows application developers to implement parts of their application using native-code languages such as C and C++ through the Android Native Development Kit (NDK). In this book, you will learn how to use the Android NDK to implement performance-critical portions of your Android applications using native-code languages.

Android C++ with the NDK provides a detailed overview of native application development, available native APIs, the troubleshooting techniques, including the step by step instructions and screenshots to help Android developers to quickly get up to speed on developing native application.

What You Will Learn

This book includes the following:

- Installing the Android native development environment on major operating systems.

- Using the Eclipse IDE to develop native code.

- Connecting native code to Java world using Java Native Interface (JNI).

- Auto-generating the JNI code using SWIG.

- Developing multithreaded native apps using the POSIX and Java threads.

- Developing networking native apps using POSIX sockets.

- Debug native code through logging, GDB, and Eclipse Debugger.

- Analyzing memory issues through Valgrind.
- Measuring application performance through GProf.
- Optimizing native code through SIMD/NEON.

Downloading the Code

The source code for this book is available to readers at www.apress.com.

Contacting the Author

Readers can contact the author through author's Android C++ with the NDK site at http://www.zdo.com/android-c++-with-the-ndk to ask questions.

Getting Started with C++ on Android

Needless to say, exploring and practicing are the best methods for learning. Having a fully functional development environment ready at the very beginning of this book will enable you to explore and experiment with the material while working through the chapters. The Android C++ development environment is mainly formed by the following components:

- Android Software Development Kit (SDK)

- Android Native Development Kit (NDK)

- Android Development Tools (ADT) Plug-In for Eclipse

- Java Development Kit (JDK)

- Apache ANT Build System

- GNU Make Build System

- Eclipse IDE

This chapter will provide step-by-step instructions for setting up the proper Android C++ development environment. Android development tools are provided for the major operating systems:

- Microsoft Windows

- Apple Mac OS X

- Linux

Since the requirements and the installation procedure vary depending on the operating system, the following sections will walk you through the steps for setting up the Android C++ development environment based on the operating system. You can skip over the ones that don't apply to you.

Microsoft Windows

Android development tools require Windows XP (32-bit only), Vista, or Windows 7. In this section, you will be downloading and installing the following components:

- Java JDK 6
- Apache ANT Build System
- Android SDK
- Cygwin
- Android NDK
- Eclipse IDE

Downloading and Installing the Java Development Kit on Windows

Android development tools require Java Development Kit (JDK) version 6 in order to run. Java Runtime Edition (JRE) itself is not sufficient. Java JDK 6 needs to be installed prior installing the Android development tools.

> **Note**   Android development tools only support Java compiler compliance level 5 or 6. Although the later versions of JDK can be configured to comply with those levels, using JDK 6 is much simpler and less prone to errors.

Multiple JDK flavors are supported by Android development tools, such as IBM JDK, Open JDK, and Oracle JDK (formerly known as Sun JDK). In this book, it is assumed that Oracle JDK will be used since it supports a broader range of platforms.

In order to download Oracle JDK, navigate to www.oracle.com/technetwork/java/javase/downloads/index.html and follow these steps:

1. Click the JDK 6 download button, as shown in Figure 1-1. At the time of this writing the latest version of Oracle JDK 6 is Update 33.

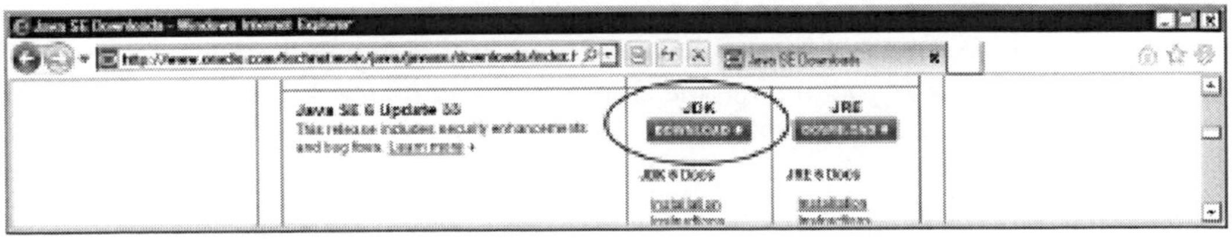

Figure 1-1. Oracle JDK 6 Download button

2. Clicking the Oracle JDK 6 Download button takes you to a page listing the Oracle JDK 6 installation packages for supported platforms.

3. Check "Accept License Agreement" and download the installation package for Windows x86, as shown in Figure 1-2.

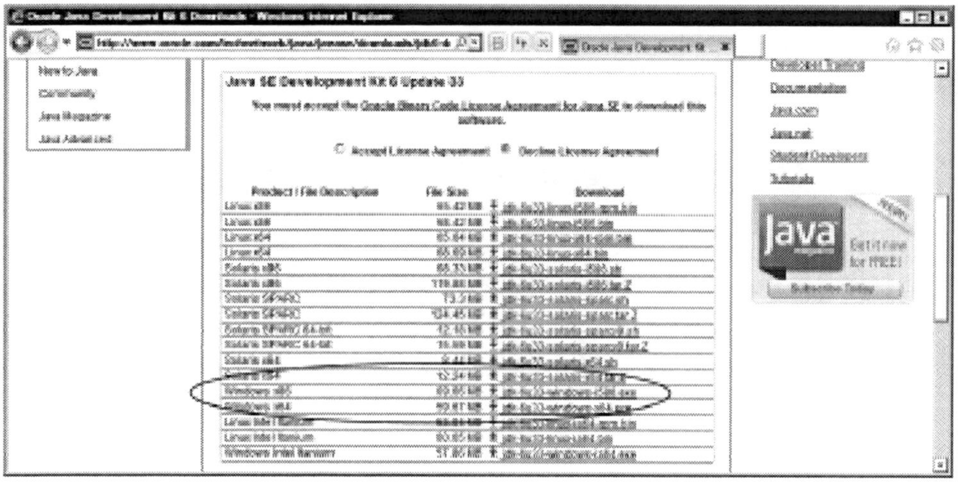

Figure 1-2. Download Oracle JDK 6 for Windows x86

Now you can install. The Oracle JDK 6 installation package for Windows comes with a graphical installation wizard. The installation wizard will guide you through the process of installing JDK. The installation wizard will first install the JDK, and then the JRE. During the installation process, the wizard will ask for the destination directories, as well as the components to be installed. You can continue with the default values here. Make a note of the installation directory for the JDK part, shown in Figure 1-3.

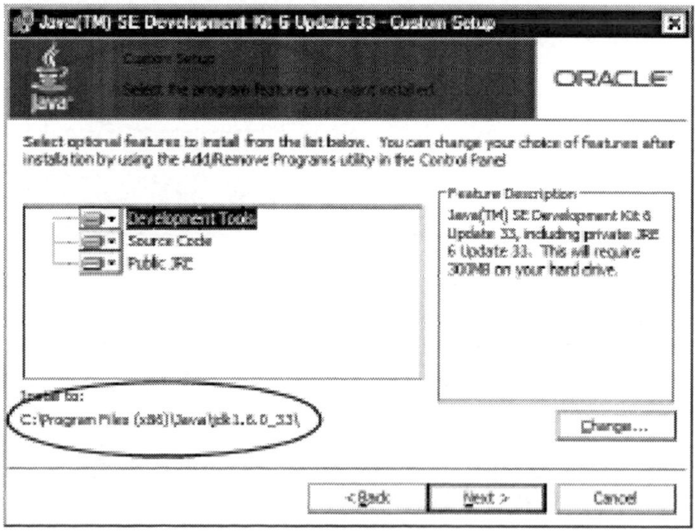

Figure 1-3. Oracle JDK 6 installation directory

The JDK will be ready to use upon completion of the installation process. The installation wizard does not automatically add the Java binary directory into the system executable search path, also known as the PATH variable. This needs to be done manually as the last step of the JDK installation.

1. Choose Control Panel from the Start button menu.

2. Click the System icon to launch the System Properties dialog.

3. Switch to the Advanced tab and click the Environment Variables button, as shown in Figure 1-4.

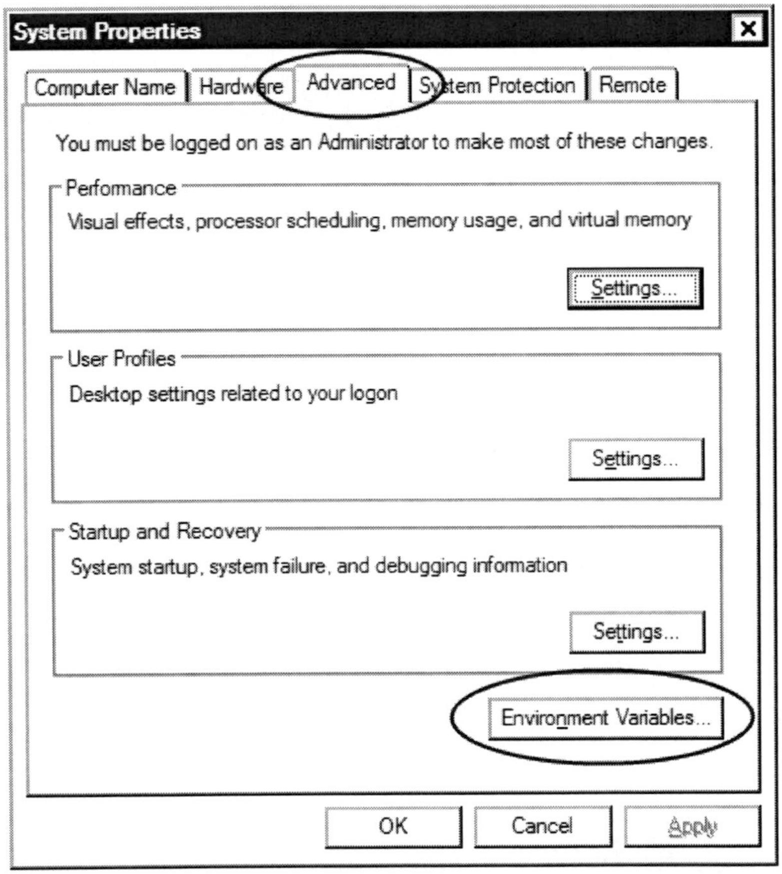

Figure 1-4. System Properties dialog

4. Clicking the Environment Variables button will launch the Environment Variables dialog. The dialog is separated into two parts: the top one is for the user and the bottom is for the system.

5. Click the New button in the system variables section to define a new environment variable, as shown in Figure 1-5.

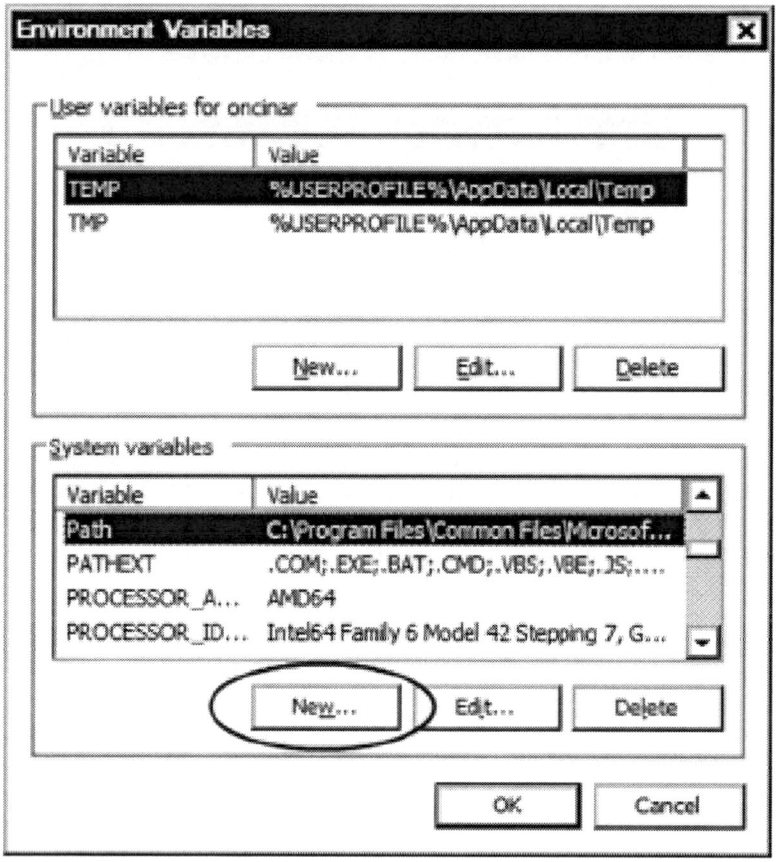

Figure 1-5. Environment Variables dialog

6. Set the variable name to JAVA_HOME and the variable value to the Oracle JDK installation directory that you noted during the Oracle JDK installation, as shown in Figure 1-6.

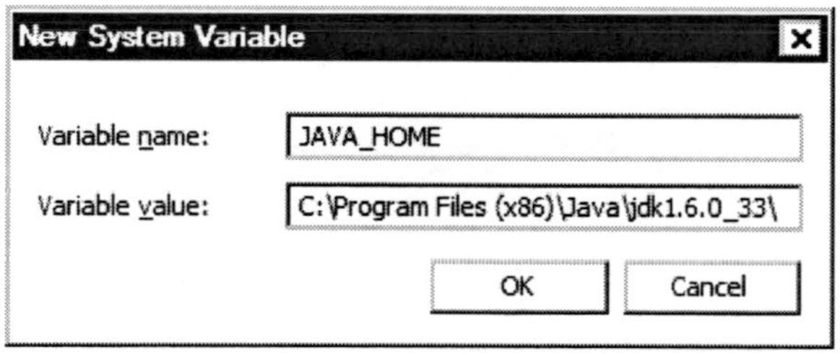

Figure 1-6. New JAVA_HOME environment variable

7. Click OK button to save the environment variable.

8. From the list of system variables, double-click the PATH variable and append
    ;%JAVA_HOME%\bin to the variable value, as shown in Figure 1-7.

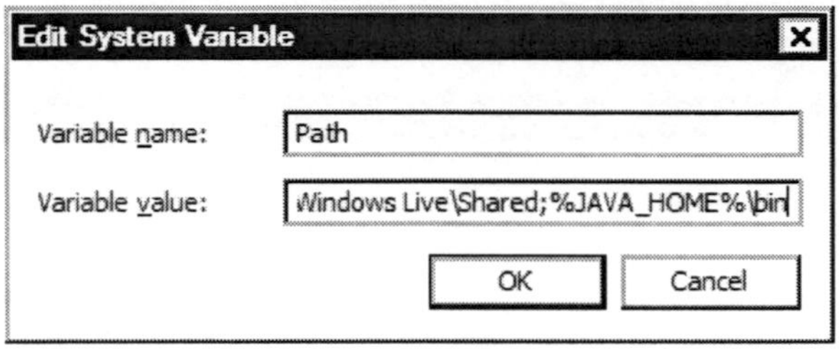

Figure 1-7. Appending Oracle JDK binary path to system PATH variable

The Oracle JDK is now part of the system executable search path and it is easily reachable. In order
to validate the installation, open a command prompt window by choosing **Start ➤ Accessories ➤
Command Prompt**. Using the command prompt, execute javac -version. If the installation was
successful, you will see the Oracle JDK version number, as shown in Figure 1-8.

Figure 1-8. Validating Oracle JDK installation

Downloading and Installing the Apache ANT on Windows

Apache ANT is a command-line build tool that whose mission is to drive any type of process that
can be described in terms of targets and tasks. Android development tools require Apache ANT
version 1.8 or later for the build process to function. At the time of this writing, the latest version of
Apache ANT is 1.8.4.

In order to download Apache ANT, navigate to http://ant.apache.org/bindownload.cgi and
download the installation package in ZIP format, as shown in Figure 1-9. Then follow these steps:

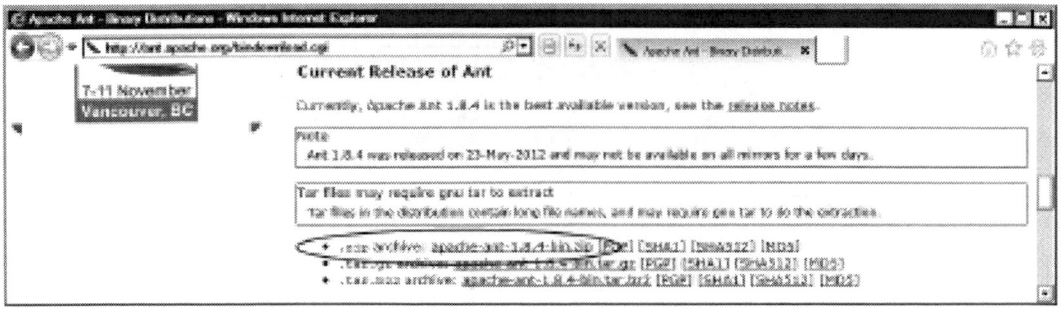

Figure 1-9. Apache ANT download package in ZIP format

1. The Windows operating system comes with native support for ZIP files. When the download completes, right-click the ZIP file.

2. Choose Extract All from the context menu to launch the Extract Compressed Folder wizard.

3. Using the Browse button, choose the destination directory, as shown in Figure 1-10. A dedicated empty destination directory is not needed since the ZIP file already contains a sub directory called `apache-ant-1.8.4` that holds the Apache ANT files. In this book, the `C:\android` directory will be used as the root directory to hold the Android development tools and dependencies. Make a note of the destination directory.

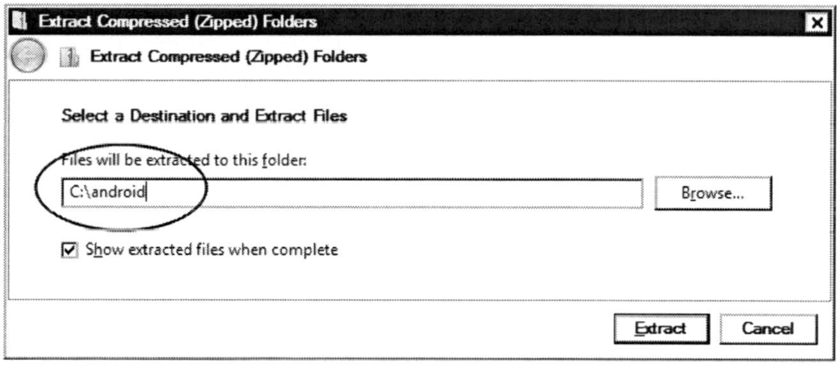

Figure 1-10. Extracting Apache ANT ZIP archive

4. Click the Extract button to install Apache ANT.

Upon installing the Apache ANT, follow these steps to append its binary path to system executable search path:

1. Launch the Environment Variables dialog from System Properties.

2. Click the New button in the system variables section to define a new environment variable.

3. Set the variable name to `ANT_HOME` and the variable value to the Apache ANT installation directory (such as `C:\android\apache-ant-1.8.4`), as shown in Figure 1-11.

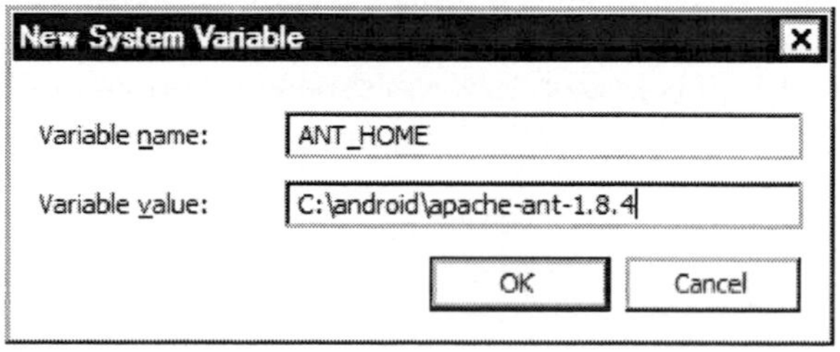

Figure 1-11. New ANT_HOME environment variable

4. Click the OK button to save the new environment variable.

5. From the list of system variables, double-click the PATH variable and append
    ;%ANT_HOME%\bin to the variable value, as shown in Figure 1-12.

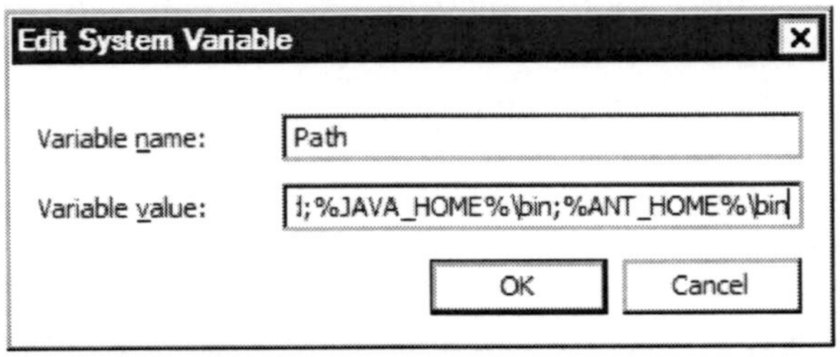

Figure 1-12. *Appending Apache ANT binary path to system PATH variable*

After completing this last installation step, Apache ANT is now added to the system executable
search path. In order to validate the installation, open a command prompt window. Using the
command prompt, execute ant -version. If the installation was successful, you will see the Apache
ANT version number, as shown in Figure 1-13.

Figure 1-13. *Validating Apache ANT installation*

Downloading and Installing the Android SDK on Windows

The Android software development kit (SDK) is the core component of the development toolchain,
providing framework API libraries and developer tools that are necessary for building, testing, and
debugging Android applications.

Navigate to http://developer.android.com/sdk/index.html to download the Android SDK. At the
time of this writing, the latest version for Android SDK is R20. Two types of installation packages are
currently provided: a graphical installer and a ZIP archive. Although the graphical installer is offered
as the main installation package, it is known to have issues on certain platforms. Click the link for

"Other Platforms" and download the Android SDK ZIP archive, as shown in Figure 1-14. Then follow these steps:

Figure 1-14. Android SDK download page

6. When the download completes, right-click the ZIP file and choose Extract All from the context menu to launch the Extract Compressed Folder wizard.

7. Using the Browse button, choose the destination directory. A dedicated empty destination directory is not needed since the ZIP file already contains a sub directory called android-sdk-windows that contains the Android SDK files. Make a note of the destination directory.

8. Click the Extract button install Android SDK.

Binary paths of Android SDK should be appended to the system executable search path. In order to do so, follow these steps:

1. Launch the Environment Variables dialog from System Properties.

2. Click the New button in the system variables section to define a new environment variable.

3. Set the variable name to ANDROID_SDK_HOME and the variable value to the Android SDK installation directory (such as C:\android\android-sdk-windows), as shown in Figure 1-15.

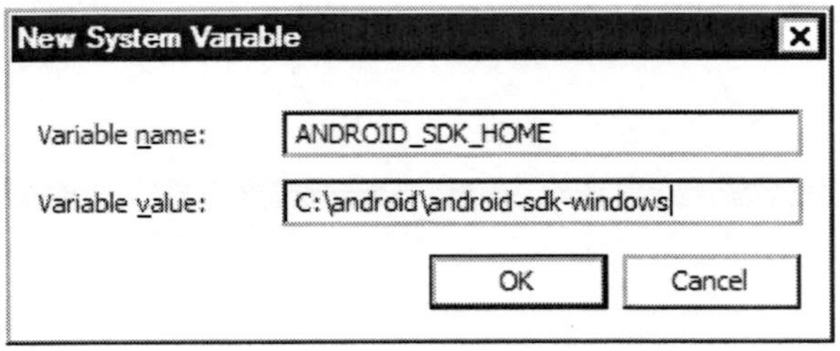

Figure 1-15. ANDROID_SDK_HOME environment variable

4. Click the OK button to save the new environment variable.

5. There are three important directories that need to be added to the system executable search path: the SDK root directory, the tools directory holding the Android platform-independent SDK Tools, and the platform-tools directory holding the Android platform tools. Ignore the fact that platform-tools directory does not exist yet. From the list of system variables on the Environment Variables dialog, double-click the PATH variable and append `;%ANDROID_SDK_HOME%;%ANDROID_SDK_HOME%\tools;%ANDROID_SDK_HOME%\platform-tools` to the variable value, as shown in Figure 1-16.

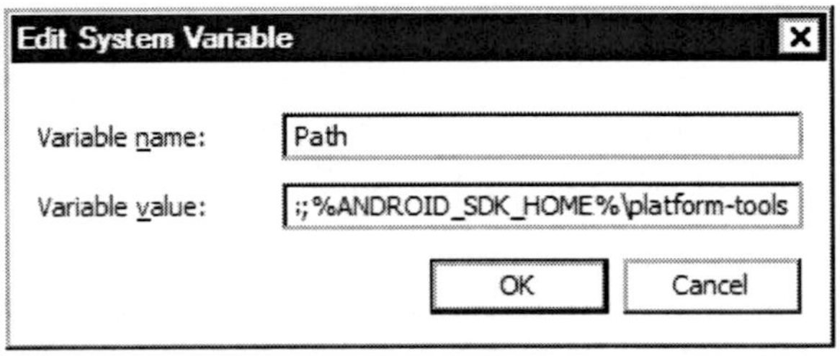

Figure 1-16. Appending Android SDK binary paths to system PATH variable

In order to validate the installation, open a command prompt window. Using the command prompt, execute `'SDK Manager'` *including the quotes*. If the installation was successful, you will see the Android SDK Manager, as shown in Figure 1-17.

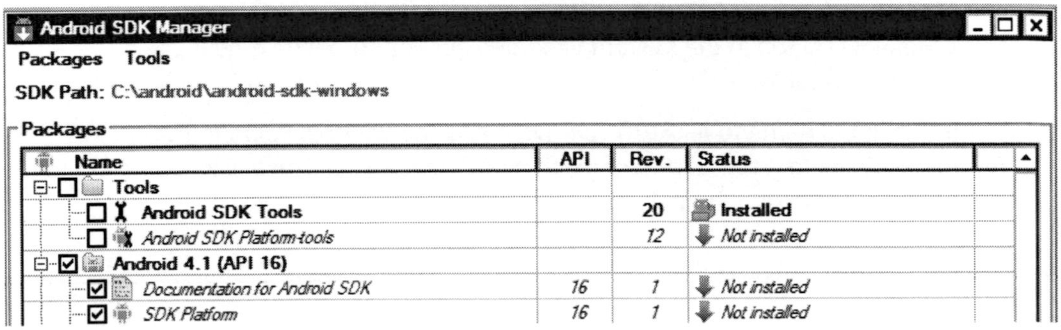

Figure 1-17. Android SDK Manager application

Downloading and Installing the Cygwin on Windows

The Android Native Development Kit (NDK) tools were initially designed to work on UNIX-like systems. Some of the NDK components are shell scripts, and they are not directly executable on the Windows operating system. Although the latest version of the Android NDK is showing progress in making itself more independent and self-packaged, it still requires Cygwin to be installed on the host machine in order to fully operate. Cygwin is a UNIX-like environment and command-line interface for the Windows operating system. It comes with base UNIX applications, including a shell that allows running the Android NDK's build system. At the time of this writing, Android NDK requires Cygwin 1.7 to be installed in order to function. Navigate to `http://cygwin.com/install.html` and download the Cygwin installer, `setup.exe` (see Figure 1-18).

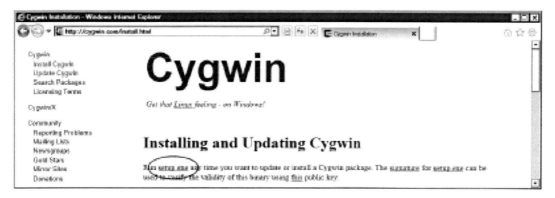

Figure 1-18. Download the Cygwin setup application

Upon starting the setup application, you will see the Cygwin installation wizard welcome screen. Click the Next button and follow these steps to proceed with the installation:

1. Installation will ask you to choose the download source. Keep the default selection of "Install from Internet" and click the Next button to proceed.

2. In the next dialog, the installer will ask you select the directory where you want to install Cygwin, as shown in Figure 1-19. By default Cygwin will be installed under C:\cygwin directory. Note the destination directory and click the Next button.

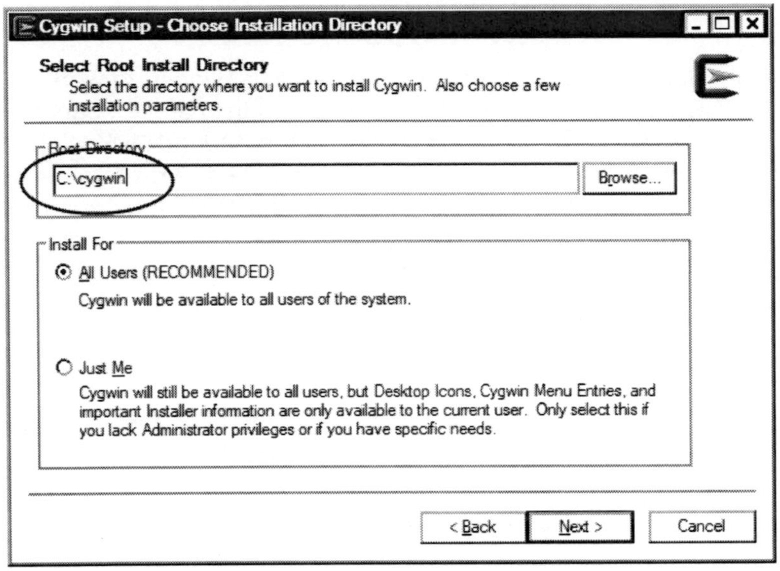

Figure 1-19. *Choosing Cygwin installation directory*

3. The next dialog will ask you select the local package directory. This is the temporary directory that will be used to download the packages. Keep the default value and click the Next button.

4. In the next dialog, you will select the Internet connection type. Unless you need to use a proxy to access the Internet, keep the default selection of "Direct Connection" and click the Next button to proceed.

5. The installer will ask you to select a download site. From the list of mirror sites, either chooses a random one or the one closest geographically to your location. Then click the Next button.

6. Cygwin is not a single application; it is a large software distribution containing multiple applications. In the next dialog, the Cygwin installer will provide you a list of all available packages. Android NDK requires GNU Make 3.8.1 or later in order to function. Using the search field, filter the package list by keyword "make," expand the Devel category, and select the GNU Make package, as shown in Figure 1-20. Click the Next button to start the installation.

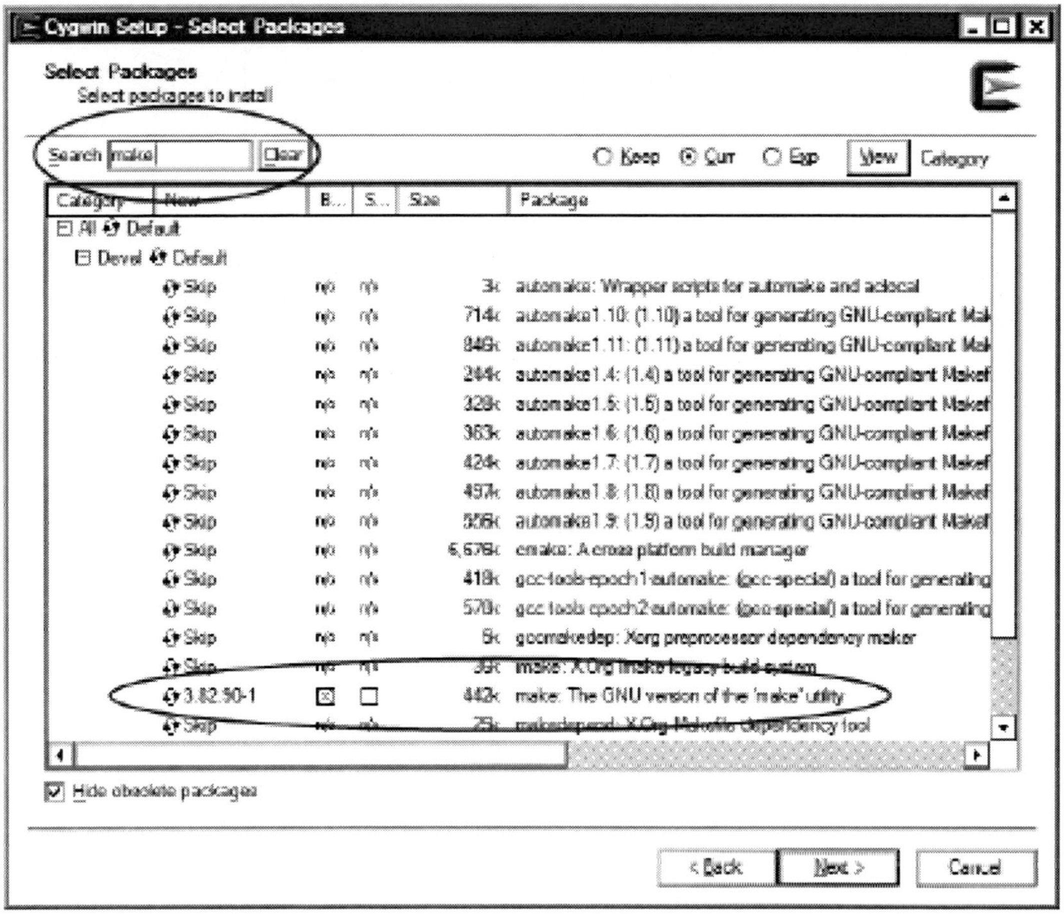

Figure 1-20. Select GNU Make package

When the installation completes, the Cygwin binary path needs to be added to the system executable search path.

1. Launch the Environment Variables dialog from System Properties.

2. Click the New button in the system variables section to define a new environment variable.

3. Set the variable name to CYGWIN_HOME and the variable value to the Cygwin installation directory (such as C:\cygwin), as shown in Figure 1-21.

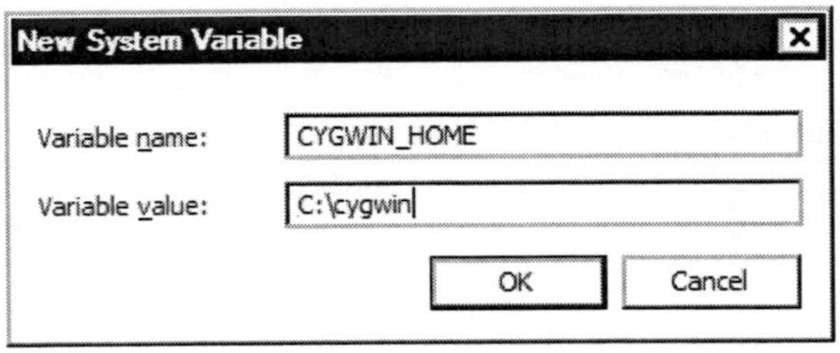

Figure 1-21. *CYGWIN_HOME environment variable*

4. From the list of system variables in the Environment Variables dialog, double-click
    the PATH variable and append ;%CYGWIN_HOME%\bin to the variable value, as shown
    in Figure 1-22.

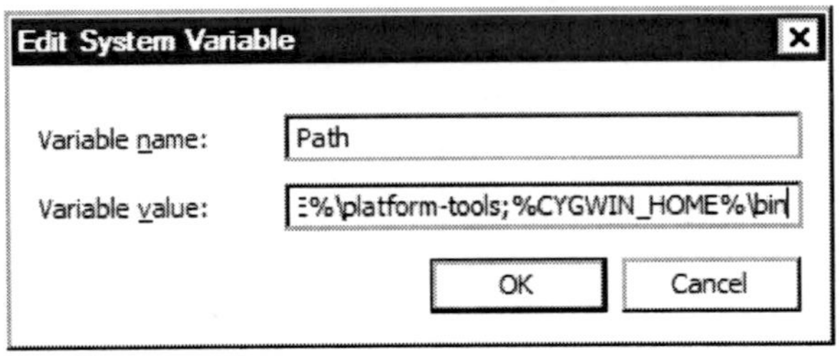

Figure 1-22. *Appending Cygwin binary path to system PATH variable*

After completing this last installation step, Cygwin tools are now part of the system executable
search path. In order to validate the installation, open a command prompt window. Using the
command prompt, execute make -version. If the installation was successful, you will see the GNU
Make version number, as shown in Figure 1-23.

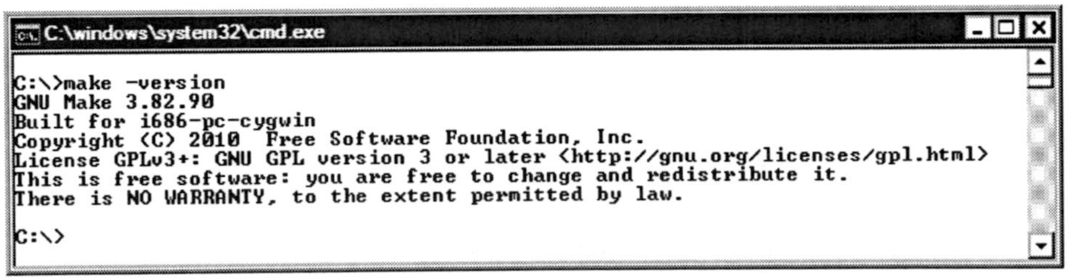

Figure 1-23. *Validating Cygwin installation*

Downloading and Installing the Android NDK on Windows

The Android Native Development Kit (NDK) is a companion tool to Android SDK that lets you develop
Android applications using native programming languages such as C++. Android NDK provide
header files, libraries, and cross-compiler toolchains. At the time of this writing, the latest version for

Android NDK is R8. In order to download the Android NDK, navigate to `http://developer.android.com/tools/sdk/ndk/index.html` and go to the Downloads section shown in Figure 1-24. Then follow these steps:

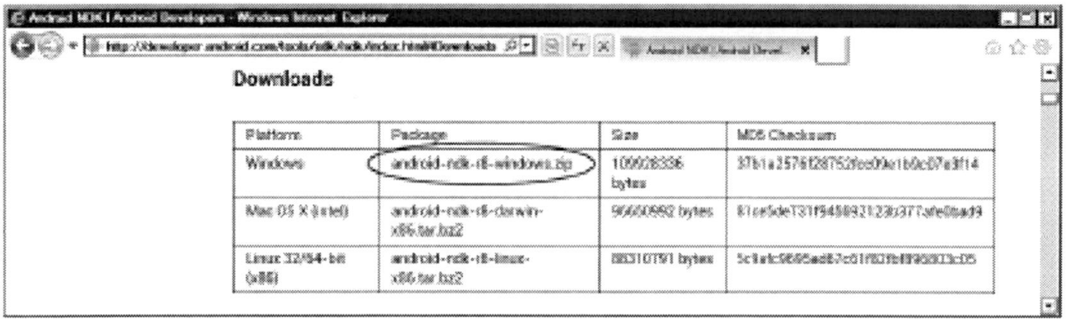

Figure 1-24. Android NDK download page

1. Android NDK installation package is provided as a ZIP archive. When the download completes, right-click the ZIP file and choose Extract All from the context menu to launch the Extract Compressed Folder wizard.

2. Using the Browse button, choose the destination directory. A dedicated empty destination directory is not needed since the ZIP file already contains a sub directory called `android-ndk-r8` that contains the Android NDK files. Make a note of the destination directory.

3. Click the Extract button to install Android NDK.

The binary paths of Android SDK can be appended to the system executable search path by following these steps:

1. Again, launch the Environment Variables dialog from System Properties.

2. Click the New button in the system variables section to define a new environment variable. Set the variable name to `ANDROID_NDK_HOME` and the variable value to the Android NDK installation directory (such as `C:\android\android-ndk-r8`), as shown in Figure 1-25.

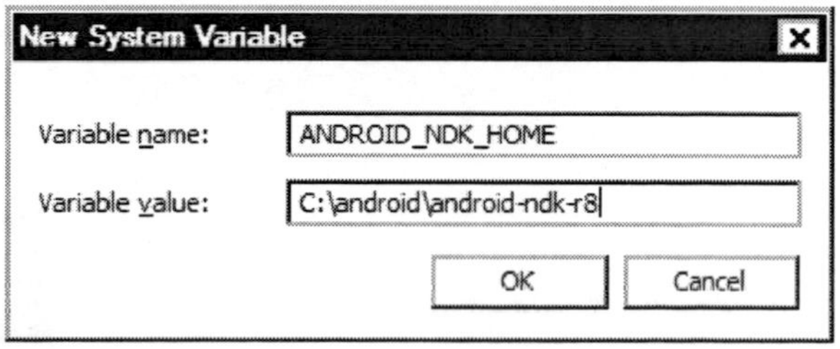

Figure 1-25. ANDROID_NDK_HOME environment variable

3.   Click the OK button to save the new environment variable.

4.   From the list of system variables in the Environment Variables dialog, double-click the PATH variable and append ;%ANDROID_NDK_HOME% to the variable value, as shown in Figure 1-26.

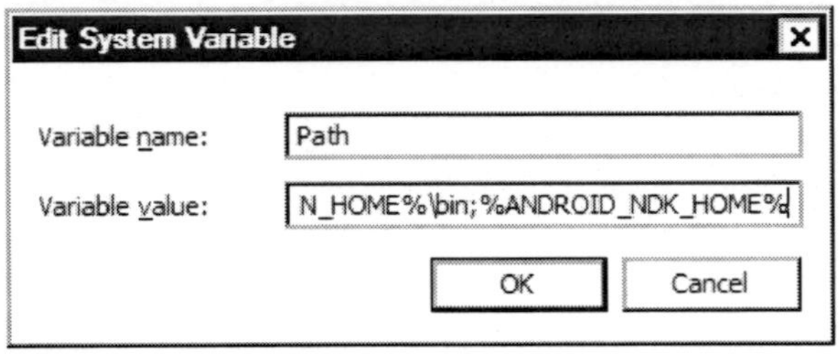

Figure 1-26. Appending Android NDK binary path to system PATH variable

Android NDK is now easily reachable. In order to validate the installation, open a command prompt window. Using the command prompt, execute ndk-build. If the installation was successful, you will see NDK build complaining about project directory, as shown in Figure 1-27, which is fine.

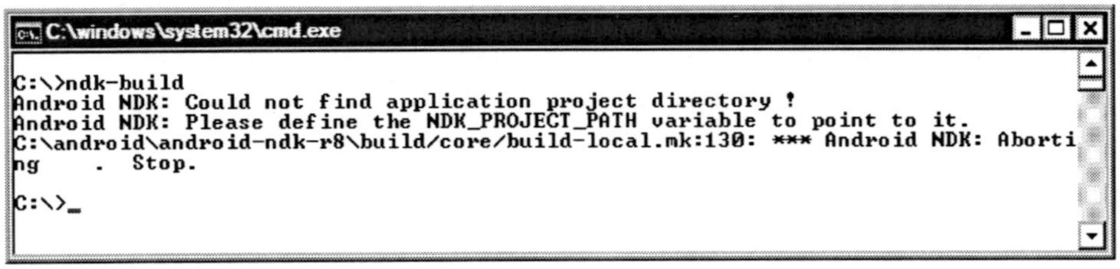

Figure 1-27. Validating Android NDK installation

Downloading and Installing the Eclipse on Windows

Eclipse is a highly extensible, multi-language integrated development environment. Although it is not a requirement for native Android development, Eclipse does provide a highly integrated coding environment, bringing Android tools to your fingertips to streamline the application development. At the time of this writing, the latest version of Eclipse is Juno 4.2. In order to download Eclipse, navigate to http://www.eclipse.org/downloads/, as shown in Figure 1-28, and follow these steps:

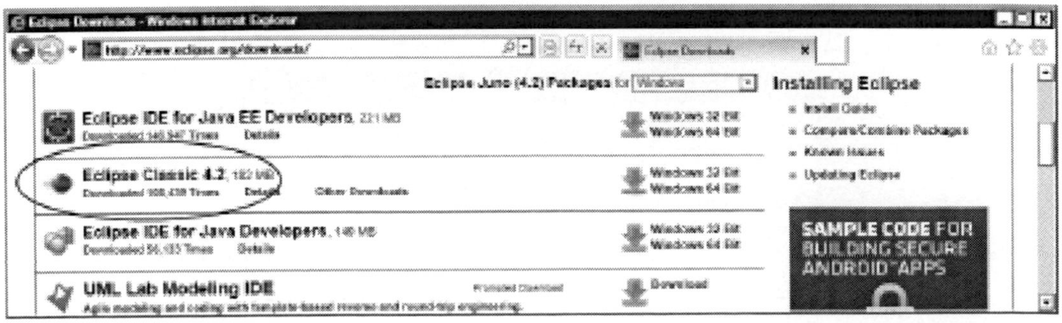

Figure 1-28. Eclipse download page

1. Download the Eclipse Classic for Windows 32 Bit from the list. The Eclipse installation package is provided as a ZIP archive.

2. When the download completes, right-click the ZIP file and choose Extract All from the context menu to launch the Extract Compressed Folder wizard.

3. Using the Browse button, choose the destination directory. A dedicated empty destination directory is not needed since the ZIP file already contains a sub directory called `eclipse` that holds the Eclipse files.

4. Click the Extract button to install Eclipse.

5. In order to make Eclipse easily accessible, go to the Eclipse installation directory.

6. Right-click the Eclipse binary and choose **Send ➤ Desktop** to make a shortcut to Eclipse on your Windows desktop.

To validate the Eclipse installation, double-click the Eclipse icon. If the installation was successful, you will see the Eclipse Workspace Launcher dialog shown in Figure 1-29.

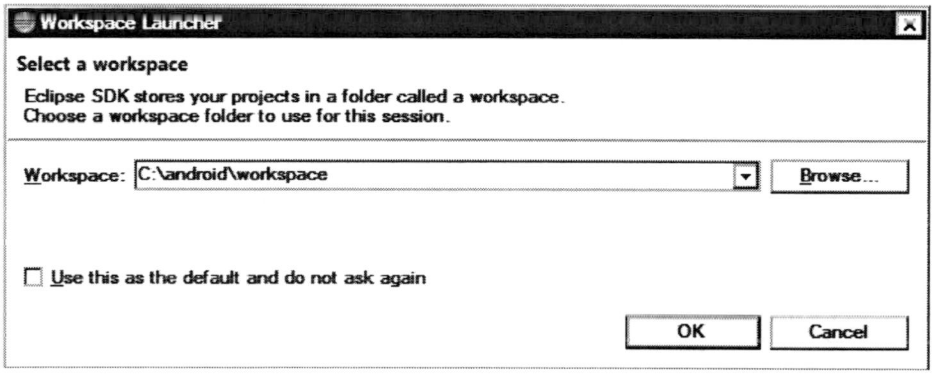

Figure 1-29. Validating Eclipse installation

Apple Mac OS X

Android development tools require Mac OS X 10.5.8 or later and an x86 system. Since Android development tools were initially designed to work on UNIX-like systems, most of its dependencies are already available on the platform either through OS X directly or through the Xcode developer tools. In this section, you will be downloading and installing the following components:

- Xcode
- Java JDK 6
- Apache ANT Build System
- GNU Make

- Android SDK
- Android NDK
- Eclipse IDE

Installing Xcode on Mac

Xcode provides developer tools for application development on the OS X platform. Xcode can be found at Mac OS X installation media or through the Mac App Store free of charge. Navigate to `https://developer.apple.com/xcode/` for more information. Starting the Xcode installer will take you to the Xcode installation wizard, which will guide you through the installation process.

1. Approve the licenses.

2. Select the destination directory.

3. The Install wizard will show the list of Xcode components that can be installed. From this list, select the UNIX Development package shown in Figure 1-30.

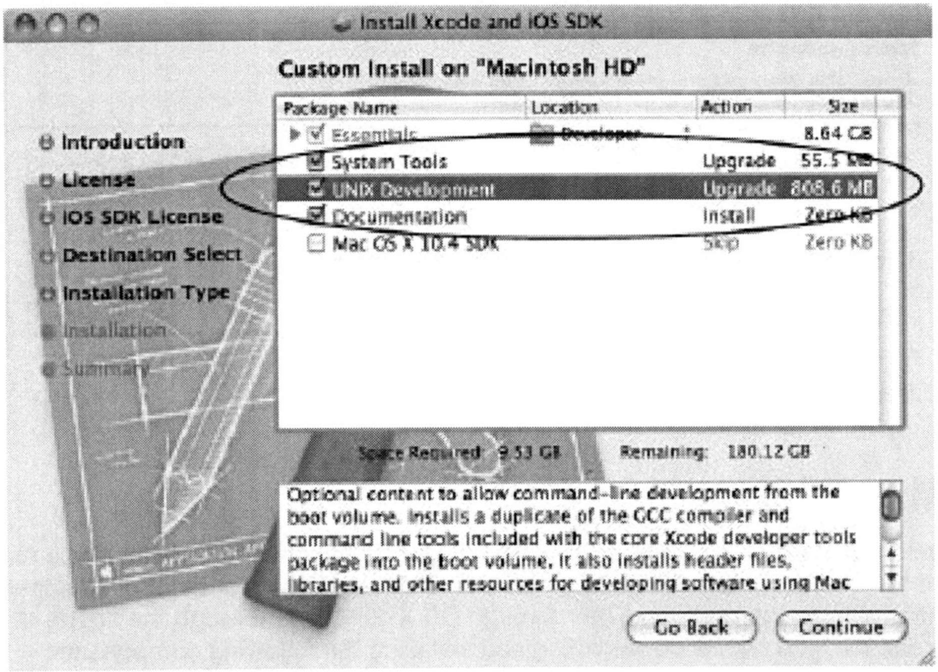

Figure 1-30. Xcode custom installation dialog

4. Click the Continue button to start the installation.

Validating the Java Development Kit on Mac

Android development tools require Java Development Kit (JDK) version 6 in order to run. The Apple Mac OS X operating system ships with the JDK already installed. It is based on the Oracle JDK but configured by Apple for better integration with Mac OS X. New versions of the JDK are available through the Software Update. Make sure that JDK 6 or later is installed. To validate the JDK installation, open a Terminal window and execute `javac -version` on the command line. If JDK is properly installed, you will see JDK version number, as shown in Figure 1-31.

```
○ ○ ○              Terminal — bash — 80×6
$ javac -version
javac 1.6.0_33
$ []
```

Figure 1-31. Validating JDK

Validating the Apache ANT on Mac

Apache ANT is a command-line build tool that drives any type of process that can be described in terms of targets and tasks. Android development tools require Apache ANT version 1.8 or later for the build process to function. Apache ANT is installed as a part of Xcode's UNIX Development package. In order to validate the Apache ANT installation, open a Terminal window and execute `ant -version` on the command line. If the installation was successful, you will see the Apache ANT version number, as shown in Figure 1-32.

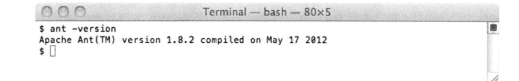

```
○ ○ ○              Terminal — bash — 80×5
$ ant -version
Apache Ant(TM) version 1.8.2 compiled on May 17 2012
$ []
```

Figure 1-32. Validating Apache ANT

Validating the GNU Make

GNU Make is a build tool that controls the generation of executables and other parts of an application from application's source code. Android NDK requires GNU Make 3.8.1 or later in order to function. GNU Make is installed as a part of Xcode's UNIX Development package. In order to validate the GNU Make installation, open a Terminal window and execute `make -version` on the command line. If the installation was successful, you will see the GNU Make version number, as shown in Figure 1-33.

```
○ ○ ○              Terminal — bash — 80×10
$ make -version
GNU Make 3.81
Copyright (C) 2006  Free Software Foundation, Inc.
This is free software; see the source for copying conditions.
There is NO warranty; not even for MERCHANTABILITY or FITNESS FOR A
PARTICULAR PURPOSE.

This program built for i386-apple-darwin10.0
$ []
```

Figure 1-33. Validating GNU Make

Downloading and Installing the Android SDK on Mac

The Android Software Development Kit (SDK) is the core component of the development toolchain, providing framework API libraries and developer tools that are necessary for building, testing, and debugging Android applications. At the time of this writing, the latest version for Android SDK is R20. Navigate to http://developer.android.com/sdk/index.html to download the Android SDK, as shown in Figure 1-34, and follow these steps:

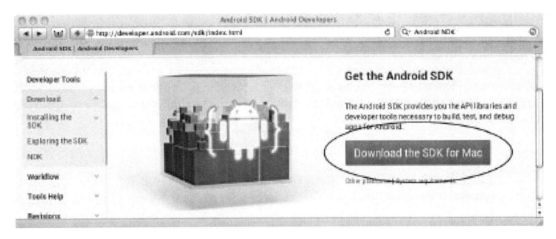

Figure 1-34. Android SDK download page

1. Click the "Download the SDK for Mac" button to start downloading the SDK installation package.

2. The Android SDK installation package is provided as a ZIP archive. OS X provides native support for ZIP archives. If you are using the Safari browser, the ZIP file will be automatically extracted after the download. Otherwise, double-click the ZIP file to open it as a compressed folder.

3. Drag and drop the android-sdk-macosx directory to its destination location using the Finder, as shown in Figure 1-35. In this book, the /android directory will be used as the root directory holding the Android development tools and dependencies.

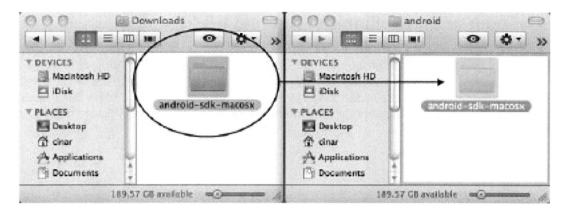

Figure 1-35. *Installing Android SDK to its destination location*

In order to make Android SDK easily accessible, the binary paths of Android SDK should be appended to the system executable search path. Open a Terminal window and execute the following commands, as shown in Figure 1-36:

Figure 1-36. *Appending Android SDK binary path to system PATH variable*

- echo export ANDROID_SDK_HOME=/android/android-sdk-macosx > > ~/.bash_profile
- echo export PATH=\$ANDROID_SDK_HOME/tools:\$ANDROID_SDK_HOME/platform-tools:\$PATH >>~/.bash_profile

In order to validate the Android SDK installation, open a new Terminal window and execute android -h on the command line. If the installation was successful, you will see the help messages shown in Figure 1-37.

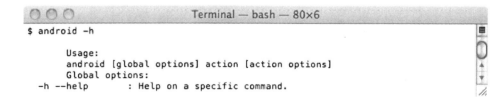

Figure 1-37. *Validating Android SDK installation*

Downloading and Installing the Android NDK on Mac

Android Native Development Kit (NDK) is a companion tool to Android SDK that lets you develop Android applications using native programming languages such as C++. The Android NDK provides header files, libraries, and cross-compiler toolchains. At the time of this writing, the latest version for Android NDK is R8. In order to download the Android NDK, navigate to `http://developer.android.com/tools/sdk/ndk/index.html` and go to the Downloads section, as shown in Figure 1-38. Then follow these steps:

Figure 1-38. Android NDK download page

1. Click to download the installation package. The Android NDK installation package is provided as a BZIP'ed TAR archive. OS X does not automatically extract this type of archive files.

2. In order to manually extract the archive file, open a Terminal window.

3. Go into the destination directory `/android`.

4. Execute `tar jxvf ~/Downloads/android-ndk-r8-darwin-x86.tar.bz2`, as shown in Figure 1-39.

```
○ ○ ○                Terminal — bash — 80×6
$ cd /android
$ tar jxvf ~/Downloads/android-ndk-r8-darwin-x86.tar.bz2
x android-ndk-r8/
x android-ndk-r8/prebuilt/
x android-ndk-r8/prebuilt/darwin-x86/
x android-ndk-r8/prebuilt/darwin-x86/bin/
```

Figure 1-39. Installing Android NDK

The binary paths of Android NDK should be appended to system-executable search path to make it easily accessible. Open a Terminal window and execute the following commands (see Figure 1-40).

Figure 1-40. Appending Android NDK binary path to system PATH variable

- echo export ANDROID_NDK_HOME=/android/android-ndk-r8 >>~/.bash_profile
- echo export PATH=\\$ANDROID_NDK_HOME:\\$PATH >>~/.bash_profile

Validate the Android NDK installation by opening a new Terminal window and executing `ndk-build` on the command line. If the installation was successful, you will see the NDK build complaining about the project directory, as shown in Figure 1-41, which is fine.

```
$ ndk-build
Android NDK: Could not find application project directory !
Android NDK: Please define the NDK_PROJECT_PATH variable to point to it.
/android/android-ndk-r8/build/core/build-local.mk:130: *** Android NDK: Aborting
  . Stop.
$ []
```

Figure 1-41. Validating Android NDK

Downloading and Installing the Eclipse on Mac

Eclipse is a highly extensible, multi-language integrated development environment. Although it is not a requirement for native Android development, Eclipse does provide a highly integrated coding environment, bringing Android tools to your fingertips to streamline the application development. At the time of this writing, the latest version of Eclipse is Juno 4.2. In order to install Eclipse, navigate to http://www.eclipse.org/downloads/, as shown in Figure 1-42, and follow these steps:

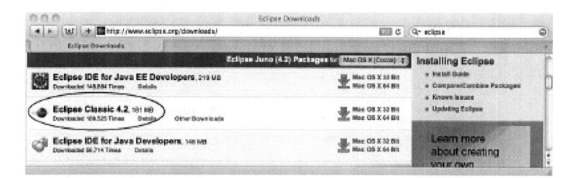

Figure 1-42. Eclipse download page

1. Download the Eclipse Classic for Mac OS X 32 Bit from the list. The Eclipse installation package is provided as a GZIP'ed TAR archive. If you are using the Safari browser, the archive file can be automatically decompressed but not extracted after the download.

2. In order to manually extract the archive, open a Terminal window and go into the destination directory of /android.

3. Execute tar xvf ~/Downloads/eclipse-SDK-4.2-macosx-cocoa.tar, as shown in Figure 1-43.

```
                     Terminal — bash — 80×6
$ cd /android
$ tar xvf ~/Downloads/eclipse-SDK-4.2-macosx-cocoa.tar
x eclipse/
x eclipse/Eclipse.app/
x eclipse/Eclipse.app/Contents/
x eclipse/Eclipse.app/Contents/Info.plist
```

Figure 1-43. Installing Eclipse

You can add Eclipse to the dock to make it easily accessible by following these steps:

1. Go to the Eclipse installation directory.

2. Drag and drop the Eclipse application to Dock, as shown in Figure 1-44.

Figure 1-44. Adding Eclipse to dock

Double-click the Eclipse icon to validate the Eclipse installation. If the installation was successful, you will see the Eclipse Workspace Launcher dialog shown in Figure 1-45.

```
○ ○ ○                    Workspace Launcher

Select a workspace

    Eclipse SDK stores your projects in a folder called a workspace.
    Choose a workspace folder to use for this session.


Workspace:  /android/workspace                              ▼    ( Browse... )



   ☐ Use this as the default and do not ask again


                                        ( Cancel )   ( OK )
```

Figure 1-45. Validating Eclipse

Ubuntu Linux

Android development tools require Ubuntu Linux version 8.04 32-bit or later or any other Linux flavor with GNU C Library (glibc) 2.7 or later. In this section, you will be downloading and installing the following components:

- Java JDK 6
- Apache ANT Build System
- GNU Make
- Android SDK
- Android NDK
- Eclipse IDE

Checking the GNU C Library Version

You can check the GNU C Library version by executing `ldd --version` on a Terminal window, as shown in Figure 1-46.

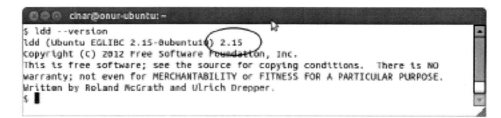

Figure 1-46. *Checking the GNU C library version*

Enabling the 32-Bit Support on 64-Bit Systems

On 64-bit Linux distributions, Android development tools require the 32-bit support package to be installed. In order to install the 32-bit support package, open a Terminal window and execute `sudo apt-get install ia32-libs-multiarch`, as shown in Figure 1-47.

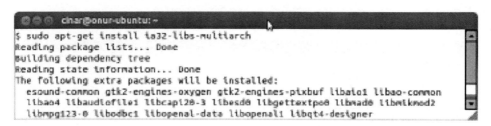

Figure 1-47. *Installing ia32-libs-multiarch*

Downloading and Installing the Java Development Kit on Linux

Android development tools require Java Development Kit (JDK) version 6 in order to run. Java Runtime Edition (JRE) itself is not sufficient. Java JDK 6 needs to be installed prior installing the Android development tools. Except for the GNU Compiler for Java (gcj), a variety of JDK flavors are supported by Android development tools, such as IBM JDK, Open JDK, and Oracle JDK (formerly known as Sun JDK). Due to licensing issues, Oracle JDK is not available in the Ubuntu software repository. In this book, it is assumed that Open JDK will be used. In order to install Open JDK, open a Terminal window and execute sudo apt-get install openjdk-6-jdk, as shown in Figure 1-48.

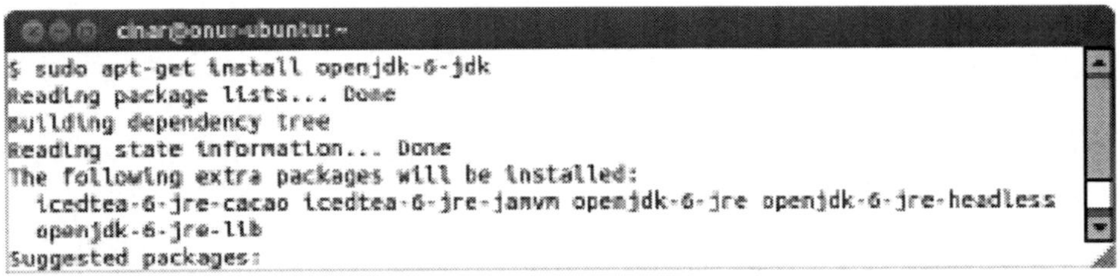

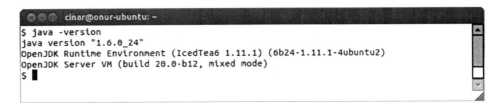

Figure 1-48. Installing Open JDK 6

In order to validate the Open JDK installation, open a Terminal window and execute java –version on the command line. If the installation was successful, you will see the Open JDK version number, as shown in Figure 1-49.

Figure 1-49. Validating Open JDK installation

Downloading and Installing the Apache ANT on Linux

Apache ANT is a command-line build tool that drives any type of process that can be described in terms of targets and tasks. Android development tools require Apache ANT version 1.8 or later for the build process to function. Apache ANT is provided through the Ubuntu software repository. In order to install Apache ANT, open a Terminal window and execute sudo apt-get install ant, as shown in Figure 1-50.

Figure 1-50. Installing Apache ANT

Open a Terminal window and execute ant -version on the command line to validate the Apache ANT installation. If the installation was successful, you will see the Apache ANT version number, as shown in Figure 1-51.

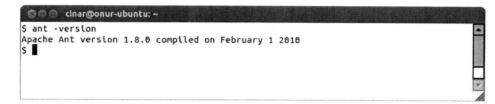

Figure 1-51. *Validating Apache ANT installation*

Downloading and Installing the GNU Make on Linux

GNU Make is a build tool that controls the generation of executables and other parts of an application from application's source code. Android NDK requires GNU Make 3.8.1 or later in order to function. GNU Make is provided through Ubuntu software repository. In order to install GNU Make, open a Terminal window and execute sudo apt-get install make, as shown in Figure 1-52.

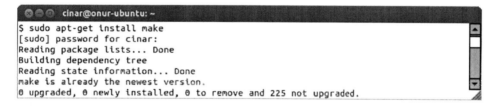

Figure 1-52. *Installing GNU Make*

Open a Terminal window and validate the GNU Make installation by executing make -version on the command line. If the installation was successful, you will see the GNU Make version number, as shown in Figure 1-53.

Figure 1-53. *Validating GNU Make installation*

Downloading and Installing the Android SDK on Linux

The Android Software Development Kit (SDK) is the core component of the development toolchain, providing framework API libraries and developer tools that are necessary for building, testing, and debugging Android applications. At the time of this writing, the latest version for Android SDK is R20. Navigate to `http://developer.android.com/sdk/index.html` to download the Android SDK, as shown in Figure 1-54. Then follow these steps to install it:

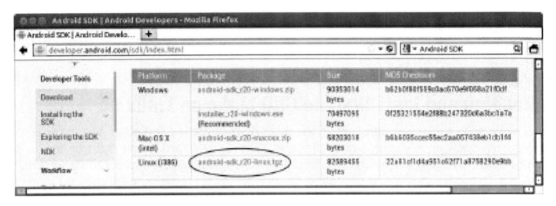

Figure 1-54. Android SDK download page

1. The Android SDK installation package is provided as a GZIP'ed TAR archive. Open a Terminal window and go to the destination directory. In this book, ~/ android directory will be used as the root directory for holding the Android development tools and dependencies.

2. Extract the Android SDK by executing `tar zxvf ~/Downloads/android-sdk_ r20-linux.tgz` on the command line, as shown in Figure 1-55.

Figure 1-55. Installing Android SDK

In order to make Android SDK easily accessible, binary paths of Android SDK should be appended to the system executable search path. Assuming that you are using the BASH shell, open a Terminal window and execute the following commands (shown in Figure 1-56):

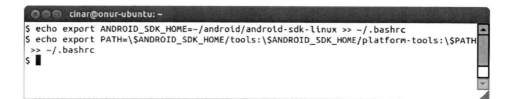

Figure 1-56. Appending Android SDK binary path to system PATH variable

- echo export ANDROID_SDK_HOME=~/android/android-sdk-linux >>~/.bashrc

- echo export PATH=\$ANDROID_SDK_HOME/tools:\$ANDROID_SDK_HOME/platform-tools:\$PATH >>~/.bashrc

In order to validate the Android SDK installation, open new a Terminal window and execute android -h on the command line. If the installation was successful, you will see the help messages shown in Figure 1-57.

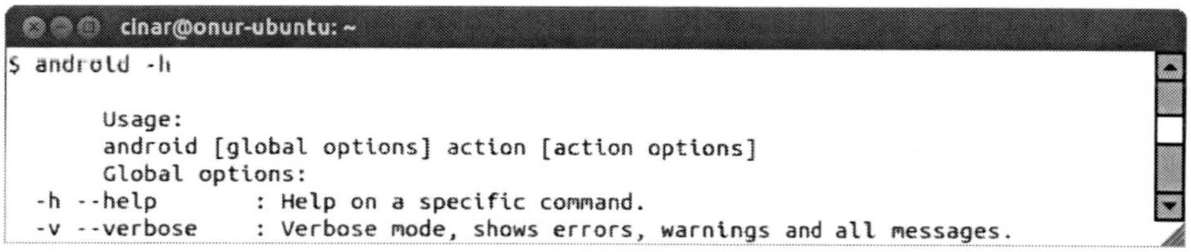

```
cinar@onur-ubuntu: ~
$ android -h

      Usage:
      android [global options] action [action options]
      Global options:
  -h --help       : Help on a specific command.
  -v --verbose    : Verbose mode, shows errors, warnings and all messages.
```

Figure 1-57. Validating Android SDK installation

Downloading and Installing the Android NDK on Linux

The Android Native Development Kit (NDK) is a companion tool to Android SDK that lets you develop Android applications using native programming languages such as C++. Android NDK provides header files, libraries, and cross-compiler toolchains. At the time of this writing, the latest version for Android NDK is R8. In order to download the Android NDK, navigate to http://developer.android.com/tools/sdk/ndk/index.html and go to the Downloads section, as shown in Figure 1-58. Follow these steps to install it:

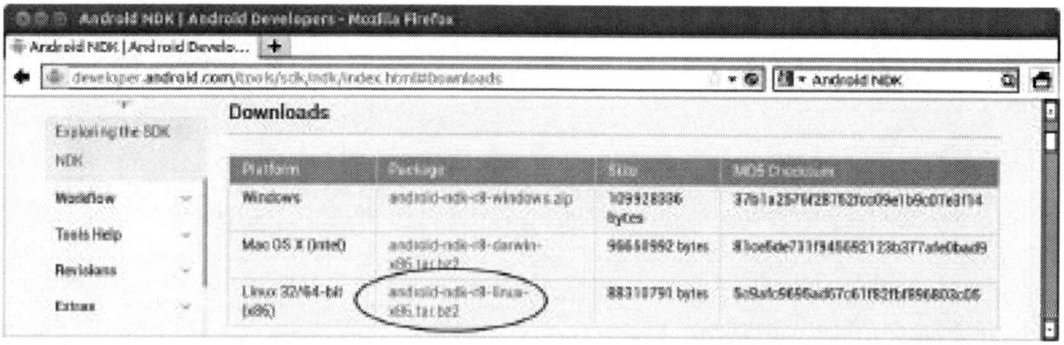

Figure 1-58. Android NDK download page

1. Open a Terminal window and go into the destination directory ~/android.

2. The Android NDK installation package is provided as a BZIP'ed TAR archive. Execute tar jxvf ~/Downloads/android-ndk-r8-linux-x86.tar.bz2, as shown in Figure 1-59, to extract the archive file.

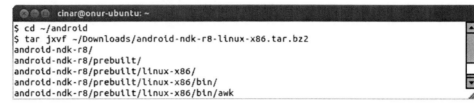

Figure 1-59. Installing Android NDK

The Binary paths of Android NDK should be appended to a system-executable search path in order to make Android NDK easily accessible. Open a Terminal window and execute the following commands (shown in Figure 1-60):

Figure 1-60. Appending Android NDK binary path to system PATH variable

- echo export ANDROID_NDK_HOME =~/android/android-ndk-r8 >>~/.bashrc

- echo export PATH=\$ANDROID_NDK_HOME:\$PATH >>~/.bashrc

Open a new Terminal window and execute ndk-build on the command line to validate the Android NDK installation. If the installation was successful, you will see NDK build complaining about project directory, as shown in Figure 1-61, which is fine.

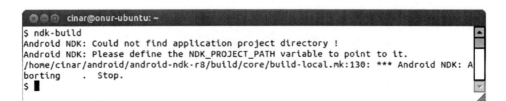

Figure 1-61. Validating Android NDK installation

Downloading and Installing the Eclipse on Linux

Eclipse is a highly extensible, multi-language integrated development environment. Although it is not a requirement for native Android development, Eclipse does provide a highly integrated coding environment, bringing Android tools to your fingertips to streamline the application development. At the time of this writing, the latest version of Eclipse is Juno 4.2. Download Eclipse by navigating to www.eclipse.org/downloads/, as shown in Figure 1-62:

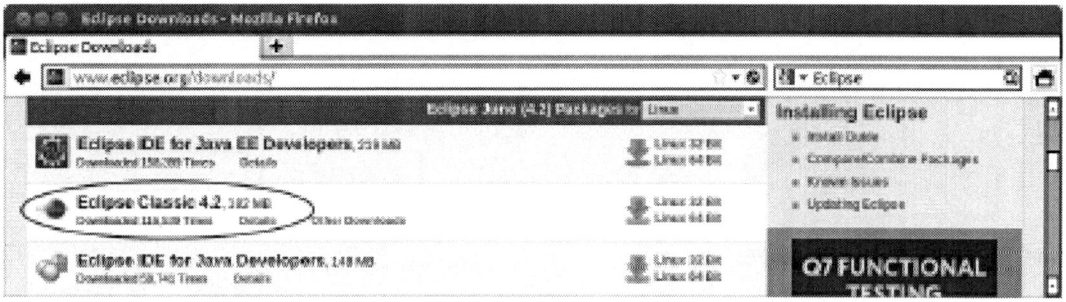

Figure 1-62. Eclipse download page

1. Download the Eclipse Classic for Linux 32 Bit from the list.

2. Open a Terminal window and go into the destination directory ~/android.

3. The Eclipse installation package is provided as a GZIP'ed TAR archive. Extract the archive by invoking tar xvf ~/Downloads/eclipse-SDK-4.2-linux-gtk.tar.gz on the command line, as shown in Figure 1-63.

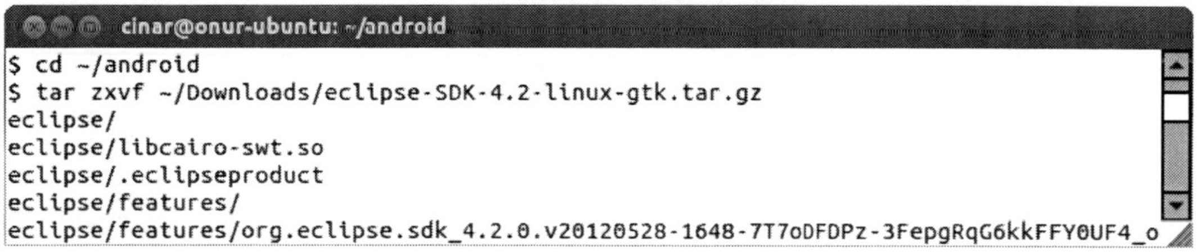

```
cinar@onur-ubuntu: ~/android
$ cd ~/android
$ tar zxvf ~/Downloads/eclipse-SDK-4.2-linux-gtk.tar.gz
eclipse/
eclipse/libcairo-swt.so
eclipse/.eclipseproduct
eclipse/features/
eclipse/features/org.eclipse.sdk_4.2.0.v20120528-1648-7T7oDFDPz-3FepgRqG6kkFFY0UF4_o
```

Figure 1-63. Installing Eclipse

To validate the Eclipse installation, go into the eclipse directory and execute ./eclipse on the command line. If the installation was successful, you will see the Eclipse Workspace Launcher dialog shown in Figure 1-64.

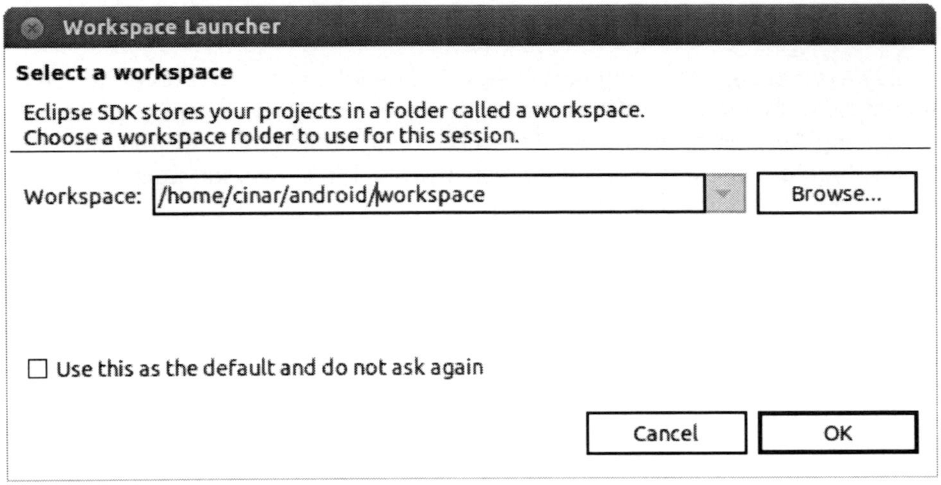

Figure 1-64. Validating Eclipse installation

Downloading and Installing the ADT

Android Development Tools (ADT) is a platform-independent component of the Android C++ development environment. It has to be installed on all three operating systems.

The Eclipse platform is structured around the concept of plug-ins. ADT is a set of plug-ins for Android application development on the Eclipse platform. ADT is free software that is provided under the open source Apache License. More information about the latest ADT version and the most current installation steps can be found at the ADT Plug-in for Eclipse page at `http://developer.android.com/sdk/eclipse-adt.html`. You will be using Eclipse's Install New Software wizard to install ADT.

1. Launch the wizard by choosing **Help ➤ Install New Software** from the top menu bar, as shown in Figure 1-65.

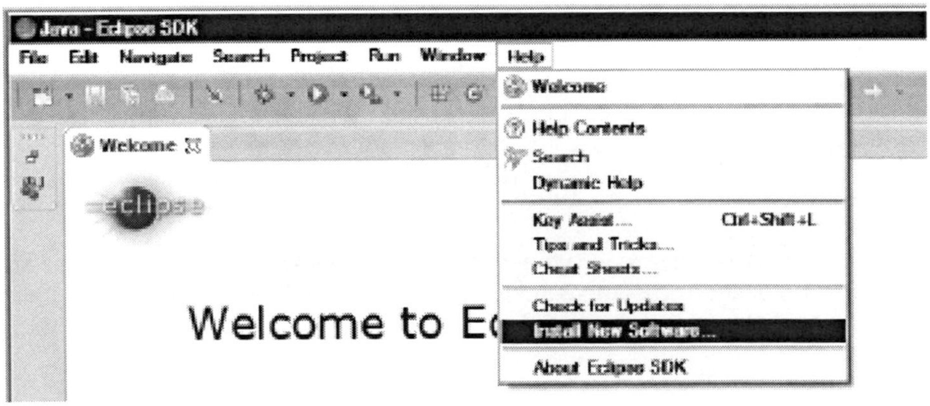

Figure 1-65. Eclipse install new software

2. The wizard will start and display a list of available plug-ins. Since ADT is not part of the official Eclipse software repository, you need to first add Android's Eclipse software repository as a new software site. To do this, click the Add button, as shown in Figure 1-66.

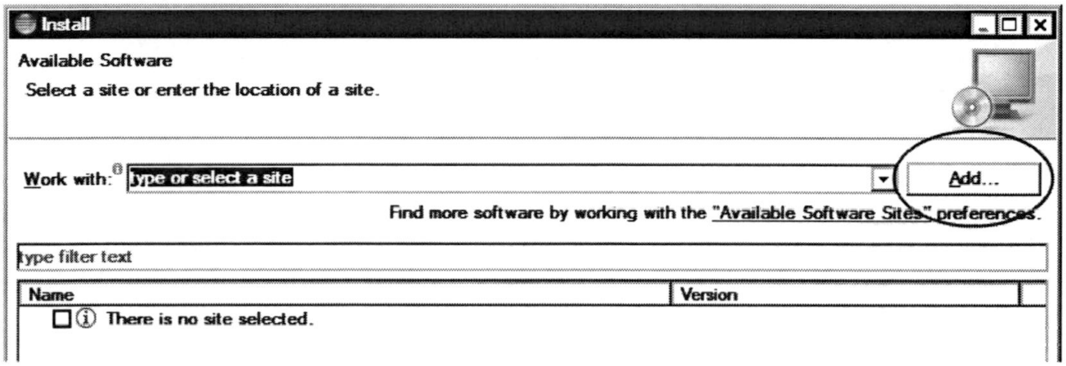

Figure 1-66. Add new software repository

3. The Add Repository dialog appears. In the Name field, enter Android ADT, and in the Location field, enter the URL for Android's Eclipse software repository: `https://dl-ssl.google.com/android/eclipse/` (see Figure 1-67).

Figure 1-67. Add Android ADT software repository

4. Click the OK button to add the new software site.

5. The Install New Software wizard will display a list of available ADT plug-ins, as shown in Figure 1-68. Each of these plug-ins is crucial for Android application development, and it is highly recommended that you install all of them.

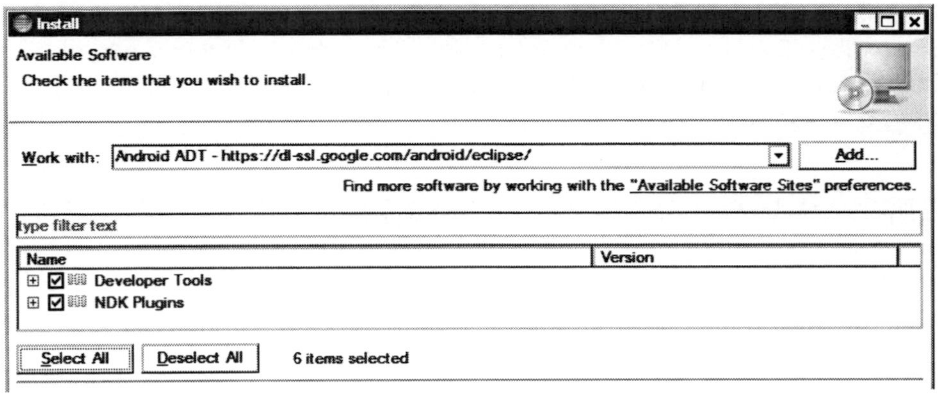

Figure 1-68. Installing ADT

6. Click the Select All button to select all of the ADT plug-ins.

7. Click the Next button to move to the next step.

8. Eclipse will go through the list of selected plug-ins to append any dependencies to the list and then will present the final download list for review. Click the Next button to move to the next step.

9. ADT contains a set of other third-party components with different licensing terms. During the installation process, Eclipse will present each software license and will ask you to accept the terms of the license agreements in order to continue with the installation. Review the license agreements, choose to accept their terms, and then click the Finish button to start the installation process.

ADT plug-ins come within unsigned JAR files, which may trigger a security warning, as shown in Figure 1-69. Click the OK button to dismiss the warning and continue the installation. When the installation of the ADT plug-ins is complete, Eclipse will need to restart in order to apply the changes.

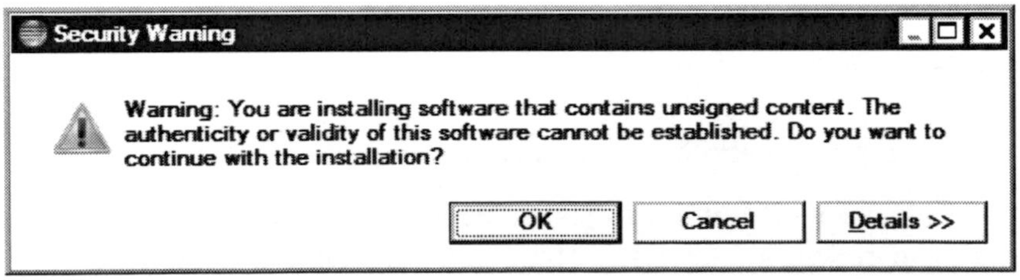

Figure 1-69. Security warning

Upon restarting, ADT will ask you for the location of the Android SDK. Choose "Use existing SDKs" and select the Android SDK installation directory using the Browse button, as shown in Figure 1-70.

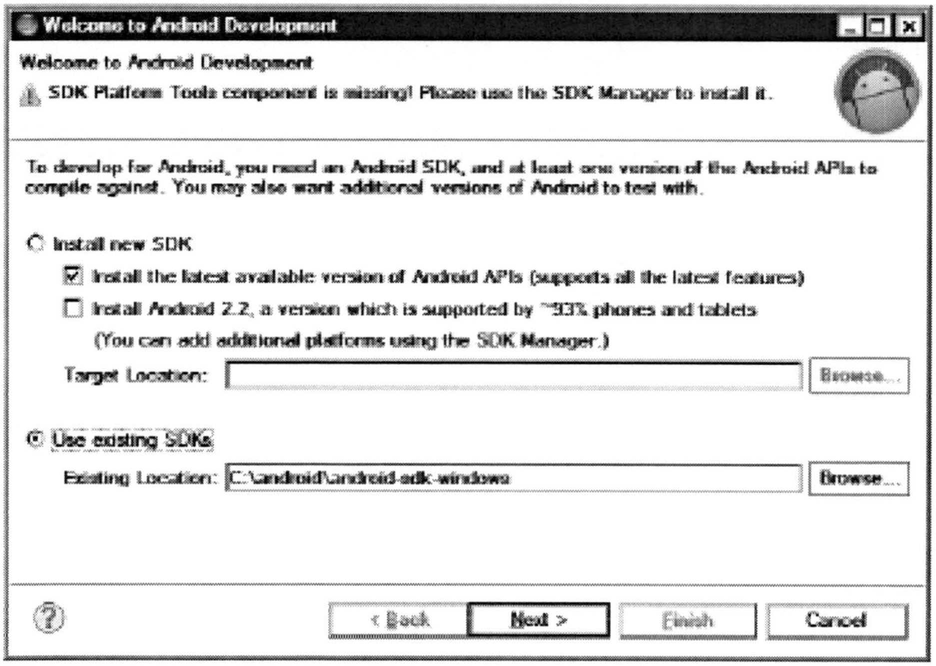

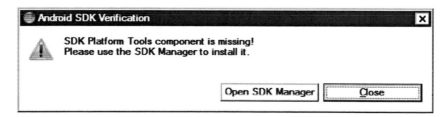

Figure 1-70. Selecting the Android SDK location

Click the Next button to proceed to next step.

Installing the Android Platform Packages

Upon selecting the Android SDK location, ADT validates the Android SDK and the Android Platform packages. The Android SDK installation only contains the Android development tools. The Android Platform packages need to be installed separately to be able to build Android applications. Upon completing the validation, a SDK validation warning dialog is displayed, as shown in Figure 1-71.

Figure 1-71. ADT Android SDK validation

Click the Open SDK Manager button to launch the Android SDK Manager. Then follow these steps, as shown in Figure 1-72:

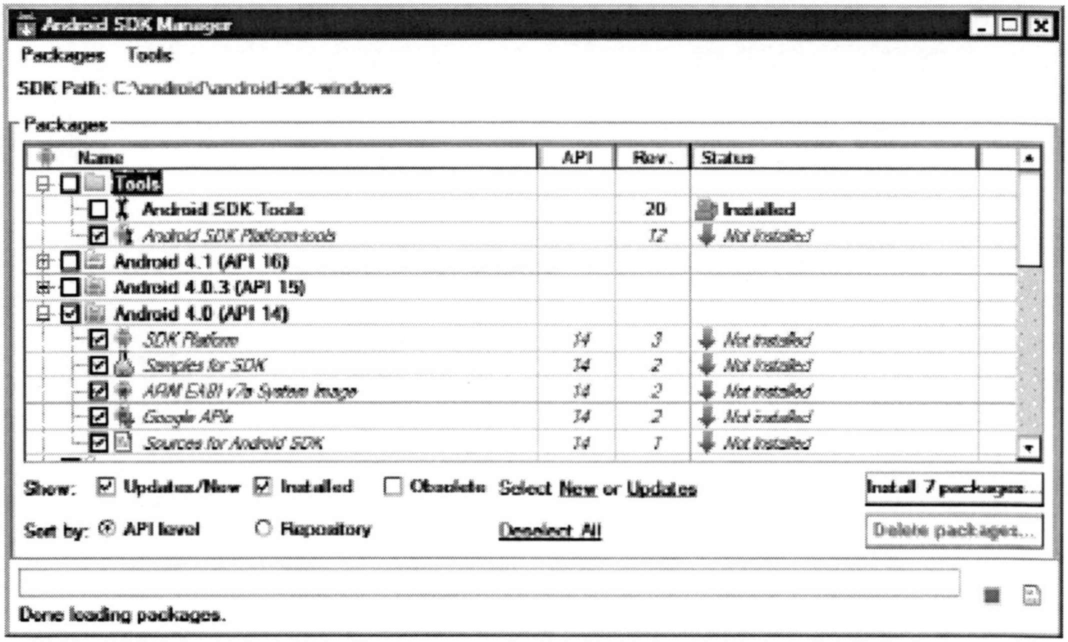

Figure 1-72. Android SDK manager

1. Expand the Tools category from the list of available packages and select Android SDK Platform-Tools.

2. Select the Android 4.0 (API 14) category.

3. Click the Install *N* Packages button to start the installation.

Android SDK manager will show the license agreements for the selected packages. Accept the license agreements to continue the installation.

Configuring the Emulator

The Android SDK comes with a full-featured emulator, a virtual device that runs on your machine. The Android emulator allows you to develop and test Android applications locally on your machine without using a physical device.

The Android emulator runs a full Android system stack, including the Linux kernel. It is a fully virtualized device that can mimic all of the hardware and software features of a real device. Each of these features can be customized by the user using the Android Virtual Device (AVD) Manager. Launch the AVD Manager, choose **Window ➤ AVD Manager** Window AVD Manager from the top menu bar, as shown in Figure 1-73.

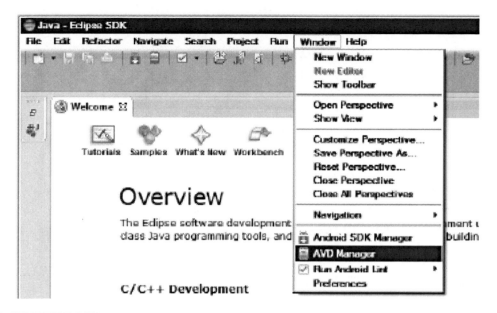

Figure 1-73. AVD Manager menu

Click the New button on right side of the AVD Manager dialog to define a new emulator configuration, as shown in Figure 1-74.

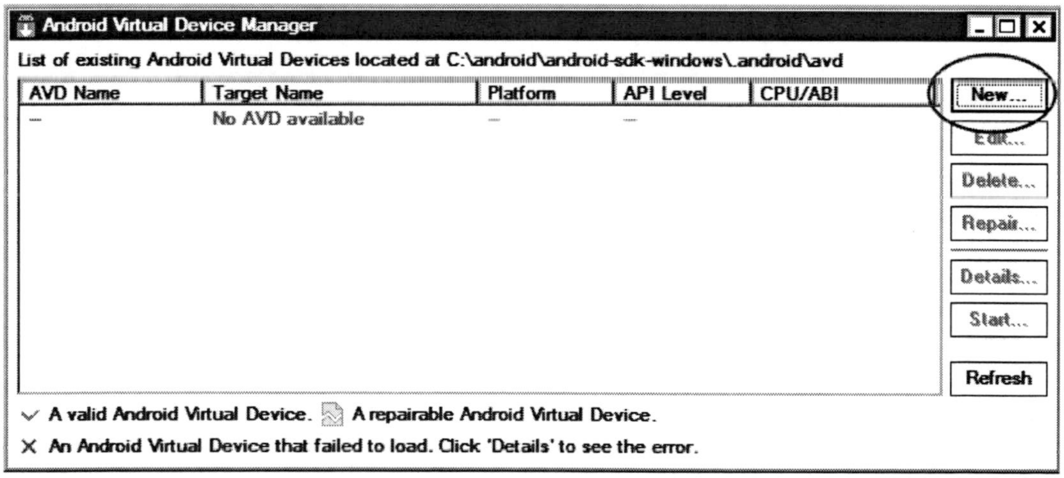

Figure 1-74. AVD Manager

In this book, you will use the Android Emulator often while working through the material. The following virtual machine configuration is recommended to execute the example code in this book. Complete the fields using the following values, as shown in Figure 1-75:

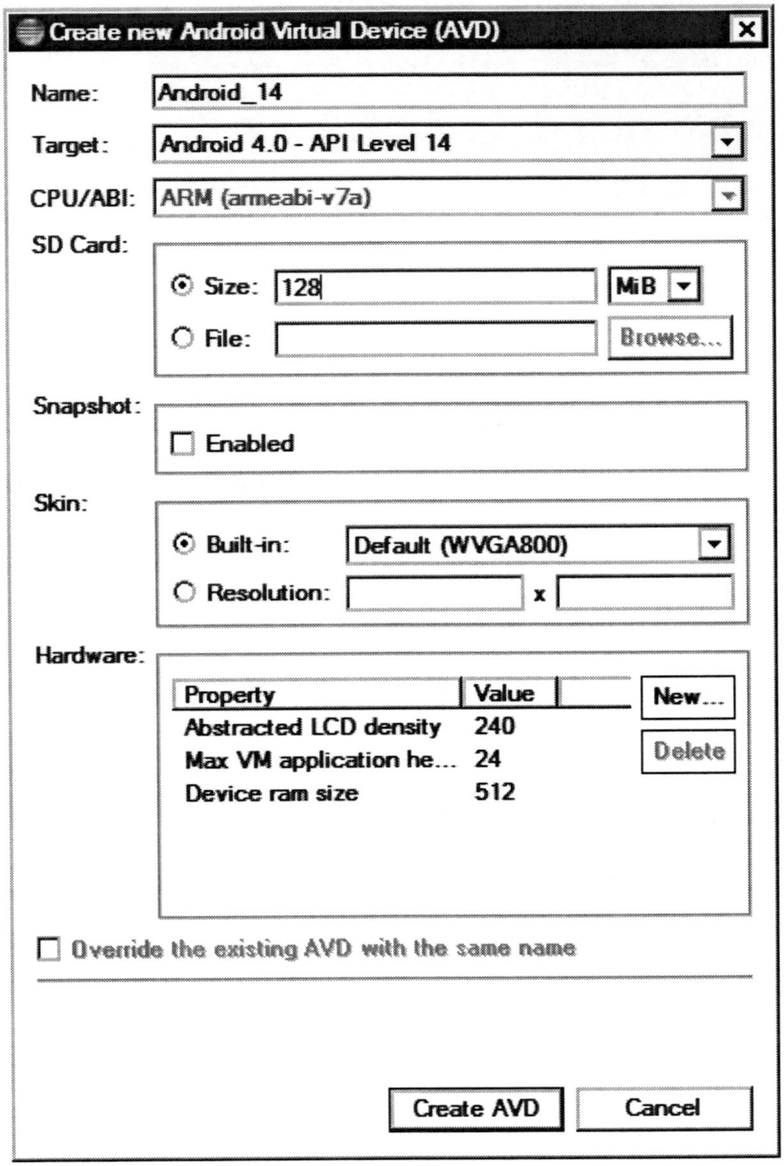

Figure 1-75. *New emulator configuration*

- The Name parameter should be set to **Android_14**.

- The Target parameter should be set to **Android 4.0 – API Level 14**.

- The SD Card size should be set to at least 128 MB.

The other settings can be left as is.

In order to validate the newly defined emulator configuration, open up the AVD Manager, select the name of the emulator configuration from the list, and click the Start button to launch the emulator instance. If the configuration was successful, the emulator will come up (see Figure 1-76).

Figure 1-76. Newly defined emulator configuration running

Summary

In this chapter you have configured your Android C++ development environment by installing the Android development tools and dependencies based on the target operating system. You have defined the Android emulator configuration to execute the example code that will be presented in the following chapters. The next chapter will provide a detailed introduction to the Android NDK.

## Chapter 2

Exploring the Android NDK

In the previous chapter, you configured your development environment by installing Android development tools and dependencies. Among these tools, the Android Native Development Kit (NDK) is the tool you will be using for C++ development on Android platform. The Android NDK is a companion toolset for the Android Software Development Kit (SDK), designed to augment the Android SDK to allow developers to implement and embed performance-critical portions of their applications using machine code-generating programming languages like C, C++, and Assembly.

In this chapter, you will start exploring the Android NDK. You will be taking the `hello-jni` sample application that comes with the Android NDK and manipulating it to demonstrate the Android NDK build system.

Components Provided with the Android NDK

The Android NDK is not a single tool; it is a comprehensive set of APIs, cross-compilers, linkers, debuggers, build tools, documentation, and sample applications. The following are some of the key components of Android NDK:

- ARM, x86, and MIPS cross-compilers
- Build system
- Java Native Interface headers
- C library
- Math library
- POSIX threads
- Minimal C++ library
- ZLib compression library
- Dynamic linker library
- Android logging library

- Android pixel buffer library

- Android native application APIs

- OpenGL ES 3D graphics library

- OpenSL ES native audio library

- OpenMAX AL minimal support

Structure of the Android NDK

During the installation process, all of the Android NDK components are installed under the target directory. The following are some of the important files and subdirectories:

- `ndk-build`: This shell script is the starting point of the Android NDK build system. This chapter will cover `ndk-build` in detail while exploring the Android NDK build system.

- `ndk-gdb`: This shell script allows debugging native components using the GNU Debugger. Chapter 5 will cover `ndk-gdb` in detail while discussing the debugging of native components.

- `ndk-stack`: This shell script helps facilitate analyzing the stack traces that are produced when native components crash. Chapter 5 will cover `ndk-stack` in detail while discussing the troubleshooting and crash dump analysis of native components.

- `build`: This directory contains the modules of the entire Android NDK build system. This chapter will cover the Android NDK build system in detail.

- `platforms`: This directory contains header files and libraries for each supported Android target version. These files are used automatically by the Android NDK build system based on the specified target version.

- `samples`: This directory contains sample applications to demonstrate the capabilities provided by the Android NDK. These sample projects are very useful for learning how to use the features provided by the Android NDK.

- `sources`: This directory contains shared modules that developers can import into their existing Android NDK projects.

- `toolchains`: This directory contains cross-compilers for different target machine architectures that the Android NDK currently supports. Android NDK currently supports ARM, x86, and MIPS machine architectures. The Android NDK build system uses the cross-compiler based on the selected machine architecture.

The most important component of the Android NDK is its build system, which brings all other components together. To better understand how the build system works, you will be starting with a working example.

Starting with an Example

You will start with the hello-jni sample application that comes with the Android NDK. Later, you will modify it to demonstrate the different functionalities provided by the Android NDK build system, such as

- Building a shared library
- Building multiple shared libraries
- Building static libraries
- Sharing common modules using shared libraries
- Sharing modules between multiple NDK projects
- Using prebuilt libraries
- Building standalone executables
- Other build system variables and macros
- Defining new variables and conditional operations

Open the Eclipse IDE that you installed in the previous chapter. Although the Android NDK does not require the use of an IDE, using one will help to visually inspect the project structure and the build flow. During the startup, Eclipse will ask you to choose the workspace; you can continue with the default.

Specifying the Android NDK Location

Since this is the first time the workspace will be used for Android NDK development, the location of the Android NDK needs to be specified.

1. On Windows and Linux platforms, choose the **Preferences** menu item from the top menu bar. On Mac OS X platform, use the application menu in Eclipse and choose the **Preferences** menu item.

2. As shown in Figure 2-1, the left pane of the Preferences dialog contains the list of preferences categories in a tree format. Expand Android and then choose NDK from the tree.

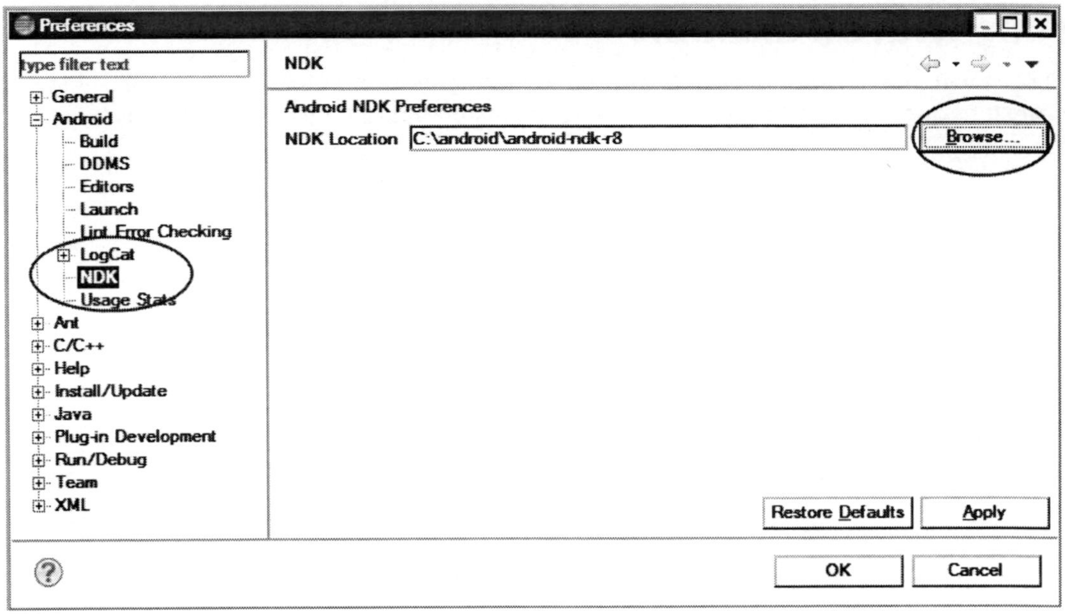

Figure 2-1. Android NDK location preference

3.   Using the right pane, click the Browse button and select the location of
     Android NDK installation using the file explorer.

The NDK location preference is only for the current Eclipse workspace. If you use another workspace later, you will need to repeat this process again.

Importing the Sample Project

As stated in the previous section, Android NDK installation contains example applications under the samples directory. You will be using one of those sample applications now.

Using the top menu bar, choose **File**, and then the **Import** menu item to launch the Import wizard. From the list of import sources, expand **Android** and choose **Existing Android Code into Workspace**, as shown in Figure 2-2. Click **Next** to proceed to the next step.

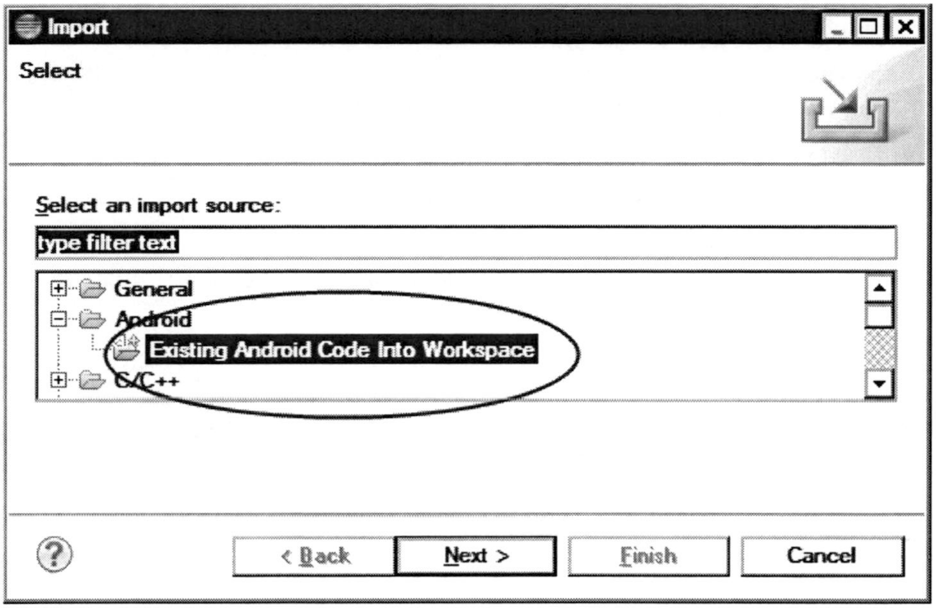

Figure 2-2. *Import existing Android code into workspace*

As shown in Figure 2-3, use the **Browse** button to launch the file explorer and navigate to <Android NDK>/samples/hello-jni directory. The hello-jni project is simple "Hello World" Android NDK project. The project directory contains both the actual project and the test project. For the sake of simplicity, uncheck the test project for now, and only keep the main project checked. It is always a good practice to not change anything in the Android NDK installation directory to keep things safe. Check the "**Copy projects into workspace**" option to ask Eclipse to copy the project code into the workspace, so that you can operate on a copy rather than the original project. Click **Next** to start importing the project into the workspace.

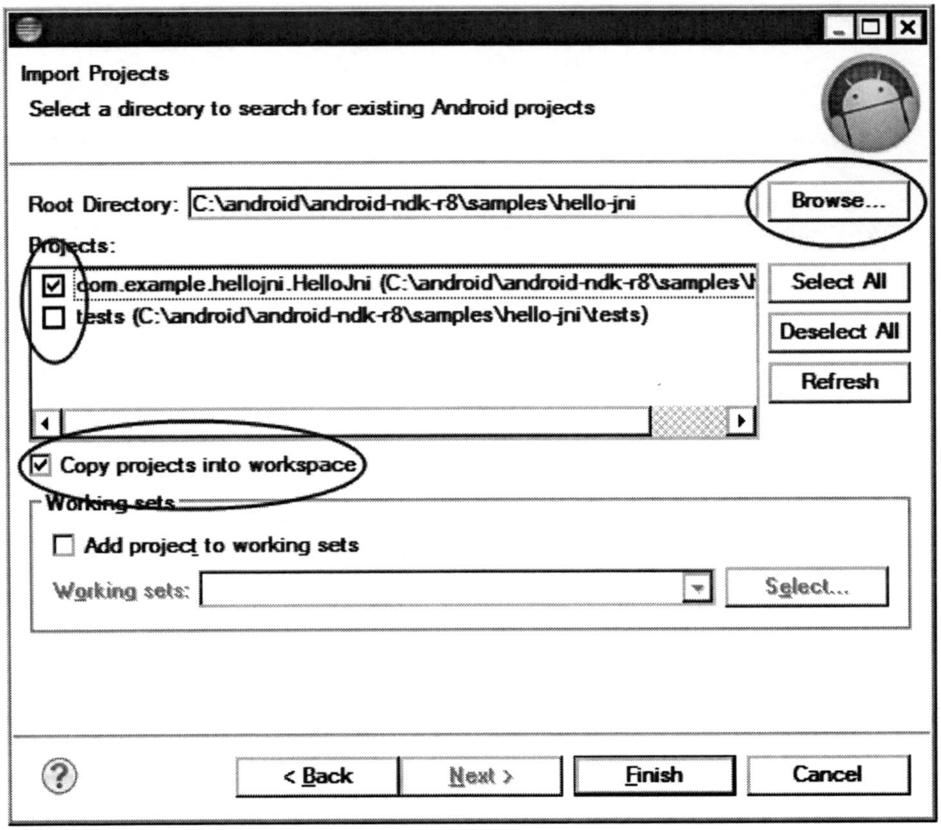

Figure 2-3. *Importing hello-jni Android NDK project*

You will notice an error message on the console at the end of the import process, as shown in Figure 2-4. As you may recall, in the previous chapter you only downloaded the platform APIs for Android 4.0 (API Level 14) using the SDK Manager. The hello-jni project is developed for Android 1.5 (API Level 3).

Figure 2-4. *Unable to resolve target API level 3*

API levels are backward compatible. Instead of downloading API Level 3, using the Project Explorer view in Eclipse, right-click to com.example.hellojni.HelloJni project, and choose Properties from the context menu to launch the project properties dialog. The right pane of the project properties dialog contains the list of project properties categories in a tree format. Choose Android from the tree, and using the right pane, select Android 4.0 as the project build target (see Figure 2-5).

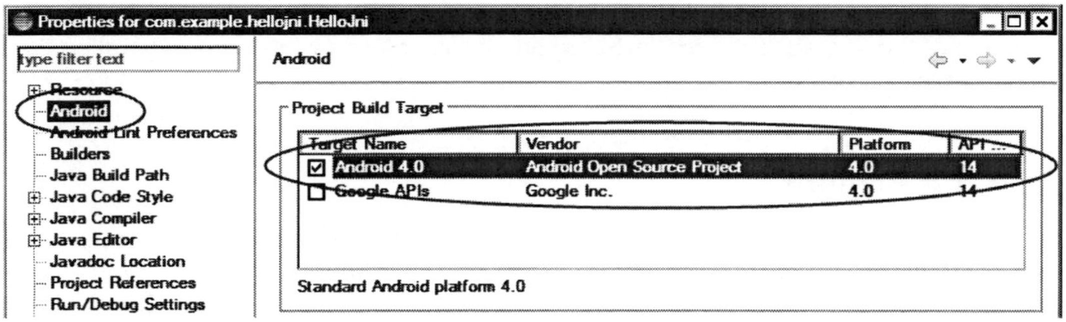

Figure 2-5. Choose Android 4.0 as the project build target

Click the **OK** button to apply the changes. Eclipse will rebuild the project using the selected project build target.

Adding Native Support to Project

The Import Android Project wizard only imports projects as Android Java projects. The native support needs to be added manually in order to include the native components into the build flow. Using the Project Explorer view in Eclipse, right-click to the `com.example.hellojni.HelloJni` project, hover on the **Android Tools** menu item, and choose "**Add Native Support**" from the context menu. The Add Android Native Support dialog will be launched, as shown in Figure 2-6. Since the project already contains a native project, you can leave the library name as is, and click to the Finish button to proceed.

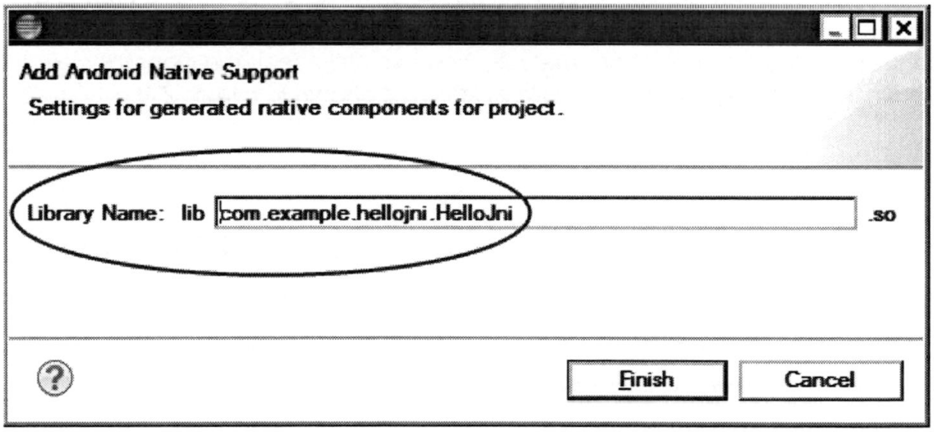

Figure 2-6. Add Android native support

If this is the first time you are adding native support to a Java-only project, you can specify the preferred name of the shared library in this dialog and it will be used while auto-generating the build files as a part of the process.

Running the Project

Now that the project is ready, you can run it on the Android emulator. Choose Run from the top menu, and select Run from the submenu. Since this is the first time you are running this project, Eclipse will ask you to select how you would like to run the project through the Run As dialog. Choose **Android Application** from the list and click **OK** button to proceed. Android Emulator will be launched; the project will be automatically deployed and executed by Eclipse, as shown in Figure 2-7. Android Emulator is a virtual machine, and it may take several minutes for it to fully launch the Android operating system.

Figure 2-7. *Android Emulator running the native project*

As you may have noticed, the process to run the project is exactly the same as running a Java-only project. Adding the native support to the project automatically incorporates the necessary steps into the build process transparently from the user. You can still check the Console view to watch the messages coming from the Android NDK build system, as shown in Figure 2-8.

```
 Problems   Tasks   Console ⊠   Properties                   ⇩ ⇧ 

CDT Build Console [com.example.hellojni.HelloJni]
15:06:05 **** Build of configuration Default for project com.example.hellojni.HelloJni ****
sh "C:\\android\\android-ndk-r8\\ndk-build" all
Gdbserver      : [arm-linux-androideabi-4.4.3] libs/armeabi/gdbserver

Gdbsetup       : libs/armeabi/gdb.setup

Cygwin         : Generating dependency file converter script

Compile thumb  : hello-jni <= hello-jni.c

SharedLibrary  : libhello-jni.so

Install        : libhello-jni.so => libs/armeabi/libhello-jni.so


15:06:09 Build Finished (took 3s.815ms)
```

Figure 2-8. *Console view showing Android NDK build messages*

Although Eclipse did a great job streamlining the entire build and deployment process for us, as stated earlier in this chapter, Eclipse is not a requirement to build Android NDK projects. The entire build process can be executed from the command line as well.

Building from the Command Line

In order to build the hello-jni project from the command line, first open up a command prompt in Windows or a Terminal window in Mac OS X or Linux, and change your directory to hello-jni project. Building an Android project with native components requires a two-step process. The first step is to build the native components, and the second step is to build the Java application and then package both Java application and its native components together. To build the native components, execute ndk-build on the command line. The ndk-build is a helper script that invokes the Android build system. As shown in Figure 2-9, Android NDK build script will output progress messages throughout the build process.

```
C:\android\workspace\com.example.hellojni.HelloJni>ndk-build
Gdbserver      : [arm-linux-androideabi 4.4.3] libs/armeabi/gdbserver
Gdbsetup       : libs/armeabi/gdb.setup
"Compile thumb : hello jni <= hello-jni.c
SharedLibrary  : libhello-jni.so
Install        : libhello-jni.so => libs/armeabi/libhello-jni.so

C:\android\workspace\com.example.hellojni.HelloJni>_
```

Figure 2-9. Building the native components using ndk-build

Now that those native components are properly built, you can proceed with the second step. The Android SDK build system is based on Apache ANT. Since this is the first time you are going to build the project from the command line, the Apache ANT build files should be generated first. Execute android update project -p . -n hello-jni -t android-14 --subprojects on the command line to generate the Apache ANT build files, as shown in Figure 2-10.

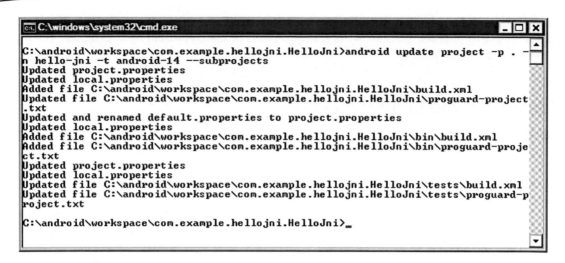

Figure 2-10. Generating Apache ANT build files

Now that the Apache ANT build files are ready, you can build the project by executing ant debug on the command line. Apache ANT will build the Java files and package them with the native components into an installable Android package file, also known as the APK file. As you can see from the multiple-step process, using Eclipse is the easiest way to build Android projects with native components, and it is less error prone since you don't have to remember each build step.

Examining the Structure of an Android NDK Project

Let's go back into Eclipse and study the structure of an Android application with native components. As shown in Figure 2-11, an Android project with native components contains a set of additional directories and files.

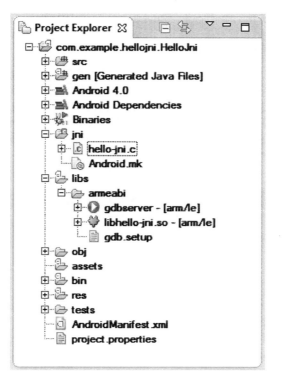

Figure 2-11. Structure of hello-jni Android NDK project

- jni: This directory contains the source code for the native components plus the Android.mk build file describing how the native components should be built. The Android NDK build system refers to this directory as the NDK project directory and it expects to find it at project root.

- libs: This directory gets created during the build process by the Android NDK build system. It contains individual subdirectories for target machine architecture that are specified, such as armeabi for the ARM. This directory gets incorporated into the APK file during the packaging process.

- obj: This directory is an intermediate directory holding the object files that are produced after compiling the source code. Developers are not expected to touch this directory.

The most important component of the Android NDK project here is the Android.mk build file, which describes the native components. Understanding the build system is the key to successfully using the Android NDK and all its components.

Build System

The Android NDK comes with its own build system that is based on GNU Make. The primary goal of this build system is to allow developers to only write very short build files to describe their native Android applications; the build system handles many details including the toolchain, platform, CPU, and ABI specifics on behalf of the developer. Having the build process encapsulated allows the later updates of the Android NDK to add support for more toolchains, platforms, and system interfaces without requiring changes in the build files.

The Android NDK build system is formed by multiple GNU Makefile fragments. The build system includes the necessary fragments based on type of the NDK project needed to render the build process. As shown in Figure 2-12, these build system fragments can be found in the build/core sub-directory of the Android NDK installation. Although developers are not expected to directly interface with these files, knowing their locations becomes highly beneficial when troubleshooting build-system–related problems.

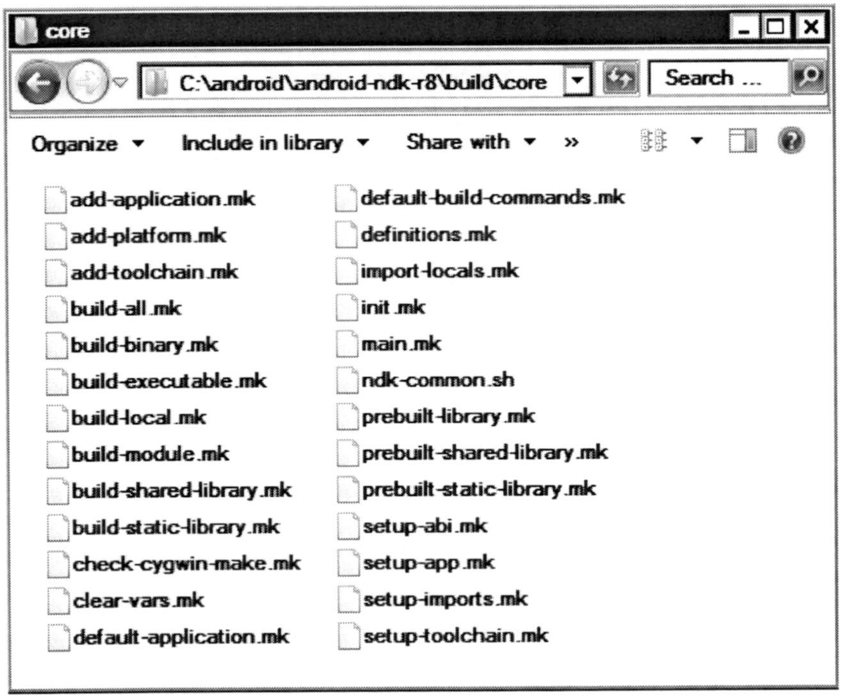

Figure 2-12. Android NDK build system fragments

In addition to those fragments, the Android NDK build system relies on two other files that are expected to be provided by the developer as a part of the NDK project: Android.mk and Application.mk. Let's review them now.

Android.mk

Android.mk is a GNU Makefile fragment that describes the NDK project to the Android NDK build system. It is a required component of every NDK project. The build system expects it to be present in the jni sub-directory. Using the Project Explorer in Eclipse, double-click the Android.mk file to open it in the editor view. Listing 2-1 shows the contents of the Android.mk file from the hello-jni project.

Listing 2-1. Contents of Android.mk File from hello-jni Project

```
# Copyright (C) 2009 The Alndroid Open Source Project
#
# Licensed under the Apache License, Version 2.0 (the "License");
# you may not use this file except in compliance with the License.
# You may obtain a copy of the License at
#
#        http://www.apache.org/licenses/LICENSE-2.0
#
# Unless required by applicable law or agreed to in writing, software
# distributed under the License is distributed on an "AS IS" BASIS,
# WITHOUT WARRANTIES OR CONDITIONS OF ANY KIND, either express or implied.
# See the License for the specific language governing permissions and
# limitations under the License.
#
LOCAL_PATH := $(call my-dir)

include $(CLEAR_VARS)

LOCAL_MODULE     := hello-jni
LOCAL_SRC_FILES := hello-jni.c

include $(BUILD_SHARED_LIBRARY)
```

Let's go through this file line by line to better understand its syntax. Since this is a GNU Makefile fragment, its syntax is exactly the same as any other Makefile. Each line contains a single instruction. The lines starting with a hash (#) sign indicate a comment and they are not processed by the GNU Make tool. By the naming convention, the variable names are upper-case.

The first instruction after the comments block is the definition of the LOCAL_PATH variable. As a requirement of the Android build system, the Android.mk file should always begin with the definition of LOCAL_PATH variable.

```
LOCAL_PATH := $(call my-dir)
```

The LOCAL_PATH is used by the Android build system to locate the source files. Since setting this variable to a hard-coded value is not appropriate, the Android build system provides a macro function called my-dir. By setting the variable to the return of the my-dir macro function, it gets set to the current directory.

The CLEAR_VARS variable gets set by the Android build system to the location of clear-vars.mk fragment. Including this Makefile fragment clears the LOCAL_<name> variables such as LOCAL_MODULE, LOCAL_SRC_FILES, etc., with the exception of LOCAL_PATH.

```
include $(CLEAR_VARS)
```

This is needed because multiple build files and module definitions are parsed by the Android build system in a single execution, and the LOCAL_<name> variables are global. Clearing them prevent conflicts. Each native component is referred to as a module.

The `LOCAL_MODULE` variable is used to name these modules with a unique name. This line sets the name of the module to `hello-jni`

```
LOCAL_MODULE    := hello-jni
```

since the module name is also used to name the generated file as a result of the build process. The build system adds the proper prefix and the suffix to the file. In this example, the `hello-jni` module will generate a shared library file, and it will be named as `libhello-jni.so` by the build system.

The list of source files that will be built and assembled to produce the module is defined using the `LOCAL_SRC_FILES` variable.

```
LOCAL_SRC_FILES := hello-jni.c
```

The `hello-jni` module is produced by only one source file, but `LOCAL_SRC_FILES` variable can contain more than one source file separated by spaces.

Until this point, the build system variables that are defined in the `Android.mk` file simply described the native project. For the build system to compile and generate the actual module, the appropriate build system fragment needs to be included, depending on the type of the preferred module.

Building a Shared Library

In order to have a consumable module by the main application, it has to become a shared library. The `BUILD_SHARED_LIBRARY` variable is set by the Android NDK build system to the location of `build-shared-library.mk` file. This Makefile fragment contains the necessary build procedure to build and assemble the source files as a shared library:

```
include $(BUILD_SHARED_LIBRARY)
```

The `hello-jni` is a simple module; however, unless your module requires any special treatment, your `Android.mk` file will contain the exact same flow and instructions.

Building Multiple Shared Libraries

Depending on your application's architecture, multiple shared library modules can also be produced from a single `Android.mk` file. In order to do so, multiple modules need to be defined in the `Android.mk` file, as shown in Listing 2-2.

Listing 2-2. Android.mk Build File with Multiple Shared Library Modules

```
LOCAL_PATH := $(call my-dir)

#
# Module 1
#
include $(CLEAR_VARS)

LOCAL_MODULE    := module1
LOCAL_SRC_FILES := module1.c
```

```
include $(BUILD_SHARED_LIBRARY)

#
# Module 2
#
include $(CLEAR_VARS)

LOCAL_MODULE     := module2
LOCAL_SRC_FILES := module2.c

include $(BUILD_SHARED_LIBRARY)
```

The Android NDK build system will produce `libmodule1.so` and `libmodule2.so` shared libraries after processing this `Android.mk` build file.

Building Static Libraries

Static libraries are also supported by the Android NDK build system. Static libraries are not directly consumable by the actual Android application, and they don't get included into the application package. Static libraries can be used to build shared libraries. For example, when integrating third party code into an existing native project, instead of including the source code directly, the third party code can be compiled as a static library and then combined into the shared library, as shown in Listing 2-3.

Listing 2-3. Android.mk File Showing the Use of Static Library

```
LOCAL_PATH := $(call my-dir)

#
# 3rd party AVI library
#
include $(CLEAR_VARS)

LOCAL_MODULE     := avilib
LOCAL_SRC_FILES := avilib.c platform_posix.c

include $(BUILD_STATIC_LIBRARY)

#
# Native module
#
include $(CLEAR_VARS)

LOCAL_MODULE     := module
LOCAL_SRC_FILES := module.c

LOCAL_STATIC_LIBRARIES := avilib

include $(BUILD_SHARED_LIBRARY)
```

Upon building the module as a static library, it can get consumed by the shared libraries by including its module name into the LOCAL_STATIC_LIBRARIES variable.

Sharing Common Modules using Shared Libraries

Static libraries allow you to keep your source code modular; however, when the static library gets linked into a shared library, it becomes part of that shared library. In the case of multiple shared libraries, linking with the same static library simply increases the application size due to multiple copies of the common module. In such cases, instead of building a static library, the common module can be built as a shared library, and the dependent modules then dynamically link to it to eliminate the duplicate copies (see Listing 2-4).

Listing 2-4. Android.mk File Showing Code Sharing Between Shared Libraries

```
LOCAL_PATH := $(call my-dir)

#
# 3rd party AVI library
#
include $(CLEAR_VARS)

LOCAL_MODULE    := avilib
LOCAL_SRC_FILES := avilib.c platform_posix.c

include $(BUILD_SHARED_LIBRARY)

#
# Native module 1
#
include $(CLEAR_VARS)

LOCAL_MODULE    := module1
LOCAL_SRC_FILES := module1.c

LOCAL_SHARED_LIBRARIES := avilib

include $(BUILD_SHARED_LIBRARY)

#
# Native module 2
#
include $(CLEAR_VARS)

LOCAL_MODULE    := module2
LOCAL_SRC_FILES := module2.c

LOCAL_SHARED_LIBRARIES := avilib

include $(BUILD_SHARED_LIBRARY)
```

Sharing Modules between Multiple NDK Projects

Using both the static and shared libraries, the common modules can be shared between modules. However, the caveat here is that all these modules should be part of the same NDK project. Starting from version R5, Android NDK also allows sharing and reusing modules between NDK projects. Considering the previous example, the avilib module can be shared between multiple NDK projects by doing the following:

■ First, move the avilib source code to a location outside the NDK project, such as C:\android\shared-modules\avilib. In order to prevent name conflicts, the directory structure can also include the module provider's name, such as C:\android\shared-modules\transcode\avilib.

> **Caution**   The Android NDK build system does not accept the space character in shared module path.

■ As a shared module, avilib requires its own Android.mk file, as shown in Listing 2-5.

Listing 2-5. Android.mk File of the Shared avilib Module

```
LOCAL_PATH := $(call my-dir)

#
# 3rd party AVI library
#
include $(CLEAR_VARS)

LOCAL_MODULE     := avilib
LOCAL_SRC_FILES := avilib.c platform_posix.c

include $(BUILD_SHARED_LIBRARY)
```

■ Now the avilib module can be removed from the Android.mk file of the NDK project. A call to function macro import-module with parameter transcode/ avilib should be added to the end of the build file, as shown in Listing 2-6, to use this shared module. The import-module function macro call should be placed at the end of the Android.mk file to prevent any build system conflicts.

Listing 2-6. NDK Project Using the Shared Module

```
#
# Native module
#
include $(CLEAR_VARS)

LOCAL_MODULE     :- module
LOCAL_SRC_FILES := module.c
```

```
            LOCAL_SHARED_LIBRARIES := avilib

            include $(BUILD_SHARED_LIBRARY)
```

$(call import-module,transcode/avilib)

- The import-module function macro needs to first locate the shared module and then import it into the NDK project. By default, only the `<Android NDK>/` sources directory is searched by the import-module function macro. In order to include the `c:\android\shared-modules` directory into the search, define a new environment variable called NDK_MODULE_PATH and set it to the root directory of shared modules, such as `c:\android\shared-modules`.

Using Prebuilt Libraries

Using the shared modules requires you to have the source code of the shared modules. The Android NDK build system simply includes these source files in the NDK project and builds them each time. Android NDK, since version R5, also provides support for prebuilt libraries. Prebuilt libraries are very useful in the following situations:

- You want to distribute your modules to other parties without distributing your source code.
- You want to use prebuilt version of your shared modules to speed up the builds.

Although they are already compiled, prebuild modules still required an Android.mk build file, as shown in Listing 2-7.

Listing 2-7. Android.mk File for Prebuilt Shared Module

```
LOCAL_PATH := $(call my-dir)

#
# 3rd party prebuilt AVI library
#
include $(CLEAR_VARS)

LOCAL_MODULE    := avilib
LOCAL_SRC_FILES := libavilib.so

include $(PREBUILT_SHARED_LIBRARY)
```

The LOCAL_SRC_FILES variable, instead of pointing to the source files, points to the location of the actual prebuilt library relative to the LOCAL_PATH.

> **Caution**   The Prebuilt library definition does not carry any information about the actual machine architecture that the prebuilt library is built for. Developers need to ensure that the prebuilt library is built for the same machine architecture as the NDK project.

The PREBUILT_SHARED_LIBRARY variable points to the prebuilt-shared-library.mk Makefile fragment. It does not build anything, but it copies the prebuilt library to the NDK project's libs directory. By using PREBUILT_STATIC_LIBRARY variable, static libraries can also be used as prebuilt libraries the same way as the shared libraries. NDK project can use the prebuilt library the same way as the ordinary shared libraries.

```
...
LOCAL_SHARED_LIBRARIES := avilib
...
```

Building Standalone Executable

The recommended and supported way of using native components on Android platform is through packaging them as shared libraries. However, in order to facilitate testing and quick prototyping, Android NDK also provides support for building a standalone executable. The standalone executables are regular Linux applications that can be copied to the Android device without being packaged into an APK file, and they can get executed directly without being loaded through a Java application. Standalone executables can be produced by importing the BUILD_EXECUTABLE variable in the Android.mk build file instead of BUILD_SHARED_LIBRARY, as shown in Listing 2-8.

Listing 2-8. Android.mk File for Standalone Executable Module

```
#
# Native module standlone executable
#
include $(CLEAR_VARS)

LOCAL_MODULE    := module
LOCAL_SRC_FILES := module.c

LOCAL_STATIC_LIBRARIES := avilib

include $(BUILD_EXECUTABLE)
```

The BUILD_EXECUTABLE variable points to the build-executable.mk Makefile fragment that contains the necessary build steps to produce a standalone executable on Android platform. The standalone executable gets placed into libs/<machine architecture> directory with the same name as the module. Although it is placed into this directory, it does not get included into the APK file during the packaging phase.

Other Build System Variables

Besides the variables covered in the previous sections, there are other variables that are supported by the Android NDK build system. This section will briefly mention them.

The variables that are defined by the build system are

- ▓ TARGET_ARCH: Name of the target CPU architecture, such as arm.
- ▓ TARGET_PLATFORM: Name of the target Android platform, such as android-3.

- TARGET_ARCH_ABI: Name of the target CPU architecture and the ABI, such as armeabi-v7a.

- TARGET_ABI: Concatenation of target platform and ABI, such as android-3-armeabi-v7a.

The variables that can be defined as a part of the module description are

- LOCAL_MODULE_FILENAME: Optional variable to redefine the name of the generated output file. By default the build system uses the value of LOCAL_MODULE as the name of the generated output file, but it can be overridden using this variable.

- LOCAL_CPP_EXTENSION: The default extension of C++ source files is .cpp. This variable can be used to specify one or more file extensions for the C++ source code.

  ```
  ...
  LOCAL_CPP_EXTENSION := .cpp .cxx
  ...
  ```

- LOCAL_CPP_FEATURES: Optional variable to indicate that the module relies on specific C++ features such as RTTI, exceptions, etc.

  ```
  ...
  LOCAL_CPP_FEATURES := rtti
  ...
  ```

- LOCAL_C_INCLUDES: Optional list of paths, relative to NDK installation directory, to search for header files.

  ```
  ...
  LOCAL_C_INCLUDES := sources/shared-module
  LOCAL_C_INCLUDES := $(LOCAL_PATH)/include
  ...
  ```

- LOCAL_CFLAGS: Optional set of compiler flags that will be passed to the compiler while compiling the C and C++ source files.

  ```
  ...
  LOCAL_CFLAGS :=-DNDEBUG -DPORT=1234
  ...
  ```

- LOCAL_CPP_FLAGS: Optional set of compiled flags that will be passed to the compiler while compiling the C++ source files only.

- LOCAL_WHOLE_STATIC_LIBRARIES: A variant of LOCAL_STATIC_LIBRARIES that indicates that the whole content of the static library should be included in the generated shared library.

> **Tip** LOCAL_WHOLE_STATIC_LIBRARIES is very useful when there are circular dependencies between several static libraries.

- LOCAL_LDLIBS: Optional list of linker flags that will be passed to the linker while linking the object files to generate the output file. It is primarily used to pass the list of system libraries to dynamically link with. For example, to link with the Android NDK logging library, use this code:

  ```
  LOCAL_LDFLAGS := -llog
  ```

- LOCAL_ALLOW_UNDEFINED_SYMBOLS: Optionally disables the checking for missing symbols in the generated file. When not defined, the linker will produce error messages indicating the missing symbols.

- LOCAL_ARM_MODE: Optional and ARM machine architecture-specific variable indicating the type of ARM binary to be generated. By default, the build system generates in thumb mode with 16-bit instructions, but this variable can be set to arm to indicate that the 32-bit instructions should be used.

  ```
  LOCAL_ARM_MODE := arm
  ```

  This variable changes the build system behavior for the entire module; the .arm extension can also be used to only build specific files in arm mode.

  ```
  LOCAL_SRC_FILES := file1.c file2.c.arm
  ```

- LOCAL_ARM_NEON: Optional and ARM machine architecture-specific variable indicating that ARM Advanced Single Instruction Multiple Date (SIMD) (a.k.a. NEON) intrinsics should be enabled in the source files.

  ```
  LOCAL_ARM_NEON := true
  ```

  This variable changes the build system behavior for the entire module; the .neon extension can also be used to only build specific files with NEON intrinsics.

  ```
  LOCAL_SRC_FILES := file1.c file2.c.neon
  ```

- LOCAL_DISABLE_NO_EXECUTE: Optional variable to disable the NX Bit security feature. NX Bit, which stands for Never Execute, is a technology used in CPUs to segregate areas of memory for use by either code or storage. This prevents malicious software from taking control of the application by inserting its code into the application's storage memory area.

- LOCAL_DISABLE_NO_EXECUTE := true

- LOCAL_EXPORT_CFLAGS: This variable allows recording a set of compiler flags that will be added to the LOCAL_CFLAGS definition of any other module that is using this module through either LOCAL_STATIC_LIBRARIES or LOCAL_SHARED_LIBRARIES.

  ```
  LOCAL_MODULE := avilib
  ```

```
...
LOCAL_EXPORT_CFLAGS := -DENABLE_AUDIO
...
LOCAL_MODULE := module1
LOCAL_CFLAGS :=-DDEBUG
...
LOCAL_SHARED_LIBRARIES := avilib
```

The compiler will get executed with flags –DENABLE_AUDIO –DDEBUG while building the module1.

■ LOCAL_EXPORT_CPPFLAGS: Same as the LOCAL_EXPORT_CLAGS but for C++ code-specific compiler flags.

■ LOCAL_EXPORT_LDFLAGS: Same as the LOCAL_EXPORT_CFLAGS but for the linker flags.

■ LOCAL_EXPORT_C_INCLUDES: This variable allows recording set include paths that will be added to the LOCAL_C_INCLUDES definition of any other module that is using this module through either LOCAL_STATIC_LIBRARIES or LOCAL_SHARED_ LIBRARIES.

■ LOCAL_SHORT_COMMANDS: This variable should be set to true for modules with a very high number of sources or dependent static or shared libraries. Operating systems like Windows only allow a maximum of 8191 characters on the command line; this variable makes the build commands shorter than this limit by breaking them. This is not recommended for smaller modules since enabling it will make the build slower.

■ LOCAL_FILTER_ASM: This variable defines the application that will be used to filter the assembly files from the LOCAL_SRC_FILES.

Other Build System Function Macros

This section covers the other function macros that are supported by the Android NDK build system.

■ all-subdir-makefiles: Returns a list of Android.mk build files that are located in all sub-directories of the current directory. For example, calling the following includes all Android.mk files in the sub-directories into the build process:

```
include $(call all-subdir-makefiles)
```

■ this-makefile: Returns the path of the current Android.mk build file.

■ parent-makefile: Returns the path of the parent Android.mk build file that included the current build file.

■ grand-parent-makefile: Same as the parent-makefile but for the grandparent.

Defining New Variables

Developers can define other variables to simplify their build files. The names beginning with LOCAL_ and NDK_ prefixes are reserved for use by the Android NDK build system. It is recommended to use MY_ prefix for variables that are defined by the developers, as shown in Listing 2-9.

Listing 2-9. Android.mk File Showing the Use of Developer-Defined Intermediate Variables

```
...
MY_SRC_FILES := avilib.c platform_posix.c
LOCAL_SRC_FILES := $(addprefix avilib/, $(MY_SRC_FILES))
...
```

Conditional Operations

The Android.mk build file can also contain conditional operations on these variables, for example, to include a different set of source files per architecture, as shown in Listing 2-10.

Listing 2-10. Android.mk Build File with Conditional Operation

```
...
ifeq ($(TARGET_ARCH),arm)
    LOCAL_SRC_FILES += armonly.c
else
    LOCAL_SRC_FILES += generic.c
endif
...
```

Application.mk

The Application.mk is an optional build file that is used by the Android NDK build system. Same as the Android.mk file, it is also placed in the jni directory. Application.mk is also a GNU Makefile fragment. Its purpose is to describe which modules are needed by the application; it also defines the variables that are common for all modules. The following variables are supported in the Application.mk build file:

- APP_MODULES: By default the Android NDK build system builds all modules that are declared by the Android.mk file. This variable can override this behavior and provide a space-separated list of modules that need to be built.

- APP_OPTIM: This variable can be set to either release or debug to alter the optimization level of the generated binaries. By default the release mode is used and the generated binaries are highly optimized. This variable can be set to debug mode to generate un-optimized binaries that are easier to debug.

- APP_CLAGS: This variable lists the compiler flags that will be passed to the compiler while compiling C and C++ source files for any of the modules.

- APP_CPPFLAGS: This variable lists the compilers flags that will be passed to the compiler while compiling the C++ source files for any of the modules.

- APP_BUILD_SCRIPT: By default the Android NDK build system looks for the Android.mk build file under the jni sub-directory of the project. This behavior can be altered by using this variable, and a different build file can be used.

- APP_ABI: By default Android NDK build system generates binaries for armeabi ABI. This variable can be used to alter this behavior and generate binaries for a different ABI, like so:

  APP_ABI := mips

  Additionally, more than one ABI can be set

  APP_ABI := armeabi mips

  in order to generate binaries for all supported ABIs

  APP_ABI := all

- APP_STL: By default the Android NDK build system uses the minimal STL runtime library, also known as the system library. This variable can be used to select a different STL implementation.

  APP_STL := stlport_shared

- APP_GNUSTL_FORCE_CPP_FEATURES: Similar to LOCAL_CPP_EXTENSIONS variable, this variable indicates that all modules rely on specific C++ features such as RTTI, exceptions, etc.

- APP_SHORT_COMMANDS: Similar to the LOCAL_SHORT_COMMANDS variable, this variable makes the build system use shorter commands on projects with high amount of source files.

Using the NDK-Build Script

As stated earlier in this chapter, the Android NDK build system is started by executing the ndk-build script. The script can take a set of arguments to allow you to easily maintain and control the build process.

- By default the ndk-build script expects to be executed within the main project directory. The -C argument can be used to specify the location the NDK project on the command line so that the ndk-build script can be started from an arbitrary location.

  ndk-build -C /path/to/the/project

- The Android NDK build system does not rebuild objects if their source file is not being modified. You can execute the ndk-build script using the -B argument to force rebuilding all source code.

  ndk-build -B

- In order to clean the generated binaries and object files, you can execute ndk-build clean on the command line. Android NDK build system removes the generated binaries.

```
ndk-build clean
```

- The Android NDK build system relies on GNU Make tool to build the modules. By default GNU Make tool executes one build command at a time, waiting for it to finish before executing the next one. GNU Make can execute build commands in parallel if the -j argument is provided on the command line. Optionally, the number of commands that can be executed in parallel can also be specified as a number following the argument.

```
ndk-build -j 4
```

Troubleshooting Build System Problems

The Android NDK build system comes with extensive logging support for troubleshooting build system related problems. This section briefly explores them.

Logging of the internal state of the Android NDK build system can be enabled by typing ndk-build NDK_LOG=1 on the command line. The Android NDK build system will produce extensive amount of logging with log messages prefixed with "Android NDK: " (see Figure 2-13).

```
C:\windows\system32\cmd.exe - ndk-build  NDK_LOG=1

C:\android\workspace\com.example.hellojni.HelloJni>ndk-build NDK_LOG=1
Android NDK: NDK installation path auto-detected: 'C:/android/android-ndk-r8'
Android NDK: GNU Make version 3.81 detected
Android NDK: Host OS was auto-detected: windows
Android NDK:  Host operating system detected: windows
Android NDK: Host CPU was auto-detected: x86
Android NDK: HOST_TAG set to windows
Android NDK: Host tools prebuilt directory: C:/android/android-ndk-r8/prebuilt/w
indows/bin
Android NDK: Host 'echo' tool: C:/android/android-ndk-r8/prebuilt/windows/bin/ec
ho.exe
Android NDK: Host 'awk' tool: C:/android/android-ndk-r8/prebuilt/windows/bin/awk
.exe
Android NDK: Host 'awk' test returned: Pass
Android NDK:  This NDK supports the following target architectures and ABIS:
Android NDK:     arm: armeabi armeabi-v7a
Android NDK:     mips: mips
Android NDK:     x86: x86
```

Figure 2-13. Ndk-build script displaying debug information

If you are only interested in seeing the actual build commands that get executed, you can type ndk-build V=1 on the command line. Android NDK will only display the build commands, as shown in Figure 2-14.

```
C:\windows\system32\cmd.exe                                          _ □ ×
C:\android\workspace\com.example.hellojni.HelloJni>ndk-build V=1
Gdbserver       : [arm-linux-androideabi-4.4.3] libs/armeabi/gdbserver
if not exist ".\libs\armeabi" md ".\libs\armeabi"
copy /b/y "C:\android\android-ndk-r8\toolchains\arm-linux-androideabi-4.4.3\preb
uilt\gdbserver" ".\libs\armeabi\gdbserver" > NUL
Gdbsetup        : libs/armeabi/gdb.setup
if not exist ".\libs\armeabi" md ".\libs\armeabi"
C:/android/android-ndk-r8/prebuilt/windows/bin/echo.exe "set solib-search-path .
/obj/local/armeabi" > ./libs/armeabi/gdb.setup
C:/android/android-ndk-r8/prebuilt/windows/bin/echo.exe "directory C:/android/an
droid-ndk-r8/platforms/android-14/arch-arm/usr/include jni C:/android/android-nd
k-r8/sources/cxx-stl/system" >> ./libs/armeabi/gdb.setup
Install         : hello-jni => libs/armeabi/hello-jni
if not exist ".\libs\armeabi" md ".\libs\armeabi"
copy /b/y ".\obj\local\armeabi\hello-jni" ".\libs\armeabi\hello-jni" > NUL
C:/android/android-ndk-r8/toolchains/arm-linux-androideabi-4.4.3/prebuilt/window
s/bin/arm-linux-androideabi-strip --strip-unneeded  ./libs/armeabi/hello-jni

C:\android\workspace\com.example.hellojni.HelloJni>
```

Figure 2-14. Ndk-build script displaying the build commands

Summary

In this chapter, you configured the Eclipse IDE to build your first NDK project. You learned a lot about the Android NDK build system in the process. In the next chapter, you will explore how the native components that you are building using Android NDK can communicate with the actual Java application.

## Chapter 3

Communicating with Native Code using JNI

In the previous chapter, you started exploring the Android NDK by going through its components, its structure, and its build system. Using this information you can now build and package any kind of native code with your Android applications. In this chapter, you will focus on the integration part by using the Java Native Interface (JNI) technology to enable the Java application and the native code to communicate with each other.

What is JNI?

The JNI is a powerful feature of the Java programming language. It allows certain methods of Java classes to be implemented natively while letting them be called and used as ordinary Java methods. These native methods can still use Java objects in the same way that the Java code uses them. Native methods can create new Java objects or use objects created by the Java application, which can inspect, modify, and invoke methods on these objects to perform tasks.

Starting with an Example

Before going into the details of JNI technology, let's walk through an example application. This will provide you with the foundation necessary to experiment with the APIs and concepts as you work through the chapter. By going through the example application, you will learn the following key concepts:

- How the native methods are called from Java code

- Declaration of native methods

- Loading the native modules from shared libraries

- Implementing the native methods in C/C++

To begin, open the Eclipse IDE and go into the hello-jni sample project that you imported in the previous chapter. The hello-jni application is a single activity Android application. Using the Project Explorer view, expand the src directory, and then expand the com.example.hellojni package. Open the HelloJni activity in the editor view by double-clicking the HelloJni.java source file.

The HelloJni activity has a very simple user interface that is formed by a single android.widget.TextView widget. In the body of activity's onCreate method, the string value of the TextView widget is set to the return value of stringFromJNI method, as shown in Listing 3-1.

Listing 3-1. HelloJni Activity onCreate Method

```
/** Called when the activity is first created. */
@Override
public void onCreate(Bundle savedInstanceState)
{
    super.onCreate(savedInstanceState);

    /* Create a TextView and set its content.
     * the text is retrieved by calling a native
     * function.
     */
    TextView tv = new TextView(this);
    tv.setText( stringFromJNI() );
    setContentView(tv);
}
```

There is nothing new here. You will find the stringFromJNI method just below the onCreate method.

Declaration of Native Methods

As shown in Listing 3-2, the method declaration of stringFromJNI contains the native keyword to inform the Java compiler that the implementation of this method is provided in another language. The method declaration is terminated with a semicolon, the statement terminator symbol, because the native methods do not have a body.

Listing 3-2. Method Declaration of Native stringFromJNI Method

```
/* A native method that is implemented by the
 * 'hello-jni' native library, which is packaged
 * with this application.
 */
public native String  stringFromJNI();
```

Although the virtual machine now knows that the method is implemented natively, it still does not know where to find the implementation.

Loading the Shared Libraries

As mentioned in the previous chapter, native methods are compiled into a shared library. This shared library needs to be loaded first for the virtual machine to find the native method implementations. The java.lang.System class provides two static methods, load and loadLibrary, for loading shared libraries during runtime. As shown in Listing 3-3, the HelloJni activity loads the shared library hello-jni.

Listing 3-3. HelloJni Activity Loading the hello-jni Shared Library

```
/* this is used to load the 'hello-jni' library on application
 * startup. The library has already been unpacked into
 * /data/data/com.example.HelloJni/lib/libhello-jni.so at
 * installation time by the package manager.
 */
static {
        System.loadLibrary("hello-jni");
}
```

The loadLibrary method is called within the static context because you want the native code implementations to be loaded as the class is loaded and initialized for the first time.

Bear in mind that Java technology is designed with the goal of being platform independent. As a part of the Java framework API, the design of loadLibrary is not any different. Although the actual shared library produced by Android NDK is named libhello-jni.so, the loadLibrary method only takes the library name, hello-jni, and adds the necessary prefix and suffix as required by the operating system in use. The library name is same as the module name that is defined in Android.mk using the LOCAL_MODULE build system variable.

The argument to loadLibrary does not include the location of the shared library either. The Java library path, system property java.library.path, holds the list of directories that the loadLibrary method will search for in the shared libraries. The Java library path on Android contains /vendor/lib and /system/lib.

The caveat here is that loadLibrary will load the shared library as soon as it finds a library with the same name while going through the Java library path. Since the first set of directories in the Java library path is the Android system directories, Android developers are strongly encouraged to pick unique names for the shared libraries in order to prevent any name clashes with the system libraries.

Now let's look into the native code to see how the native method is declared and implemented.

Implementing the Native Methods

Using the Project Explorer view, expand the jni directory and double-click the hello-jni.c source file to open it in the editor view. The C source code starts by including the jni.h header file, as shown in Listing 3-4. This header file contains definitions of JNI data types and functions.

Listing 3-4. Native Implementation of stringFromJNI Method

```
#include<string.h>
#include<jni.h>
```

```
...
jstring
Java_com_example_hellojni_HelloJni_stringFromJNI( JNIEnv* env,
                                                  jobject thiz )
{
    return (*env)->NewStringUTF(env, "Hello from JNI !");
}
```

The stringFromJNI native method is also declared with a fully qualified function named
Java_com_example_hellojni_HelloJni_stringFromJNI. This explicit function naming allows the
virtual machine to automatically find native functions in loaded shared libraries.

C/C++ Header Generator: javah

Keeping the native function names and list of arguments aligned to their original declaration in Java
class files can be a cumbersome and redundant task. The JDK comes with a command line tool,
known as **javah**, to automate this task. The **javah** tool parses a Java class file for native methods
and generates a header file consisting of native method declarations.

Running from Command Line

Using the command line, change the directory to <Eclipse Workspace>/com.example.hellojni.
HelloJni, where the HelloJni project is imported. The javah tool operates on compiled Java class
files. Invoke the javah tool with the location of compiled class files and the name of the Java class to
parse, like so:

```
javah –classpath bin/classes com.example.hellojni.HelloJni
```

The javah tool will parse the com.example.hellojni.HelloJni class file, and it will generate the
C/C++ header file as com_example_hellojni_HelloJni.h, as shown in Listing 3-5.

Listing 3-5. The com_example_hellojni_HelloJni.h Header File

```
/* DO NOT EDIT THIS FILE - it is machine generated */
#include <jni.h>
/* Header for class com_example_hellojni_HelloJni */

#ifndef _Included_com_example_hellojni_HelloJni
#define _Included_com_example_hellojni_HelloJni
#ifdef __cplusplus
extern "C" {
#endif
/*
 * Class:     com_example_hellojni_HelloJni
 * Method:    stringFromJNI
 * Signature: ()Ljava/lang/String;
 */
JNIEXPORT jstring JNICALL Java_com_example_hellojni_HelloJni_stringFromJNI
  (JNIEnv *, jobject);
```

```
/*
 * Class:     com_example_hellojni_HelloJni
 * Method:    unimplementedStringFromJNI
 * Signature: ()Ljava/lang/String;
 */
JNIEXPORT jstring JNICALL Java_com_example_hellojni_HelloJni_unimplementedStringFromJNI
  (JNIEnv *, jobject);

#ifdef __cplusplus
}
#endif
#endif
```

The C/C++ source file simply needs to include this header file and provide the implementation for the native methods, as shown in Listing 3-6.

Listing 3-6. The com_example_hellojni_HelloJni.c Source File

```
#include "com_example_hellojni_HelloJni.h"

JNIEXPORT jstring JNICALL Java_com_example_hellojni_HelloJni_stringFromJNI
  (JNIEnv * env, jobject thiz)
{
    return (*env)->NewStringUTF(env, "Hello from JNI !");
}
```

Instead of running the javah tool each time from the command line, it can be integrated into Eclipse as an external tool to streamline the process of generating the header files.

Running from Eclipse IDE

Open the Eclipse IDE, and choose **Run ➤** External Tools External Tools Configurations from the top menu bar. Using the External Tools Configurations dialog, select Program, and then click the New launch configuration button. Using the Main tab, fill in the tool information as follows and as shown in Figure 3-1:

- Name: Generate C and C++ Header File
- Location: ${system_path:javah}
- Working Directory: ${project_loc}/jni
- Arguments: -classpath "${project_classpath};${env_var:ANDROID_SDK_HOME}/platforms/android-14/android.jar" ${java_type_name}

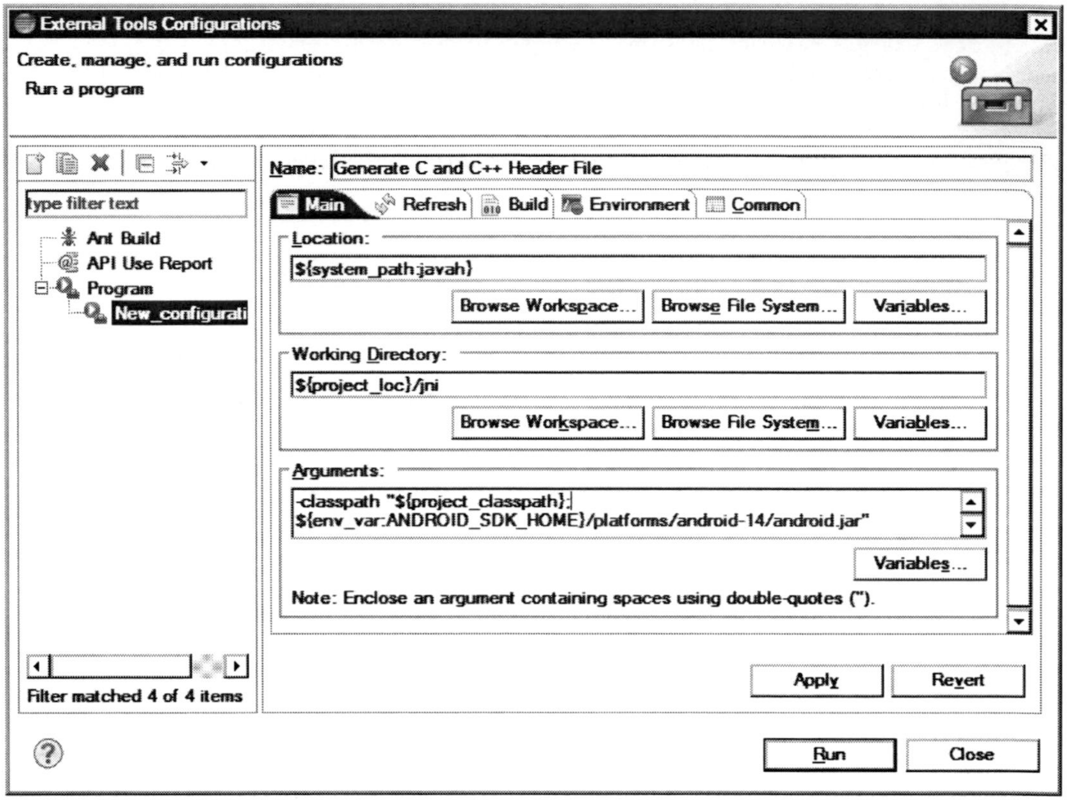

Figure 3-1. *The javah external tool configuration*

You will need to replace the semicolon symbol with colon symbol on Mac OS X and Linux platforms. Switch to the Refresh tab; put a checkmark next to the "Refresh resource upon completion" and select "The project containing the selected resource" from the list, as shown in Figure 3-2.

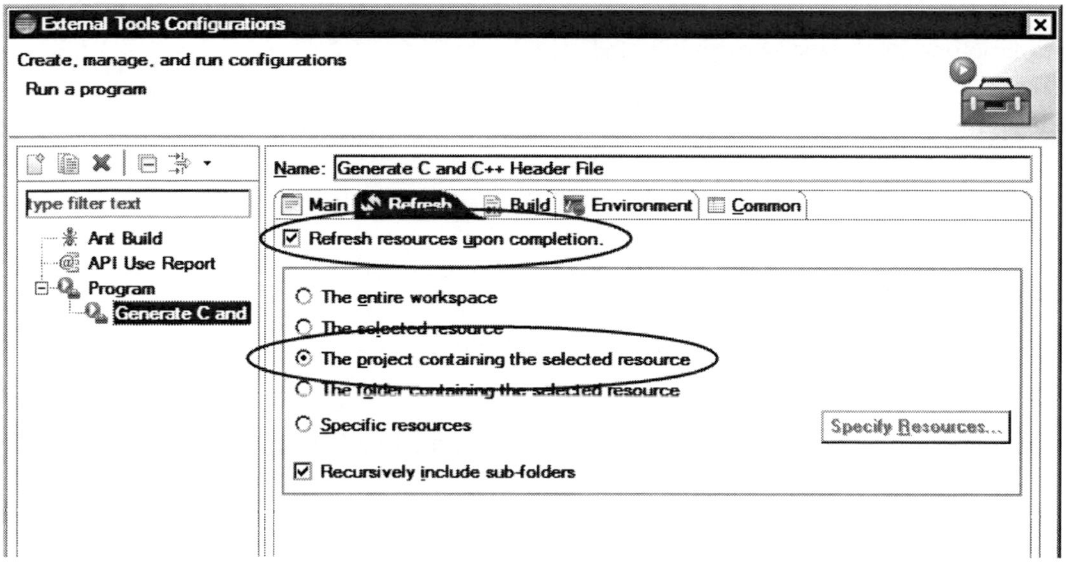

Figure 3-2. Refresh project upon running the javah tool

Switch to the Common tab, and put a checkmark next to the External Tools under the "Display in favorites menu" group, as shown in Figure 3-3.

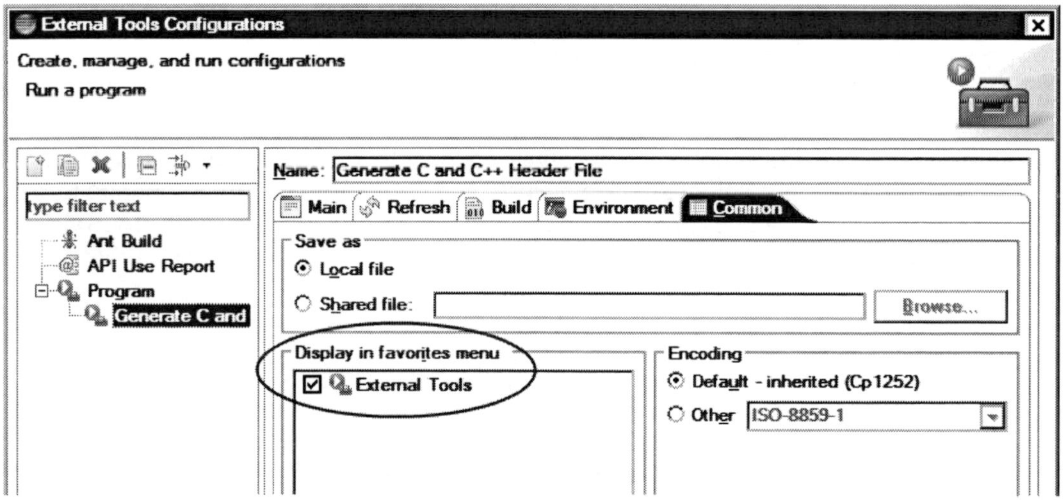

Figure 3-3. Display the javah tool in the favorites menu

Click the OK button to save the external tool configuration. In order to test the new configuration, using the Project Explorer view, select the HelloJni class, then choose **Run ➤ External Tools ➤ Generate C and C++ Header File**. The javah tool will parse the selected class file for native methods, and it will generate a C/C++ header file called com_example_hellojni_HelloJni.h under the jni directory with the method descriptions.

Now that you have automated the way to generate the native method declarations, let's look into the generated method declarations more in detail.

Method Declarations

Although the Java method `stringFromJNI` does not take any parameters, the native function takes two parameters, as shown in Listing 3-7.

Listing 3-7. Mandatory Parameters of Native Methods

```
JNIEXPORT jstring JNICALL Java_com_example_hellojni_HelloJni_stringFromJNI
  (JNIEnv *, jobject);
```

The first parameter, `JNIEnv`, is an interface pointer that points to a function table of available JNI functions. The second parameter, `jobject`, is a Java object reference to the `HelloJni` class instance.

JNIEnv Interface Pointer

Native code accesses the virtual machine functionality through the various functions exposed by the `JNIEnv` interface pointer. `JNIEnv` is a pointer to thread-local data, which in turn contains a pointer to a function table. Functions that implement a native method take the `JNIEnv` interface pointer as their first argument.

> **Caution**   The `JNIEnv` interface pointer that is passed into each native method call is also valid in the thread associated with the method call. It cannot be cached and used by other threads.

Depending on whether the native code is a C or C++ source file, the syntax for calling JNI functions differs. In C code, `JNIEnv` is a pointer to JNINativeInterface structure. This pointer needs to be dereferenced first in order to access any JNI function. Since the JNI functions in C code do not know the current JNI environment, the `JNIEnv` instance should be passed as the first argument to each JNI function call, like so:

```
return (*env)->NewStringUTF(env, "Hello from JNI !");
```

In C++ code, `JNIEnv` is actually a C++ class instance. JNI functions are exposed as member functions. Since JNI methods have access to the current JNI environment, the JNI method calls do not require the `JNIEnv` instance as an argument. In C++, the same code looks like

```
return env->NewStringUTF("Hello from JNI !");
```

Instance vs. Static Methods

The Java programming language has two types of methods: instance methods and static methods. Instance methods are associated with a class instance, and they can only be called on a class instance. Static methods are not associated with a class instance, and they can be called directly from a static context. Both instance and static methods can be declared as native, and their implementations can be provided as native code through the JNI technology. Native instance methods get the instance reference as their second parameter as a jobject value, as shown in Listing 3-8.

Listing 3-8. Native Instance Method Definition

```
JNIEXPORT jstring JNICALL Java_com_example_hellojni_HelloJni_stringFromJNI
  (JNIEnv * env, jobject thiz);
```

Since static methods are not tied to an instance, they get the class reference instead as their second parameter as a jclass value, shown in Listing 3-9.

Listing 3-9. Native Static Method Definition

```
JNIEXPORT jstring JNICALL Java_com_example_hellojni_HelloJni_stringFromJNI
  (JNIEnv * env, jclass clazz);
```

As you may have noticed in the method definitions that JNI provides its own data types to expose Java types to native code.

Data Types

There are two kinds of data types in Java:

- ▓ Primitive types: boolean, byte, char, short, int, long, float, and double
- ▓ Reference types: String, arrays, and other classes

Let's take a closer look at each of these data types.

Primitive Types

Primitive types are directly mapped to C/C++ equivalents, as shown in Table 3-1. The JNI uses type definitions to make this mapping transparent to developers.

Table 3-1. *Java Primitive Data Types*

Java Type	JNI Type	C/C++ Type	Size
Boolean	Jboolean	unsigned char	Unsigned 8 bits
Byte	Jbyte	char	Signed 8 bits
Char	Jchar	unsigned short	Unsigned 16 bits
Short	Jshort	short	Signed 16 bits
Int	Jint	Int	Signed 32 bits
Long	Jlong	long long	Signed 64 bits
Float	Jfloat	float	32 bits
Double	Jdouble	double	64 bits

Reference Types

Unlike the primitive data types, the reference types are passed as opaque references to native methods. The reference type mapping is shown in Table 3-2. Their internal data structure is not exposed directly to native code.

Table 3-2. *Java Reference Type Mapping*

Java Type	Native Type
java.lang.Class	jclass
java.lang.Throwable	jthrowable
java.lang.String	jstring
Other objects	jobject
java.lang.Object[]	jobjectArray
boolean[]	jbooleanArray
byte[]	jbyteArray
char[]	jcharArray
short[]	jshortArray
int[]	jintArray
long[]	jlongArray
float[]	jfloatArray
double[]	jdoubleArray
Other arrays	Jarray

Operations on Reference Types

Reference types are passed as opaque references to the native code rather than native data types, and they cannot be consumed and modified directly. JNI provides a set of APIs for interacting with these reference types. These APIs are provided to the native function through the JNIEnv interface pointer. In this section, you will briefly explore these APIs pertinent to the following types and components:

- Strings
- Arrays
- NIO Buffers
- Fields
- Methods

String Operations

Java strings are handled by the JNI as reference types. These reference types are not directly usable as native C strings. JNI provides the necessary functions to convert these Java string references to C strings and back. Since Java string objects are immutable, JNI does not provide any function to modify the content of an existing Java string.

JNI supports both Unicode and UTF-8 encoded strings, and it provides two sets of functions through the JNIEnv interface pointer to handle each of these string encodings.

New String

New string instances can be constructed from the native code by using the functions NewString for Unicode strings and NewStringUTF for UTF-8 strings. As shown in Listing 3-10, these functions take a C string and returns a Java string reference type, a jstring value.

Listing 3-10. New Java String from a Given C String

```
jstring javaString;
javaString = (*env)->NewStringUTF(env, "Hello World!");
```

In case of a memory overflow, these functions return NULL to inform the native code that an exception has been thrown in the virtual machine so the native code should not continue. We will get back to the topic of exception handling later in this chapter.

Converting a Java String to C String

In order to use a Java string in native code, it needs to be converted to a C string first. Java strings can be converted to C strings using the functions GetStringChars for Unicode strings and GetStringUTFChars for UTF-8 strings. These functions take an optional third argument, a pass-by-reference output parameter called isCopy that can allow the caller to determine whether the returned C string address points to a copy or the pinned object in the heap. This is shown in Listing 3-11.

Listing 3-11. Converting a Java String to C String

```
const jbyte* str;
jboolean isCopy;

str = (*env)->GetStringUTFChars(env, javaString, &isCopy);
if (0 != str) {
    printf("Java string: %s", str);

    if (JNI_TRUE == isCopy) {
        printf("C string is a copy of the Java string.");
    } else {
        printf("C string points to actual string.");
    }
}
```

Releasing Strings

C strings obtained though the JNI GetStringChars and GetStringUTFChars functions need to be properly released after the native code is finished using them, or memory leaks will occur. As shown in Listing 3-12, JNI provides ReleaseStringChars for Unicode strings and ReleaseStringUTFChars for UTF-8 encoded strings.

Listing 3-12. Releasing the C Strings Returned by JNI Functions

```
(*env)->ReleaseStringUTFChars(env, javaString, str);
```

Array Operations

Java arrays are handled by the JNI as reference types. The JNI provides the necessary functions to access and manipulate Java arrays.

New Array

New array instances can be constructed from the native code using the New<*Type*>Array function, with the <Type> being Int, Char, Boolean, etc. such as NewIntArray. As shown in Listing 3-13, the size of the array should be provided as a parameter when invoking these functions.

Listing 3-13. New Java Array from Native Code

```
jintArray javaArray;
javaArray = (*env)->NewIntArray(env, 10);
if (0 != javaArray) {
    /* You can now use the array. */
}
```

Same as the NewString function, in case of a memory overflow, the New<Type>Array function will return NULL to inform the native code that an exception has been thrown in the virtual machine and that the native code should not continue.

Accessing the Array Elements

JNI provides two types of access to Java array elements. Code can either get a copy of the array as a C array, or it can ask JNI to get a direct pointer to the array elements.

Operating on a Copy

The Get<Type>ArrayRegion function copies the given primitive Java array to the given C array, as shown in Listing 3-14.

Listing 3-14. Getting a Copy of Java Array Region as a C Array

```
jint nativeArray[10];
(*env)->GetIntArrayRegion(env, javaArray, 0, 10, nativeArray);
```

The native code can then use and modify the array elements as an ordinary C array. When the native code wants to commit its changes back to the Java array, the Set<Type>ArrayRegion function can be used to copy the C array back to Java array, as shown in Listing 3-15.

Listing 3-15. Committing Back the Changes from C Array to Java Array

```
(*env)->SetIntArrayRegion(env, javaArray, 0, 10, nativeArray);
```

When the array sizes are big, copying the array in order to operate on them causes performance problems. In such cases, the native code should either only get or set the region of the array elements instead of getting the entire array, if possible. Otherwise, JNI provides a different set of functions to obtain a direct pointer to the array elements instead of their copies.

Operating on Direct Pointer

The Get <Type>ArrayElements function allows the native code to get a direct pointer to array elements, when possible. As shown in Listing 3-16, the function takes a third optional parameter, a pass-by-reference output parameter called isCopy that can allow the caller to determine whether the returned C array points to a copy or the pinned array in the heap.

Listing 3-16. Getting a Direct Pointer to Java Array Elements

```
jint* nativeDirectArray;
jboolean isCopy;

nativeDirectArray = (*env)->GetIntArrayElements(env, javaArray, &isCopy);
```

JNI does not provide a set method, since the array elements can be accessed and manipulated as an ordinary C array. JNI requires the native code to release these pointers when it finishes; otherwise memory leaks happen. JNI provides the Release<Type>ArrayElemens functions to enable native code to release the C arrays that are returned by Get<Type>ArrayElements function calls, as shown in Listing 3-17.

Listing 3-17. Releasing the Direct Pointer to Java Array Elements

```
(*env)->ReleaseIntArrayElements(env, javaArray, nativeDirectArray, 0);
```

This function takes a fourth parameter, the release mode. Table 3-3 contains a list of supported release modes.

Table 3-3. Supported Release Modes

Release Mode	Action
0	Copy back the content and free the native array.
JNI_COMMIT	Copy back the content but do not free the native array. This can be used for periodically updating a Java array.
JNI_ABORT	Free the native array without copying its content.

NIO Operations

Native I/O (NIO) provides improved performance in the areas of buffer management, scalable network and file I/O, and character-set support. JNI provides functions to use the NIO buffers from native code. Compared to array operations, NIO buffers deliver much better performance, and they are highly suitable for delivering vast amount of data between the native code and the Java application.

New Direct Byte Buffer

Native code can create a direct byte buffer that will be used by the Java application by providing a native C byte array as the basis. The NewDirectByteBuffer is used in Listing 3-18.

Listing 3-18. New Byte Buffer Based on the Given C Byte Array

```
unsigned char* buffer = (unsigned char*) malloc(1024);
...
jobject directBuffer;
directBuffer = (*env)->NewDirectByteBuffer(env, buffer, 1024);
```

> **Note** The memory allocated in native methods is out of the scope and control of the virtual machine's garbage collector. Native functions should manage their memory properly by freeing the unused allocations to prevent memory leaks.

Getting the Direct Byte Buffer

The direct byte buffer can also be created in the Java application. Native code can use the GetDirectBufferAddress function call to obtain the memory address of the native byte array, as shown in Listing 3-19.

Listing 3-19. Getting the Native Byte Array from the Java Byte Buffer

```
unsigned char* buffer;
buffer = (unsigned char*) (*env)->GetDirectBufferAddress(env,
    directBuffer);
```

Accessing Fields

Java has two types of fields: instance fields and static fields. Each instance of a class owns its copy of the instance fields, whereas all instances of a class share the same static fields.

The JNI provides functions to access both field types. Listing 3-20 shows an example of a Java class with one static and one instance field.

Listing 3-20. Java Class with Both Static and Instance Fields

```
public class JavaClass {
    /** Instance field */
    private String instanceField = "Instance Field";

    /** Static field */
    private static String staticField = "Static Field";

    ...
}
```

Getting the Field ID

The JNI provides access to both types of fields through field IDs. You can obtain field IDs through the class object for the given instance. The class object is obtained through the GetObjectClass function, as shown in Listing 3-21.

Listing 3-21. Getting the Class from an Object Reference

```
jclass clazz;
clazz = (*cnv)->GetObjectClass(env, instance);
```

Depending on the field type, there are two functions to obtain the field ID from the class. The GetFieldId function is for instance fields, as shown in Listing 3-22.

Listing 3-22. Getting the Field ID of an Instance Field

```
jfieldID instanceFieldId;
instanceFieldId = (*env)->GetFieldID(env, clazz,
    "instanceField", "Ljava/lang/String;");
```

The GetStaticFieldId is for static fields, as shown in Listing 3-23. Both functions return the field ID as a jfieldID type.

Listing 3-23. Getting the Field ID of a Static Field

```
jfieldID staticFieldId;
staticFieldId = (*env)->GetStaticFieldID(env, clazz,
    "staticField", "Ljava/lang/String;");
```

The last parameter of both functions takes the field descriptor that represents the field type in Java. In the example code, "Ljava/lang/String" indicates that the field type is a String. We will get back to this later in this chapter.

> **Tip**   The field IDs can be cached in order to improve application performance. Always cache the most frequently used field ids.

Getting the Field

After you obtain the field ID, you can get the actual field through the Get<*Type*>Field function for instance fields, as shown in Listing 3-24.

Listing 3-24. Getting an Instance Field

```
jstring instanceField;
instanceField = (*env)->GetObjectField(env, instance, instanceFieldId);
```

Use the GetStatic<*Type*>Field function for static fields, as shown in Listing 3-25.

Listing 3-25. Getting a Static Field

```
jstring staticField;
staticField = (*env)->GetStaticObjectField(env, clazz, staticFieldId);
```

In case of a memory overflow, both of these functions can return NULL, and the native code should not continue to execute.

> **Tip**   Getting the value of a single field takes two or three JNI function calls. Native code reaching back to Java to obtain values of each individual field adds extra overhead to the application and leads to poorer performance. It is strongly recommended to pass all needed parameters to native method calls instead of having the native code reach back to Java.

Calling Methods

As with fields, there are two types of methods in Java: instance methods and static methods. The JNI provides functions to access both types. Listing 3-26 shows a Java class that contains one static method and one instance method.

Listing 3-26. Java Class with Both Instance and Static Methods

```
public class JavaClass {
    /**
     * Instance method.
     */
    private String instanceMethod() {
        return "Instance Method";
    }

    /**
     * Static method.
     */
    private static String staticMethod() {
        return "Static Method";
    }

    ...
}
```

Getting the Method ID

The JNI provides access to both types of methods through method IDs. You can obtain method IDs through the `class` object for the given instance. Use the `GetMethodID` function to obtain the method ID of an instance method, as shown in Listing 3-27.

Listing 3-27. Getting the Method ID of an Instance Method

```
jmethodID instanceMethodId;
instanceMethodId = (*env)->GetMethodID(env, clazz,
    "instanceMethod", "()Ljava/lang/String;");
```

Use the `GetStaticMethodID` function to get the method ID of a static field, as shown in Listing 3-28. Both functions return the method ID as a `jmethodID` type.

Listing 3-28. Getting the Method ID of a Static Method

```
jmethodID staticMethodId;
staticMethodId = (*env)->GetStaticMethodID(env, clazz,
    "staticMethod", "()Ljava/lang/String;");
```

Like the field ID getter methods, the last parameter of both functions takes the method descriptor. It represents the method signature in Java.

> **Tip**   The method IDs can be cached in order to improve application performance. Always cache the most frequently used method ids.

Calling the Method

Using the method ID, you can call the actual method through the Call<*Type*>Method function for instance methods, as shown in Listing 3-29.

Listing 3-29. Calling an Instance Method

```
jstring instanceMethodResult;
instanceMethodResult = (*env)->CallStringMethod(env,
    instance, instanceMethodId);
```

Use the CallStatic<*Type*>Field function for static methods, as shown in Listing 3-30.

Listing 3-30. Calling a Static Method

```
jstring staticMethodResult;
staticMethodResult = (*env)->CallStaticStringMethod(env,
    clazz, staticMethodId);
```

In case of a memory overflow, both of these functions can return NULL and the native code should not continue executing.

Tip   Transitions between Java and native code is a costly operation. It is strongly recommended that you take this into account when deciding to split between Java and native code. Minimizing these transitions can benefit the application performance greatly.

Field and Method Descriptors

As mentioned in the previous two sections, getting both the field ID and the method ID requires the field and method descriptors. Both the field and the method descriptors can be generated by using the Java type signature mapping shown in Table 3-4.

Table 3-4. *Java Type Signature Mapping*

Java Type	Signature
Boolean	Z
Byte	B
Char	C
Short	S
Int	I
Long	J
Float	F
Double	D
fully-qualified-class	Lfully-qualified-class;
type[]	[type
method type	(arg-type)ret-type

Manually producing the field and method descriptors by using the type signature mapping and keeping them in sync with the Java code can be a cumbersome task.

Java Class File Disassembler: javap

JDK comes with a command line Java class file disassembler called javap. This tool can be used to extract the field and method descriptors from the compiled class files.

Running from Command Line

Using the command line, change the directory to `<Eclipse Workspace>`/com.example.hellojni. HelloJni, where the HelloJni project is imported. The javap tool operates on compiled Java class files. Invoke the javap tool with the location of compiled class files and the name of the Java class to disassemble, like so:

```
javap –classpath bin/classes –p –s com.example.hellojni.HelloJni
```

The javap tool will disassemble the com.example.hellojni.HelloJni class file and will output the field and method signatures, as shown in Figure 3-4.

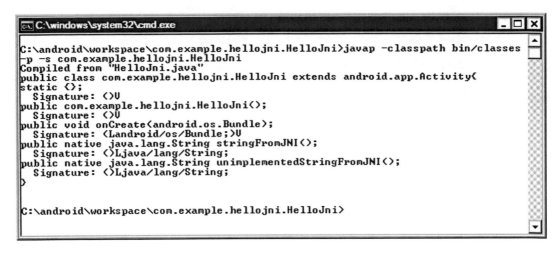

Figure 3-4. The javap tool output

Instead of running the javap tool each time from the command line, it can be integrated into Eclipse as an external tool to streamline the process of extracting the field and method signatures.

Running from Eclipse IDE

Open the Eclipse IDE, and choose **Run ➤ External Tools** Configurations… from the top menu bar. Using the External Tool Configurations dialog, select Program, and then click the New launch configuration button. Using the Main tab, fill in the tool information as follows and as shown in Figure 3-5:

- Name: `Java Class File Disassembler`
- Location: `${system_path:javap}`
- Working Directory: `${project_loc}`
- Arguments: `-classpath "${project_classpath};${env_var:ANDROID_SDK_HOME}/platforms/android-14/android.jar" -p -s ${java_type_name}`

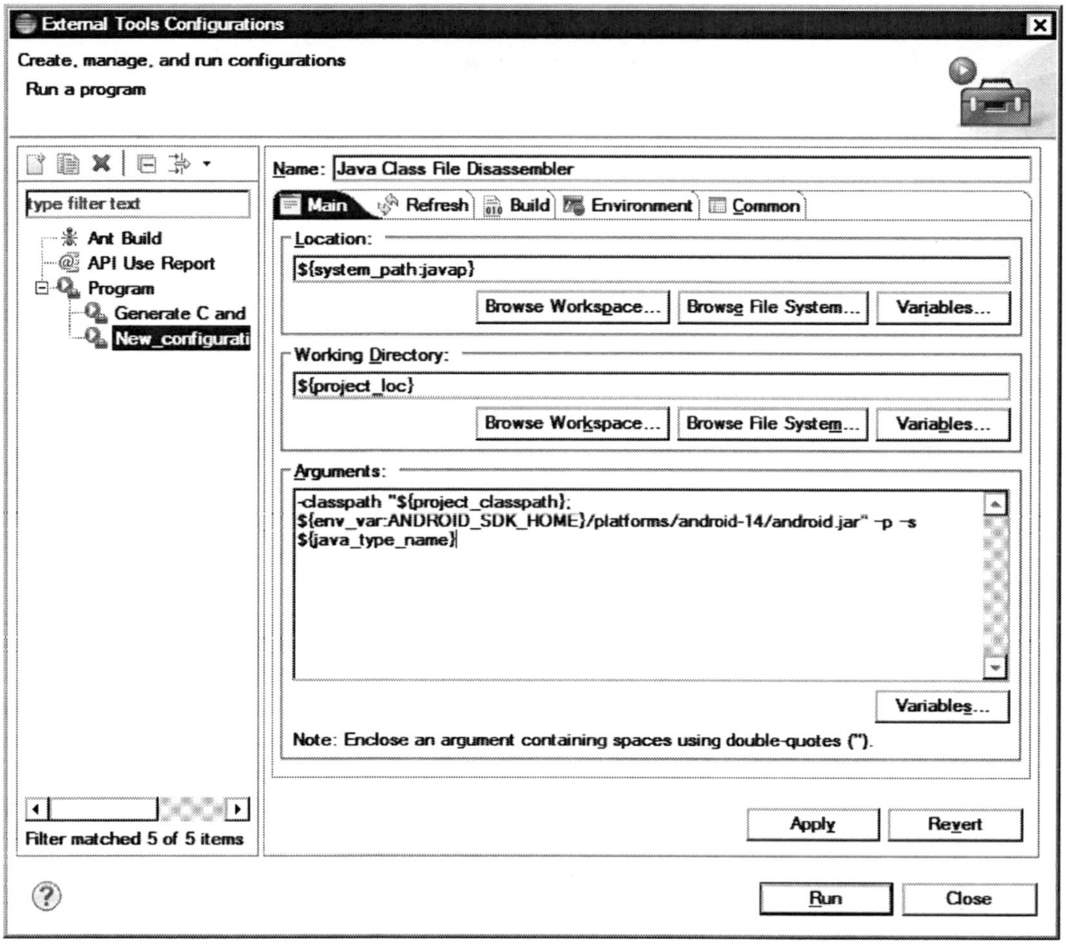

Figure 3-5. The javap external tool configuration

You will need to replace the semicolon symbol with colon symbol on Mac OS X and Linux platforms. Switch to the Common tab, and put a checkmark next to the External Tools under the "Display in favorites menu" group, as described earlier.

Click the OK button to save the external tool configuration. In order to test the new configuration, using the Project Explorer view, select the HelloJni class, then choose **Run ➤ External Tools ➤** Java Class File Disassembler. The console view will show the output of the javah tool, as shown in Figure 3-6.

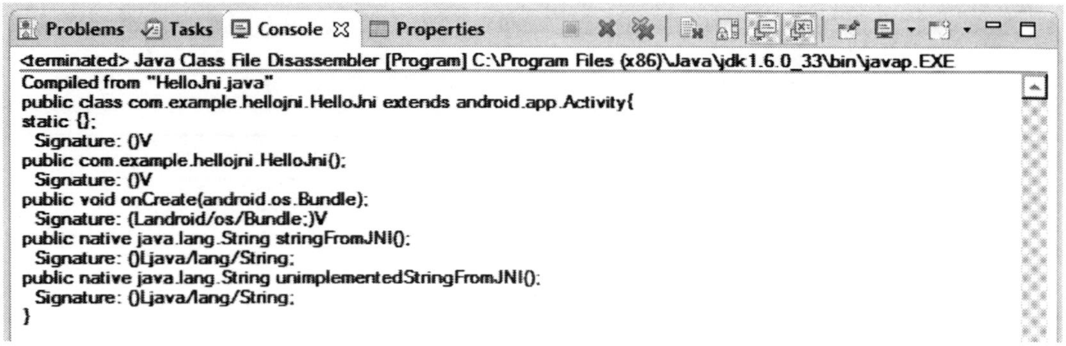

Figure 3-6. Console showing the javap tool output

The native methods are not prone to exceptions. Manipulating fields and calling Java methods can result in Java exceptions.

Exception Handling

Exception handling is an important aspect of the Java programming language. Exceptions behave differently in the JNI than they do in Java. In Java, when an exception is thrown, the virtual machine stops the execution of the code block and goes through the call stack in reverse order to find an exception handler code block that can handle the specific exception type. This is also called *catching an exception*. The virtual machine clears the exception and transfers the control to the exception handler block. In contrast, the JNI requires developers to explicitly implement the exception handling flow after an exception has occurred.

Catching Exceptions

The JNIEnv interface provides a set of functions related to exceptions. To see these functions in action, use the Java class, shown in Listing 3-31, as an example.

Listing 3-31. Java Example That Throws an Exception

```java
public class JavaClass {
    /**
     * Throwing method.
     */
    private void throwingMethod() throws NullPointerException {
        throw new NullPointerException("Null pointer");
    }

    /**
     * Access methods native method.
     */
    private native void accessMethods();
}
```

The accessMethods native method needs to explicitly do the exception handling while calling the throwingMethod method. The JNI provides the ExceptionOccurred function to query the virtual machine if there is a pending exception. The exception handler needs to explicitly clear the exception using the ExceptionClear function after it finishes with it, as shown in Listing 3-32.

Listing 3-32. Exception Handling in Native Code

```
jthrowable ex;
...
(*env)->CallVoidMethod(env, instance, throwingMethodId);
ex = (*env)->ExceptionOccurred(env);
if (0 != ex) {
    (*env)->ExceptionClear(env);

    /* Exception handler. */
}
```

Throwing Exceptions

The JNI allows the native code to throw exceptions as well. Since exceptions are Java classes, the exception class should be obtained first using the FindClass function. The ThrowNew function can be used to initiate and throw the new exception, as shown in Listing 3-33.

Listing 3-33. Throwing an Exception from Native Code

```
jclass clazz;
...
clazz = (*env)->FindClass(env, "java/lang/NullPointerException");
if (0 != clazz) {
    (*env)->ThrowNew(env, clazz, "Exception message.");
}
```

As the code execution of native functions are not under the control of the virtual machine, throwing an exception does not stop the execution of the native function and transfer control to the exception handler. Upon throwing an exception, the native function should free any allocated native resources, such as the memory, and properly return. The references obtained through the JNIEnv interface are local references and they get freed automatically by the virtual machine as soon as the native function returns.

Local and Global References

References play an important role in Java programming. The virtual machine manages the lifetime of class instances by tracking their references and garbage-collecting the ones that are no longer referenced. Since native code is not a managed environment, the JNI provides a set of functions to allow native code to explicitly manage the object references and lifetimes. The JNI supports three type kinds of references: local references, global references, and weak global references, as described in the following sections.

Local References

Most JNI functions return local references. Local references cannot be cached and reused in subsequent invocations since their lifetime is limited to the native method. Local references are freed once the native function returns. For example, the FindClass function returns a local reference; it is freed automatically when the native method returns. Native code can also be freed explicitly through the DeleteLocalRef function, as shown in Listing 3-34.

Listing 3-34. Deleting a Local Reference

```
jclass clazz;
clazz = (*env)->FindClass(env, "java/lang/String");
...
(*env)->DeleteLocalRef(env, clazz);
```

Based on the JNI specification, the virtual machine should allow minimum of 16 local references to be created for the native code. Best practice is to delete unused local references while doing multiple memory-intensive operations within a single method invocation. If that is not possible, the native code can use the EnsureLocalCapacity method to request more local reference slots from the virtual machine prior using them.

Global References

Global references remain valid across subsequent invocations of the native methods until they are explicitly freed by the native code.

New Global Reference

Global references can be initiated from local references through the NewGlobalRef function, as shown in Listing 3-35.

Listing 3-35. New Global Reference from a Given Local Reference

```
jclass localClazz;
jclass globalClazz;
...
localClazz = (*env)->FindClass(env, "java/lang/String");
globalClazz = (*env)->NewGlobalRef(env, localClazz);
...
(*env)->DeleteLocalRef(env, localClazz);
```

Deleting a Global Reference

When a global reference is no longer needed by the native code, you can free it at any time through the DeleteGlobalRef function, as shown in Listing 3-36.

Listing 3-36. Deleting a Global Reference

```
(*env)->DeleteGlobalRef(env, globalClazz);
```

Weak Global References

Another flavor of global reference is the weak global reference. Like global references, weak global references remain valid across subsequent invocations of the native methods. Unlike global references, weak global references do not prevent the underlying object from being garbage-collected.

New Weak Global Reference

Weak global references can be initiated using the NewWeakGlobalRef function, as shown in Listing 3-37.

Listing 3-37. New Weak Global Reference from a Given Local Reference

```
jclass weakGlobalClazz;
weakGlobalClazz = (*env)->NewWeakGlobalRef(env, localClazz);
```

Validating a Weak Global Reference

To determine if the weak global reference is still pointing to a live class instance, you can use the IsSameObject function, as shown in Listing 3-38.

Listing 3-38. Checking if Weak Global Reference is Still Valid

```
if (JNI_FALSE == (*env)->IsSameObject(env, weakGlobalClazz, NULL)) {
    /* Object is still live and can be used. */
} else {
    /* Object is garbage collected and cannot be used. */
}
```

Deleting a Weak Global Reference

Weak global references can be freed at any time using the DeleteWeakGlobalRef function, as shown in Listing 3-39.

Listing 3-39. Deleting a Weak Global Reference

```
(*env)->DeleteWeakGlobalRef(env, weakGlobalClazz);
```

Until they get explicitly freed, the global references remains valid, and they can be used by other native function calls as well as the native threads.

Threading

The virtual machine supports running native code as a part of the multithreaded environment. There are certain constraints of JNI technology to keep in mind while developing native components:

- Local references are valid only during the execution of the native method and in the thread context that is executing the native method. Local references cannot be shared among multiple threads. Only global references can be shared by multiple threads.

- The JNIEnv interface pointer that is passed into each native method call is also valid in the thread associated with the method call. It cannot be cached and used by other threads.

Synchronization

Synchronization is an important aspect of multithreaded programming. Similar to Java's synchronized blocks, JNI's monitors allow the native code to synchronize using Java objects. The virtual machine guarantees that the thread that acquired the monitor executes safely, while the other threads wait until the monitored object becomes available. The synchronized block in a Java application is shown in Listing 3-40.

Listing 3-40. Java Synchronized Code Block

```
synchronized(obj) {
    /* Synchronized thread-safe code block. */
}
```

In the native code, the same level of synchronization can be achieved using the JNI's monitor methods, as shown in Listing 3-41.

Listing 3-41. Native Equivalent of Java Synchronized Code Block

```
if (JNI_OK == (*env)->MonitorEnter(env, obj)) {
    /* Error handling. */
}

/* Synchronized thread-safe code block. */

if (JNI_OK == (*env)->MonitorExit(env, obj)) {
    /* Error handling. */
}
```

> **Caution**   The call to the MonitorEnter function should be matched with a call to MonitorExit in order to prevent deadlocks in the code.

Native Threads

These native components may use native threads in order to execute certain tasks in parallel. Since the native threads are not known to the virtual machine, they cannot directly communicate with the Java components. Native threads should be attached to the virtual machine first in order to interact with the remaining portion of the application.

The JNI provides the AttachCurrentThread function, through the JavaVM interface pointer, to allow native code to attach native threads to the virtual machine, as shown in Listing 3-42. The JavaVM interface pointer should be cached earlier since it cannot be obtained otherwise.

Listing 3-42. Attaching and Detaching the Current Thread to the Virtual Machine

```
JavaVM* cachedJvm;
...
JNIEnv* env;
...
/* Attach the current thread to virtual machine. */
(*cachedJvm)->AttachCurrentThread(cachedJvm, &env, NULL);

/* Thread can communicate with the Java application
   using the JNIEnv interface. */

/* Detach the current thread from virtual machine. */
(*cachedJvm)->DetachCurrentThread(cachedJvm);
```

The call to the AttachCurrentThread function allows the application to obtain a JNIEnv interface pointer that is valid for the current thread. There is no side effect of attaching an already attached native thread. When the native thread completes, it can be detached from the virtual machine by using the DetachCurrentThread function.

Summary

In this chapter, you learned how to communicate between the Java application and the native code using the JNI technology. More information on the JNI technology and available JNI APIs can be found in Oracle's JNI documentation at http://docs.oracle.com/javase/1.5.0/docs/guide/jni/spec/jniTOC.html.

As you may have noticed, doing any operation in JNI takes two or three function calls. Implementing a large number of native methods and keeping them in sync with the Java classes can easily become a cumbersome task. In the next chapter, you will evaluate some open source solutions that can automatically generate the JNI code for you based on the existing native code interfaces.

## Chapter 4

Auto-Generate JNI Code Using SWIG

In the previous chapter you explored JNI technology and you learned how to connect native code to a Java application. As noted, implementing JNI wrapper code and handling the translation of data types is a cumbersome and time-consuming development task. This chapter will introduce the Simplified Wrapper and Interface Generator (SWIG), a development tool that can simplify this process by automatically generating the necessary JNI wrapper code.

SWIG is not an Android- and Java-only tool. It is a highly extensive tool that can generate code in many other programming languages. As SWIG is rather large, this chapter will only cover the following key SWIG concepts and APIs that will get you started:

- Defining a SWIG interface for native code.
- Generating JNI code based on the interface.
- Integrating SWIG into the Android Build process.
- Wrapping C and C++ code.
- Exception handling.
- Using memory management.
- Calling Java from native code.

As SWIG simplifies the development of JNI code, you will be using SWIG often in the next chapters.

What is SWIG?

SWIG is a compile-time software development tool that can produce the code necessary to connect native modules written in C/C++ with other programming languages, including Java. SWIG is an interface compiler, merely a code generator; it does not define a new protocol nor is it a component framework or a specialized runtime library. SWIG takes an interface file as its input and produces the necessary code to expose that interface in Java. SWIG is not a stub generator; it produces code that is ready to be compiled and run.

SWIG was originally developed in 1995 for scientific applications; it has since evolved into a general-purpose tool that is distributed under GNU GPL open source license. More information about SWIG can be found at `www.swig.org`.

Installation

SWIG works on all major platforms, including Windows, Mac OS X, and Linux. At the time of this writing, the latest version of SWIG is 2.0.7. The latest version of SWIG is provided as a source code package through its official website at `www.swig.org`. The binaries for SWIG, except the Windows binaries, are provided through operating system-specific repositories. This section will provide detailed instructions on where SWIG binaries can be downloaded from and installed to for each major operating system.

Installing on Windows

SWIG binaries for Windows platform are provided through the SWIG download page at `www.swig.org/download.html`. As shown in Figure 4-1, click on the link to download the SWIG installation package.

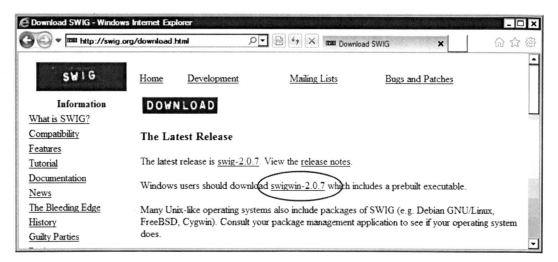

Figure 4-1. SWIG for Windows download link

The SWIG installation package comes as a ZIP archive file. The Windows OS comes with native support for ZIP format. When the download completes, right-click on the ZIP file and choose Extract All from the context menu to launch the Extract Compressed Folder wizard. Using the

Browse button, choose the destination directory where you want the extracted SWIG files to go. As mentioned, the C:\android directory is used as the root directory to hold the development tools. Select C:\android as the destination directory. A dedicated empty destination directory is not needed since the ZIP file already contains a sub directory called swigwin-2.0.7 to hold the SWIG. Click the Extract button to start the installation process.

Similar to the other development tools that you have installed, in order to have SWIG easily reachable, its installation directory should be appended to system executable search path. Launch the Environment Variables dialog from System Properties, and click the New button. As shown in Figure 4-2, using the New System Variable, set the variable name to SWIG_HOME and the variable value to the SWIG installation directory, such as C:\android\swigwin-2.0.7.

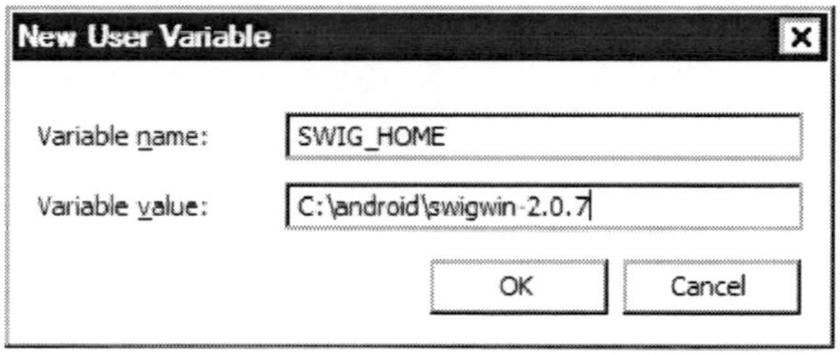

Figure 4-2. New SWIG_HOME environment variable

From the list of system variables, double-click on the PATH variable, and append ;%SWIG_HOME% to the variable value, as shown in Figure 4-3.

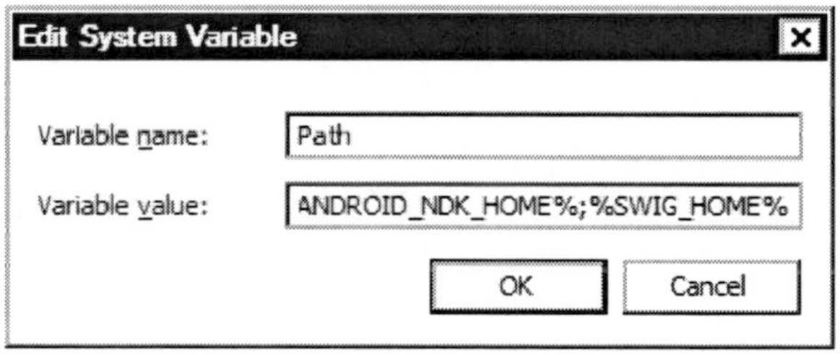

Figure 4-3. Appending SWIG binary path to system PATH variable

If the installation was successful, you will see the SWIG version number, as shown in Figure 4-4.

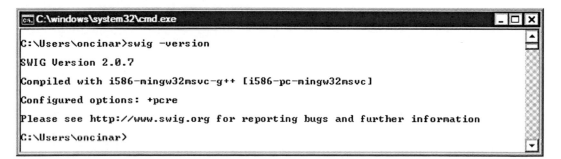

Figure 4-4. Validating SWIG installation

Installing on Mac OS X

The SWIG web site does not provide an installation package for Mac OS X platform. A Homebrew package manager will be used to download and install SWIG. In order to use Homebrew, it needs to be installed on the host machine as well. Homebrew comes with a console-based installation application. Copy the install command from the Homebrew installation page, as shown in Figure 4-5.

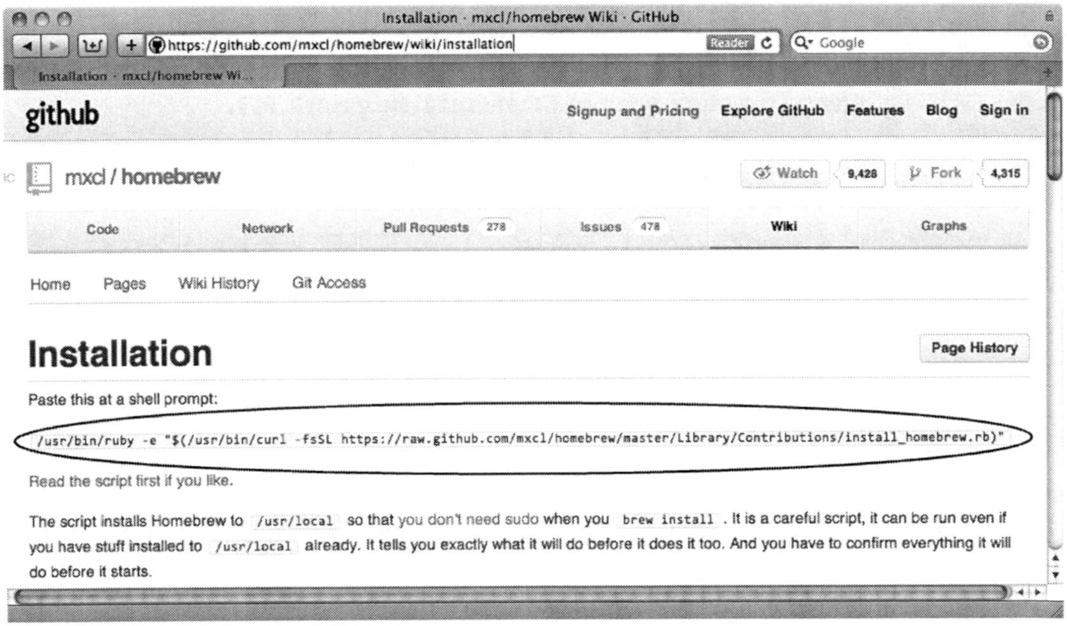

Figure 4-5. Installation command for Homebrew

Open a Terminal window. At the command prompt, paste the install command, as shown in Figure 4-6, and press the Enter key to start the installation process. The command will first download the Homebrew installation script and it will execute it using Ruby. Follow the on-screen instructions to complete the installation process.

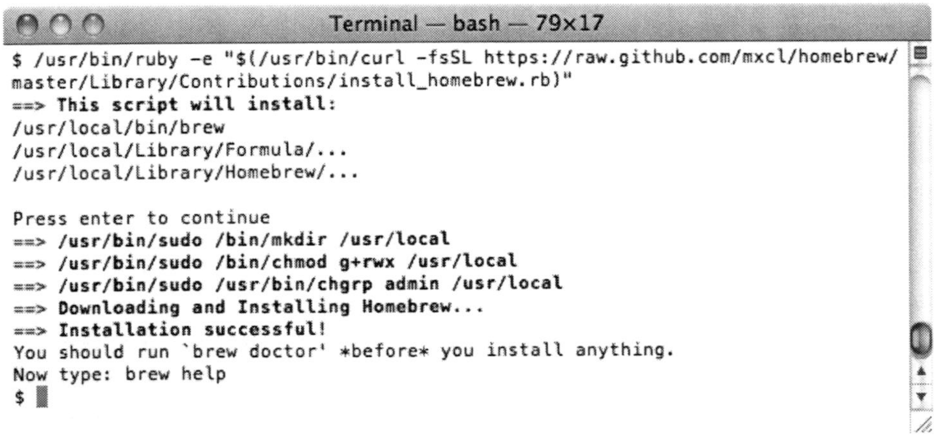

Figure 4-6. Installing Homebrew from command line

Upon completing the installation of Homebrew, SWIG can now be installed. Using the Terminal window, execute brew install swig on the command prompt. As shown in Figure 4-7, Homebrew will download the source code of SWIG and its dependencies, and then it will compile and install it automatically.

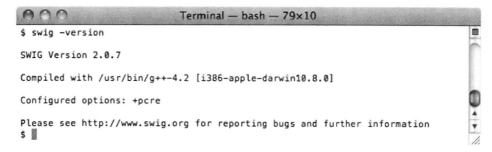

```
$ brew install swig
==> Installing swig dependency: pcre
==> Downloading ftp://ftp.csx.cam.ac.uk/pub/software/programming/pcre/pcre-8.31
######################################################################## 100.0%
==> ./configure --prefix=/usr/local/Cellar/pcre/8.31 --enable-utf8 --enable-uni
==> make test
==> make install
/usr/local/Cellar/pcre/8.31: 130 files, 3.2M, built in 54 seconds
==> Installing swig
==> Downloading http://downloads.sourceforge.net/project/swig/swig/swig-2.0.7/s
######################################################################## 100.0%
==> ./configure --prefix=/usr/local/Cellar/swig/2.0.7
==> make
==> make install
/usr/local/Cellar/swig/2.0.7: 598 files, 6.2M, built in 66 seconds
$ 
```

Figure 4-7. Installing SWIG using Homebrew

In order to validate the installation, open a new Terminal window and execute swig -version on the command line. If the installation was successful, you will see the SWIG version number, as shown in Figure 4-8.

```
$ swig -version

SWIG Version 2.0.7

Compiled with /usr/bin/g++-4.2 [i386-apple-darwin10.8.0]

Configured options: +pcre

Please see http://www.swig.org for reporting bugs and further information
$ 
```

Figure 4-8. Validating the SWIG installation

Installing on Ubuntu Linux

The SWIG web site does not provide an installation package for Linux flavors. The Ubuntu Linux software repository contains the latest version of SWIG, and it can be installed using the system package manager. Again, open a Terminal window. At the command prompt, execute sudo apt-get install swig, as shown in Figure 4-9. The system package manager will download and install SWIG and its dependencies automatically.

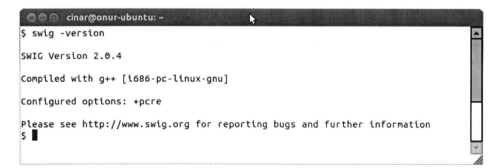

Figure 4-9. Installing SWIG from command line

In order to validate the installation, open a new Terminal window. Using the Terminal window, execute `swig -version` on the command line. If the installation was successful, you will see the SWIG version number, as shown in Figure 4-10.

Figure 4-10. Validating SWIG installation

Experimenting with SWIG Through an Example

Before learning the details of SWIG, you will walk through an example application to better understand how SWIG works. The Android platform is built on top of the Linux OS, a multiuser platform. It runs the applications within a virtual machine sandbox and treats them as different users on the system to keep the platform secure. On Linux, each user gets assigned a user ID, and this user ID can be queried by using the POSIX OS API `getuid` function. As a platform-independent programming language, Java does not provide access to these functions. As a part of this example application, you will be

- Writing a SWIG interface file to expose the getuid function.
- Integrating SWIG into the Android build process.
- Adding SWIG-generated source files into the Android.mk build file.
- Use the SWIG-generated proxy classes to query the getuid.
- Display the result on the screen.

You will be using the hello-jni sample project as a testbed. Open Eclipse IDE, and go into the hello-jni project. As mentioned earlier, SWIG operates on interface files.

Interface File

SWIG interface files contain function prototypes, classes, and variable declarations. Its syntax is the same as any ordinary C/C++ header file. In addition to C/C++ keywords and preprocessor directives, the interface files can also contain SWIG specific preprocessor directives that can enable tuning the generated wrapper code.

In order to expose getuid, an interface file needs to be defined. Using the Project Explorer, right-click on jni directory under the hello-jni project, and choose **New ➤ File** from the context menu to launch the New File dialog. As shown in Figure 4-11, set file name to Unix.i and click the Finish button.

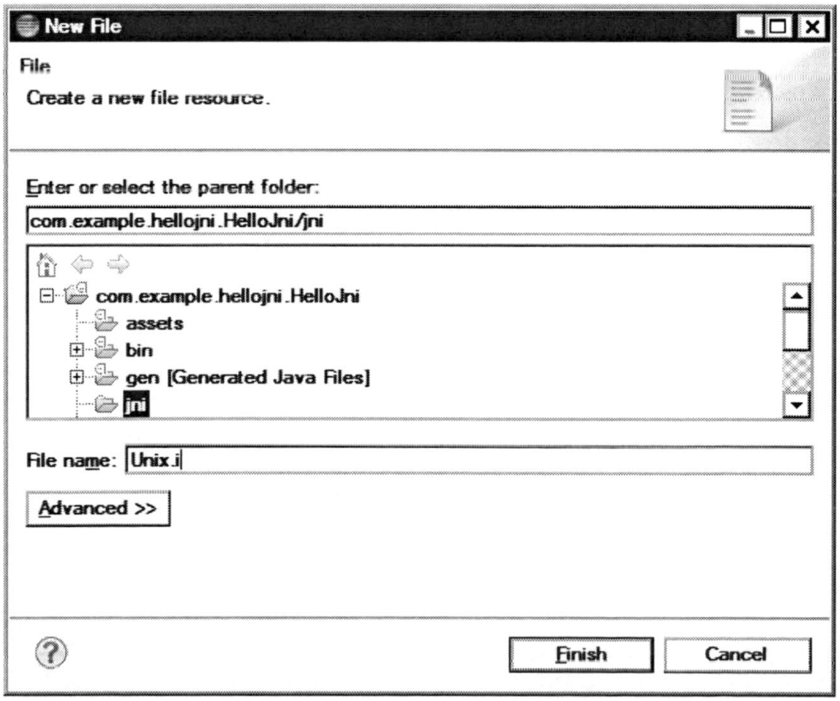

Figure 4-11. Creating the Unix.i SWIG interface file

Using the Editor view, populate the content of Unix.i, as shown in Listing 4-1.

Listing 4-1. Unix.i Interface File Content

```
/* Module name is Unix. */
%module Unix

%{
/* Include the POSIX operating system APIs. */
#include<unistd.h>
%}

/* Tell SWIG about uid_t. */
typedef unsigned int uid_t;

/* Ask SWIG to wrap getuid function. */
extern uid_t getuid(void);
```

Before moving to the next step (invoking SWIG), let's briefly go through the interface file.

Comments

The Unix.i interface file starts with a C style comment line starting with /* and ending with */ characters, as shown in Listing 4-2. Like the compilers, SWIG does not process comment lines. They are merely for annotating the interface files for developers.

Listing 4-2. Unix.i Starting with a Comment

```
/* Module name is Unix. */
...
```

Module Name

Each invocation of SWIG requires a module name to be specified. The module name is used to name the resulting wrapper files. The module name is specified using the SWIG specific preprocessor directive %module, and it should appear at the beginning of every interface file. Complying with this rule, the Unix.i interface file also starts by defining its module name as Unix, as shown in Listing 4-3.

Listing 4-3. Unix.i Defining Its Module Name

```
%module Unix
```

User-Defined Code

SWIG only uses the interface file while generating the wrapper code; its content does not go beyond this point. It is often necessary to include user-defined code in the generated files, such as any header file that is required to compile the generated code. When SWIG generates a wrapper code, it is broken up to into five sections. SWIG provides preprocessor directives to enable developers to specify the code snippets that should be included in any of these five sections. The syntax for SWIG preprocessor directive is shown in Listing 4-4.

Listing 4-4. Syntax for SWIG insert preprocessor directive

```
%<section>%{
  ...
  This code block will be included into generated code as is.
  ...
%}
...
```

The `<section>` portion can take following values:

- begin: Places the code block at the beginning of the generated wrapper file. It is mostly used for defining preprocessor macros that are used in the later part of the file.

- runtime: Places the code block next to SWIG's internal type-checking and other support functions.

- header: Places the code block into the header section next to header files and other helper functions. This is the default place to inject code into the generated files. The `%{ ... %}` can also be used the short form.

- wrapper: Places the code block next to generated wrapper functions.

- init: Places the code block into to function that will initialize the module upon loading.

As shown in Listing 4-5, the `Unix.i` interface file injects a header file into the generated wrapper code using the short form of insert header preprocessor directive.

Listing 4-5. Unix.i Inserting a Header into Generated Wrapper Code

```
%{
/* Include the POSIX operating system APIs. */
#include<unistd.h>
%}
```

Type Definitions

SWIG can understand all C/C++ data types but treats anything else as objects and wraps them as pointers. The declaration of the `getuid` function suggests that its return type is uid_t, which is not a standard C/C++ data type. As is, SWIG will treat it as an object, and it will wrap it as a pointer. This is not the preferred behavior since uid_t is nothing more than a simple typedef-name based on unsigned integer, not an object. As shown in Listing 4-6, the `Unix.i` interface file uses a typedef to inform SWIG about the actual return type of `getuid` function.

Listing 4-6. Type Definition for uid_t

```
/* Tell SWIG about uid_t. */
typedef unsigned int uid_t;
```

Function Prototypes

The Unix.i interface file ends with the function prototype for the getuid function as shown in Listing 4-7.

Listing 4-7. Function Prototype for getuid

```
/* Ask SWIG to wrap getuid function. */
extern uid_t getuid(void);
```

This was a brief explanation of how SWIG gets instructed to generate wrapper code to expose native functions to Java.

Invoking SWIG from Command Line

Now that the interface file is ready, SWIG can be invoked to generate the necessary wrapper code to expose getuid function to Java. SWIG will generate two sets of files: wrapper C/C++ code to expose the native function and Java proxy classes to provide access to the exposed function.

Java Package for Proxy Classes

The Java package directory should be created in advance of invoking SWIG. Using the Project Explorer, right-click on the src directory and select **New ➤ Package** to launch the New Java Package dialog. As shown in Figure 4-12, set the package name to com.apress.swig and click the Finish button.

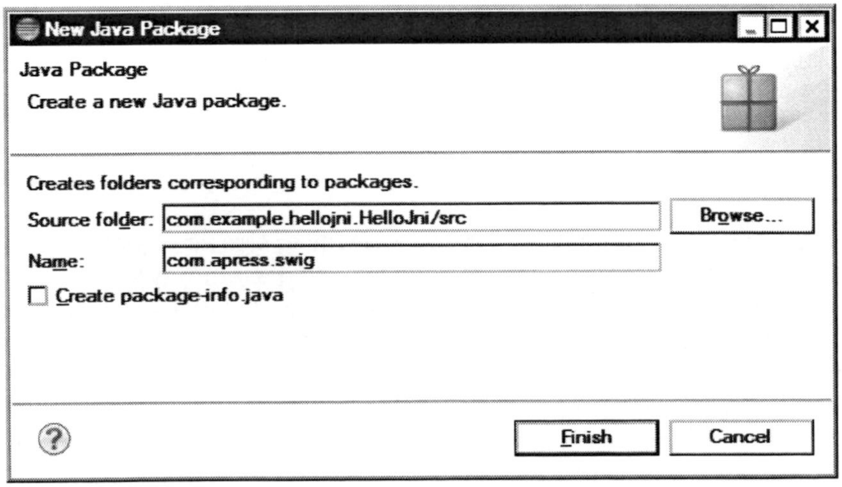

Figure 4-12. Java package for SWIG files

Invoking SWIG

You are now ready to invoke SWIG. Open a Terminal window or a command prompt, and go in to the directory where the hello-jni project is imported, such as C:\android\workspace\com.example. hellojni.HelloJni. As shown in Figure 4-13, execute swig -java -package com.apress.swig -outdir src/com/apress/swig jni/Unix.i on the command line.

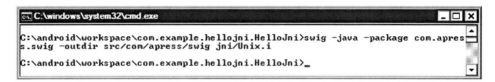

Figure 4-13. *Invoking SWIG on the command line*

SWIG parses the Unix.i interface file and generates the Unix_wrap.c C/C++ wrapper code in the jni directory plus the UnixJNI.java and Unix.java Java proxy classes in the com.apress.swig package.

Before starting to explore these files, let's streamline the process. SWIG can be integrated into the Android build process, instead of being manually executed from the command line.

Integrating SWIG into Android Build Process

In order to integrate SWIG into Android build process, you will define a Makefile fragment.

Android Build System Fragment for SWIG

Using the Project Explorer, right-click the jni directory and choose **New ➤ File** from the menu. Using the New File dialog, create a file named my-swig-generate.mk. The contents of this Makefile fragment are shown in Listing 4-8.

Listing 4-8. Contents of my-swig-generate.mk File

```
#
# SWIG extension for Android build system.
#
# @author Onur Cinar
#

# Check if the MY_SWIG_PACKAGE is defined
ifndef MY_SWIG_PACKAGE
  $(error MY_SWIG_PACKAGE is not defined.)
endif

# Replace dots with slashes for the Java directory
MY_SWIG_OUTDIR :- $(NDK_PROJECT_PATH)/src/$(subst .,/,$(MY_SWIG_PACKAGE))
```

```
# Default SWIG type is C
ifndef MY_SWIG_TYPE
  MY_SWIG_TYPE := c
endif

# Set SWIG mode
ifeq ($(MY_SWIG_TYPE),cxx)
  MY_SWIG_MODE :=-c++
else
  MY_SWIG_MODE :=
endif

# Append SWIG wrapper source files
LOCAL_SRC_FILES+= $(foreach MY_SWIG_INTERFACE,\
  $(MY_SWIG_INTERFACES),\
  $(basename $(MY_SWIG_INTERFACE))_wrap.$(MY_SWIG_TYPE))

# Add .cxx as a C++ extension
LOCAL_CPP_EXTENSION+= .cxx

# Generate SWIG wrapper code (indention should be tabs for this block)
%_wrap.$(MY_SWIG_TYPE) : %.i
        $(call host-mkdir,$(MY_SWIG_OUTDIR))
        swig -java \
        $(MY_SWIG_MODE) \
        -package $(MY_SWIG_PACKAGE) \
        -outdir $(MY_SWIG_OUTDIR) \
        $<
```

Integrating SWIG into Android.mk

In order to use this build system fragment, the existing Android.mk file needs to be modified. The build system fragment requires three new variables to be defined in Android.mk file in order to operate:

- MY_SWIG_PACKAGE: Defines the Java package where SWIG will generate the proxy classes. In your example, this will be the com.apress.swig package.

- MY_SWIG_INTERFACES: Lists the SWIG interface file that should be processed. In your example, this will be the Unix.i file.

- MY_SWIG_MODE: Instructs SWIG to generate the wrapper code in either C or C++. In your example, this will be C code.

Using the Project Explorer, expand the jni directory under the project root, and open Android.mk in editor view. Let's now define these new variables for the project. The additions to the Android.mk file are shown in Listing 4-9 as bold.

Listing 4-9. Defining SWIG Variables in Android.mk file

```
LOCAL_PATH := $(call my-dir)

include $(CLEAR_VARS)

LOCAL_MODULE    := hello-jni
LOCAL_SRC_FILES := hello-jni.c

MY_SWIG_PACKAGE := com.apress.swig
MY_SWIG_INTERFACES := Unix.i
MY_SWIG_TYPE := c

include $(LOCAL_PATH)/my-swig-generate.mk

include $(BUILD_SHARED_LIBRARY)
```

After defining these new variables, the Androd.mk file includes the my-swig-generate.mk build system fragment that you defined earlier in this section. The build system fragment first creates the Java package directory and then invokes SWIG by setting the proper parameters based on these variables. This should happen before building the shared library since the wrapper code that will be generated by SWIG should also get compiled into the shared library. The build system fragment automatically appends the generated wrapper files into the LOCAL_SRC_FILES variable.

Choose **Project ➤ Build** All from the top menu to rebuild the current project. As shown in Figure 4-14, the Android NDK build logs indicate that the Unix_wrapper.c wrapper code is getting compiled into the shared library.

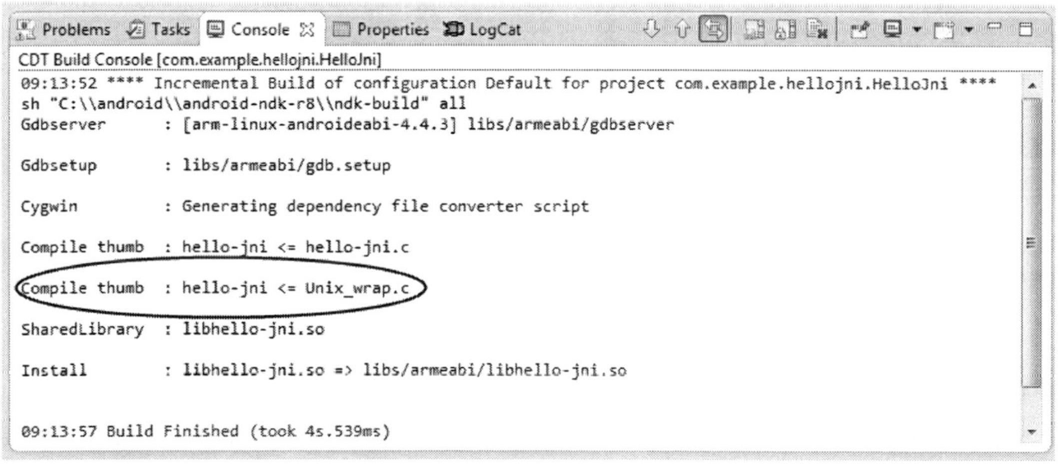

Figure 4-14. Build logs showing the wrapper code getting compiled

Updating the Activity

The getuid function is now properly exposed through the Unix proxy Java class. In order to validate it, you will be modifying the HelloJni activity to show its return value on the display. Using the

Project Explorer, expand the `src` directory and then the `com.example.hellojni` Java package. Open `HelloJni` in editor view, and modify the body of `onCreate` method as shown in Listing 4-10.

Listing 4-10. Invoking getuid Function from Unix Proxy Class

```
@Override
public void onCreate(Bundle savedInstanceState)
{
    super.onCreate(savedInstanceState);

    . . .

    TextView  tv = new TextView(this);
    tv.setText("UID: "+Unix.getuid());
    setContentView(tv);
}
```

Executing the Application

The application is now ready. Choose Run ➤ Run from the top menu bar to launch the application. As shown in Figure 4-15, activity will call the `getuid` function and the result will be displayed on the screen.

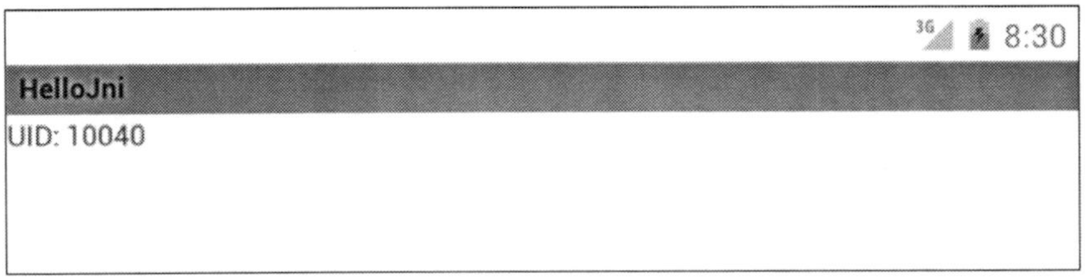

Figure 4-15. Activity displaying the user ID

As demonstrated with this example, SWIG can automatically generate all of the necessary JNI and Java code to expose a native function to Java.

Exploring Generated Code

In order to make the native function reachable from Java, SWIG has generated two Java classes and one C/C++ wrapper:

- `Unix_wrap.c`: Contains the JNI wrapper functions to handle the type mapping and to expose the selected native functions to Java. The generated wrapper function is shown in Listing 4-11.

Listing 4-11. Generated Wrapper Function for getuid

```
SWIGEXPORT jlong JNICALL Java_com_apress_swig_UnixJNI_getuid(JNIEnv *jenv, jclass jcls)
{
  jlong jresult = 0 ;
  uid_t result;

  (void)jenv;
  (void)jcls;
  result = (uid_t)getuid();
  jresult = (jlong)result;
  return jresult;
}
```

■ UnixJNI.java: Intermediary JNI class containing the Java native function declaration for all functions that are exposed by the wrapper. It is generated in the com.apress.swig Java package as specified in Android.mk file. The generated intermediary JNI class is shown in Listing 4-12.

Listing 4-12. Generated Intermediary JNI Class

```
package com.apress.swig;

public class UnixJNI {
  public final static native long getuid();
}
```

■ Unix.java: Module class containing all methods and global variable getter and setters. It wraps the calls in the intermediary JNI class to implement static type checking. You will revisit this subject when you start exploring how SWIG handles the objects. It is generated in com.apress.swig Java package as well. The generated module class is shown in Listing 4-13.

Listing 4-13. Generated Module Class

```
package com.apress.swig;

public class Unix {
  public static long getuid() {
    return UnixJNI.getuid();
  }
}
```

Wrapping C Code

In the previous example, you learned how the functions get exposed through SWIG. In this section, you will explore how other components get wrapped by SWIG. Note that the components that are defined in the interface file are merely for SWIG to expose them to Java; they do not get included into the generated files unless they are also declared in insert preprocessor declaration. SWIG assumes that all exposed components are defined elsewhere in the code. If the component is not defined, the build will simply fail during compile-time.

Global Variables

Although there is no such thing as a Java global variable, SWIG does support global variables. SWIG generates getter and setter methods in the module class to provide access to native global variables. In order to expose a global variable to Java, simply add it to the interface file as shown in Listing 4-14.

Listing 4-14. Interface File Exposing the Counter Global Variable

```
%module Unix
...
/* Global counter. */
extern int counter;
```

Upon processing the interface file, SWIG will generate the corresponding getter and setter methods to provide access to the global variable from the Java application, as shown in Listing 4-15.

Listing 4-15. Getter and Setter Methods for Counter Global Variable

```
package com.apress.swig;

public class Unix {
  ...

  public static void setCounter(int value) {
    UnixJNI.counter_set(value);
  }

  public static int getCounter() {
    return UnixJNI.counter_get();
  }
}
```

Besides the variables, SWIG also provides support for those constants that are associated with a value that cannot be altered during runtime.

Constants

Constants can be defined in the interface file either through #define or %constant preprocessor directives, as shown in Listing 4-16.

Listing 4-16. Interface File Defining Two Constants

```
%module Unix
...
/* Constant using define directive. */
#define MAX_WIDTH 640
```

```
/* Constant using %constant directive. */
%constant int MAX_HEIGHT = 320;
```

SWIG generates a Java interface called <Module>Constant, and the constants are exposed as static final variables on that interface, as shown in Listing 4-17.

Listing 4-17. UnixConstants Interface Exposing Two Constants

```
package com.apress.swig;

public interface UnixConstants {
  public final static int MAX_WIDTH = UnixJNI.MAX_WIDTH_get();
  public final static int MAX_HEIGHT = UnixJNI.MAX_HEIGHT_get();
}
```

By default SWIG generates runtime constants. The values of the constants are initialized by making JNI function calls to the native code at runtime. This can be changed by using the %javaconst preprocessor directive in interface file, as shown in Listing 4-18.

Listing 4-18. Instructions to Generate Compile-time Constant for MAX_WIDTH

```
%module Unix
...
/* Constant using define directive. */
%javaconst(1);
#define MAX_WIDTH 640

/* Constant using %constant directive. */
%javaconst(0);
%constant int MAX_HEIGHT = 320;
```

This preprocessor directive instructs SWIG to generate a compile-time constant for MAX_WIDTH and a run-time constant for MAX_HEIGHT. The Java constants interface now looks like Listing 4-19.

Listing 4-19. UnixConstants Interface Exposing the Compile-time Constant

```
package com.apress.swig;

public interface UnixConstants {
  public final static int MAX_WIDTH = 640;
  public final static int MAX_HEIGHT = UnixJNI.MAX_HEIGHT_get();
}
```

In certain situation you may want to limit the write access on a variable and expose it as read-only to Java.

Read-Only Variables

SWIG provides the %immutable preprocessor directive to mark a variable as read-only, as shown in Listing 4-20.

Listing 4-20. Enabling and Disabling Read-only Mode in the Interface File

```
%module Unix
...
/* Enable the read-only mode. */
%immutable;

/* Read-only variable. */
extern int readOnly;

/* Disable the read-only mode. */
%mutable;

/* Read-write variable. */
extern int readWrite;
```

The setter method will not be generated for the read-only variable, as shown in Listing 4-21.

Listing 4-21. Setter Method Is Not Generated for the Read-only Variable

```
package com.apress.swig;

public class Unix implements UnixConstants {
  ...

  public static int getReadOnly() {
    return UnixJNI.readOnly_get();
  }

  public static void setReadWrite(int value) {
    UnixJNI.readWrite_set(value);
  }

  public static int getReadWrite() {
    return UnixJNI.readWrite_get();
  }
}
```

Besides the constants and read-only variables, enumerations are also frequently used in applications. Enumerations are set of named constant values.

Enumerations

SWIG can handle both named and anonymous enumerations. Depending on the developer's choice or the target Java version, it can generate enumerations in four different ways.

Anonymous

Anonymous enumerations can be declared in the interface file, as shown in Listing 4-22.

Listing 4-22. Anonymous Enumeration

```
%module Unix
...
/* Anonymous enumeration. */
enum { ONE = 1, TWO = 2, THREE, FOUR };
```

SWIG generates the final static variables in the `<Module>Constants` Java interface for each enumeration, as shown in Listing 4-23. Like the constants, the enumerations are also generated as run-time enumerations. The `%javaconst` preprocessor directive can be used to generate compile-time enumeration.

Listing 4-23. Anonymous Enumeration Exposed Through Constants Interface

```
package com.apress.swig;

public interface UnixConstants {
  ...
  public final static int ONE = UnixJNI.ONE_get();
  public final static int TWO = UnixJNI.TWO_get();
  public final static int THREE = UnixJNI.THREE_get();
  public final static int FOUR = UnixJNI.FOUR_get();
}
```

Type-Safe

Named enumerations can be declared in interface file, as shown in Listing 4-24. Unlike the anonymous enumerations, they get exposed to Java as type-safe enumerations.

Listing 4-24. Named Enumeration

```
%module Unix
...
/* Named enumeration. */
enum Numbers { ONE = 1, TWO = 2, THREE, FOUR };
```

SWIG defines a separate class with the enumeration's name, and the enumeration values are exposed as final static member fields, as shown in Listing 4-25.

Listing 4-25. Named Enumeration Exposed as a Java Class

```
package com.apress.swig;

public final class Numbers {
  public final static Numbers ONE = new Numbers(
    "ONE", UnixJNI.ONE_get());
```

```
  public final static Numbers TWO = new Numbers(
    "TWO", UnixJNI.TWO_get());
  public final static Numbers THREE = new Numbers("THREE");
  public final static Numbers FOUR = new Numbers("FOUR");


  ...
  /* Helper methods. */
  ...
}
```

This type of enumeration allows type checking and it is much safer than the constants based approach, although it cannot be used in switch statements.

Type-Unsafe

The third approach is a combination of previous two approaches. Enumeration gets wrapped into its on class but the enumeration values are exposed as static final variables. A named enumeration can be marked as type-unsafe exposure by including the enumtypeunsafe.swg extension, as shown in Listing 4-26.

Listing 4-26. Named Enumeration Exposed as Type Unsafe

```
%module Unix
...
/* Type Unsafe */
%include "enumtypeunsafe.swg"

/* Named enumeration. */
enum Numbers { ONE = 1, TWO = 2, THREE, FOUR };
```

The generated Java class for the enumeration is shown in Listing 4-27. This type of enumerations can be used in switch statements since they are constants-based.

Listing 4-27. Type Unsafe Enumeration Exposed as a Java Class

```
package com.apress.swig;

public final class Numbers {
  public final static int ONE = UnixJNI.ONE_get();
  public final static int TWO = UnixJNI.TWO_get();
  public final static int THREE = UnixJNI.THREE_get();
  public final static int FOUR = UnixJNI.FOUR_get();
}
```

Java Enumerations

Named enumerations can also be exposed to Java as proper Java enumerations. This type of enumerations is type checked, and they can also be used in switch statements. Named enumerations can be marked as Java enumeration exposure by including the enums.swg extension, as shown in Listing 4-28.

Listing 4-28. Java Enumeration

```
%module Unix
...
/* Java enumeration. */
%include "enums.swg"

/* Named enumeration. */
enum Numbers { ONE = 1, TWO = 2, THREE, FOUR };
```

The generated Java class is shown in Listing 4-29.

Listing 4-29. Generated Java Enumeration Class

```
package com.apress.swig;

public enum Numbers {
  ONE(UnixJNI.ONE_get()),
  TWO(UnixJNI.TWO_get()),
  THREE,
  FOUR;

  ...
  /* Helper methods. */
  ...
}
```

Structures are widely used in C/C++ applications. They aggregate a set of named variables into a single data type.

Structures

Structures are also supported by SWIG, and they can be declared in the interface file, as shown in Listing 4-30.

Listing 4-30. Point Structure That Is Declared in the Interface File

```
%module Unix
...
/* Point structure. */
struct Point {
  int x;
  int y;
};
```

They get wrapped as Java classes with getters and setters for the member variables, as shown in Listing 4-31.

Listing 4-31. Generated Point Java Class

```
package com.apress.swig;

public class Point {
  private long swigCPtr;
  protected boolean swigCMemOwn;

  protected Point(long cPtr, boolean cMemoryOwn) {
    swigCMemOwn = cMemoryOwn;
    swigCPtr = cPtr;
  }

  protected static long getCPtr(Point obj) {
    return (obj == null) ? 0 : obj.swigCPtr;
  }

  protected void finalize() {
    delete();
  }

  public synchronized void delete() {
    if (swigCPtr ! = 0) {
      if (swigCMemOwn) {
        swigCMemOwn = false;
        UnixJNI.delete_Point(swigCPtr);
      }
      swigCPtr = 0;
    }
  }

  public void setX(int value) {
    UnixJNI.Point_x_set(swigCPtr, this, value);
  }

  public int getX() {
    return UnixJNI.Point_x_get(swigCPtr, this);
  }

  public void setY(int value) {
    UnixJNI.Point_y_set(swigCPtr, this, value);
  }

  public int getY() {
    return UnixJNI.Point_y_get(swigCPtr, this);
  }

  public Point() {
    this(UnixJNI.new_Point(), true);
  }
}
```

Another widely used C/C++ data type is pointers, a memory address whose value refers directly to value elsewhere in the memory.

Pointers

SWIG also provides support for pointers. As seen in the previous example, SWIG stores the C pointer of the actual C structure instance in the Java class. SWIG stores the pointers using the long data type. It manages the life cycle of the C components aligned with the life cycle of the associated Java class through the use of the finalize method.

Wrapping C++ Code

In the previous section you explored the basics of wrapping C components. Now you will focus on wrapping the C++ code. First, you need to modify the Android.mk file to instruct SWIG to generate C++ code. In order to do so, open the Android.mk file in the editor view and set MY_SWIG_TYPE variable to cxx, as shown in Listing 4-32.

Listing 4-32. Android.mk Instructing SWIG to Generate C+ Code

```
MY_SWIG_PACKAGE := com.apress.swig
MY_SWIG_INTERFACES := Unix.i
MY_SWIG_TYPE := cxx
```

SWIG will now generate the wrapper in C++ instead of C code. You have already learned the function generation, so you'll now focus on the type of arguments that can be passed to these functions.

Pointers, References, and Values

In C/C++, function can take arguments in many different ways, such as through pointers, references, or by simply value (see Listing 4-33).

Listing 4-33. Functions with Different Argument Types

```
/* By pointer. */
void drawByPointer(struct Point* p);

/* By reference */
void drawByReference(struct Point& p);

/* By value. */
void drawByValue(struct Point p);
```

In Java there are no such types. SWIG unifies these types together in the wrapper code as object instance reference, as shown in Listing 4-34.

Listing 4-34. Unified Methods in Generated Java Class

```
package com.apress.swig;

public class Unix implements UnixConstants {
  ...

  public static void drawByPointer(Point p) {
    UnixJNI.drawByPointer(Point.getCPtr(p), p);
  }

  public static void drawByReference(Point p) {
    UnixJNI.drawByReference(Point.getCPtr(p), p);
  }

  public static void drawByValue(Point p) {
    UnixJNI.drawByValue(Point.getCPtr(p), p);
  }
}
```

Although the declaration in C code is different, all of the calls shown in Listing 4-35 are correct based on the generated code.

Listing 4-35. Unified Methods Getting Called with the Same Argument Type

```
Point p;
...
Unix.drawByPointer(p);
Unix.drawByReference(p);
Unix.drawByValue(p);
```

The C/C++ programming language allows functions to specify default values for some of their arguments. When these functions are called by omitting these arguments, the default values are used.

Default Arguments

Although default arguments are not supported by Java, SWIG provides support for functions with default arguments by generating additional functions for each argument that is defaulted. Functions with default arguments can be decelerated in the interface file, as shown in Listing 4-36.

Listing 4-36. Function with Default Arguments in the Interface File

```
%module Unix
...
/* Function with default arguments. */
void func(int a = 1, int b = 2, int c = 3);
```

Generated additional functions will be exposed through the module Java class, as shown in Listing 4-37.

Listing 4-37. Additional Functions Generated to Support Default Arguments

```
package com.apress.swig;

public class Unix {
  ...

  public static void func(int a, int b, int c) {
    UnixJNI.func__SWIG_0(a, b, c);
  }

  public static void func(int a, int b) {
    UnixJNI.func__SWIG_1(a, b);
  }

  public static void func(int a) {
    UnixJNI.func__SWIG_2(a);
  }

  public static void func() {
    UnixJNI.func__SWIG_3();
  }
}
```

Function overloading allows applications to define multiple functions having the same name but different arguments.

Overloaded Functions

SWIG easily supports the overloaded functions since Java already provides support for them. Overloaded functions can be declared in the interface file, as shown in Listing 4-38.

Listing 4-38. Overloaded Functions Declared in the Interface File

```
%module Unix
...
/* Overloaded functions. */
void func(double d);
void func(int i);
```

SWIG exposes the overloaded functions through the module Java class, as shown in Listing 4-39.

Listing 4-39. Overloaded Functions Exposed Through the Module Java Class

```
package com.apress.swig;

public class Unix {
  ...
```

```
  public static void func(double d) {
    UnixJNI.func__SWIG_0(d);
  }

  public static void func(int i) {
    UnixJNI.func__SWIG_1(i);
  }
}
```

SWIG resolves overloaded functions using a disambiguation scheme that ranks and sorts declarations according to a set of type-precedence rules. Besides the functions and primitive data types, SWIG can also translate C++ classes.

Classes

Similar to structures, classes are also wrapped as Java classes. SWIG generates the necessary getter and setter methods for all public class variables. Classes can be declared in the interface file, as shown in Listing 4-40.

Listing 4-40. Class Declaration in the Interface File

```
%module Unix
...
/* Class A. */
class A {
public:
  A();
  A(int value);
  ~A();

  void print();

  int value;
private:
  void reset();
};
```

SWIG generates the corresponding Java class, as shown in Listing 4-41. The value member variable is public, and the corresponding getter and setter methods are automatically generated by SWIG. The reset method does not get exposed to Java since it is declared in private in the class declaration.

Listing 4-41. C/C++ Exposed to Java

```
package com.apress.swig;

public class A {
  private long swigCPtr;
  protected boolean swigCMemOwn;
```

```java
  protected A(long cPtr, boolean cMemoryOwn) {
    swigCMemOwn = cMemoryOwn;
    swigCPtr = cPtr;
  }

  protected static long getCPtr(A obj) {
    return (obj == null) ? 0 : obj.swigCPtr;
  }

  protected void finalize() {
    delete();
  }

  public synchronized void delete() {
    if (swigCPtr ! = 0) {
      if (swigCMemOwn) {
        swigCMemOwn = false;
        UnixJNI.delete_A(swigCPtr);
      }
      swigCPtr = 0;
    }
  }

  public A() {
    this(UnixJNI.new_A__SWIG_0(), true);
  }

  public A(int value) {
    this(UnixJNI.new_A__SWIG_1(value), true);
  }

  public void print() {
    UnixJNI.A_print(swigCPtr, this);
  }

  public void setValue(int value) {
    UnixJNI.A_value_set(swigCPtr, this, value);
  }

  public int getValue() {
    return UnixJNI.A_value_get(swigCPtr, this);
  }
}
```

SWIG provides support for inheritance as well. Those classes are wrapped into a hierarchy of
Java classes reflecting the same inheritance relationship. Since Java does not support multiple
inheritance, any C++ class with multiple inheritance will trigger an error during the code generation
phase.

Exception Handling

In native code, C/C++ functions can throw exceptions or return error codes. SWIG allows developers to inject exception handling code into the generated wrapper code by using the %exception preprocessor directive to translate the C/C++ exceptions and error codes into Java exceptions. Exception handling code can be defined in the interface file, as shown in Listing 4-42. The exception handling code should be defined before the actual function declaration.

Listing 4-42. Exception Handling Code for getuid Function

```
/* Exception handling for getuid. */
%exception getuid {
  $action
  if (!result) {
    jclass clazz = jenv->FindClass("java/lang/OutOfMemoryError");
    jenv->ThrowNew(clazz, "Out of Memory");
    return $null;
  }
}

/* Ask SWIG to wrap getuid function. */
extern uid_t getuid(void);
```

Compared to Listing 4-11, the generated wrapper code for getuid function now looks like Listing 4-43.

Listing 4-43. Wrapper Code with Exception Handling

```
SWIGEXPORT jlong JNICALL Java_com_apress_swig_UnixJNI_getuid(JNIEnv *jenv, jclass jcls) {
  jlong jresult = 0 ;
  uid_t result;

  (void)jenv;
  (void)jcls;
  {
    result = (uid_t)getuid();
    if (!result) {
      jclass clazz = jenv->FindClass("java/lang/OutOfMemoryError");
      jenv->ThrowNew(clazz, "Out of Memory");
      return 0;
    }
  }
  jresult = (jlong)result;
  return jresult;
}
```

The generated Java code did not change since the code is throwing a run-time exception. If a checked exception is thrown, SWIG can be instructed through the %javaexception preprocessor directive to reflect that accordingly to the generated Java methods, as shown in Listing 4-44.

Listing 4-44. Instructing SWIG That a Checked Exception May Be Thrown

```
/* Exception handling for getuid. */
%javaexception("java.lang.IllegalAccessException") getuid {
  $action
  if (!result) {
    jclass clazz = jenv->FindClass("java/lang/IllegalAccessException");
    jenv->ThrowNew(clazz, "Illegal Access");
    return $null;
  }
}
```

The generated Java method signature now reflects the checked exception that may be thrown, as shown in Listing 4-45.

Listing 4-45. Java Class Reflecting the Thrown Exception

```
package com.apress.swig;

public class Unix {
  public static long getuid() throws java.lang.IllegalAccessException {
    return UnixJNI.getuid();
  }
}
```

Memory Management

Each proxy class that is generated by SWIG contains an ownership flag called swigCMemOwn. This flag specifies who is responsible for cleaning up the underlying C/C++ component. If the proxy class owns the underlying component, the memory will get freed by the finalize method of the Java class when it gets garbage collected. Memory can be freed without waiting for the garbage collector by simply invoking the delete method of the Java class. During runtime the Java class can be instructed to release or take ownership of the underlying C/C++ component's memory through the swigReleaseOwnership and swigTakeOwnership methods.

Calling Java from Native Code

Until this point you have always called from Java to C/C++ code. In certain cases, you may need to call from C/C++ code back to Java code as well, such as for callbacks. SWIG does also provide support calling from C/C++ code to Java by the use of virtual methods.

Asynchronous Communication

In order to demonstrate the flow, you will convert the getuid function call to an asynchronous mode by wrapping it in a C/C++ class and returning its result through a callback. For this experiment, you can place the class declaration and definition into the SWIG interface file, as shown in Listing 4-46.

Listing 4-46. Declaration and Definition of AsyncUidProvider Class

```
%module Unix
...
%{
/* Asynchornous user ID provider. */
class AsyncUidProvider {
public:
  AsyncUidProvider() {
  }

  virtual~AsyncUidProvider() {
  }

  void get() {
    onUid(getuid());
  }

  virtual void onUid(uid_t uid) {
  }
};
%}

/* Asynchornous user ID provider. */
class AsyncUidProvider {
public:
  AsyncUidProvider();
  virtual~AsyncUidProvider();

  void get();
  virtual void onUid(uid_t uid);
};
```

Enabling Directors

SWIG provides support for cross language polymorphism using directors feature. The directors feature is disabled by default. In order to enable it, the %module preprocessor directive should be modified to include the directors flag. After enabling the directors extension, the feature should be applied to AsyncUidProvider class using the %feature preprocessor directive. Both changes are shown in Listing 4-47.

Listing 4-47. Enabling Directors Extension and Applying the Feature

```
/* Module name is Unix. */
%module(directors=1) Unix

/* Enable directors for AsyncUidProvider. */
%feature("director") AsyncUidProvider;
```

In order to bridge calls from C/C++ code to Java, the directors extension relies on Run-Time Type Information (RTTI) feature of the compiler.

Enabling RTTI

By default, RTTI is turned off on Android NDK build system. In order to enable it, modify the Android.mk file as shown in Listing 4-48.

Listing 4-48. Enabling RTTI in Android.mk File

```
# Enable RTTI
LOCAL_CPP_FEATURES+= rtti
```

The native code portion is now ready. Choose **Project ➤ Build All** from the top menu to rebuild the current project.

Overriding the Callback Method

On the Java side, you need to extend the exposed AsyncUidProvider class and override the onUid method to receive the result of the getuid function call, as shown in Listing 4-49.

Listing 4-49. Extending the AsyncUidProvider in Java

```java
package com.example.hellojni;

import android.widget.TextView;

import com.apress.swig.AsyncUidProvider;

public class UidHandler extends AsyncUidProvider {
  private final TextView textView;

  UidHandler(TextView textView) {
    this.textView = textView;
  }

  @Override
  public void onUid(long uid) {
    textView.setText("UID: "+uid);
  }
}
```

Updating the HelloJni Activity

As the last step, the HelloJni activity needs to be modified to use the UidHandler class. The modified content of onCreate method is shown in Listing 4-50.

Listing 4-50. Modified onCreate Method Using the New UidHandler

```
@Override
public void onCreate(Bundle savedInstanceState)
{
  ...

  TextView  tv = new TextView(this);
  setContentView(tv);

  UidHandler uidHandler = new UidHandler(tv);
  uidHandler.get();
}
```

Now you can choose **New ➤ File** from the top menu to launch the application. Upon invoking the get method of the `AsnycUidProvider`, the C/C++ code will call back to Java with the result of the `getuid` function call and it will get displayed.

Summary

As you can see, SWIG simplifies the process of connecting native code to the Java layer by automatically producing all necessary JNI wrapper code. Although the process is highly transparent to the developers, SWIG still provides the necessary functionality to enable developers to expand the generated code to match their unique requirements. More information about SWIG features can be found in SWIG Documentation at `http://swig.org/Doc2.0/index.html`. You will be using SWIG often in the next chapters, and you will continue exploring the other unique features offered.

## Chapter 5

Logging, Debugging, and Troubleshooting

In previous chapters, you explored the Android NDK build system and how to connect the native code to the Java application using the JNI technology. Needless to say, learning application development on a new platform involves much experimentation; it takes time to get things right. It is vital to gain the troubleshooting skills pertaining to Android platform before starting to experiment with the native APIs offered, as it can catalyze the learning phase greatly by helping you to spot problems quickly. Your existing troubleshooting skills may not directly apply since the development and execution of Android applications happens on two different machines. In this chapter you will explore logging, debugging, and troubleshooting tools and techniques including:

- An Introduction to Android Logging framework
- Debugging native code through Eclipse and command line
- Analyzing stack traces from crashes
- Using CheckJNI mode to spot problems earlier
- Troubleshooting memory issues using libc and Valgrind
- Using strace to monitor native code execution

Logging

Logging is the most important part of troubleshooting, but it is tricky to achieve, especially on mobile platforms where the development and the execution of the application happen on two different machines. Android has an extensive logging framework that promotes system-wide centralized logging of information from both the Android system itself and the applications. A set of user-level applications is also provided to view and filter these logs, such as the logcat and Dalvik Debug Monitor Server (DDMS) tools.

Framework

The Android logging framework is implemented as a kernel module known as the *logger*. The amount of information being logged on the platform at any given time makes the viewing and analysis of these log messages very difficult. In order to simplify this procedure, the Android logging framework groups the log messages into four separate log buffers:

- *Main*: Main application log messages
- *Events*: System events
- *Radio*: Radio-related log messages
- *System*: Low-level system debug messages for debugging

These four buffers are kept as pseudo-devices under the /dev/log system directory. Since input and output (I/O) operations on mobile platforms are very costly, the log messages are not saved in persistent storage; instead, they are kept in memory. In order to keep the memory utilization of the log messages under control, the logger module puts them in fixed-sized buffers. Main, radio, and system logs are kept as free-form text messages in 64KB log buffers. The event log messages carry additional information in binary format, so they are kept in a 256KB log buffer.

Native Logging APIs

Developers are not expected to directly interact with the logger kernel module. The Android runtime provides a set of API calls to allow both Java and the native code to easily send log messages to the logger kernel module. The logging API for the native code is exposed through the android/log.h header file. In order to use the logging functions, native code should include this header file first.

```
#include <android/log.h>
```

In addition to including the proper header file, the Android.mk file needs to be modified dynamically to link the native module with the log library. This is achieved through the use LOCAL_LDLIBS build system variable, as shown in Listing 5-1. This build system variable must be placed before the include statement for the shared library build fragment; otherwise, it will not have any affect.

Listing 5-1. Dynamically Linking the Native Module with Log Library

```
LOCAL_MODULE := hello-jni
...
LOCAL_LDLIBS += -llog
...
include $(BUILD_SHARED_LIBRARY)
```

Log Message

Each log entry that is dispatched to the logger module through the logging APIs has the following fields:

- *Priority*: Can be verbose, debug, info, warning, error, or fatal to indicate the severity of the log message. Supported log priority levels are declared in the android/log.h header file, as shown in Listing 5-2.

Listing 5-2. Supported Log Priority Levels

```
typedef enum android_LogPriority {
  ...
  ANDROID_LOG_VERBOSE,
  ANDROID_LOG_DEBUG,
  ANDROID_LOG_INFO,
  ANDROID_LOG_WARN,
  ANDROID_LOG_ERROR,
  ANDROID_LOG_FATAL,
  ...
} android_LogPriority;
```

- *Tag*: Identifies the component that emits the log message. The logcat and DDMS tools can filter the log messages based on this tag value. The tag value is expected to be reasonably small.

- *Message*: Text payload carrying the actual log message. The newline character gets automatically appended to each log message. Since the circular log buffers are pretty small, it is strongly recommended that the applications keep the size of log message at a reasonable level.

Logging Functions

The android/log.h header file also declares a set of functions for the native code to emit log messages.

- __android_log_write: Can be used to emit a simple string as a log message. It takes log priority, log tag, and a log message, as shown in Listing 5-3.

Listing 5-3. Logging a Simple Message

```
__android_log_write(ANDROID_LOG_WARN, "hello-jni", "Warning log.");
```

- __android_log_print: Can be used to emit a formatted string as a log message. It takes log priority, log tag, string format, and variable numbers of other parameters as specified in the format, as shown in Listing 5-4. For the syntax of the format string, please refer to ANSI C printf documentation.

Listing 5-4. Logging a Formatted Message

```
__android_log_print(ANDROID_LOG_ERROR, "hello-jni",
    "Failed with errno %d", errno);
```

■ __android_log_vprint: It behaves exactly as the __android_log_print
function except the additional parameters are passed as a va_list instead of
a succession of parameters. This is very useful if you are planning to call the
logging function with variable number of parameters that are passed to the
current function, as shown in Listing 5-5.

Listing 5-5. Logging a Message by Using the Variable Number of Parameters That Are Passed In

```
void log_verbose(const char* format, ...)
{
    va_list args;

    va_start(args, format);
    __android_log_vprint(ANDROID_LOG_VERBOSE, "hello-jni", format, args);
    va_end(args);
}
...
void example()
{
    log_verbose("Errno is now %d", errno);
}
```

■ __android_log_assert: Can be used to log assertion failures. Compared to other
logging functions, it does not take a log priority and always emits logs as fatal,
as shown in Listing 5-6. If a debugger is attached, it also SIGTRAP's the current
process to enable further inspection through the debugger.

Listing 5-6. Logging an Assertion Failure

```
if (0 != errno)
{
    __android_log_assert("0 != errno", "hello-jni",
        "There is an error.");
}
```

Controlled Logging

Like their Java counterparts, the native logging APIs only let you emit log messages to the logger
kernel module. In real life, you would neither use asserts nor log at the same granularity in your
release and debug builds. Unfortunately, the Android logging API does not provide any capability to
suppress log messages based on their priorities. It is not as advanced as other logging frameworks
such as Log4J or Log4CXX. The Android logging framework assumes that you will somehow take
out the unnecessary logging calls from your release builds. Although this can very easily be done in
Java applications by relying on Proguard, there is no easy recipe for the native code.

Log Wrapper

This section will introduce a preprocessor based solution to this problem. To see it in action, you will modify the `hello-jni` native project that you imported earlier. Open Eclipse and, using the Project Explorer, right-click on the `jni` sub-directory. From the context menu, choose New Header File to launch the New Header File dialog. Set the header file name as `my_log.h`, and click the Finish button to proceed. The content of the `my_log.h` header file is shown in Listing 5-7.

Listing 5-7. The Content of my_log.h Header File

```
#pragma once

/**
 * Basic logging framework for NDK.
 *
 * @author Onur Cinar
 */

#include <android/log.h>

#define MY_LOG_LEVEL_VERBOSE 1
#define MY_LOG_LEVEL_DEBUG 2
#define MY_LOG_LEVEL_INFO 3
#define MY_LOG_LEVEL_WARNING 4
#define MY_LOG_LEVEL_ERROR 5
#define MY_LOG_LEVEL_FATAL 6
#define MY_LOG_LEVEL_SILENT 7

#ifndef MY_LOG_TAG
#     define MY_LOG_TAG __FILE__
#endif

#ifndef MY_LOG_LEVEL
#     define MY_LOG_LEVEL MY_LOG_LEVEL_VERBOSE
#endif

#define MY_LOG_NOOP (void) 0

#define MY_LOG_PRINT(level,fmt,...) \
        __android_log_print(level, MY_LOG_TAG, "(%s:%u) %s: " fmt, \
                __FILE__, __LINE__, __PRETTY_FUNCTION__, ##__VA_ARGS__)

#if MY_LOG_LEVEL_VERBOSE >= MY_LOG_LEVEL
#     define MY_LOG_VERBOSE(fmt,...) \
        MY_LOG_PRINT(ANDROID_LOG_VERBOSE, fmt, ##__VA_ARGS__)
#else
#     define MY_LOG_VERBOSE(...) MY_LOG_NOOP
#endif

#if MY_LOG_LEVEL_DEBUG >= MY_LOG_LEVEL
#     define MY_LOG_DEBUG(fmt,...) \
        MY_LOG_PRINT(ANDROID_LOG_DEBUG, fmt, ##__VA_ARGS__)
```

```
#else
#    define MY_LOG_DEBUG(...) MY_LOG_NOOP
#endif

#if MY_LOG_LEVEL_INFO >= MY_LOG_LEVEL
#    define MY_LOG_INFO(fmt,...) \
        MY_LOG_PRINT(ANDROID_LOG_INFO, fmt, ##__VA_ARGS__)
#else
#    define MY_LOG_INFO(...) MY_LOG_NOOP
#endif

#if MY_LOG_LEVEL_WARNING >= MY_LOG_LEVEL
#    define MY_LOG_WARNING(fmt,...) \
        MY_LOG_PRINT(ANDROID_LOG_WARN, fmt, ##__VA_ARGS__)
#else
#    define MY_LOG_WARNING(...) MY_LOG_NOOP
#endif

#if MY_LOG_LEVEL_ERROR >= MY_LOG_LEVEL
#    define MY_LOG_ERROR(fmt,...) \
        MY_LOG_PRINT(ANDROID_LOG_ERROR, fmt, ##__VA_ARGS__)
#else
#    define MY_LOG_ERROR(...) MY_LOG_NOOP
#endif

#if MY_LOG_LEVEL_FATAL >= MY_LOG_LEVEL
#    define MY_LOG_FATAL(fmt,...) \
        MY_LOG_PRINT(ANDROID_LOG_FATAL, fmt, ##__VA_ARGS__)
#else
#    define MY_LOG_FATAL(...) MY_LOG_NOOP
#endif

#if MY_LOG_LEVEL_FATAL >= MY_LOG_LEVEL
#    define MY_LOG_ASSERT(expression, fmt, ...) \
        if (!(expression)) \
        { \
            __android_log_assert(#expression, MY_LOG_TAG, \
                fmt, ##__VA_ARGS__); \
        }
#else
#    define MY_LOG_ASSERT(...) MY_LOG_NOOP
#endif
```

Through a set of preprocessor directives, the my_log.h header file defines a basic logging framework for native code. These preprocessor directives wrap the Android logging functions and allow them to be toggled during the compile time.

Adding Logging

You can now add logging statements into the native code. Using the Project Explorer, double-click the hello-jni.c source file to open it in the Editor view. In order to use the basic logging framework, the my_log.h header file needs to be included first. There is no need to include the android/log.h anymore, since it is already included through my_log.h.

```
#include "my_log.h"
```

You can now add the logging statements into the native function, as shown in Listing 5-8.

Listing 5-8. Adding Logging Statements into Native Function

```
jstring
Java_com_example_hellojni_HelloJni_stringFromJNI( JNIEnv* env,
                                                  jobject thiz )
{
    MY_LOG_VERBOSE("The stringFromJNI is called.");

    MY_LOG_DEBUG("env=%p thiz=%p", env, thiz);

    MY_LOG_ASSERT(0 != env, "JNIEnv cannot be NULL.");

    MY_LOG_INFO("Returning a new string.");

    return (*env)->NewStringUTF(env, "Hello from JNI !");
}
```

Updating Android.mk

You can now update the Android.mk file to tune the basic logging framework. Using the Project Explorer, double-click on the Android.mk source file to open it in the Editor view.

Log Tag

As mentioned, each log message contains a log tag identifying the component that is emitting the log message. The log tag for the module can be defined in the Android.mk file, as shown in Listing 5-9.

Listing 5-9. Defining the Log Tag Through MY_LOG_TAG Build Variable

```
LOCAL_MODULE := hello-jni
...
# Define the log tag
MY_LOG_TAG := \"hello-jni\"
```

Log Level

The main advantage of the basic logging framework is the ability to define a log level. As you would not log at the same granularity in your release and debug builds, the Android.mk file can be modified to define different log levels for debug and release builds, as shown in Listing 5-10.

Listing 5-10. Defining the Default Logging Levels

```
LOCAL_MODULE := hello-jni
...
# Define the log tag
MY_LOG_TAG := \"hello-jni\"

# Define the default logging level based build type
ifeq ($(APP_OPTIM),release)
  MY_LOG_LEVEL := MY_LOG_LEVEL_ERROR
else
  MY_LOG_LEVEL := MY_LOG_LEVEL_VERBOSE
endif
```

As mentioned in Chapter 2, the APP_OPTIM build system variable indicates whether the build type is release or debug. Based on the value of APP_OPTIM, the value of MY_LOG_LEVEL can be set to the preferred log level.

Applying the Logging Configuration

Upon defining the MY_LOG_TAG and MY_LOG_LEVEL build system variables, the logging system configuration can be applied to the module, as shown in Listing 5-11.

Listing 5-11. Applying the Logging Configuration to the Module

```
LOCAL_MODULE := hello-jni
...
# Define the log tag
MY_LOG_TAG := hello-jni

# Define the default logging level based build type
ifeq ($(APP_OPTIM),release)
  MY_LOG_LEVEL := MY_LOG_LEVEL_ERROR
else
  MY_LOG_LEVEL := MY_LOG_LEVEL_VERBOSE
endif

# Appending the compiler flags
LOCAL_CFLAGS += -DMY_LOG_TAG=$(MY_LOG_TAG)
LOCAL_CFLAGS += -DMY_LOG_LEVEL=$(MY_LOG_LEVEL)

# Dynamically linking with the log library
LOCAL_LDLIBS += -llog
```

Observing Log Messages Through Logcat

Upon executing the hello-jni application, the log messages can be observed through the Logcat view, as shown in Figure 5-1.

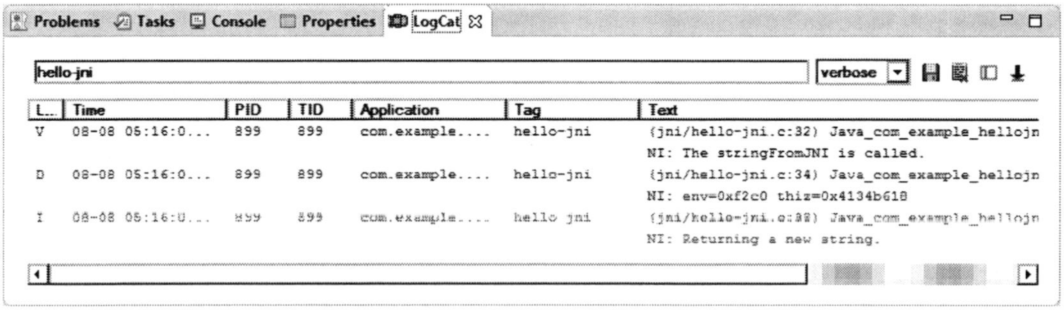

Figure 5-1. Log messages from the native code

Console Logging

When integrating third party libraries and legacy modules into an Android application project, changing their logging mechanism to Android-specific logging may not be possible. Most logging mechanisms either log messages to a file or directly to the console.

The console file descriptors, STDOUT and STDERR, are not visible by default on the Android platform. To redirect these log messages to the Android system log, open a command prompt or a Terminal window and execute the ADB commands shown in Listing 5-12.

Listing 5-12. Redirecting Console Log to Android System Log

```
adb shell stop
adb shell setprop log.redirect-stdio true
adb shell start
```

Upon restarting the application, the console log messages will be visible through the Logcat view, as shown in Figure 5-2.

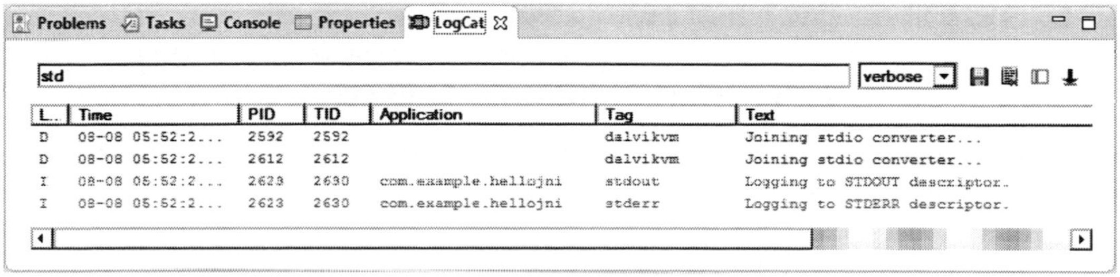

Figure 5-2. Log messages re-directed from STDOUT and STDERR descriptors

The system retains this setting until the device reboots. If you want to make these settings the default, add them to the /data/local.prop file on the device or emulator.

Debugging

Logging allows you to output messages from a running application, exposing its current state. When troubleshooting problems, the granularity of the log messages from the concerned portion of the code may not be sufficient. New log messages can be implanted into the code to expose more information about its current state but this simply slows down the troubleshooting process. Using a debugger to properly observe the application state is the most convenient way of troubleshooting. Android NDK supports debugging of native code through the GNU Debugger (GDB).

Prerequisites

In order to debug the native code, the following conditions should be met:

- Native code should be compiled either through ndk-build command from the command line, or through the Eclipse IDE using Android Development Tools. The NDK build system generates a set of files during the build process to remote debugging possible.

- The application should be set as debuggable in its AndroidManifest.xml file through the android:debuggable attribute of the application tag, as shown in Listing 5-13.

Listing 5-13. Declaring the Application as Debuggable

```
<?xml version="1.0" encoding="utf-8"?>
<manifest xmlns:android="http://schemas.android.com/apk/res/android"
    package="com.example.hellojni"
    android:versionCode="1"
    android:versionName="1.0">

  ...
  <application android:label="@string/app_name"
              android:debuggable="true">

  ...
  </application>
</manifest>
```

- The device or the emulator should be running Android version 2.2 or higher. Native code debugging is not supported in earlier versions.

The ndk-gdb script handles many of the error conditions and outputs informative error messages to let you know if any of these conditions have not been met.

Debug Session Setup

The ndk-gdb script that takes care of setting up the debug session on behalf of the developer but knows the sequence of events happening during the debug session setup, which is very beneficial to understanding the caveats of debugging native code on Android. The complete sequence of events during the debug session setup is shown in Figure 5-3.

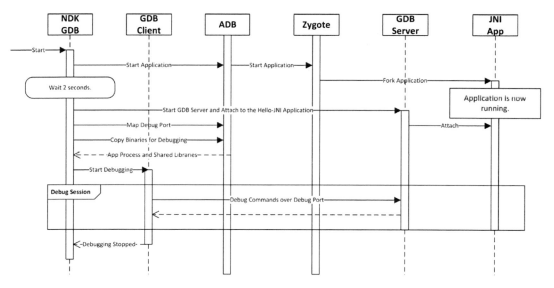

Figure 5-3. Debug session setup sequence diagram

The ndk-gdb script launches the target application by using the application manager through ADB. The application manager simply relays the request to Zygote process.

Zygote, also known as the "app process," is one of the core processes started when the Android system boots. Its role within the Android platform is to start the Dalvik virtual machine and initialize all core Android services. As a mobile operating system, Android needs to keep the startup time of applications as small as possible in order to provide a highly responsive user experience. In order to achieve that, instead of starting a new process from scratch for the applications, Zygote simply relies on forking. In computing, forking is the operation to clone an existing process. The new process has an exact copy of all memory segments of the parent process, although both processes execute independently.

At this point in time, the application is started and is executing code. As you may have noticed, the debug session is not established yet at this point.

> **Note** Due to the way Zygote works, the GDB cannot start the application, but it can simply attach to an already running application process. If you want to prevent your application from executing code prior to when GDB attaches, you need to use the Java Debugger to set a breakpoint at a proper position in the code.

Upon obtaining the process ID of the application, the ndk-gdb script starts the GDB Server on Android and has it attach to the running application. The ndk-gdb script configures port forwarding using ADB to make the GDB Server accessible from the host machine. Later, it copies the binaries for Zygote and the shared libraries to the host machine prior starting the GDB Client. After the binaries are copied, the ndk-gdb script starts the GDB Client and the debug session becomes active. After this point, you can start debugging the application.

Setting up the Example for Debugging

In order to see the native code debugging in action, you will be using the hello-jni sample project. To simplify the debug process, you will make a slight change in the HelloJni activity's onCreate method. Using Eclipse, open up the HelloJni activity in the Editor View, as described earlier. Modify the onCreate method as shown in Listing 5-14.

Listing 5-14. Modified onCreate Method to Delay the Native Call

```
@Override
public void onCreate(Bundle savedInstanceState)
{
    super.onCreate(savedInstanceState);

    Button button = new Button(this);
    button.setText("Call Native");
    button.setOnClickListener(new OnClickListener() {
        public void onClick(View button) {
            ((Button) button).setText(stringFromJNI());
        }
    });

    setContentView(button);
}
```

From the menu bar, choose **Source ➤ Organize Imports** to get Eclipse to add the necessary import statements to the source file. For the OnClickListener class, Eclipse will propose more than one alternative to import. Select android.view.View.OnClickListener and proceed. The modified onCreate method places a button to the display. Clicking that button will initiate the native call. This will let you to make sure that the native call is initiated after the debug session is properly set up.

Starting the Debugger

Debugging of native code can be done through both the command line and from within Eclipse. This section will demonstrate both methods.

Fix for Windows Users

On Windows platform, there is a known bug in the Android NDK that prevents the GDB from locating the binaries properly. The ndk-gdb script configures the GDB Client using a GDB script file. On the Windows platform, this script file gets generated with extra carriage returns, causing this issue.

In order to fix it, using Eclipse, open the <ANDROID_NDK_HOME>/ndk-gdb script in the Editor view. Go to the end of the file, and add fix as shown in Listing 5-15.

Listing 5-15. Fixing the GDB Setup Script Generation

```
# Fix the line endings.
sed -i 's/\r\r//' 'native_path $GDBSETUP'

$GDBCLIENT -x 'native_path $GDBSETUP'
```

Using Eclipse

Like running applications, Eclipse requires having a debug configuration defined in order establish a debug session.

1. From the menu bar, choose **Run ➤ Debug Configurations** to launch the Debug Configurations dialog, as shown in Figure 5-4.

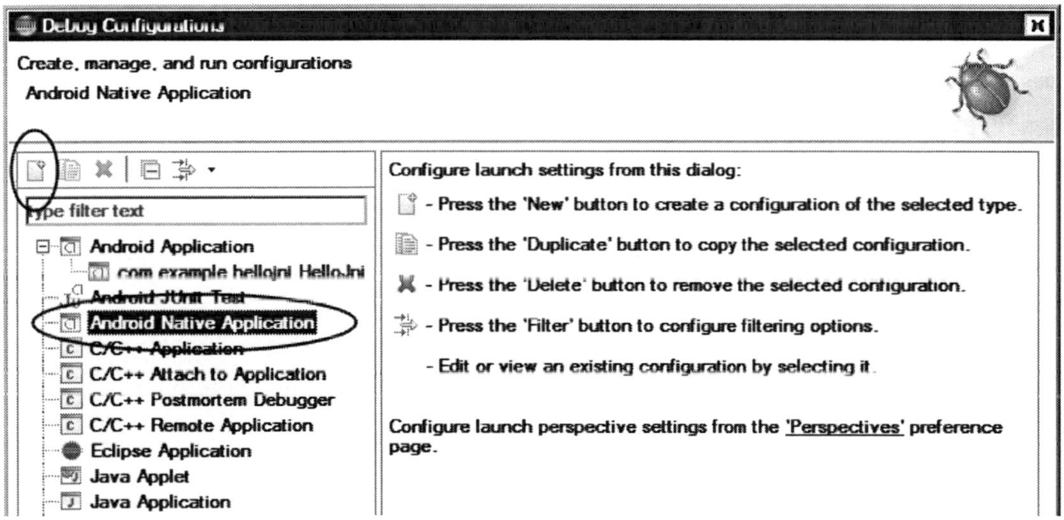

Figure 5-4. New Android native application configuration

2. From the right panel, select Android Native Application.

3. Click the new configuration icon on the dialog toolbar.

4. As shown in Figure 5-5, using the right panel, use the Browse button to select the current project.

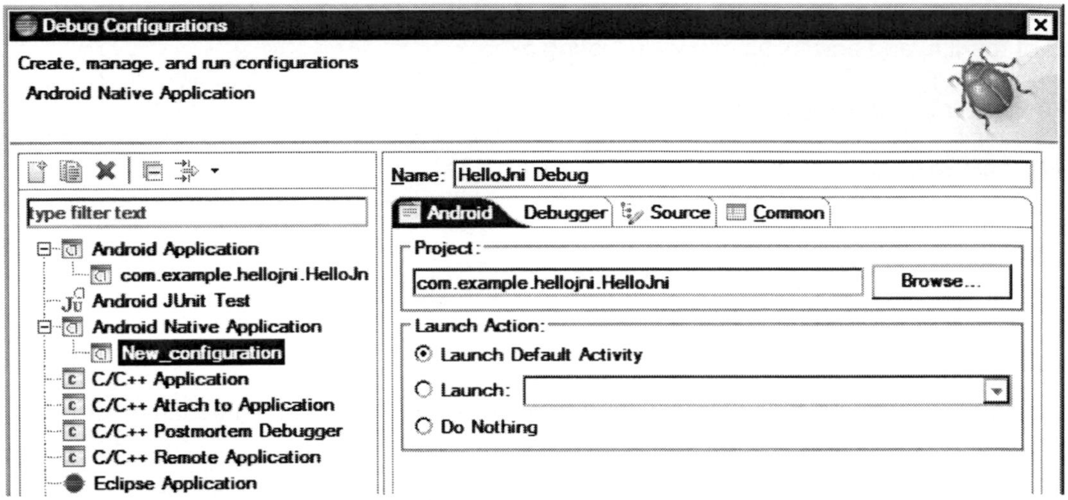

Figure 5-5. *Defining the native debug configuration*

5. Click the Apply button to store the debug configuration.

6. Close the debug configurations dialog and go back to Eclipse workbench.

You will now place a breakpoint into the native code to stop the process in the debugger. In order to do so, follow these steps:

1. Open up the hello-jni.c source file in Editor view, as described earlier.

2. Go into the native function, and right-click on the marker area, the left border of the Editor view.

3. As shown in Figure 5-6, choose from the context menu to place a breakpoint. A blue point will be placed on the marker bar indicating the breakpoint.

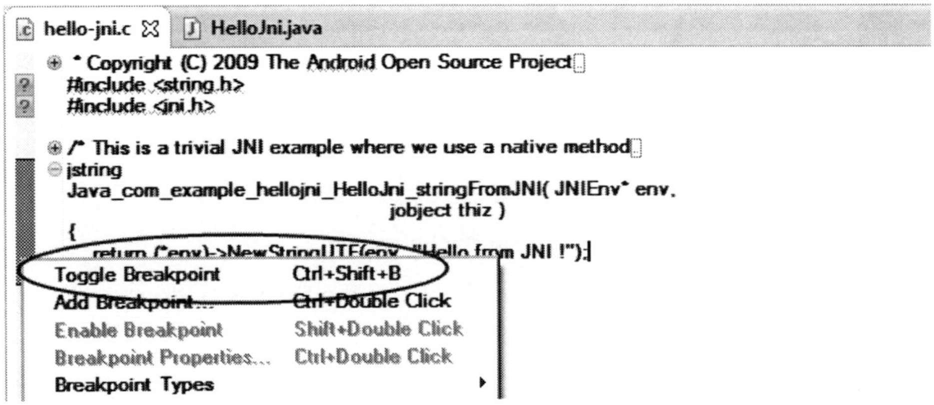

Figure 5-6. *Toggle breakpoint*

Tip   Using the same context menu, you can also place a conditional breakpoint as well as enable and disable existing breakpoints.

4.   Now that the breakpoint is placed, using the top menu bar, choose **Run ➤ Debug Configurations** to launch the Debug Configurations dialog.

5.   Select the debug configuration that you defined earlier.

6.   Click the Debug button.

7.   Eclipse supports different perspectives, workbench layouts, for different tasks. Upon clicking the Debug button, Eclipse will ask you if you would like to switch to the Debug perspective, as shown in Figure 5-7. Click Yes to proceed.

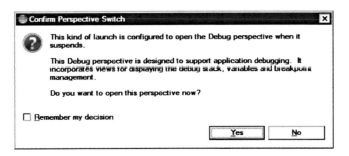

Figure 5-7. Switching to the debug perspective

8.   Using the Android device or the emulator, click the Call Native button to invoke the native function.

As soon as the native code hits the breakpoint, the application will stop and give the control to the debugger, as shown in Figure 5-8.

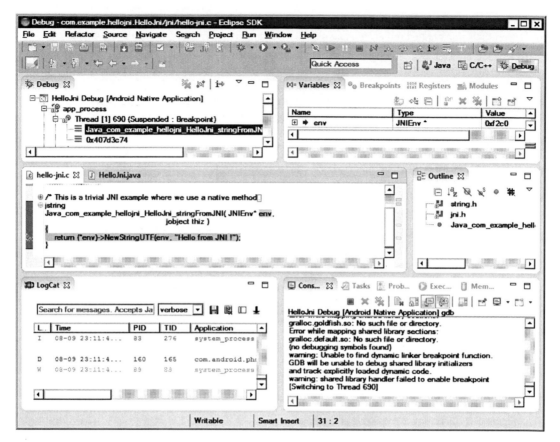

Figure 5-8. Eclipse debug perspective in action

The debug perspective gives you a full snapshot of the native code's current state. On the top left, the Debug view shows the list of running threads and the function that they are currently running. On the top right corner, the Variables view gives you access to the native variables and lets you to inspect their current values. In the center area, the native source code is shown in the Editor view, and an arrow is shown on the marker bar next to the line that will be executed next. As shown in Figure 5-9, using the debug toolbar, you can control the execution of the application.

Figure 5-9. Debug toolbar

The following actions are provided through the debug toolbar:

- *Skip All Breakpoints*: Allows you to disable all breakpoints.

- *Resume*: Resumes the execution of the native code until the next breakpoint.

- *Suspend*: Suspends the execution of native code by sending the SIGINT interrupt signal to the process, which allows you to investigate the current state of the native code.

- *Step Into*: Follows the next native call by going into it.

- *Step Over*: Executes the next native call and then stops.

- *Step Return*: Executes until the native function returns.

- *Terminate*: Terminates the debug session.

Debugging of native applications is not only possible through Eclipse. The same level of debugging functionality can also be achieved through the command line as well.

The Command Line

Native code can be debugged using the ndk-gdb script from the command line. Currently the ndk-gdb script requires a UNIX shell to run. On the Windows platform, you will use Cygwin instead of the command prompt for debugging. First, open Cygwin or the Terminal window, based on your platform. You will use the hello-jni sample project for this experiment.

1. Make sure that Eclipse is no longer running in order to prevent any conflicts.

2. Change the current directory to the hello-jni project directory.

3. Delete any leftover files from the Eclipse by issuing rm -rf bin obj libs.

4. Compile the native module by issuing ndk-build on the command line.

5. In order to compile and package the application from command line, make sure that the ANT build script build.xml file exists in project directory. If this is the first time you are building this project from the command line, issue android update project -p to generate the necessary build files. If you are using Cygwin, use android.bat instead of android.

6. Compile and package the project in debug mode by issuing ant debug on the command line.

7. Deploy the application to the device or the emulator by issuing ant installd on the command line.

8. By default, the ndk-gdb script searches for an already running application process; however, you can use the --start or --launch=<activity> arguments to automatically start the application before the debugging session. Start the debugging session by issuing ndk-gdb --start from the command. When GDB successfully attaches to the hello-jni application, it will show the GDB prompt.

9. Add a breakpoint to the hello-jni.c souce file at line 30 by issuing b hello-jni.c:30 on the GDB prompt.

10. Now that the breakpoint is defined, issue c on the GDB prompt to continue the execution of the native application.

11. Using the Android device or emulator, click the Native Call button to invoke the native function.

> **Note**   It is normal to see a long list of error messages saying that GDB cannot be able locate various system library files. You can safely ignore these messages since symbol/debug versions of these libraries are not available.

When the native function hits the breakpoint, the application will stop and you can inspect the current state of the native code using GDB, as shown in Figure 5-10.

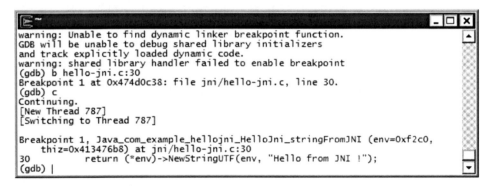

```
warning: Unable to find dynamic linker breakpoint function.
GDB will be unable to debug shared library initializers
and track explicitly loaded dynamic code.
warning: shared library handler failed to enable breakpoint
(gdb) b hello-jni.c:30
Breakpoint 1 at 0x474d0c38: file jni/hello-jni.c, line 30.
(gdb) c
Continuing.
[New Thread 787]
[Switching to Thread 787]

Breakpoint 1, Java_com_example_hellojni_HelloJni_stringFromJNI (env=0xf2c0,
    thiz=0x413476b8) at jni/hello-jni.c:30
30          return (*env)->NewStringUTF(env, "Hello from JNI !");
(gdb) |
```

Figure 5-10. Command line debug session

Useful GDB Commands

Here is a list of useful GDB commands that you can use through the GDB prompt to debug the native code:

- break <where>: Places a breakpoint to the location specified. The location can be a function name, or a file name and a line number such as file.c:10.

- enable/disable/delete <#>: Enables, disables, or deletes the breakpoint with the given number.

- clear: Clears all breakpoints.

- next: Goes to the next instruction.

- continue: Continues execution of the native code.

- backtrace: Shows the call stack.

- backtrace full: Shows the call stack including the local variables in each frame.

- ▨ `print <what>`: Prints the content of the variable, expression, memory address, or register.

- ▨ `display <what>`: Same as the print, but continues printing the value after each step instruction.

- ▨ `what is <variable>`: Shows the type of the variable.

- ▨ `info threads`: Lists all running threads.

- ▨ `thread <thread>`: Operates on the selected thread.

- ▨ `help`: Help screen to get a list of all commands.

- ▨ `quit`: Terminates the debug session.

Note   The debugged application will be stopped when quitting the GDB prompt. This is a known limitation.

For more information on GDB, please check the GDB documentation at `www.gnu.org/software/gdb/documentation/`.

Troubleshooting

During the development phase, logging allows you to decide and expose the information about the application's state that will be beneficial in solving problems later. Debugging comes into play when the information exposed through logging is simply not enough, but you have an idea of where the problem could be. When you are facing the unexpected, troubleshooting skills becomes a life saver. Knowing the right tools and techniques enables you to rapidly resolve problems. In this section, you will briefly explore some of them.

Stack Trace Analysis

In order to observe stack trace analysis in action, you will implant a bug into the `hello-jni` sample application that will cause a crash. Using Eclipse, open up the `hello-jni.c` source file. Modify the content of the native function as shown in Listing 5-16.

Listing 5-16. Bug Injected into the Native Function

```
static jstring func1( JNIEnv* env )
{
    /* BUG BEGIN */
    env = 0;
    /* BUG END */

    return (*env)->NewStringUTF(env, "Hello from JNI !");
}
```

```
jstring
Java_com_example_hellojni_HelloJni_stringFromJNI( JNIEnv* env,
                                                  jobject thiz )
{
    return func1(env);
}
```

By setting the value of the JNIEnv interface pointer to zero, you will trigger the crash. Now build and run the application. When the application starts, click the Call Native method to invoke the native function. The application will crash, and a stack trace will be displayed in logcat, as shown in Figure 5-11.

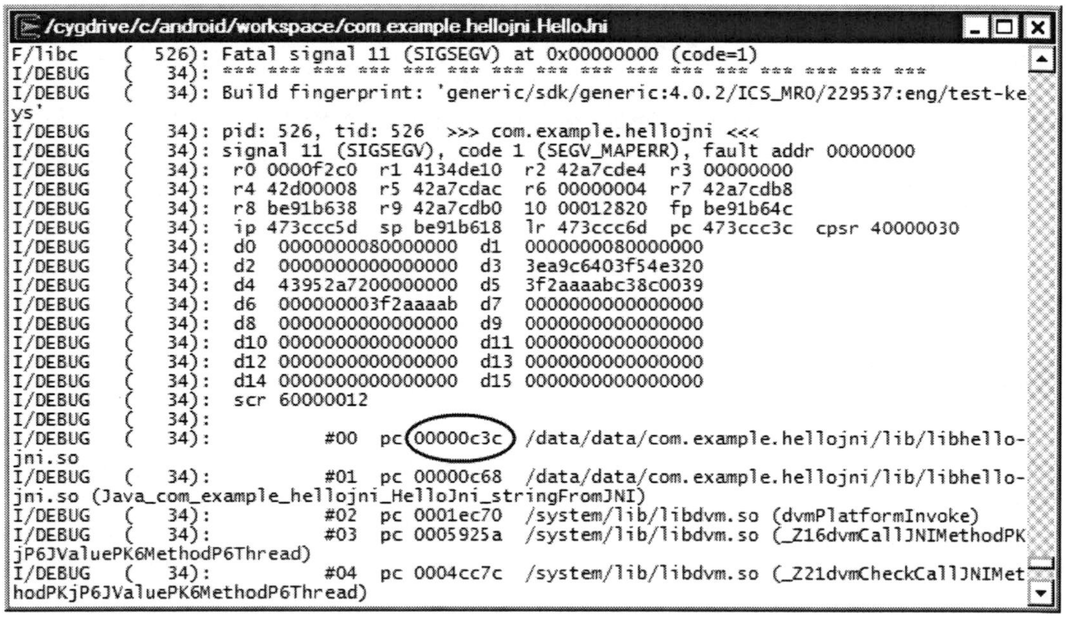

Figure 5-11. Logcat displaying the stack trace after the crash

The lines starting with the hash sign indicates the call stack. The first line that starts with #00 is where the crash occurred; the next line, #01, is the previous function call, and so on. The number following the pc is the code's address. As seen in the stack trace, the native code crashed at address 00000c3c, and the previous function call was the stringFromJNI native function. The address 00000c3c itself may not tell you much, but using the right tools this address can be used to find the actual file and line number that the crash occurred. Android NDK comes with a tool called ndk-stack that can translate the stack trace to the actual file names and line numbers. On the command line, go into the project root directory, and issue

```
adb logcat | ndk-stack -sym obj/local/armeabi
```

The ndk-stack tool will translate the stack trace, as shown in Figure 5-12. The address got translated to jni/hello-jni.c in source file line 33. Having this information makes the troubleshooting much easier. By simply putting a breakpoint at this address you can stop the application and inspect the application state.

```
/cygdrive/c/android/workspace/com.example.hellojni.HelloJni                    _ □ ×
$ adb logcat | ndk-stack -sym obj/local/armeabi
********** Crash dump: **********
Build fingerprint: 'generic/sdk/generic:4.0.2/ICS_MR0/229537:eng/test-keys'
pid: 526, tid: 526  >>> com.example.hellojni <<<
signal 11 (SIGSEGV), code 1 (SEGV_MAPERR), fault addr 00000000
Stack frame #00  pc 00000c3c  /data/data/com.example.hellojni/lib/libhello-jni.s
o( Routine func1 in jni/hello-jni.c:33
Stack frame #01  pc 00000c68  /data/data/com.example.hellojni/lib/libhello-jni.s
o (Java_com_example_hellojni_HelloJni_stringFromJNI): Routine Java_com_example_h
ellojni_HelloJni_stringFromJNI in jni/hello-jni.c:40
Stack frame #02  pc 0001ec70  /system/lib/libdvm.so (dvmPlatformInvoke)
Stack frame #03  pc 0005925a  /system/lib/libdvm.so (_Z16dvmCallJNIMethodPKjP6JV
aluePK6MethodP6Thread)
Stack frame #04  pc 0004cc7c  /system/lib/libdvm.so (_Z21dvmCheckCallJNIMethodPK
jP6JValuePK6MethodP6Thread)
Stack frame #05  pc 0005af84  /system/lib/libdvm.so (_Z22dvmResolveNativeMethodP
KjP6JValuePK6MethodP6Thread)
Stack frame #06  pc 00030a8c  /system/lib/libdvm.so
Stack frame #07  pc 000342ac  /system/lib/libdvm.so (_Z12dvmInterpretP6ThreadPKG
MethodP6JValue)
Stack frame #08  pc 0006c93e  /system/lib/libdvm.so (_Z15dvmInvokeMethodP6Object
PK6MethodP11ArrayObjectS5_P11ClassObjectb)
Stack frame #09  pc 00073d4a  /system/lib/libdvm.so
Stack frame #10  pc 00030a8c  /system/lib/libdvm.so
```

Figure 5-12. Ndk-stack translates the code address.

Extended Checking of JNI

By default, JNI functions do a very little error checking. Errors usually result in a crash. Android provides an extended checking mode for JNI calls, known as CheckJNI. When enabled, JavaVM and JNIEnv interface pointers gets switched to tables of functions that perform an extended level of error checking before calling the actual implementation. CheckJNI can detect the following problems:

■ Attempt to allocate a negative sized array

■ Bad or NULL pointers passed to JNI functions

■ Syntax errors while passing class names

■ Making JNI calls while in critical section

■ Bad arguments passed to NewDirectByeBuffer

■ Making JNI calls when an exception is pending

■ JNIEnv interface pointer used in wrong thread

■ Field type and Set<Type>Field function mismatch

■ Method type and Call<Type>Method function mismatch

■ DeleteGlobalRef/DeleteLocalRef called with wrong reference type

■ Bad release mode passed to Release<Type>ArrayElement function

■ Incompatible type returned from native method

■ Invalid UTF-8 sequence passed to a JNI call

By default, the CheckJNI mode is only enabled in the emulator, not on the regular Android devices, due to its effect on the overall performance of the system.

Enabling CheckJNI

On a regular device, using the command line, you can enable the CheckJNI mode by issuing the following:

```
adb shell setprop debug.checkjni 1
```

This won't affect the running applications but any application launched afterwards will have CheckJNI enabled. CheckJNI status is also displayed in the logcat, as shown in Figure 5-13.

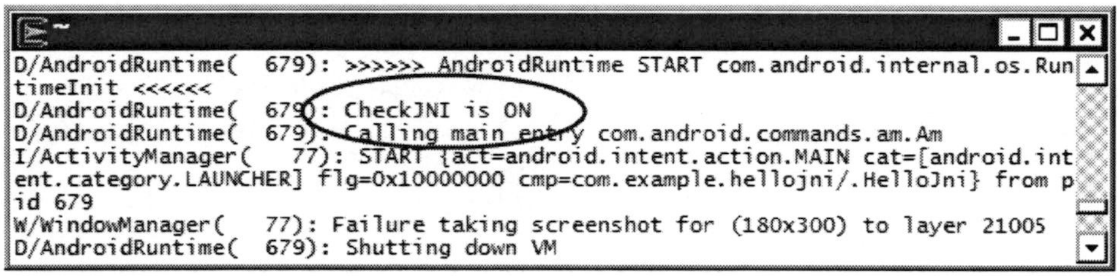

Figure 5-13. CheckJNI status displayed in logcat

In order to see CheckJNI in action, using Eclipse, open up hello-jni.c source code. Modify the native function as shown in Listing 5-17.

Listing 5-17. Creating an Array with Native Size

```
jstring
Java_com_example_hellojni_HelloJni_stringFromJNI( JNIEnv* env,
                                                  jobject thiz )
{
    jintArray javaArray = (*env)->NewIntArray(env, -1);

    return (*env)->NewStringUTF(env, "Hello from JNI !");
}
```

You will be creating a new integer array with a negative size. Build and run the application on the emulator. When the application starts, click the Call Native button to invoke the native function. As shown in Figure 5-14, CheckJNI will display a warning message on logcat and abort the execution.

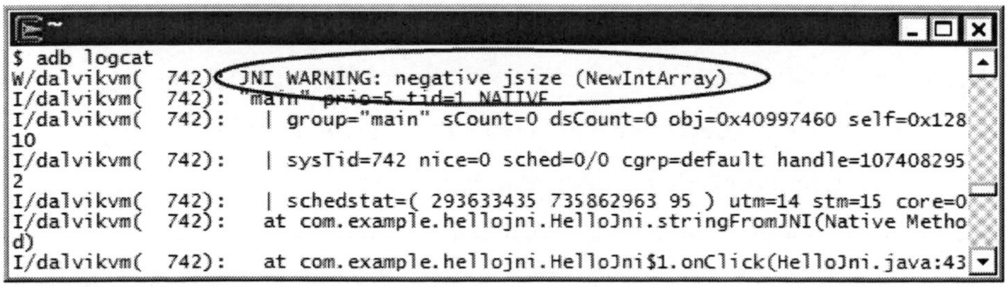

Figure 5-14. JNI warning about negative-sized array

Memory Issues

Memory issues are very hard to troubleshoot in the absence of right tools. In this section you will briefly explore two methods for analyzing the memory issues.

Using Libc Debug Mode

Using the emulator, the libc debug mode can be enabled to troubleshoot memory issues. In order to enable libc debug mode, using the commands as shown in Listing 5-18.

Listing 5-18. Enabling libc debug mode

```
adb shell setprop libc.debug.malloc 1
adb shell stop
adb shell start
```

Supported libc debug mode values are

- 1: Perform leak detection.
- 5: Fill allocated memory to detect overruns.
- 10: Fill memory and add sentinel to detect overruns.

In order to see Libc debug mode in action, using Eclipse, open up hello-jni.c source code. Modify the native function as shown in Listing 5-19.

Listing 5-19. Modifying a Memory Beyond the Allocated Buffer

```
jstring
Java_com_example_hellojni_HelloJni_stringFromJNI( JNIEnv* env,
                                                  jobject thiz )
{
    char* buffer;
    size_t i;

    buffer = (char*) malloc(1024);
    for (i = 0; i < 1025; i++)
    {
        buffer[i] = 'a';
    }

    free(buffer);

    return (*env)->NewStringUTF(env, "Hello from JNI !");
}
```

You will be allocating 1024 bytes, but the code will be modifying an extra byte beyond the allocated size, causing a memory corruption. Enable the libc debug mode by issuing the commands shown in Listing 5-20.

Listing 5-20. Enable libc Debug Mode for Memory Corruption Detection

```
adb shell setprop libc.debug.malloc 10
adb shell stop
adb shell start
```

Build and run the application on the emulator. When the application starts, click the Call Native button to invoke the native function. As shown in Figure 5-15, libc debug mode will display a warning message about the memory corruption on logcat and abort the execution.

```
I/libc     ( 3817): app_process using MALLOC_DEBUG = 10 (sentinels, fill)


E/libc     ( 3828): *** FREE CHECK: buffer 0xa5218, size=1024, corrupted 1 bytes
after allocation
E/libc     ( 3828): call stack:
E/libc     ( 3828):  0: 40069f1c
E/libc     ( 3828):  1: 40069fe4
E/libc     ( 3828):  2: 4006a010
E/libc     ( 3828):  3: 4001a0be
```

Figure 5-15. Libc debug mode displaying memory corruption error

Valgrind

Libc debug mode allows you to do basic troubleshooting for memory issues. Valgrind can be used for more advanced memory analysis. It is an open source tool for memory debugging, memory leak detection, and profiling. For this experiment, you can either download the prebuilt Valgrind binaries from book's web site or you can build it on your machine. If you would like build it, skip to the "Building from Source Code" section.

Using the Prebuilt Binaries

Using your web browser, download the Valgrind binaries for ARM emulator as a zip file from `http://zdo.com/valgrind-arm-emulator-3.8.0.zip`. Extract the content of the zip file and take a note of its location. You can now skip to the "Installing to Emulator" section.

Building from Source Code

In order to properly build Valgrind for Android from the source code, you will need a Linux host system. Official distribution of Valgrind now comes with Android support. Download the latest version of Valgrind from `http://valgrind.org/downloads/current.html`. At the time of this writing, the latest version of Valgrind was 3.8.0. and it comes as a BZip2 compressed TAR archive. Using the command line, extract it by issuing

```
tar jxvf valgrind-3.8.0.tar.bz2
```

Upon extracting the Valgrind source code, using your editor, open up `README.android` file for the up to date build instructions. Since you will be using Valgrind in an Android emulator, please make sure to set `HWKIND` to emulator by issuing

```
export HWKIND=emulator
```

Upon properly building Valgrind, the binaries and the other necessary components will be placed in `Inst` sub-directory.

Deploying Valgrind to Emulator

Valgrind needs to be deployed into the emulator first before it can be used. In order to do so, open up Cygwin or a Terminal window, and go in to the root directory where you have extracted the zip file if you are using the prebuilt binaries or to the root directory of Valgrind source code, and issue the following on the command line:

```
adb push Inst /
```

This will deploy the Valgrind files to `/data/local/Inst` directory on the emulator. Upon deploying the files to the device, the execution bits should be fixed. In order to do so, issue the following command:

```
adb shell chmod 755 \
    $(find Inst -type f -exec file {} \; | \
                grep executable | \
                sed -n -e 's/^Inst\([^:]*\).*$/\1/gp' | \
                xargs)
```

Valgrind Wrapper

In addition to Valgrind binaries, a helper script is also needed. Using Eclipse or your favorite editor, create new file called `valgrind_wrapper.sh` with the content shown in Listing 5-21.

Listing 5-21. Valgrind Wrapper Shell Script

```
#!/system/bin/sh

export TMPDIR=/sdcard
exec /data/local/Inst/bin/valgrind --error-limit=no $*
```

Fix the wrapper script's line ending, deploy it to the Emulator, and grant executable permission by issuing the commands shown in Listing 5-22.

Listing 5-22. Deploying the Valgrind Wrapper Script

```
dos2unix.exe valgrind_wrapper.sh
adb push valgrind_wrapper.sh /data/local/Inst/bin
adb shell chmod 755 /data/local/Inst/bin/valgrind_wrapper.sh
```

Running Valgrind

In order to run the application under Valgrind, inject the wrapper script into the startup sequence by issuing the command shown in Listing 5-23.

Listing 5-23. Injecting Valgrind Wrapper into Startup Sequence

```
adb shell setprop wrap.com.example.hellojni \
    "logwrapper /data/local/Inst/bin/valgrind_wrapper.sh"
```

The format for the property key is wrap.<package name>. To run your other applications under Valgrind, simply substitute the package name with the proper value. Stop and restart the application. Valgrind messages will be displayed on logcat, as shown in Figure 5-16.

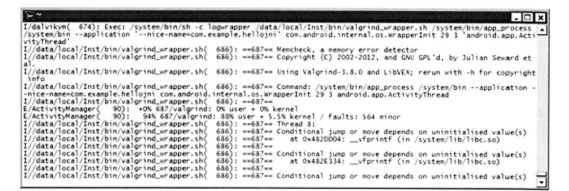

Figure 5-16. Logcat displaying Valgrind messages

> **Note**   Running application under Valgrind will slow down the application at a very high rate. Android may complain about process not responding. Please click Wait button to give Valgrind more time in such cases.

Strace

In certain cases you may want to monitor every activity of your application without attaching a debugger or adding numerous log messages. The strace tool can be used to easily achieve that. It is a useful diagnostic tool because it intercepts and records the system calls that are called by the application and the signals that are received. The name of each system call, its arguments, and its return value are printed. Note that strace comes with the Android emulator.

In order to see strace in action, using Eclipse, open the hello-jni.c source code. Modify the source file as shown in Listing 5-24.

Listing 5-24. Native Source Code with Two System Calls Added

```
#include <unistd.h>
...
jstring
Java_com_example_hellojni_HelloJni_stringFromJNI( JNIEnv* env,
                                                  jobject thiz )
```

```
{
    getpid();
    getuid();

    return (*env)->NewStringUTF(env, "Hello from JNI !");
}
```

Build and run the application on the emulator. Open up Cygwin or a Terminal window. When the application starts, issue the following command to obtain the process ID of the application:

adb shell ps | grep com.example.hellojni

The process ID is the number on the third column, as shown in Figure 5-17.

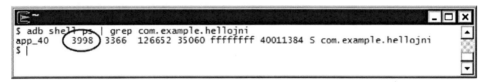

Figure 5-17. Getting the process ID of the application

Issue the following command to attach strace to the running application process by substituting the process ID:

adb shell strace -v -p <Process ID>

As you can see, strace will attach to the application process and it will intercept and print the system calls with their parameters and return values. Click the Call Native button to invoke the native function, and strace will display two system calls that you have introduced into the native code, as shown in Figure 5-18.

```
$ adb shell strace -v -p 3998
Process 3998 attached - interrupt to quit
msgget(0x1, 0xbefae640, 0xbefae640, 0x40103ee0) = 0
semget(0x22, 0xbefae4e0, 0x10, 0xffffffff) = 1
read(46, "D", 1)                            = 1
ioctl(45, 0x40087707, 0xbefae430)           = 0
write(33, "W", 1)                           = 1
msgget(0x1, 0xbefae640, 0xbefae640, 0x40103ee0) = 0
msgget(0x1, 0xbefae640, 0xbefae640, 0x40103ee0) = 0
msgget(0x1, 0xbefae640, 0xbefae640, 0x40103ee0) = 0
write(47, "f", 1)                           = 1
getpid()                                    = 3998
getuid32()                                  = 10040
semget(0x22, 0xbefae4e0, 0x10, 0)           = 2
read(28, "W", 16)                           = 1
read(46, "D", 1)                            = 1
```

Figure 5-18. Strace printing the system calls

Strace is a very useful tool for troubleshooting both open and closed code applications.

Summary

In this chapter, you explored the tools and the techniques for effective logging, debugging, and troubleshooting on Android platform. The concepts presented in this chapter will be highly beneficial when experimenting with the native APIs offered by the Android platform, as you will see in the following chapters.

## Chapter 6

Bionic API Primer

In previous chapter, you explored the logging, debugging, and troubleshooting tools and techniques pertaining to Android native application development. Starting with this chapter, you will be exploring the native APIs provided by the Android NDK.

Bionic is the POSIX standard C library that is provided by the Android platform for native application development using C and C++ programming languages. Bionic is a derivation of BSD standard C library by Google for the Android operating system. The name "Bionic" comes from the fact that it consists of a mixture of BSD C library pieces with custom Linux-specific bits for handling threads, processes, and signals.

Bionic is a highly vital subject for native application development, since it provides the minimal set of constructs that are needed to develop any type of functional native code on Android platform. In the following chapters, you will be relying heavily on the functionality provided by the Bionic. Before getting into Bionic specifics, let's quickly review standard libraries in general.

Reviewing Standard Libraries

A *standard library* for a programming language provides frequently needed constructs, algorithms, data structures, and an abstract interface to tasks that would normally depend heavily on the hardware and operating system, such as network access, multi-threading, memory management, and file I/O. Depending on the philosophy behind the programming language itself, the scope of the standard library varies greatly. It can either be fairly minimal with only a set of constructs for vital tasks, or in contrast, it can be highly extensive. In all cases, the standard library is conventionally made available in every implementation of the programming language in order to provide a consistent base for application development.

There is a standard library for almost every programming language. The Java platform comes with the Java Class Library (JCL), a standard library for Java programming language that contains a comprehensive set of standard class libraries for common operations such as sorting, string manipulation, and an abstract interface to underlying operating system services such as the stream I/O for interacting with the files and the network. The Android framework extends the JCL by incorporating additional constructs that are specific to Android application development.

For the C programming language, the ANSI C standard defines the scope of the standard library. This standard library is known as C standard library, or simply as libc. Implementations of the C programming language also accompanied with an implementation of the C standard library. On top of the standard C library specification, the POSIX C library specification declares the additional constructs that should be included in such standard library on POSIX compliant systems.

Yet Another C Library?

Google's motivation behind creating a new C library instead of reusing the existing GNU C Library (glibc) or the C Library for Embedded Linux (uClibc) can be summarized under the three main goals behind its design:

- *License*: Both the glibc and uClibc are available under GNU Lesser General Public License (LGPL), thus restricting the way they can be used by proprietary applications. Instead, Bionic is published under the BSD license, a highly permissive license that does not set any restriction on the use of the library.

- *Speed*: Bionic is specifically crafted for mobile computing. It is tailored to work efficiently despite the limited CPU cycles and memory available on the mobile devices.

- *Size*: Bionic is designed with the core philosophy of keeping it simple. It provides lightweight wrappers around kernel facilities and a lesser set of APIs, making it smaller compared to other alternatives. This chapter will cover these APIs.

Binary Compatibility

Even though it is a C standard library, Bionic is not in any way binary-compatible with other C libraries. Object files and static libraries that are produced against other C libraries should not be *dynamically linked* with Bionic. Doing so will usually result in the inability to link or execute your native applications properly.

Besides that, any application that is generated by *statically linking* with other C libraries and not mixed with Bionic can run on the Android platform without any issues, unless it is dynamically loading any other system library during runtime.

What is Provided?

Bionic provides C standard library macros, type definitions, functions, and small number of Android-specific features that can be itemized under these functionality domains:

- Memory Management
- File Input and Output
- String Manipulation
- Mathematics

- Date and Time

- Process Control

- Signal Handling

- Socket Networking

- Multithreading

- Users and Groups

- System Configuration

- Name Service Switch

What is Missing?

As mentioned, Bionic is specifically designed for Android platform and tuned for mobile computing. Not every function in the standard C library is supported by Bionic. Android NDK documentation does provide a full list of missing functionality; however, such information is available within the actual header files itself. Bionic header files can be located platforms/android-<api-level>/ arch-<architecture>/usr/include under the ANDROID_NDK_HOME directory.

Each header file in this directory contains a section clearly marking the list of missing functions. As an example, the section listing the missing functions in stdio.h header file is shown in Listing 6-1.

Listing 6-1. Missing Functions in Bionic Implementation

```
#if o /* MISSING FROM BIONIC */
char    *ctermid(char *);
char    *cuserid(char *);
#endif /* MISSING */
```

The pre-processor if statement is used to disable these lines in the header file, and the associated comment indicates that the section contains the list of missing functions. In addition to this list, the Android NDK documentation also cites the functions that are exposed through Bionic but implemented as a stub only, without any or minimal functionality.

Memory Management

Memory is the most basic resource available to a process. For Java applications, the memory is managed by the virtual machine. Memory gets allocated as new objects are created, and through the garbage collector, the unused memory automatically gets returned to the system. However, in the native space, the applications are expected to manage their own memory explicitly. Managing the memory properly is vital in native application development since failure to do so will result in exhausting available system memory and will deeply impact the stability of the application as well as the system in general.

Memory Allocation

There are three types of memory allocation that are supported by the C/C++ programming language:

- *Static allocation*: For each static and global variable that is defined in the code, static allocation happens automatically when the application starts.

- *Automatic allocation*: For each function argument and local variable, automatic allocation happens when the compound statement containing the declaration is entered; it's freed automatically when compound statement is exited.

- *Dynamic allocation*: Both static and automatic allocation assumes that the required memory size and its scope are fixed and defined during the compile-time. Dynamic allocation comes into play when the size and the scope of memory allocation depends on runtime factors that are not known in advance.

This section will focus on the dynamic memory management for both C and C++ based applications.

Dynamic Memory Management for C

The C programming language does not provide built-in support for dynamic memory management. The Bionic C library provides a set of functions to enable the use of dynamic memory in C code.

Allocating Dynamic Memory in C

In the C programming language, dynamic memory can be allocated during runtime using the standard C library function `malloc`.

```
void* malloc(size_t size);
```

In order to use this function, the stdlib.h standard C library header file should be included first. As shown in Listing 6-2, malloc takes a single argument, the size of memory to be allocated as number of bytes, and returns a pointer to the newly allocated memory.

Listing 6-2. Dynamic Memory Allocation in C Code Using malloc

```
/* Include standard C library header. */
#include < stdlib.h>

...

/* Allocate an integer array of 16 elements. */
int* dynamicIntArray = (int*) malloc(sizeof(int) * 16);
if (NULL == dynamicIntArray) {
    /* Unable to allocate enough memory. */
    ...
} else {
    /* Use the memory through the integer pointer. */
    *dynamicIntArray   = 0;
    dynamicIntArray[8] = 8;
    ...
```

```
    /* Free the memory allocation. */
    free(dynamicIntArray);
    dynamicIntArray = NULL;
}
```

> **Tip**   Since malloc takes the size of memory as number of bytes, the C keyword sizeof can be used
> to extract the size of a data types.

If the requested memory size is not achievable, malloc returns NULL to indicate that. Applications should check the value returned from malloc prior using it. Once allocated, the dynamic memory can be used by ordinary C code through the pointers, until it gets freed.

Freeing Dynamic Memory in C

Dynamic memory should be explicitly freed by the application when it is no longer needed. The standard C library function free is used to release the dynamic memory.

```
void free(void* memory);
```

The free function takes a pointer the previously allocated dynamic memory and releases it, as shown in Listing 6-3.

Listing 6-3. Releasing the Dynamic Memory in C Code Using free

```
int* dynamicIntArray = (int*) malloc(sizeof(int) * 16);
...
/* Use the allocated memory. */
...
free(dynamicIntArray);
dynamicIntArray = NULL;
```

Note that the pointer's value does not change after this function call even though the memory that it is pointing to got released. Any attempt to use this invalid pointer results in segmentation violation. It is a good practice to set the pointer to NULL immediately after freeing it in order to prevent accidental use of the invalid pointers.

Changing Dynamic Memory Allocation in C

Once the memory is allocated, its size can be changed through the realloc function that is provided by the standard C library.

```
void* realloc(void* memory, size_t size);
```

The size of dynamic memory allocation gets either expanded or reduced based on its new size. The realloc function takes the original dynamic memory allocation as its first argument and the new size as the second argument, as shown in Listing 6-4.

Listing 6-4. Reallocating Dynamic Memory Allocation Using realloc

```
int* newDynamicIntArray = (int*) realloc(
        dynamicIntArray, sizeof(int) * 32);

if (NULL == newDynamicIntArray) {
    /* Unable to reallocate enough memory. */
    ...
} else {
    /* Update the memory pointer. */
    dynamicIntArray = newDynamicIntArray;
    ...
}
```

The `realloc` function returns the pointer to reallocated dynamic memory. The function may move the memory to a new location by preserving its content, in which case the new location is returned. If the function fails, it keeps the original dynamic memory allocation unchanged and returns NULL.

Dynamic Memory Management for C++

The C++ programming language does provide built-in support for dynamic memory management. The C++ `new` and `delete` keywords can be used to manage dynamic memory allocation instead of standard C library memory functions.

When dealing with C++ objects, it is highly recommended to use these C++ keywords instead of the functions provided through the standard C library. Unlike the standard C library functions, the C++ dynamic memory management keywords are type-aware, and they support C++ object lifecycle. In addition to allocating memory, the `new` keyword also invokes the class' constructor; likewise, the `delete` keyword invokes the class' destructor prior releasing the memory.

Allocating Dynamic Memory in C++

Memory is allocated using the `new` keyword followed by the data type, as shown in Listing 6-5.

Listing 6-5. Dynamic Memory Allocation for Single Element in C++ Code

```
int* dynamicInt = new int;
if (NULL == dynamicInt) {
    /* Unable to allocate enough memory. */
    ...
} else {
    /* Use the allocated memory. */
    *dynamicInt = 0;
    ...
}
```

If an array of elements needs to be allocated, the number of elements is specified using the brackets, as shown in Listing 6-6.

Listing 6-6. Dynamic Memory Allocation for Multiple Elements in C++ Code

```
int* dynamicIntArray = new int[16];
if (NULL == dynamicIntArray) {
    /* Unable to allocate enough memory. */
    ...
} else {
    /* Use the allocated memory. */
    dynamicIntArray[8] = 8;
    ...
}
```

Freeing Dynamic Memory in C++

Dynamic memory should be explicitly freed using the C++ delete keyword by the application when it is no longer needed, as shown in Listing 6-7.

Listing 6-7. Freeing Single Element Dynamic Memory Using the delete Keyword

```
delete dynamicInt;
dynamicInt = 0;
```

If an array of elements needs to be freed, the C++ delete[] keyword should be used instead, as shown in Listing 6-8.

Listing 6-8. Freeing Array Dynamic Memory Using delete[ ]

```
delete[] dynamicIntArray;
dynamicIntArray - 0;
```

Take care to use the proper delete keyword; failure to do so will result in memory leaks in the native application.

Changing Dynamic Memory Allocation in C++

The C++ programming language does not have built-in support for reallocating dynamic memory. The memory allocation is done based on the size of the data type and the number of elements. If the application logic requires increasing or decreasing the number of elements during runtime, it is highly recommended to use the suitable Standard Template Library (STL) container classes.

Mixing the Memory Functions and the Keywords

Developers must use the proper function and keyword pairs when dealing with dynamic memory. Memory blocks that are allocated through malloc must be released through the free keyword; likewise, memory blocks that are allocated through new keyword must be released with the delete keyword accordingly. Failure to do so will result in unknown application behavior.

Standard File I/O

Native applications can interact with the file system through the Standard File I/O (`stdio`) functions that are provided by the standard C library. Two flavors of file I/O are provided through the standard C library:

- *Low-level I/O*: Primitive I/O functions with finer grade of control over the data source.
- *Stream I/O*: Higher-level, buffered I/O functions more suitable for dealing with data streams.

The stream based I/O is more flexible and convenient when dealing with regular files. This section will focus on the stream I/O functions. Low-level I/O functions will be partially covered in the socket communication section of this chapter.

Standard Streams

Through the stream I/O, there are three predefined streams available to the native code immediately. These represent the standard input and output channels for the native application. They are defined in the standard I/O header file as the following variables:

- `stdin`: Standard input stream for the application
- `stdout`: Standard output stream for the application
- `stderr`: Standard error stream for the application

As the native application on Android runs as a module behind the graphical user interface (GUI), these streams are not very useful. While integrating legacy code, you should make sure that any use of these standard streams is properly handled through the GUI. As explained in the "Console Logging" section in Chapter 5, the `stdout` and `stderr` streams can be directed to Android system log by setting the `log.redirect-stdio` system property prior starting the application.

Using the Stream I/O

Stream I/O constructs and functions are defined in the `stdio.h` standard C library header file. In order to use stream I/O in native applications, this header file should be included in advance, as shown in Listing 6-9.

Listing 6-9. Including Standard I/O Header File to Use the Stream I/O

```
#include<stdio.h>
```

For historical reasons, the type of data structure representing a stream is called `FILE`, not a stream, in the standard C library. A `FILE` object holds all of the internal state information for the stream I/O connection. The `FILE` object is created and maintained by the stream I/O functions and is not expected to be directly manipulated by the application code.

Opening Streams

A new stream to a new or an existing file can be opened through the stream I/O fopen function. The fopen function takes the name of the file, and the open type as arguments, and returns a pointer to the stream.

```
FILE* fopen(const char* filename, const char* opentype);
```

The second argument to fopen function, the opentype, is a string that controls how the file is opened. It should begin with one of the following open types:

- r: Opens an existing file as read-only.
- w: Opens the file as write-only. If the file already exists, it gets truncated to zero length.
- a: Opens the file in append mode. File content is preserved, and the new output gets appended to the end of the file. If the file does not exist, a new file is opened.
- r+: Opens the file in read-write mode.
- w+: Opens the file in read-write mode. If the file already exists, it gets truncated to zero length.
- a+: Opens the file for reading and appending. The initial file position is set to the beginning for reading and to the end of the file for appending.

> **Note** The buffers should be flushed using the fflush function prior to switching between reading and writing if the file is opened in dual-mode with either r+, w+, or a +.

If the file could not be opened with the requested mode, the fopen function returns a NULL pointer. In case of success, a stream pointer, a FILE pointer, is returned for communicating with the stream, as shown in Listing 6-10.

Listing 6-10. Opening a Stream in Write-Only Mode

```
#include<stdio.h>
...
FILE* stream = fopen("/data/data/com.example.hellojni/test.txt", "w");
if (NULL == stream)
{
    /* File could not be opened for writing. */
}
else
{
    /* Use the stream. */

    /* Close the stream. */
}
```

Once the stream is opened, it can be used for reading and writing until it gets closed.

Writing to Streams

Stream I/O provides four functions for writing to a stream. This section will briefly explore these functions.

Writing Block of Data to Streams

The fwrite function can be used for writing blocks of data to the streams.

```
size_t fwrite(const void* data, size_t size, size_t count, FILE* stream);
```

As shown in Listing 6-11, the fwrite function writes count number of elements of size size from the buffer data to given stream stream.

Listing 6-11. Writing Block of Data to Stream Using fwrite

```
char data[] = { 'h', 'e', 'l', 'l', 'o', '\n' };
size_t count = sizeof(data) / sizeof(data[0]);

/* Write data to stream. */
if (count ! = fwrite(data, sizeof(char), count, stream))
{
    /* Error occured while writing to stream. */
}
```

It returns the number of elements actually written to the stream. In case of success, the returned value should be equal to the value given as the count; otherwise, it indicates an error in writing.

Writing Character Sequences to Streams

Sequence of null-terminated characters can be written to a stream using the fputs function.

```
int fputs(const char* data, FILE* stream);
```

As shown in Listing 6-12, the fputs function writes the given character sequence data to the given stream, named stream.

Listing 6-12. Writing Character Sequence to the Stream Using fputs

```
/* Writing character sequence to stream. */
if (EOF == fputs("hello\n", stream))
{
    /* Error occured while writing to the stream. */
}
```

If the character sequence cannot be written to the stream, fputs function returns EOF.

Writing a Single Character to Streams

A single character or byte can be written to a stream using the fputc function.

```
int fputc(int c, FILE* stream);
```

As shown in Listing 6-13, the fputc function takes the single character c as an integer and converts it to a unsigned char prior writing to the given stream, named stream.

Listing 6-13. Writing a Single Character to Stream Using fputc

```
char c = 'c';

/* Writing a single character to stream. */
if (c ! = fputc(c, stream))
{
    /* Error occured while writing character to string.
}
```

If the character cannot be written to the stream, fputc function returns EOF; otherwise it returns the character itself.

Writing Formatted Data to Streams

The fprintf function can be used to format and output variable number of arguments to the given stream.

```
int fprintf(FILE* stream, const char* format, ...);
```

It takes a pointer to the stream, the format string, and variable number of arguments that are referenced in the format. The format string consists of a mix of ordinary characters and format specifiers. Ordinary characters in the format string are passed unchanged into the stream. Format specifiers cause the fprintf function to format and write the given arguments to the stream accordingly. The most frequently used specifiers are

- %d, %i: Formats the integer argument as signed decimal.
- %u: Formats the unsigned integer as unsigned decimal.
- %o: Formats the unsigned integer argument as octal.
- %x: Formats the unsigned integer argument as hexadecimal.
- %c: Formats the integer argument as a single character.
- %f: Formats the double precision argument as floating point number.
- %e: Formats the double precision argument in fixed format.
- %s: Prints the given NULL-terminated character array.
- %p: Print the given pointer as memory address.
- %%: Writes a % character.

As shown in Listing 6-14, the order and the type of the provided arguments to `fprintf` function should match the specifiers in the format string.

Listing 6-14. Writing Formatted Data to the Stream

```
/* Writes the formatted data. */
if (0>fprintf(stream, "The %s is %d.", "number", 2))
{
    /* Error occurred while writing formatted data. */
}
```

The `fprintf` function returns the number of characters written to the stream. In case of an error, it returns a negative value. More information on the format string, including the full list of specifiers and other modifiers, can be found in `fprintf` manual page at `http://pubs.opengroup.org/onlinepubs/009695399/functions/fprintf.html`.

Flushing the Buffer

Stream I/O accumulates the written data and asynchronously transmits it to the underlying file instead of writing it immediately. Similarly, stream I/O reads from files in blocks instead of character-by-character basis. This is known as buffering.

Flushing the buffer means transmitting all accumulated data to the underlying file. Flushing happens automatically in certain cases:

- Normal termination of the application.
- When a newline is written in case of line buffering.
- When the buffer is full.
- When the stream is closed.

Stream I/O also provides the `fflush` function to enable applications to manually flush the buffer as needed.

```
int fflush(FILE* stream);
```

As shown in Listing 6-15, the `fflush` function takes the stream pointer and flushes the output buffer.

Listing 6-15. Flushing the Buffer Using fflush Function

```
char data[] = { 'h', 'e', 'l', 'l', 'o', '\n' };
size_t count = sizeof(data) / sizeof(data[0]);

/* Write data to stream. */
fwrite(data, sizeof(char), count, stream);

/* Flush the output buffer. */
if (EOF == fflush(stream))
{
    /* Error occured while flushing the buffer. */
}
```

If the buffer cannot be written to the actual file, fflush function returns EOF; otherwise, it returns zero.

Reading from Streams

Similar to writing, stream I/O provides four functions for reading from a stream.

Reading Block of Data from Streams

The fread function can be used for reading blocks of data from the stream.

```
size_t fread(void* data, size_t size, size_t count, FILE* stream);
```

As shown in Listing 6-16, the fread function reads count number of elements of size (size) into the buffer data from the given stream, named stream. It returns the number of elements actually read.

Listing 6-16. Reading Block Data of Four Characters from the Stream

```
char buffer[5];
size_t count = 4;

/* Read 4 characters from the stream. */
if (count ! = fread(buffer, sizeof(char), count, stream))
{
    /* Error occured while reading from the stream. */
}
else
{
    /* Null terminate. */
    buffer[4] = NULL;

    /* Output buffer. */
    MY_LOG_INFO("read: %s", buffer);
}
```

In the case of success, the returned number of elements should be equal to the value passed as count.

Reading Character Sequences from Streams

The fgets function can be used to read a newline-terminated character sequence from the given stream.

```
char* fgets(char* buffer, int count, FILE* stream);
```

As shown in Listing 6-17, the fgets function reads at most count-1 characters up to and including the newline character into the character array buffer from the given stream, named stream.

Listing 6-17. Reading a Newline-Terminated Character Sequence

```
char buffer[1024];

/* Read newline terminated character sequence from the stream. */
if (NULL == fgets(buffer, 1024, stream))
{
    /* Error occured while reading the stream. */
}
else
{
    MY_LOG_INFO("read: %s", buffer);
}
```

In the case of success, it returns the buffer pointer; otherwise, it returns the NULL pointer.

Reading a Single Character from Streams

The fgetc function can be used to read a single unsigned char from the streams.

```
int fgetc(FILE* stream);
```

As shown in Listing 6-18, the fgetc functions reads a single character from the stream and returns it as an integer.

Listing 6-18. Reading a Single Character from the Stream

```
unsigned char ch;
int result;

/* Read a single character from the stream. */
result = fgetc(stream);
if (EOF == result)
{
    /* Error occured while reading from the stream. */
}
else
{
    /* Get the actual character. */
    ch = (unsigned char) result;
}
```

If end-of-file indicator for the stream is set, it returns EOF.

Reading Formatted Data from Streams

The fscanf function can be used to read formatted data from the streams. It works in a way similar to the fprintf function, except that it reads the data based on the given format into the provided arguments.

```
int fscanf(FILE* stream, const char* format, ...);
```

It takes a pointer to the stream, the format string, and variable number of arguments that are referenced in the format. The format string consists of a mix of ordinary characters and format specifiers. Ordinary characters in the format string are used to specify characters that must be present in the input. Format specifiers cause the fscanf function to read and place the data into the given arguments. The most frequently used specifiers are

- %d, %i: Reads a signed decimal.

- %u: Reads an unsigned decimal.

- %o: Reads an octal number as unsigned integer.

- %x: Reads a hexadecimal number as unsigned integer.

- %c: Reads a single character.

- %f: Reads a floating point number.

- %e: Reads a fixed format floating point number.

- %s: Scans a string.

- %%: Escapes the % character.

As shown in Listing 6-19, the order and the type of the provided arguments to fscanf function should match the specifiers in the format string.

Listing 6-19. Reading Formatted Data from the Stream

```
char s[5];
int i;

/* Stream has "The number is 2" */
/* Reads the formatted data. */
if (2 != fscanf(stream, "The %s is %d", s, &i))
{
    /* Error occured while reading formatted data. */
}
```

On success, the fscanf function returns the number of items read. In case of an error, EOF is returned. More information on the format string, including the full list of specifiers and other modifiers, can be found in fscanf manual page at http://pubs.opengroup.org/onlinepubs/009695399/functions/fscanf.html.

Checking for End of File

When reading from a stream, the feof function can be used to check if the end-of-file indicator for the stream is set.

```
int feof(FILE* stream);
```

As shown in Listing 6-20, the feof function takes the stream pointer as an argument and returns a non-zero value if the end of file is reached; otherwise, it returns zero if more data can be read from the stream.

Listing 6-20. Reading Strings from stream Until the End of the File

```
char buffer[1024];

/* Until the end of the file. */
while (0 == feof(stream))
{
    /* Read and output string. */
    fgets(buffer, 1024, stream);
    MY_LOG_INFO("read: %s", buffer);
}
```

Seeking Position

The position within the stream can also be changed through the fseek function.

```
int fseek(FILE* stream, long offset, int whence);
```

The fseek function uses the stream pointer, the relative offset, and the whence as the reference point for the offset. The whence can take following values:

- SEEK_SET: Offset is relative to the beginning of stream.
- SEEK_CUR: Offset is relative to current position.
- SEEK_END: Offset is relative to the end of the stream.

The example code, shown in Listing 6-21, writes four characters, rewinds back the stream 4 bytes, and overwrites them with a different set of characters.

Listing 6-21. Rewinding the Stream for 4 Bytes

```
/* Write to the stream. */
fputs("abcd", stream);

/* Rewind for 4 bytes. */
fseek(stream, -4, SEEK_CUR);

/* Overwrite abcd with efgh. */
fputs("efgh", stream);
```

Error checking is omitted in the example code. The fseek function returns zero if the operation is successful; otherwise a non-zero value indicates the failure.

Checking Errors

Most stream I/O functions returns EOF to indicate both the errors as well as to report end-of-file. The ferror function can be used to check if an error has occurred on a previous operation.

```
int ferror(FILE* stream);
```

As shown in Listing 6-22, the ferror function returns a non-zero value if the error flag is set for the given stream.

Listing 6-22. Checking for the Errors

```
/* Check for the errors. */
if (0 != ferror(stream))
{
    /* Error occured on the previous request. */
}
```

Closing Streams

Streams can be closed using the fclose function. Any buffered output gets written to the stream, and any buffered input is discarded.

```
int fclose(FILE* stream);
```

The fclose function takes the stream pointer as argument. It returns zero in case of success and EOF if an error is occurred while closing the stream, as shown in Listing 6-23.

Listing 6-23. Closing a Stream Using fclose Function

```
if (0 != fclose(stream))
{
    /* Error occured while closing the stream. */
}
```

The error may indicate that the buffered output could not be written to the stream due to insufficient space on the disk. It is always a good practice to check the return value of the fclose function.

Interacting with Processes

Bionic enables native applications to start and interact with other native processes. Native code can execute shell commands; it can execute a process in the background and communicate to it. This section will briefly mention some of the key functions.

Executing a Shell Command

The system function can be used to pass a command to the shell. In order to use this function, the stdlib.h header file should be included first.

```
#include<stdlib.h>
```

As shown in Listing 6-24, the function blocks the native code until the command finishes executing.

Listing 6-24. Executing a Shell Command Using the System Function

```
int result;

/* Execute the shell command. */
result = system("mkdir /data/data/com.example.hellojni/temp");
if (-1 == result || 127 == result)
{
    /* Execution of the shell failed. */
}
```

Communicating with the Child Process

The system command does not provide a communication channel for the native application to either receive the output of the process or to send commands to the running process. The native code waits until the command finishes executing. In certain cases, having a communication channel between the native code and the executed process is needed.

The popen function can be used to open a bidirectional pipe between the parent process and the child process. In order o use this function, the stdio.h standard header file should be included first.

```
FILE *popen(const char* command, const char* type);
```

The popen function takes the command to be executed and the type of the requested communication channel as arguments and returns a stream pointer. In case of an error, it returns NULL. As shown in Listing 6-25, the stream I/O functions that you explorer earlier in this chapter can be used to communicate with the child process as interacting with a file.

Listing 6-25. Opening a Channel to ls Command and Printing the Output

```
#include<stdio.h>
...
FILE* stream;

/* Opening a read-only channel to ls command. */
stream = popen("ls", "r");
if (NULL == stream)
{
    MY_LOG_ERROR("Unable to execute the command.");
}
```

```
else
{
    char buffer[1024];
    int status;

    /* Read each line from command output. */
    while (NULL != fgets(buffer, 1024, stream))
    {
        MY_LOG_INFO("read: %s", buffer);
    }

    /* Close the channel and get the status. */
    status = pclose(stream);
    MY_LOG_INFO("process exited with status %d", status);
}
```

> **Note**   The popen streams are fully buffered by default. You will need to use `fflush` function to flush the buffer as needed.

When the child process finishes executing, the stream should be closed using the `pclose` function.

```
int pclose(FILE* stream);
```

It takes the stream pointer as the argument and waits for the child process to terminate and returns the exit status.

System Configuration

The Android platform holds the system properties as a simple key-value pair. Bionic provides a set of functions to enable native applications to query the system properties. In order to use these functions, the system properties header file should be included first.

```
#include <sys/system_properties.h>
```

The system properties header file declares the necessary structures and functions. Each system property consists of a maximum of `PROP_NAME_MAX` character long name for the property and a maximum of `PROP_VALUE_MAX` characters long value.

Getting a System Property Value by Name

The `__system_property_get` function can be used to look up a system property by name.

```
int __system_property_get(const char* name, char* value);
```

As shown in Listing 6-26, it copies the null-terminated property value to the provided value pointer and returns the size of the value. The total bytes copied will not be greater than PROP_VALUE_MAX.

Listing 6-26. Getting a System Property Value by Name

```
char value[PROP_VALUE_MAX];

/* Gets the product model system property. */
if (0 == __system_property_get("ro.product.model", value))
{
    /* System property is not found or it has an empty value. */
}
else
{
    MY_LOG_INFO("product model: %s", value);
}
```

If a property is not defined, a value with size zero is returned.

Getting a System Property by Name

The __system_property_find function can be used to get a direct pointer to the system property.

```
const prop_info* __system_property_find(const char* name);
```

It searches the system property by name and returns a pointer to it if it is found; otherwise it returns NULL. The returned pointer remains valid for the lifetime of the system, and it can be cached to avoid future lookups. As shown in Listing 6-27, the __system_property_read function can be used to obtain the property value from this pointer.

Listing 6-27. Getting a System Property by Name

```
const prop_info* property;

/* Gets the product model system property. */
property = __system_property_find("ro.product.model");
if (NULL == property)
{
    /* System property is not found. */
}
else
{
    char name[PROP_NAME_MAX];
    char value[PROP_VALUE_MAX];

    /* Get the system property name and value. */
    if (0 == __system_property_read(property, name, value))
```

```
    {
        MY_LOG_INFO("%s is empty.");
    }
    else
    {
        MY_LOG_INFO("%s: %s", name, value);
    }
}
```

The __system_property_read function takes pointers to the system property and two other character array pointers to return the system property name and value.

```
int __system_property_read(const prop_info* pi, char* name, char* value);
```

It copies the null-terminated property value to the provided value pointer, and returns the size of the value. The total characters copied will not be greater than PROP_VALUE_MAX. The name argument is optional; if a character array is supplied, it copies the system property name to the given value pointer. The total characters copied will not be greater than PROP_NAME_MAX.

Users and Groups

The Linux kernel is designed for multiuser platforms. Although Android is meant to be used by a single handset user, it still takes advantage of the user-based permission model.

- Android runs the applications within a virtual machine sandbox and treats them as different users on the system. By simply relying on the user-based permission model, Android easily secures the system by preventing the applications from accessing other applications' data and memory.

- Services and hardware resources are also protected through the user-based permission model. Each of these resources has its own protection group. During application deployment, the application requests access to those resources. The application won't be allowed to access any additional resources if it is not a member of the proper resource group.

Bionic provides basic support for the user and group information functions, and most of these functions are only stubs with minimal or no functionality. This section covers the key ones. In order to use these functions, the unistd.h standard header file needs to be included first.

```
#include <unistd.h>
```

Getting the Application User and Group IDs

Each installed application gets its own user and group ID starting from 10000. The lower IDs are used for system services. The user ID for the current application can be obtained using the getuid function, as shown in Listing 6-28.

Listing 6-28. Getting the Application User ID Using the getuid Function

```
uid_t uid;

/* Get the application user ID. */
uid = getuid();

MY_LOG_INFO("Application User ID is %u", uid);
```

Similar to the user ID, the group ID for the current application can be obtained through the getgid function, as shown in Listing 6-29.

Listing 6-29. Getting the Application Group ID Using the getgid Function

```
gid_t gid;

/* Get the application group ID. */
gid = getgid();

MY_LOG_INFO("Application Group ID is %u", gid);
```

Getting the Application User Name

Each installed application gets assigned a user name prefixed with "app_" followed by the application number. For example, the user name for application with user ID 10040 will be app_40. The user name be obtained through the getlogin function, as shown in Listing 6-30.

Listing 6-30. Getting the Application User Name Using the getlogin Function

```
char* username;

/* Get the application user name. */
username = getlogin();

MY_LOG_INFO("Application user name is %s", username);
```

Inter-Process Communication

Bionic does not provide support for System V inter-process communication (IPC), in order to avoid denial-of-service attacks and kernel resource leakage. Although System V IPC is not supported, the Android platform architecture makes heavy use of IPC using its own flavor known as Binder. Android applications communicate with the system, services, and each other through the Binder interface. At the time of this writing, Bionic does not provide any official APIs to enable native applications to interact with the Binder interface. Currently, the Binder interface is only accessible through the Android Java APIs.

Summary

In this chapter, you started exploring Bionic, a derivation of the BSD standard C library by Google for the Android operating system. You studied the standard C library functions that are exposed to the native applications through Bionic, such as memory management, standard I/O, process control, system configuration, plus user and group management functions. Beside the APIs mentioned, Bionic also provides multi-threading and networking APIs for the native applications. You will explore these APIs separately in individual chapters.

Chapter 7

Native Threads

A *thread* is a mechanism enabling a single process to perform multiple tasks concurrently. Threads are lightweight processes sharing the same memory and resources of the same parent process. A single process can contain multiple threads executing in parallel. As part of the same process, threads can communicate with each other and share data. Android supports threads in both Java and the native code. In this chapter, you will be exploring different strategies and APIs that can be used for concurrent programming pertaining to native code. The following key topics are covered in this chapter:

- Java vs. POSIX Threads
- Thread synchronization
- Controlling the thread lifecycle
- Thread priorities and scheduling strategies
- Interacting with Java from within native threads

Creating the Threads Example Project

Before going into the details of having multithreading in native code, you will create a simple example application that will act as a testbed. The example application will provide the following:

- An Android application project with native code support.
- A simple GUI to define the number of threads, the number of iterations per worker, a button to start threads, and a text view showing the progress messages from the native workers during runtime.
- A native worker function mimicking a long-lasting task.

While working through the chapter, you will expand this example application to demonstrate different techniques and APIs pertaining to multithreading in native code.

Creating the Android Project

Start by creating a new Android application project.

1. Open the Eclipse IDE and choose **File ➤ New ➤ Other** from the top menu bar to launch the New dialog, as shown in Figure 7-1.

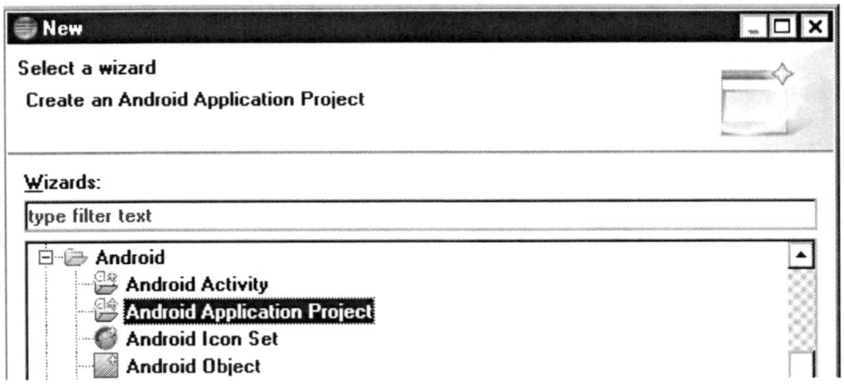

Figure 7-1. New dialog

2. From the list of wizards, expand the Android category.

3. Choose Android Application Project from the sub-list.

4. Click the Next button to launch the New Android App wizard, as shown in Figure 7-2.

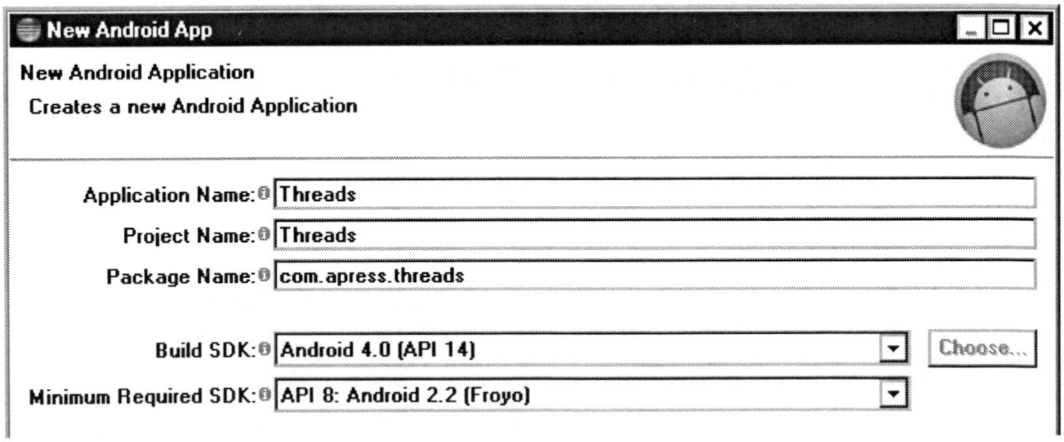

Figure 7-2. New Android App dialog

5.   Set Application Name to Threads.

6.   Set Project Name to Threads.

7.   Set Package Name to `com.apress.threads`.

8.   Set Build SDK to Android 4.0.

9.   Set Minimum Required SDK to API 8.

10. Click the Next button to proceed.

11. Keep the default settings for the launcher icon by clicking the Next button.

12. Select the Create activity.

13. Choose Blank Activity from the template list.

14. Click the Next button to proceed.

15. In the New Blank Activity step, accept the default values by clicking the Finish button.

Adding the Native Support

Native support should be added to the new Android project in order to use native code. Using the Project Explorer view, right-click the Threads project, and choose **Android Tools ➤ Add Native Support** from the context menu. As shown in Figure 7-3, the Add Android Native Support dialog will be launched.

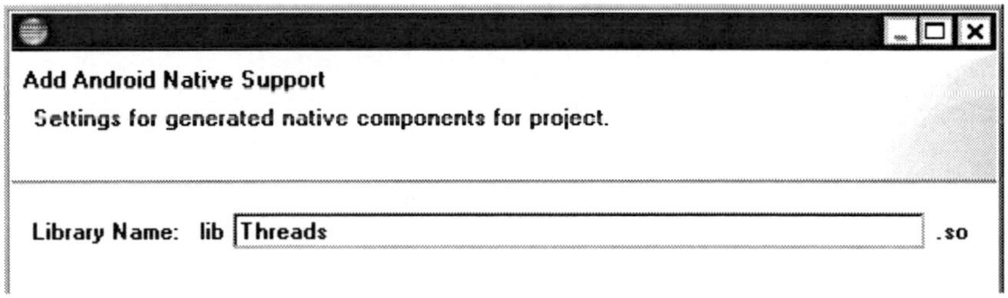

Figure 7-3. Add Android Native Support dialog

Set the Library Name to Threads and click the Finish button. Native code support will be added to the project.

Declaring the String Resources

The application's user interface will be referring to a set of string resources. Using the Project Explorer view, expand the `res` directory for resources. Expand the `values` subdirectory, and double-click on `strings.xml` to open the string resources in the editor. Replace the content as shown in Listing 7-1.

Listing 7-1. Content of res/values/strings.xml File

```
<resources>
    <string name="app_name">Threads</string>
    <string name="menu_settings">Settings</string>
    <string name="title_activity_main">Threads</string>
    <string name="threads_edit">Thread Count</string>
    <string name="iterations_edit">Iteration Count</string>
    <string name="start_button">Start Threads</string>
</resources>
```

Creating a Simple User Interface

The application will have a simple user interface with fields for the number of threads and the number of iterations, a button for starting the threads, and a text view for monitoring the thread progress (see Figure 7-4).

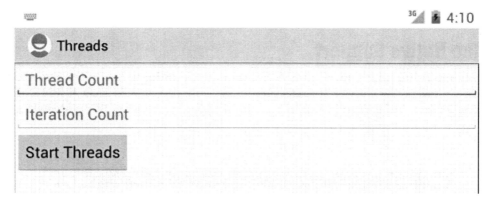

Figure 7-4. Simple user interface for the example application

Using the Project Explorer view, expand the `layout` subdirectory under the `res` directory. Double-click the `activity_main.xml` layout file to open it in the editor. Replace the content as shown in Listing 7-2.

Listing 7-2. Content of res/layout/activity_main.xml File

```
<LinearLayout xmlns:android="http://schemas.android.com/apk/res/android"
    xmlns:tools="http://schemas.android.com/tools"
    android:layout_width="match_parent"
    android:layout_height="match_parent"
    android:orientation="vertical" >

    <EditText
        android:id="@+id/threads_edit"
        android:layout_width="match_parent"
        android:layout_height="wrap_content"
        android:ems="10"
```

```
        android:hint="@string/threads_edit"
        android:inputType="number" >

        <requestFocus />
    </EditText>

    <EditText
        android:id="@+id/iterations_edit"
        android:layout_width="match_parent"
        android:layout_height="wrap_content"
        android:ems="10"
        android:hint="@string/iterations_edit"
        android:inputType="number" />

    <Button
        android:id="@+id/start_button"
        android:layout_width="wrap_content"
        android:layout_height="wrap_content"
        android:text="@string/start_button" />

    <ScrollView
        android:id="@+id/scrollView1"
        android:layout_width="match_parent"
        android:layout_height="wrap_content" >

        <TextView
            android:id="@+id/log_view"
            android:layout_width="match_parent"
            android:layout_height="wrap_content" />

    </ScrollView>

</LinearLayout>
```

Implementing the Main Activity

The main activity will be presenting the user interface that you defined in the previous section, and it will enable the user interface to configure and control the threads and the workers during runtime. Before going through the functions that are provided in the main activity, using the Project Explorer view, expand the src directory, and select com.apress.thread Java package. Double-click the MainActivity.java file, and replace the content as shown in Listing 7-3.

Listing 7-3. Content of src/com/apress/threads/MainActivity.java File

```java
package com.apress.threads;

import android.app.Activity;
import android.os.Bundle;
import android.view.View;
import android.view.View.OnClickListener;
import android.widget.Button;
```

```java
import android.widget.EditText;
import android.widget.TextView;

/**
 * Main activity.
 *
 * @author Onur Cinar
 */
public class MainActivity extends Activity {
    /** Threads edit. */
    private EditText threadsEdit;

    /** Iterations edit. */
    private EditText iterationsEdit;

    /** Start button. */
    private Button startButton;

    /** Log view. */
    private TextView logView;

    @Override
    public void onCreate(Bundle savedInstanceState) {
        super.onCreate(savedInstanceState);
        setContentView(R.layout.activity_main);

        // Initialize the native code
        nativeInit();

        threadsEdit = (EditText) findViewById(R.id.threads_edit);
        iterationsEdit = (EditText) findViewById(R.id.iterations_edit);
        startButton = (Button) findViewById(R.id.start_button);
        logView = (TextView) findViewById(R.id.log_view);

        startButton.setOnClickListener(new OnClickListener() {
            public void onClick(View view) {
                int threads = getNumber(threadsEdit, 0);
                int iterations = getNumber(iterationsEdit, 0);

                if (threads > 0 && iterations > 0) {
                    startThreads(threads, iterations);
                }
            }
        });
    }

    @Override
    protected void onDestroy() {
        // Free the native resources
        nativeFree();

        super.onDestroy();
    }
```

```java
/**
 * On native message callback.
 *
 * @param message
 *            native message.
 */
private void onNativeMessage(final String message) {
    runOnUiThread(new Runnable() {
        public void run() {
            logView.append(message);
            logView.append("\n");
        }
    });
}

/**
 * Gets the value of edit text as integer. If the value
 * is empty or count not be parsed, it returns the
 * default value.
 *
 * @param editText edit text.
 * @param defaultValue default value.
 * @return numeric value.
 */
private static int getNumber(EditText editText, int defaultValue) {
    int value;

    try {
        value = Integer.parseInt(editText.getText().toString());
    } catch (NumberFormatException e) {
        value = defaultValue;
    }

    return value;
}

/**
 * Starts the given number of threads for iterations.
 *
 * @param threads thread count.
 * @param iterations iteration count.
 */
private void startThreads(int threads, int iterations) {
    // We will be implementing this method as we
    // work through the chapter
}

/**
 * Initializes the native code.
 */
private native void nativeInit();
```

```
    /**
     * Free the native resources.
     */
    private native void nativeFree();

    /**
     * Native worker.
     *
     * @param id worker id.
     * @param iterations iteration count.
     */
    private native void nativeWorker(int id, int iterations);

    static {
        System.loadLibrary("Threads");
    }
}
```

Besides the usual methods that are necessary to present and bind to the user interface components, the main activity provides the following key methods:

- onNativeMessage is a callback function that will be invoked by the native code to send progress messages to the UI. Android does not allow code running in a different thread than the main UI thread to access or manipulate the UI components. As the native worker functions are expected to execute within a different thread, the onNativeMessage method simply schedules the actual update operation in UI thread through the runOnUiThread method of the android.app.Activity class.

- startThreads method will simply dispatch the start request to the proper threading example. As you work through the chapter, you will be experimenting with different features of threading. The startThreads method will facilitate switching between these different examples.

- nativeInit method is implemented in the native code. It handles the initialization of the native code prior executing the individual threads.

- nativeFree method is implemented in the native code. It frees the native resources when the activity is getting destroyed.

- nativeWorker method is implemented in native code and mimics a long-lasting task. It takes two arguments, the worked ID and the iterations count.

Generating the C/C++ Header File

In order to generate the function signatures for these two native methods, first select the MainActivity.java source file using the Project Explorer, and choose **Run ➤ External Tools ➤ Generate C and C++ Header File** from the top menu bar. The javah tool will generate the header file in the jni directory with the content shown in Listing 7-4.

Listing 7-4. Content of jni/com_apress_threads_MainActivity.h File

```
/* DO NOT EDIT THIS FILE - it is machine generated */
#include <jni.h>
/* Header for class com_apress_threads_MainActivity */

...

/*
 * Class:      com_apress_threads_MainActivity
 * Method:     nativeInit
 * Signature: ()V
 */
JNIEXPORT void JNICALL Java_com_apress_threads_MainActivity_nativeInit
  (JNIEnv *, jobject);

/*
 * Class:      com_apress_threads_MainActivity
 * Method:     nativeFree
 * Signature: ()V
 */
JNIEXPORT void JNICALL Java_com_apress_threads_MainActivity_nativeFree
  (JNIEnv *, jobject);

/*
 * Class:      com_apress_threads_MainActivity
 * Method:     nativeWorker
 * Signature: (II)V
 */
JNIEXPORT void JNICALL Java_com_apress_threads_MainActivity_nativeWorker
  (JNIEnv *, jobject, jint, jint);
```

Implementing the Native Functions

Based on the function signatures that were generated in the previous section, you will now be
implementing the native functions.

1. Using the Project Explorer, right-click on jni directory.

2. Choose **New ➤ Other** from the context menu to launch the New dialog.

3. From the list of wizards, expand the C/C++ category.

4. Select the Source File wizard.

5. Click the Next button.

6. Using the New Source File dialog, set the source file to
   com_apress_threads_MainActivity.cpp.

7. Click the Finish button.

The new source file will be opened in the editor. Replace its content as shown in Listing 7-5.

Listing 7-5. Content of jni/com_apress_threads_MainActivity.cpp File

```cpp
#include <stdio.h>
#include <unistd.h>

#include "com_apress_threads_MainActivity.h"

// Method ID can be cached
static jmethodID gOnNativeMessage = NULL;

void Java_com_apress_threads_MainActivity_nativeInit (
        JNIEnv* env,
        jobject obj)
{
    // If method ID is not cached
    if (NULL == gOnNativeMessage)
    {
        // Get the class from the object
        jclass clazz = env->GetObjectClass(obj);

        // Get the method id for the callback
        gOnNativeMessage = env->GetMethodID(clazz,
                "onNativeMessage",
                "(Ljava/lang/String;)V");

        // If method could not be found
        if (NULL == gOnNativeMessage)
        {
            // Get the exception class
            jclass exceptionClazz = env->FindClass(
                    "java/lang/RuntimeException");

            // Throw exception
            env->ThrowNew(exceptionClazz, "Unable to find method");
        }
    }
}

void Java_com_apress_threads_MainActivity_nativeFree (
        JNIEnv* env,
        jobject obj)
{

}

void Java_com_apress_threads_MainActivity_nativeWorker (
        JNIEnv* env,
        jobject obj,
        jint id,
        jint iterations)
```

```
{
    // Loop for given number of iterations
    for (jint i = 0; i < iterations; i++)
    {
        // Prepare message
        char message[26];
        sprintf(message, "Worker %d: Iteration %d", id, i);

        // Message from the C string
        jstring messageString = env->NewStringUTF(message);

        // Call the on native message method
        env->CallVoidMethod(obj, gOnNativeMessage, messageString);

        // Check if an exception occurred
        if (NULL != env->ExceptionOccurred())
            break;

        // Sleep for a second
        sleep(1);
    }
}
```

The native source file contains three native functions:

- Java_com_apress_threads_MainActivity_nativeInit function initializes the native code by locating the method ID for the onNativeMessage callback function and caching it in the gOnNativeMessage global variable.

- Java_com_apress_threads_MainActivity_nativeFree function is a placeholder for releasing the native resources. You will implement this function as you work through the chapter.

- Java_com_apress_threads_MainActivity_nativeWorker function mimics a long-lasting task through a for loop. It loops based on the specified number of iterations and sleeps a second between iterations. It communicates the iteration status to the UI by invoking the onNativeMessage callback method.

Updating the Android.mk Build Script

The new source file should be added to the Android.mk build script for the Android build system to compile it as part of the shared library. Using the Project Explorer, expand the jni directory, and double-click the Android.mk file to open it in the editor. Replace the content as shown in Listing 7-6.

Listing 7-6. Content of jni/Android.mk File

```
LOCAL_PATH := $(call my-dir)

include $(CLEAR_VARS)
```

```
LOCAL_MODULE    := Threads
LOCAL_SRC_FILES := com_apress_threads_MainActivity.cpp

include $(BUILD_SHARED_LIBRARY)
```

The example application is now ready. You can validate the example project by running it in the Android Emulator. Since the startThreads method is not implemented yet, the application will not function, although the UI will be displayed. In the next section, you will add multithreading functionality to the example application.

Java Threads

The easiest way to benefit from multithreading in native code is by simply using the Java threads. A java.lang.Thread instance can be created in Java space using pure Java code, and it can invoke the native method within its context. The main advantage of this approach is that it does not require any change in the native code.

Updating the Example Application to use Java Threads

Using the Project Explorer, open the MainActivity.java source file in the editor. Add the javaThreads method into the MainActivity class as shown in Listing 7-7.

Listing 7-7. Adding the javaThreads Method to MainActivity Class

```java
public class MainActivity extends Activity {
    ...
    /**
     * Using Java based threads.
     *
     * @param threads thread count.
     * @param iterations iteration count.
     */
    private void javaThreads(int threads, final int iterations) {
        // Create a Java based thread for each worker
        for (int i = 0; i < threads; i++) {
            final int id = i;

            Thread thread = new Thread() {
                public void run() {
                    nativeWorker(id, iterations);
                }
            };

            thread.start();
        }
    }
    ...
}
```

The javaThreads method takes two arguments, number of threads and the number of iterations for each worker, and it does the following:

- Creates the requested number of java.lang.Thread objects.

- Overrides the run method of java.lang.Thread class to invoke the nativeWorker method in the thread context.

- Starts each thread instance.

In order to use the javaThreads method, you need to modify the startThreads method to point to it. As you work through this chapter, you will be repeating the same procedure for other examples so that you can easily switch between examples. Update the startThreads method as shown in Listing 7-8.

Listing 7-8. Modified startThreads Method Invoking javaThreads Method

```
public class MainActivity extends Activity {
    ...
    /**
     * Starts the given number of threads for iterations.
     *
     * @param threads thread count.
     * @param iterations iteration count.
     */
    private void startThreads(int threads, int iterations) {
        javaThreads(threads, iterations);
    }
    ...
}
```

Executing the Java Threads Example

Run the example application on the Android Emulator, and follow these steps:

1. Set the Thread Count to 2 to have two threads run concurrently.

2. Set the Iteration Count to 10 to have each thread worker iterate through ten steps.

3. Click the Start Threads button to start the Java threads.

The javaThreads method will create two threads, and each of these threads will run the nativeWorker function with ten iterations. The threads will run for ten seconds. The nativeWorker function, while starting each iteration step, will inform the UI by sending an update message, as shown in Figure 7-5.

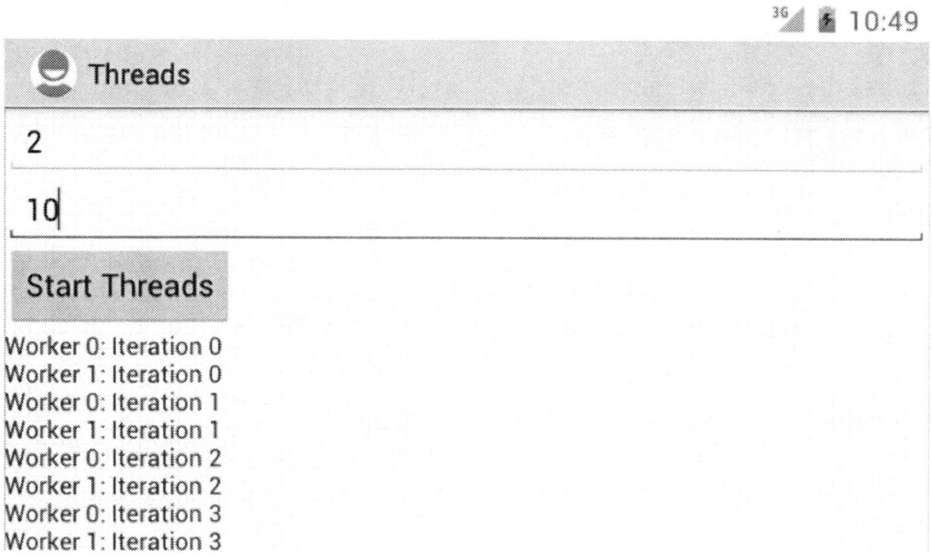

Figure 7-5. Native code running in multiple Java threads

> **Note**   Depending on the screen size you may need to scroll the results to see the latest update messages.

Pros and Cons of using Java Threads for Native Code

Using Java threads for native code has the following advantages compared to native threads:

- It's much easier to set up.

- It does not require any change in the native code.

- It does not require being explicitly attached to the virtual machine, as Java threads are already part of the Java platform. Native code can communicate with the Java code using the supplied thread-specific JNIEnv interface pointer.

- The methods provided through the java.lang.Thread class can be used to seamlessly interact with the thread instance from the Java code.

Besides its advantages, the Java threads have the following major shortcomings compared to native threads when used for multithreading the native code:

- Assumes that the logic to assign tasks to threads is part of the Java code, since there is no API in native space to create Java threads.

- Assumes that the native code is thread-safe, since Java-based threading is transparent to the native code.

- Native code cannot benefit from other concurrent programming concepts and components, such as semaphores, since no APIs for Java threads are available in native space.

- Native code running in separate threads cannot communicate or share resources directly.

> **Note**   Although some of these shortcomings of Java threads can be resolved by using JNI to invoke the necessary Java APIs, this approach is not preferable since passing through the JNI boundary is a relatively expensive operation.

In the next section, you will start exploring the native threads.

POSIX Threads

POSIX Threads, also known as simply Pthreads, is a POSIX standard for threads. Prior to 1995, several different threading APIs existed. The POSIX.1c, Threading Extensions, standard was published in 1995 and defined a common API for creating and manipulating threads. Many of the major operating systems, including Microsoft Windows, Mac OS X, BSD, and Linux provide multithreading support conforming to the POSIX Threads standard. As it is based on the Linux operating system, Android also provides non-compliant implementation of POSIX Threads for native code. As POSIX Threads standard is rather large, this section will only cover the APIs that are fully supported by Android platform.

Using POSIX Threads in Native Code

The POSIX Thread API is declared through the pthread.h header file. In order to use POSIX Threads in native code, this header file needs to be included first.

```
#include <pthread.h>
```

The Android implementation of POSIX Threads is part of the Bionic standard C standard library. Unlike other platforms, it does not require linking of any additional library during compile-time.

Creating Threads using pthread_create

The POSIX Threads are created through the pthread_create function.

```
int pthread_create(pthread_t* thread,
    pthread_attr_t const* attr,
    void* (*start_routine)(void*),
    void* arg);
```

The function takes the following arguments:

- Pointer to a thread_t type variable that will be used by the function to return the handle for the new thread.

- Attributes for the new thread in the form of a pointer to a pthread_attr_t structure. Stack base, stack size, guard size, scheduling policy, and scheduling priority for the new thread can be specified through the attributes. You will learn about some of these attributes later in the chapter. It can be NULL if the default attributes are going to be used.

- A function pointer to the start routine for the thread. The start routine function signature should look like the following:

  ```
  void* start_rountine (void* args)
  ```

  The start routine takes the thread arguments as a void pointer, and it returns a result as a void pointer.

- Any arguments should be passed to the start routine when the thread gets executed in the form of a void pointer. It can be NULL if not arguments needs to be passed.

In case of success, the pthread_create function returns zero; otherwise it returns an error code.

Updating the Example Application to use POSIX Threads

You can now expand the example application to use POSIX Threads in order to experiment with the pthread_create function.

Updating the Main Activity

Using the Project Explorer, open the MainActivity.java source file in the editor. Add the native posixThreads method into the MainActivity class as shown in Listing 7-9.

Listing 7-9. Adding the Native posixThreads Method to MainActivity Class

```
public class MainActivity extends Activity {
    ...
    /**
     * Using the POSIX threads.
     *
     * @param threads thread count.
     * @param iterations iteration count.
     */
    private native void posixThreads(int threads, int iterations);
    ...
}
```

Similar to the javaThreads method, the posixThreads method also takes two arguments, number of threads and the number of iterations for each worker. In order to use the posixThreads method, you need to modify the startThreads method to point to it instead of the javaThreads method. Update the startThreads method as shown in Listing 7-10.

Listing 7-10. Modified startThreads Method Invoking posixThreads Method

```
public class MainActivity extends Activity {
    ...
    /**
     * Starts the given number of threads for iterations.
     *
     * @param threads thread count.
     * @param iterations iteration count.
     */
    private void startThreads(int threads, int iterations) {
        posixThreads(threads, iterations);
    }
    ...
}
```

Regenerating the C/C++ Header File for posixThreads Method

As you will be using the POSIX Threads, the implementation of the posixThreads method will happen in native code instead of Java. Upon making these changes on the MainActivity class, the com_apress_threads_MainActivity.h header file should be updated. Select the MainActivity.java source file using the Project Explorer, and then choose **Run ➤ External Tools ➤ Generate C and C++ Header File** from the top menu bar. The updated header file will contain the function declaration the posixThreads native method, as shown in Listing 7-11.

Listing 7-11. Generated Function Signature for posixThreads

```
/*
 * Class:     com_apress_threads_MainActivity
 * Method:    posixThreads
 * Signature: (II)V
 */
JNIEXPORT void JNICALL Java_com_apress_threads_MainActivity_posixThreads
  (JNIEnv *, jobject, jint, jint);
```

Updating the Native Code

You will now update the native code for POSIX Threads. As the POSIX Threads are not part of the Java platform, multiple changes will be needed in the native code in order to provide the same functionality. Using the Project Explorer, expand the jni directory, and double-click on the com_apress_threads_MainActivity.cpp source file to open it. Then follow these steps:

1. Include the pthread.h in the source file in order to utilize the POSIX Thread APIs in the native code, as shown in Listing 7-12.

Listing 7-12. Including the pthread.h header File for POSIX Threads

```
#include <stdio.h>
#include <unistd.h>

#include <pthread.h>

#include "com_apress_threads_MainActivity.h"
...
```

2. As mentioned earlier, the pthread_create function can pass a single void pointer argument to the start routine when running a new thread. The com_apress_threads_nativeWorker function requires two task specific arguments, the worker ID and the iteration count to be supplied. In order to pass more than one argument to the start routine, a new structure is needed to wrap these multiple arguments. Add the definition of NativeWorkerArgs structure, as shown in Listing 7-13.

Listing 7-13. Defining the NativeWorkerArgs Structure

```
#include "com_apress_threads_MainActivity.h"

// Native worker thread arguments
struct NativeWorkerArgs
{
    jint id;
    jint iterations;
};

// Method ID can be cached
static jmethodID gOnNativeMessage = NULL;
```

3. As the POSIX Threads are not part of the Java platform, they are not known to the virtual machine. The POSIX Threads should first attach themselves to the virtual machine in order to interact with the Java space. The Java VM interface pointer should be available to the POSIX Threads in order to properly attach them. Once they are attached, the worker code running in the POSIX Threads needs to invoke the onNativeMessage callback method to inform the UI. This requires having a reference to the MainActivity class instance. The object reference that is provided with the JNI method call cannot be cached here since it is a local reference. A global reference should be created and stored for the threads to use. Add the two global variables in Listing 7-14 to the native code.

Listing 7-14. Global Variables to Hold Java VM Interface Pointer and Global Reference to Object Instance

```
// Method ID can be cached
static jmethodID gOnNativeMessage = NULL;

// Java VM interface pointer
static JavaVM* gVm = NULL;

// Global reference to object
static jobject gObj = NULL;

void Java_com_apress_threads_MainActivity_nativeInit (
        JNIEnv* env,
        jobject obj)
```

4. There are multiple ways to get the Java VM interface pointer in native code. The easiest and most proper way of doing it is through the JNI_OnLoad function. This function gets invoked automatically by the virtual machine when the shared library gets loaded. The function takes the Java VM interface pointer as one of its arguments. As shown in Listing 7-15, add the JNI_OnLoad function to the native code in order to store the Java VM interface pointer in the gVm global variable that was defined in the previous step.

Listing 7-15. JNI OnLoad Function to Store Java VM Interface Pointer

```
jint JNI_OnLoad (JavaVM* vm, void* reserved)
{
    // Cache the JavaVM interface pointer
    gVm = vm;

    return JNI_VERSION_1_4;
}
```

5. The object reference to MainActivity class instance is needed in order to invoke the onNativeMessage callback method to deliver updates to the UI from the native code. As shown in Listing 7-16, update the Java_com_apress_threads_MainActivity_nativeInit method to create a global reference that can be used by the threads.

Listing 7-16. Creating a Global Reference for the Object Instance

```
void Java_com_apress_threads_MainActivity_nativeInit (
        JNIEnv* env,
        jobject obj)
{
    // If object global reference is not set
    if (NULL == gObj)
    {
```

```
        // Create a new global reference for the object
        gObj = env->NewGlobalRef(obj);

        if (NULL == gObj)
        {
            goto exit;
        }
    }

    // If method ID is not cached
    if (NULL == gOnNativeMessage)
    ...

exit:
    return;
}
```

6. Global references should be properly deleted when they are no longer needed; otherwise memory leaks will occur. Update the Java_com_apress_threads_MainActivity_nativeFree function to delete the global reference once the activity has stopped, as shown in Listing 7-17.

Listing 7-17. Updated nativeFree Method Deleting the Global Reference

```
void Java_com_apress_threads_MainActivity_nativeFree (
        JNIEnv* env,
        jobject obj)
{
    // If object global reference is set
    if (NULL != gObj)
    {
        // Delete the global reference
        env->DeleteGlobalRef(gObj);
        gObj = NULL;
    }
}
...
```

7. In order to run the Java_com_apress_threads_MainActivity_nativeWorker function within the POSIX Thread, an intermediate start routine is required to properly attach the POSIX Thread to the Java virtual machine, obtain a valid JNIEnv interface pointer, and execute the native worker with the proper set of arguments. As shown in Listing 7-18, add the nativeWorkerThread start routine.

Listing 7-18. Adding the Start Routine for Native Worker Threads

```
static void* nativeWorkerThread (void* args)
{
    JNIEnv* env = NULL;
```

```
    // Attach current thread to Java virtual machine
    // and obrain JNIEnv interface pointer
    if (0 == gVm->AttachCurrentThread(&env, NULL))
    {
        // Get the native worker thread arguments
        NativeWorkerArgs* nativeWorkerArgs = (NativeWorkerArgs*) args;

        // Run the native worker in thread context
        Java_com_apress_threads_MainActivity_nativeWorker(env,
                gObj,
                nativeWorkerArgs->id,
                nativeWorkerArgs->iterations);

        // Free the native worker thread arguments
        delete nativeWorkerArgs;

        // Detach current thread from Java virtual machine
        gVm->DetachCurrentThread();
    }

    return (void*) 1;
}
```

8. As all the prerequisites have been satisfied, the Java_com_apress_threads_
   MainActivity_posixThreads function can be implemented in the native code.
   The function creates new threads using the pthread_create function and
   supplies the worker arguments wrapped in a NativeWorkerArgs structure
   that was defined earlier. In case of an error, the function throws a
   java.lang.RuntimeException and terminates. As shown in Listing 7-19, add
   the function to the native code.

Listing 7-19. The posixThreads Native Method Implementation

```
void Java_com_apress_threads_MainActivity_posixThreads (
        JNIEnv* env,
        jobject obj,
        jint threads,
        jint iterations)
{
    // Create a POSIX thread for each worker
    for (jint i = 0; i < threads; i++)
    {
        // Native worker thread arguments
        NativeWorkerArgs* nativeWorkerArgs = new NativeWorkerArgs();
        nativeWorkerArgs->id = i;
        nativeWorkerArgs->iterations = iterations;

        // Thread handle
        pthread_t thread;
```

```
            // Create a new thread
            int result = pthread_create(
                    &thread,
                    NULL,
                    nativeWorkerThread,
                    (void*) nativeWorkerArgs);

            if (0 != result)
            {
                // Get the exception class
                jclass exceptionClazz = env->FindClass(
                        "java/lang/RuntimeException");

                // Throw exception
                env->ThrowNew(exceptionClazz, "Unable to create thread");
            }
        }
    }
```

The POSIX Threads are now integrated into the native code.

Executing the POSIX Threads Example

Run the example application on the Android Emulator, and follow the same steps that were provided for the Java threads to test the application using POSIX Threads. The application should execute identically, although the underlying threading mechanism is different.

Return Result from POSIX Threads

Threads can return a result back when they are terminating. This is achieved through the void pointer that is returned from the thread start routine. In the previous example, the Java_com_apress_threads_MainActivity_posixThreads function is designed to return immediately after executing the threads. The function can be modified to wait for threads to finish their work and return. A function can wait for a thread to terminate by using the pthread_join function.

```
int pthread_join(pthread_t thread, void** ret_val);
```

The pthread_join function takes the following arguments:

- Thread handle that is returned from the pthread_create function for the target thread.

- Pointer to a void pointer for obtaining the returned result from the start routine.

It suspends the execution of the calling thread until the target thread terminates. If the ret_val is not NULL, the function will set the value of ret_val pointer to the result returned from the start routine. In case of success, pthread_join function returns zero; otherwise it returns the error code.

Updating the Native Code to Use pthread_join

In order to see pthread_join in action, you will update the example application. Using the Project Explorer, expand the jni directory, double-click the com_apress_threads_MainActivity.cpp source file to open it in the editor, and update the Java_com_apress_threads_MainActivity_posixThreads function as shown in Listing 7-20.

Listing 7-20. Adding pthread_join to Native Code

```
void Java_com_apress_threads_MainActivity_posixThreads (
        JNIEnv* env,
        jobject obj,
        jint threads,
        jint iterations)
{
    // Thread handles
    pthread_t* handles = new pthread_t[threads];

    // Create a POSIX thread for each worker
    for (jint i = 0; i < threads; i++)
    {
        // Native worker thread arguments
        NativeWorkerArgs* nativeWorkerArgs = new NativeWorkerArgs();
        nativeWorkerArgs->id = i;
        nativeWorkerArgs->iterations = iterations;

        // Create a new thread
        int result = pthread_create(
                &handles[i],
            NULL,
            nativeWorkerThread,
            (void*) nativeWorkerArgs);

        if (0 != result)
        {
            // Get the exception class
            jclass exceptionClazz = env->FindClass(
                    "java/lang/RuntimeException");

            // Throw exception
            env->ThrowNew(exceptionClazz, "Unable to create thread");
             goto exit;
        }
    }

    // Wait for threads to terminate
    for (jint i = 0; i < threads; i++)
    {
        void* result = NULL;

        // Join each thread handle
        if (0 != pthread_join(handles[i], &result))
```

```
        {
            // Get the exception class
            jclass exceptionClazz = env->FindClass(
                    "java/lang/RuntimeException");

            // Throw exception
            env->ThrowNew(exceptionClazz, "Unable to join thread");
        }
        else
        {
            // Prepare message
            char message[26];
            sprintf(message, "Worker %d returned %d", i, result);

            // Message from the C string
            jstring messageString = env->NewStringUTF(message);

            // Call the on native message method
            env->CallVoidMethod(obj, gOnNativeMessage, messageString);

            // Check if an exception occurred
            if (NULL != env->ExceptionOccurred())
            {
                goto exit;
            }
        }
    }

exit:
    return;
}
```

Upon making the necessary changes, run the example application on the Android Emulator. Set both the thread count and the iteration count to a small number, such as 2, and click the Start Threads button. You will immediately notice that the UI will hang for few seconds. This is due to pthread_join function suspending the execution of the main UI thread until the created threads terminates. The UI will show the returned result from the threads.

Synchronizing POSIX Threads

As they are running within the same process space, threads share the same memory and resources. This makes it very easy for threads to communicate and share data, although it makes two kinds of problems possible: thread interference and memory inconsistency due to concurrent modification of shared resources. Thread synchronization becomes vital in these situations. Thread synchronization provides the mechanism to ensure that two concurrently running threads do not execute specific portions of the code at the same time. Similar to Java threads, the POSIX Thread API also provides synchronization functionality. In this chapter, you will mainly focus on the two most frequently used synchronization mechanisms offered by the POSIX Threads:

- *Mutexes* allow mutual exclusion in the code where specific portions of the code do not execute at the same time.

- *Semaphores* control access to a resource based on a defined number of available resources. If no resource is available, the calling thread simply waits on the semaphore until a resource becomes available.

Synchronizing POSIX Threads using Mutexes

POSIX Thread API exposes mutexes to the native code through the pthread_mutex_t data type. The POSIX Thread API provides a set of functions for interacting with mutexes from the native code. Prior to being used, the mutex variables should be initialized first.

Initializing Mutexes

The POSIX Thread API provides two ways of initializing the mutexes: pthread_mutex_init function and the PTHREAD_MUTEX_INITIALIZER macro. The pthread_mutex_init function can be used to initialize the mutexes.

```
int pthread_mutex_init(pthread_mutex_t* mutex,
        const pthread_mutexattr_t* attr);
```

The pthread_mutex_init function takes two arguments, a pointer to the mutex variable to initialize and a pointer to the pthread_mutextattr_t structure defining the attributes for the mutex. If the second argument is set to NULL, the default attributes gets used. If the default attributes are enough, instead of the pthread_mutex_init function, the PTHREAD_MUTEX_INITIALIZER macro is more appropriate.

```
pthread_mutex_t mutex = PTHREAD_MUTEX_INITIALIZER;
```

Upon successful initialization, the state of the mutex becomes initialized and unlocked, and the function returns zero; otherwise it returns the error code.

Locking Mutexes

The pthread_mutex_lock function can be used to gain mutual exclusion by locking an already initialized mutex.

```
int pthread_mutex_lock(pthread_mutex_t* mutex);
```

The function takes a pointer to the mutex variable. If the mutex is already being locked, the calling thread gets suspended until the mutex becomes available. In case of success, the function returns zero; otherwise it returns the error code.

Unlocking Mutexes

Upon completing executing the critical code section, the mutex can be unlocked using the `pthread_mutex_unlock` function.

```
int pthread_mutex_unlock(pthread_mutex_t* mutex);
```

The function takes a pointer to the mutex variable and unlocks it. The scheduling policy decides which thread waiting on the mutex gets executed next. In case of success, the function returns zero; otherwise it returns the error code.

Destroying Mutexes

Once the mutex is no longer needed, it can be destroyed through the `pthread_mutex_destroy` function. The function takes a pointer to the mutex variable and destroys it. Attempting to destroy a locked mutex may result in undefined behavior.

```
int pthread_mutex_destroy(pthread_mutex_t* mutex);
```

Updating the Example Application to Use a Mutex

Now you'll update the native code to experiment with the mutexes. Using the Project Explorer, expand the `jni` directory, double-click the `com_apress_threads_MainActivity.cpp` source file to open it, and follow these steps.

1. Add the mutex variable to the native code as shown in Listing 7-21.

    Listing 7-21. Adding the Mutex Variable to the Native Code

    ```
    // Global reference to object
    static jobject gObj = NULL;

    // Mutex instance
    static pthread_mutex_t mutex;

    jint JNI_OnLoad (JavaVM* vm, void* reserved)
    ```

2. The mutex variable should be initialized prior being used. As shown in Listing 7-22, update the `Java_com_paress_threads_MainActivity_nativeInit` function to initialize the mutex.

    Listing 7-22. Initializing the Mutex Variable

    ```
    void Java_com_apress_threads_MainActivity_nativeInit (
            JNIEnv* env,
            jobject obj)
    {
        // Initialize mutex
        if (0 != pthread_mutex_init(&mutex, NULL))
    ```

```
{
    // Get the exception class
    jclass exceptionClazz = env->FindClass(
            "java/lang/RuntimeException");

    // Throw exception
    env->ThrowNew(exceptionClazz, "Unable to initialize mutex");
    goto exit;
}
...
}
```

3. Once the mutex is no longer needed, it should be destroyed. Update the
    Java_com_apress_threads_MainActivity_nativeFree function as shown in
    Listing 7-23.

Listing 7-23. Destroying the Mutex Variable

```
void Java_com_apress_threads_MainActivity_nativeFree (
        JNIEnv* env,
        jobject obj)
{
    ...
    // Destory mutex
    if (0 != pthread_mutex_destroy(&mutex))
    {
        // Get the exception class
        jclass exceptionClazz = env->FindClass(
                "java/lang/RuntimeException");

        // Throw exception
        env->ThrowNew(exceptionClazz, "Unable to destroy mutex");
    }
}
```

4. The thread worker can now lock the mutex at the beginning of the code
    section and then unlock it when the code section terminates. Update the
    Java_com_apress_threads_MainActivity_nativeWorker function as shown in
    Listing 7-24.

Listing 7-24. Locking and Unlocking the Mutex Variable

```
void Java_com_apress_threads_MainActivity_nativeWorker (
        JNIEnv* env,
        jobject obj,
        jint id,
        jint iterations)
{
    // Lock mutex
    if (0 != pthread_mutex_lock(&mutex))
```

```
        {
            // Get the exception class
            jclass exceptionClazz = env->FindClass(
                    "java/lang/RuntimeException");

            // Throw exception
            env->ThrowNew(exceptionClazz, "Unable to lock mutex");
            goto exit;
        }

        ...

        // Unlock mutex
        if (0 != pthread_mutex_unlock(&mutex))
        {
            // Get the exception class
            jclass exceptionClazz = env->FindClass(
                    "java/lang/RuntimeException");

            // Throw exception
            env->ThrowNew(exceptionClazz, "Unable to unlock mutex");
        }

exit:
    return;
}
```

You can now run the example application on the Android Emulator. As the native code is now using the mutex, threads will no longer execute concurrently. Only the thread with the mutex lock will execute and send update messages to UI; the other threads will be suspended, waiting for the mutex to become available.

Synchronizing POSIX Threads Using Semaphores

Unlike the other POSIX functions, the POSIX semaphores are declared in a different header file, the semaphore.h.

```
#include <semaphore.h>
```

The POSIX semaphores are exposed to native code through the sem_t data type. The POSIX Semaphore API provides a set of functions for interacting with the semaphores from the native code. Prior being used, the semaphore variables should be initialized first.

Initializing Semaphores

The POSIX Semaphore API provides the `sem_init` function to initialize the semaphore variables.

```
extern int sem_init(sem_t* sem, int pshared, unsigned int value);
```

It takes three arguments: a pointer to the semaphore variable that will be initialized, the share flag, and its initial value. On success, the function returns zero; otherwise −1 is returned.

Locking Semaphores

Once the semaphore is properly initialized, threads can use the `sem_wait` function to decrease the number of the semaphore.

```
extern int sem_wait(sem_t* sem);
```

The function takes a pointer to the semaphore variable. If semaphore's value is greater than zero, the locking succeeds and the value of the semaphore gets decremented accordingly. If the value of the semaphore is zero, then the calling thread gets suspended until the semaphore value gets incremented by another thread through unlocking it. On success, the function returns zero; otherwise −1 is returned.

Unlocking Semaphores

Upon finishing executing the critical code section, the thread can unlock the semaphore using the `sem_post` function.

```
extern int sem_post(sem_t* sem);
```

When the semaphore gets unlocked by the `sem_post` function, its value gets incremented by one. Scheduling policy decides which thread waiting on the semaphore gets executed next. On success, the function returns zero; otherwise −1 is returned.

Destroying Semaphores

Once the semaphore is no longer needed, it can be destroyed through the `sem_destory` function.

```
extern int sem_destroy(sem_t* sem);
```

The function takes a pointer to the semaphore variables that will be destroyed. Destroying a semaphore that another thread is currently blocked on may result in undefined behavior. On success, the function returns zero; otherwise −1 is returned.

Priority and Scheduling Strategy for POSIX Threads

Scheduling policies, with the thread priorities, orders the list of threads in a certain execution order. This section will briefly explore these scheduling strategies and the thread priorities.

POSIX Thread Scheduling Strategy

The POSIX Thread specification requires a set of scheduling strategies to be implemented. The most frequently used scheduling policies are the following:

- SCHED_FIFO: The first in, first out scheduling policy orders the list of threads based on the time the thread has been on the list. Based on its priority, the thread can also move within the thread list.

- SCHED_RR: the round-robin scheduling policy is identical to the SCHED_FIFO scheduling policy with the addition of limiting the duration of the thread execution to prevent any thread monopolizing the available CPU cycles.

These scheduling policy constants are defined in the `sched.h` header file. The scheduling strategy can either be defined using the `sched_policy` field of the thread attributes structure `pthread_attr_t` while creating a new thread using the `pthread_create` function, or during runtime through the `pthread_setschedparam` function.

```
int pthread_setschedparam(pthread_t thid,
    int poilcy,
    struct sched_param const* param);
```

The function takes a pointer to the target thread handle, the scheduling policy, and the parameters for the scheduling policy.

POSIX Thread Priority

The POSIX Thread API also provides functions to adjust the priority of the threads based on the scheduling policy. The thread priority can either be defined using the `sched_priority` field of the thread attributes structure `pthread_attr_t` while creating a new thread using the `pthread_create` function, or during runtime through the `pthread_setschedparam` function and proving the thread priority in `sched_param` structure. The minimum and maximum priority value differs based on the scheduling policy in use. The application can query for these number by using the `sched_get_priority_max` and `sched_get_priority_min` function.

Summary

In this chapter, you explored the possible multithreading mechanisms that are provided through Java threads and POSIX Threads in the native space. The chapter provided a comparison of these threading mechanisms. Then the chapter focused on POSIX Threads to provide a quick overview of the threading APIs provided in the native space, such as synchronization, priority, and scheduling pertaining to POSIX Threads.

POSIX Socket API: Connection-Oriented Communication

As they get executed in an isolated environment distant from the user, native code applications require a medium of communication either with their parent applications or the external world in order to provide any services. In Chapter 3, you explored the JNI technology enabling the native code to communicate with its parent Java application. Starting with this chapter, you will start exploring the POSIX Socket APIs available through Bionic that enable the native code to communicate with the external world directly without calling into the Java layer.

A socket is a connection end-point that can be named and addressed in order to transmit data between applications that are running either on the same machine or another machine on the network. The POSIX Socket API, previously known as the Berkeley Socket API, is designed in a highly generic fashion, enabling the applications to communicate over various protocol families through the same set of API functions.

This chapter will give a brief overview of the POSIX Socket APIs for connection-oriented communication with emphasis on the following key topics pertaining to Android platform:

- Overview of POSIX sockets
- Socket families
- Connection-oriented sockets

Prior to going into the details of the POSIX Socket APIs for connection-oriented communication, you will create a simple example application called Echo. This example application will act as a testbed enabling you to better understand the different aspects of socket programming as you work through the material presented in this chapter and the next two chapters of the book.

Echo Socket Example Application

The example application will provide the following:

- A simple user interface for defining the parameters necessary to configure the sockets.

- Service logic for a simple echo service repeating the received bytes back to the sender.

- Boilerplate native code snippets to facilitate socket programming for Android in native layer.

- A connection-oriented socket communication example.

- A connectionless socket communication example.

- A local socket communication example.

Echo Android Application Project

Open the Eclipse IDE, and follow these steps in order to create the Echo application.

1. Launch the Android Application Project dialog.

2. Set Application Name to Echo.

3. Set Project Name to Echo.

4. Set Package Name to com.apress.echo.

5. Set Build SDK to Android 4.1.

6. Set Minimum Required SDK to API 8.

7. Click the Next button to accept the default values for all other settings.

8. Click the Next button to accept the default launcher icon.

9. Uncheck the Create activity, and click the Finish button to create the empty project.

10. From the Project Explorer view, launch the Android Native Support wizard through the Android Tools context menu item.

11. Set Library Name to Echo.

12. Follow the wizard to add native support to the project.

Abstract Echo Activity

In order to facilitate the reuse of common functionality, you will create an abstract activity class prior defining the actual activities. Using the Project Explorer view, expand the `src` directory, right-click on the `com.apress.echo` package, and choose **New ➤ Class** from the context menu. Set the Name to `AbstractEchoActivity` and click the Finish button. Using the Editor view, populate the content of the new class file as shown in Listing 8-1.

Listing 8-1. Content of AbstractEchoActivity.java Class File

```java
package com.apress.echo;

import android.app.Activity;
import android.os.Bundle;
import android.os.Handler;
import android.view.View;
import android.view.View.OnClickListener;
import android.widget.Button;
import android.widget.EditText;
import android.widget.ScrollView;
import android.widget.TextView;

/**
 * Abstract echo activity object.
 *
 * @author Onur Cinar
 */
public abstract class AbstractEchoActivity extends Activity implements
        OnClickListener {
    /** Port number. */
    protected EditText portEdit;

    /** Server button. */
    protected Button startButton;

    /** Log scroll. */
    protected ScrollView logScroll;

    /** Log view. */
    protected TextView logView;

    /** Layout ID. */
    private final int layoutID;

    /**
     * Constructor.
     *
     * @param layoutID
```

```
 *            layout ID.
 */
public AbstractEchoActivity(int layoutID) {
    this.layoutID = layoutID;
}

public void onCreate(Bundle savedInstanceState) {
    super.onCreate(savedInstanceState);
    setContentView(layoutID);

    portEdit = (EditText) findViewById(R.id.port_edit);
    startButton = (Button) findViewById(R.id.start_button);
    logScroll = (ScrollView) findViewById(R.id.log_scroll);
    logView = (TextView) findViewById(R.id.log_view);

    startButton.setOnClickListener(this);
}

public void onClick(View view) {
    if (view == startButton) {
        onStartButtonClicked();
    }
}

/**
 * On start button clicked.
 */
protected abstract void onStartButtonClicked();

/**
 * Gets the port number as an integer.
 *
 * @return port number or null.
 */
protected Integer getPort() {
    Integer port;

    try {
        port = Integer.valueOf(portEdit.getText().toString());
    } catch (NumberFormatException e) {
        port = null;
    }

    return port;
}

/**
 * Logs the given message.
 *
 * @param message
 *            log message.
 */
```

```java
protected void logMessage(final String message) {
    runOnUiThread(new Runnable() {
        public void run() {
            logMessageDirect(message);
        }
    });
}

/**
 * Logs given message directly.
 *
 * @param message
 *            log message.
 */
protected void logMessageDirect(final String message) {
    logView.append(message);
    logView.append("\n");
    logScroll.fullScroll(View.FOCUS_DOWN);
}

/**
 * Abstract async echo task.
 */
protected abstract class AbstractEchoTask extends Thread {
    /** Handler object. */
    private final Handler handler;

    /**
     * Constructor.
     */
    public AbstractEchoTask() {
        handler = new Handler();
    }

    /**
     * On pre execute callback in calling thread.
     */
    protected void onPreExecute() {
        startButton.setEnabled(false);
        logView.setText("");
    }

    public synchronized void start() {
        onPreExecute();
        super.start();
    }

    public void run() {
        onBackground();
```

```
            handler.post(new Runnable() {
                public void run() {
                    onPostExecute();
                }
            });
        }

        /**
         * On background callback in new thread.
         */
        protected abstract void onBackground();

        /**
         * On post execute callback in calling thread.
         */
        protected void onPostExecute() {
            startButton.setEnabled(true);
        }
    }

    static {
        System.loadLibrary("Echo");
    }
}
```

The AbstractEchoActivity, besides handling the housekeeping tasks such as binding the user interface components, provides a simple thread implementation enabling the application to execute the network operations in a separate thread than the UI thread.

Echo Application String Resources

Using the Project Explorer view, expand the res directory for resources. Expand the values subdirectory, and double-click strings.xml to open the string resources in the Editor view. Replace the content as shown in Listing 8-2.

Listing 8-2. Content of res/values/strings.xml Resource File

```
<resources>

    <string name="app_name">Echo</string>
    <string name="title_activity_echo_server">Echo Server</string>
    <string name="port_edit">Port Number</string>
    <string name="start_server_button">Start Server</string>
    <string name="title_activity_echo_client">Echo Client</string>
    <string name="ip_edit">IP Address</string>
    <string name="start_client_button">Start Client</string>
    <string name="send_button">Send</string>
```

```
<string name="message_edit">Message</string>
<string name="title_activity_local_echo">Local Echo</string>
<string name="local_port_edit">Port Name</string>
```

```
</resources>
```

The application's user interface layouts will be referring to these common string resources.

Native Echo Module

The native echo module will provide the implementations of native socket methods to the Java application. Using the Project Explorer view, expand the jni directory for native source files, and double-click the Echo.cpp C++ source file. Replace its content as shown in Listing 8-3 with a set of helper functions that will facilitate the implementation of the socket communication examples.

Listing 8-3. Content of jni/Echo.cpp File

```
// JNI
#include <jni.h>

// NULL
#include <stdio.h>

// va_list, vsnprintf
#include <stdarg.h>

// errno
#include <errno.h>

// strerror_r, memset
#include <string.h>

// socket, bind, getsockname, listen, accept, recv, send, connect
#include <sys/types.h>
#include <sys/socket.h>

// sockaddr_un
#include <sys/un.h>

// htons, sockaddr_in
#include <netinet/in.h>

// inet_ntop
#include <arpa/inet.h>

// close, unlink
#include <unistd.h>
```

```
// offsetof
#include <stddef.h>

// Max log message length
#define MAX_LOG_MESSAGE_LENGTH 256

// Max data buffer size
#define MAX_BUFFER_SIZE 80

/**
 * Logs the given message to the application.
 *
 * @param env JNIEnv interface.
 * @param obj object instance.
 * @param format message format and arguments.
 */
static void LogMessage(
        JNIEnv* env,
        jobject obj,
        const char* format,
        ...)
{
    // Cached log method ID
    static jmethodID methodID = NULL;

    // If method ID is not cached
    if (NULL == methodID)
    {
        // Get class from object
        jclass clazz = env->GetObjectClass(obj);

        // Get the method ID for the given method
        methodID = env->GetMethodID(clazz, "logMessage",
                "(Ljava/lang/String;)V");

        // Release the class reference
        env->DeleteLocalRef(clazz);
    }

    // If method is found
    if (NULL != methodID)
    {
        // Format the log message
        char buffer[MAX_LOG_MESSAGE_LENGTH];

        va_list ap;
        va_start(ap, format);
        vsnprintf(buffer, MAX_LOG_MESSAGE_LENGTH, format, ap);
        va_end(ap);
```

```
        // Convert the buffer to a Java string
        jstring message = env->NewStringUTF(buffer);

        // If string is properly constructed
        if (NULL != message)
        {
            // Log message
            env->CallVoidMethod(obj, methodID, message);

            // Release the message reference
            env->DeleteLocalRef(message);
        }
    }
}

/**
 * Throws a new exception using the given exception class
 * and exception message.
 *
 * @param env JNIEnv interface.
 * @param className class name.
 * @param message exception message.
 */
static void ThrowException(
        JNIEnv* env,
        const char* className,
        const char* message)
{
    // Get the exception class
    jclass clazz = env->FindClass(className);

    // If exception class is found
    if (NULL != clazz)
    {
        // Throw exception
        env->ThrowNew(clazz, message);

        // Release local class reference
        env->DeleteLocalRef(clazz);
    }
}

/**
 * Throws a new exception using the given exception class
 * and error message based on the error number.
 *
 * @param env JNIEnv interface.
 * @param className class name.
 * @param errnum error number.
 */
```

```
static void ThrowErrnoException(
        JNIEnv* env,
        const char* className,
        int errnum)
{
    char buffer[MAX_LOG_MESSAGE_LENGTH];

    // Get message for the error number
    if (-1 == strerror_r(errnum, buffer, MAX_LOG_MESSAGE_LENGTH))
    {
        strerror_r(errno, buffer, MAX_LOG_MESSAGE_LENGTH);
    }

    // Throw exception
    ThrowException(env, className, buffer);
}
```

You will be heavily modifying this source file as you work through this chapter by adding the implementations of various socket functions.

Connection-Oriented Communication through TCP Sockets

Connection-oriented communication through TCP sockets provides a robust, error-free communication medium for the applications. This type of connection maintains an open connection throughout the lifetime of the communication, and handles the ordering and error checking of the packets transparently from the application. You will modify the example Echo application to include both TCP server and client activities in order to demonstrate the connection establishment and message exchange using the sockets.

Echo Server Activity Layout

Using the Project Explorer view, expand the res directory for resources. Expand the layout subdirectory, and create a new layout file called activity_echo_server.xml. Using the Editor view, replace its content as shown in Listing 8-4.

Listing 8-4. Content of res/layout/activty_echo_server.xml File

```
<LinearLayout xmlns:android="http://schemas.android.com/apk/res/android"
    xmlns:tools="http://schemas.android.com/tools"
    android:layout_width="match_parent"
    android:layout_height="match_parent"
    android:orientation="vertical" >

    <LinearLayout
        android:layout_width="match_parent"
        android:layout_height="wrap_content" >
```

```
<EditText
    android:id="@+id/port_edit"
    android:layout_width="wrap_content"
    android:layout_height="wrap_content"
    android:layout_weight="1"
    android:hint="@string/port_edit"
    android:inputType="number" >

    <requestFocus />
</EditText>

<Button
    android:id="@+id/start_button"
    android:layout_width="wrap_content"
    android:layout_height="wrap_content"
    android:layout_weight="1"
    android:text="@string/start_server_button" />

</LinearLayout>

<ScrollView
    android:id="@+id/log_scroll"
    android:layout_width="match_parent"
    android:layout_height="match_parent" >

    <TextView
        android:id="@+id/log_view"
        android:layout_width="match_parent"
        android:layout_height="wrap_content" />
</ScrollView>

</LinearLayout>
```

The Echo Server provides a simple user interface to obtain the port number to bind the server and also to present the status updates from the native TCP server while it is running.

Echo Server Activity

Using the Project Explorer view, create a new class file called EchoServerActivity.java under the src directory. Using the Editor view, populate its content as shown in Listing 8-5.

Listing 8-5. Content of EchoServerActivity.java File

```
package com.apress.echo;

/**
 * Echo server.
 *
 * @author Onur Cinar
 */
```

```java
public class EchoServerActivity extends AbstractEchoActivity {
    /**
     * Constructor.
     */
    public EchoServerActivity() {
        super(R.layout.activity_echo_server);
    }

    protected void onStartButtonClicked() {
        Integer port = getPort();
        if (port != null) {
            ServerTask serverTask = new ServerTask(port);
            serverTask.start();
        }
    }

    /**
     * Starts the TCP server on the given port.
     *
     * @param port
     *             port number.
     * @throws Exception
     */
    private native void nativeStartTcpServer(int port) throws Exception;

    /**
     * Starts the UDP server on the given port.
     *
     * @param port
     *             port number.
     * @throws Exception
     */
    private native void nativeStartUdpServer(int port) throws Exception;

    /**
     * Server task.
     */
    private class ServerTask extends AbstractEchoTask {
        /** Port number. */
        private final int port;

        /**
         * Constructor.
         *
         * @param port
         *             port number.
         */
        public ServerTask(int port) {
            this.port = port;
        }
```

```
    protected void onBackground() {
        logMessage("Starting server.");

        try {
            nativeStartTcpServer(port);
        } catch (Exception e) {
            logMessage(e.getMessage());
        }

        logMessage("Server terminated.");
    }
  }
}
```

The EchoServerActivity acquires the necessary parameters from the user and starts the nativeStartTcpServer function, native TCP client implementation, within a separate thread.

Implementing the Native TCP Server

Using the Project Explorer, select the EchoServerActivity, and then choose "Generate C and C++ Header File" from the External Tools menu to generate the native header files. Using the Project Explorer, expand the jni sub-directory, and open the Echo.cpp source file in the editor. Go the top of the source file, and insert the include statement shown in Listing 8-6 in order to include the native method declarations.

Listing 8-6. Including the EchoServerActivity Header File

```
#include "com_apress_echo_EchoServerActivity.h"
```

Creating a Socket: socket

A socket is represented through an integer called the socket descriptor. Socket API functions, other than the one creating the socket itself, require a valid socket descriptor in order to function. A socket can be created using the socket function.

```
int socket(int domain, int type, int protocol);
```

The socket function requires the following arguments to be provided in order to create a new socket:

- Domain specifies the socket domain where the communication will take place and selects the protocol family that will be used. At the time of this writing, the following protocol families are supported on Android platform:

  - PF_LOCAL: Host-internal communication protocol family. This protocol family enables applications that are running physically on the same device to use the Socket APIs to communicate with each other.

  - PF_INET: Internet version 4 protocol family. This protocol family enables applications to communicate with applications that are running elsewhere on the network.

- Type specifies the semantics of the communication. The following major socket types are supported:

  - SOCK_STREAM: Stream socket type provides connection-oriented communication using the TCP protocol.

  - SOCK_DGRAM: Datagram socket type provides connectionless communication using the UDP protocol.

- Protocol specifies the protocol that will be used. For most protocol families and types, there is only one possible protocol that can be used. In order to pick the default protocol, this argument can be set to zero.

If the socket is properly created, the socket function returns the associated socket descriptor; otherwise, it returns -1 and the errno global variable is set to the appropriate error.

Using the Editor view, append the NewTcpSocket helper function to the Echo.cpp native module source file, as shown in Listing 8-7.

Listing 8-7. NewTcpSocket Native Helper Function

```
/**
 * Constructs a new TCP socket.
 *
 * @param env JNIEnv interface.
 * @param obj object instance.
 * @return socket descriptor.
 * @throws IOException
 */
static int NewTcpSocket(JNIEnv* env, jobject obj)
{
    // Construct socket
    LogMessage(env, obj, "Constructing a new TCP socket...");
    int tcpSocket = socket(PF_INET, SOCK_STREAM, 0);

    // Check if socket is properly constructed
    if (-1 == tcpSocket)
    {
        // Throw an exception with error number
        ThrowErrnoException(env, "java/io/IOException", errno);
    }

    return tcpSocket;
}
```

This helper function creates a new TCP socket and throws a java.lang.IOException in case of a failure.

Binding the Socket to an Address: bind

When a socket is created through the socket function, it exists in a socket family space without having a protocol address assigned to it. For clients to be able to locate and connect to this socket, it needs to be bound to an address first. A socket can be bound to an address using the bind function.

```
int bind(int socketDescriptor, const struct sockaddr* address,
        socklen_t addressLength);
```

The bind function requires the following arguments in order to bind the socket to an address:

- The socket descriptor specifies the socket instance that will be bound to the given address.

- The address specifies the protocol address where the socket will be bound.

- The address length specifies the size of the protocol address structure that is passed to the function.

Depending on the protocol family, a different flavor of protocol address gets used. For PF_INET protocol family, the sockaddr_in structure is used to specify the protocol address. The definition of sockaddr_in structure is shown in Listing 8-8.

Listing 8-8. The sockaddr_in address Structure

```
struct sockaddr_in {
    sa_family_t sin_family;
    unsigned short int sin_port;
    struct in_addr sin_addr;
}
```

If the socket is properly bound, the bind function returns zero; otherwise, it returns -1 and the errno global variable is set to the appropriate error.

Using the Editor view, append the BindSocketToPort helper function to the Echo.cpp native module source file, as shown in Listing 8-9.

Listing 8-9. BindSocketToPort Native Helper Function

```
/**
 * Binds socket to a port number.
 *
 * @param env JNIEnv interface.
 * @param obj object instance.
 * @param sd socket descriptor.
 * @param port port number or zero for random port.
 * @throws IOException
 */
```

```
static void BindSocketToPort(
        JNIEnv* env,
        jobject obj,
        int sd,
        unsigned short port)
{
    struct sockaddr_in address;

    // Address to bind socket
    memset(&address, 0, sizeof(address));
    address.sin_family = PF_INET;

    // Bind to all addresses
    address.sin_addr.s_addr = htonl(INADDR_ANY);

    // Convert port to network byte order
    address.sin_port = htons(port);

    // Bind socket
    LogMessage(env, obj, "Binding to port %hu.", port);
    if (-1 == bind(sd, (struct sockaddr*) &address, sizeof(address)))
    {
        // Throw an exception with error number
        ThrowErrnoException(env, "java/io/IOException", errno);
    }
}
```

If the port number is set to zero in the address structure, the bind function allocates the first available port number for the socket. This port number can be retrieved from the socket using the getsockname function. Using the Editor view, append the GetSocketPort helper function to the Echo. cpp native module source file, as shown Listing 8-10.

Listing 8-10. GetSocketPort Native Helper Function

```
/**
 * Gets the port number socket is currently binded.
 *
 * @param env JNIEnv interface.
 * @param obj object instance.
 * @param sd socket descriptor.
 * @return port number.
 * @throws IOException
 */
static unsigned short GetSocketPort(
        JNIEnv* env,
        jobject obj,
        int sd)
{
    unsigned short port = 0;
```

```
    struct sockaddr_in address;
    socklen_t addressLength = sizeof(address);

    // Get the socket address
    if (-1 == getsockname(sd,
        (struct sockaddr*) &address,
        &addressLength))
    {
        // Throw an exception with error number
        ThrowErrnoException(env, "java/io/IOException", errno);
    }
    else
    {
        // Convert port to host byte order
        port = ntohs(address.sin_port);

        LogMessage(env, obj, "Binded to random port %hu.", port);
    }

    return port;
}
```

As you may have noticed, the port number does not get passed directly into the sockaddr_in structure. Instead, the htons function is used to make a conversion first. This is due to the difference between the host and the network byte ordering.

Network Byte Ordering

Different machine architectures use different conventions for ordering and representing data at the hardware level. This is known as the machine *byte ordering*, or *endianness*. For example:

- *Big-endian* byte ordering stores the most significant byte first.
- *Little-endian* byte ordering stores the least significant byte first.

Machines with different byte ordering conventions cannot directly exchange data. In order to enable machines with different byte order conventions to communicate over the network, the Internet Protocol declares big-endian byte ordering as the official network byte ordering convention for data transmission.

As a Java virtual machine already uses big-endian byte ordering, this could be the first time you are hearing about the endianness of data. Java applications do not have to do any conversions on the data while communicating over the network. In contrast, as native components are not executed by the Java virtual machine, they use the machine byte ordering.

- ARM and x86 machine architectures use little-endian byte ordering.
- MIPS machine architecture uses big-endian byte ordering.

When communicating over the network, the native code should do the necessary conversion between the machine byte ordering and network byte ordering.

The socket library provides a set of convenience functions to enable native applications to transparently handle the byte ordering conversions. These functions are declared through the sys/endian.h header file.

```
#include <sys/endian.h>
```

The following convenience functions are provided through this header file:

- htons function converts an unsigned short from host machine byte ordering to network byte ordering.

- ntohs function does the reverse of htons by converting an unsigned short from network byte ordering to host machine byte ordering.

- htonl function converts an unsigned integer from host machine byte ordering to network byte ordering.

- ntohl function does the reverse of htonl by converting an unsigned integer from network byte ordering to host machine byte ordering.

Using these convenience methods is highly beneficial as their implementations get defined during compile-time based on the target machine architecture. If the machine byte ordering is different from the network byte ordering, these functions get mapped to the proper conversion functions; otherwise, they don't perform any operation on the data. Throughout this chapter, you will be frequently using these convenience functions.

Having the port bound to an address is not enough to have client connect to it. The application should explicitly start listening on the socket for incoming connections.

Listen for Incoming Connections: listen

Listening on a socket is achieved through the listen function.

```
int listen(int socketDescriptor, int backlog);
```

The listen function requires the following arguments to be provided in order to start listening for incoming connections on the given socket:

- The socket descriptor specifies the socket instance that the application wants to start listening for incoming connections.

- The backlog specifies the size of the queue to hold the pending incoming connections. If the application is busy serving a client, other incoming connections get queued up to the number of pending connections specified by the backlog. When the backlog limit is reached, other incoming connections get refused.

If the function is successful, it returns zero; otherwise, it returns -1 and the errno global variable is set to the appropriate error. Using the Editor view, append the ListenOnSocket helper function to the Echo.cpp native module source file, as shown in Listing 8-11.

Listing 8-11. ListenOnSocket Native Helper Function

```
/**
 * Listens on given socket with the given backlog for
 * pending connections. When the backlog is full, the
 * new connections will be rejected.
 *
 * @param env JNIEnv interface.
 * @param obj object instance.
 * @param sd socket descriptor.
 * @param backlog backlog size.
 * @throws IOException
 */
static void ListenOnSocket(
        JNIEnv* env,
        jobject obj,
        int sd,
        int backlog)
{
    // Listen on socket with the given backlog
    LogMessage(env, obj,
            "Listening on socket with a backlog of %d pending connections.",
            backlog);

    if (-1 == listen(sd, backlog))
    {
        // Throw an exception with error number
        ThrowErrnoException(env, "java/io/IOException", errno);
    }
}
```

Listening for incoming connections through the listen function simply puts the incoming connections into a queue and waits for the application to explicitly accept them.

Accepting Incoming Connections: accept

The accept function is used to explicitly pull an incoming connection from the listen queue and to accept it.

```
int accept(int socketDescriptor, struct sockaddr* address, socklen_t* addressLength);
```

The accept function is a blocking function. If there is no pending incoming connection request in the listen queue, it puts the calling process into a suspended state until a new incoming connection arrives. The accept function requires the following arguments to be provided in order to accept a pending incoming connection:

- The socket descriptor specifies the socket instance that the application wants to accept a pending incoming connection on.

- The address pointer provides an address structure that gets filled with the protocol address of the connecting client. If this information is not needed by the application, it can be set to NULL.

- The address length pointer provides memory space for the size of the protocol address of the connecting client to be filled in. If this information is not needed, it can be set to NULL.

If the accept request is successful, the function returns the client socket descriptor that will be used to interact with this connection instance; otherwise, it returns -1 and the errno global variable is set to the appropriate error.

In the example application you will obtain the information about the connecting client and display that information on the activity. Using the Editor view, append the LogAddress helper function to the Echo.cpp native module source file, as shown in Listing 8-12, that will be used to extract and display the necessary information.

Listing 8-12. LogAddress Native Helper Function

```
/**
 * Logs the IP address and the port number from the
 * given address.
 *
 * @param env JNIEnv interface.
 * @param obj object instance.
 * @param message message text.
 * @param address adress instance.
 * @throws IOException
 */
static void LogAddress(
        JNIEnv* env,
        jobject obj,
        const char* message,
        const struct sockaddr_in* address)
{
    char ip[INET_ADDRSTRLEN];

    // Convert the IP address to string
    if (NULL == inet_ntop(PF_INET,
            &(address->sin_addr),
            ip,
            INET_ADDRSTRLEN))
```

```
    {
        // Throw an exception with error number
        ThrowErrnoException(env, "java/io/IOException", errno);
    }
    else
    {
        // Convert port to host byte order
        unsigned short port = ntohs(address->sin_port);

        // Log address
        LogMessage(env, obj, "%s %s:%hu.", message, ip, port);
    }
}
```

Using the Editor view, append the AcceptOnSocket helper function to the Echo.cpp native module source file, as shown in Listing 8-13. This function will be used by the application to accept pending incoming connections, as mentioned earlier.

Listing 8-13. AcceptOnSocket Native Helper Function

```
/**
 * Blocks and waits for incoming client connections on the
 * given socket.
 *
 * @param env JNIEnv interface.
 * @param obj object instance.
 * @param sd socket descriptor.
 * @return client socket.
 * @throws IOException
 */
static int AcceptOnSocket(
        JNIEnv* env,
        jobject obj,
        int sd)
{
    struct sockaddr_in address;
    socklen_t addressLength = sizeof(address);

    // Blocks and waits for an incoming client connection
    // and accepts it
    LogMessage(env, obj, "Waiting for a client connection...");

    int clientSocket = accept(sd,
            (struct sockaddr*) &address,
            &addressLength);

    // If client socket is not valid
    if (-1 == clientSocket)
```

```
    {
        // Throw an exception with error number
        ThrowErrnoException(env, "java/io/IOException", errno);
    }
    else
    {
        // Log address
        LogAddress(env, obj, "Client connection from ", &address);
    }

    return clientSocket;
}
```

Upon accepting a pending connection, the new socket descriptor that is returned by the accept function can be used to exchange data with the client.

Receiving Data from the Socket: recv

Receiving data from a socket is achieved through the recv function.

```
ssize_t recv(int socketDescriptor, void* buffer, size_t bufferLength,
        int flags);
```

The recv function is also a blocking function. If there is no data that can be received from the given socket, it puts the calling process into suspended state until data becomes available. The recv function requires the following arguments to be provided in order to accept a pending incoming connection:

- The socket descriptor specifies the socket instance that the application wants to receive data from.

- The buffer pointer to a memory address that will be filled with the data received from the socket.

- The buffer length specifies the size of the buffer. The recv function will only fill the buffer up to this size and return.

- Flags specify additional flags for receiving.

If the recv function is successful, it returns the number of bytes received from the socket; otherwise, it returns -1 and the errno global variable is set to the appropriate error. If the function returns zero, it indicates that the socket is disconnected. Using the Editor view, append the ReceiveFromSocket helper function to the Echo.cpp native module source file, as shown in Listing 8-14.

Listing 8-14. ReceiveFromSocket Native Helper Function

```
/**
 * Block and receive data from the socket into the buffer.
 *
 * @param env JNIEnv interface.
 * @param obj object instance.
 * @param sd socket descriptor.
```

```
 * @param buffer data buffer.
 * @param bufferSize buffer size.
 * @return receive size.
 * @throws IOException
 */
static ssize_t ReceiveFromSocket(
        JNIEnv* env,
        jobject obj,
        int sd,
        char* buffer,
        size_t bufferSize)
{
    // Block and receive data from the socket into the buffer
    LogMessage(env, obj, "Receiving from the socket...");
    ssize_t recvSize = recv(sd, buffer, bufferSize - 1, 0);

    // If receive is failed
    if (-1 == recvSize)
    {
        // Throw an exception with error number
        ThrowErrnoException(env, "java/io/IOException", errno);
    }
    else
    {
        // NULL terminate the buffer to make it a string
        buffer[recvSize] = NULL;

        // If data is received
        if (recvSize > 0)
        {
            LogMessage(env, obj, "Received %d bytes: %s",
                    recvSize, buffer);
        }
        else
        {
            LogMessage(env, obj, "Client disconnected.");
        }
    }

    return recvSize;
}
```

The ReceiveFromSocket function uses the recv function to receive data from the given socket into the given buffer. In case of an error, it throws an IOException. Sending data through a socket is done in a similar way.

Sending Data to the Socket: send

Sending data to the socket is achieved through the send function.

```
ssize_t send(int socketDescriptor, void* buffer, size_t bufferLength,
        int flags);
```

Like the recv function, the send function is also a blocking function. If the socket is busy sending data, it puts the calling process into a suspended state until the socket becomes available to transmit the data. The send function requires the following arguments to be provided in order to accept a pending incoming connection:

- The socket descriptor specifies the socket instance that the application wants to send data to.

- The buffer pointer to a memory address that will be sent through the given socket.

- The buffer length specifies the size of the buffer. The send function will only transmit the buffer up to this size and return.

- Flags specify additional flags for sending.

If the sending operation is successful, the send function returns the number of bytes transmitted; otherwise, it returns -1 and the errno global variable is set to the appropriate error. Like the recv function, if the function returns zero, it indicates that the socket is disconnected. Using the Editor view, append the SendToSocket helper function to the Echo.cpp native module source file, as shown in Listing 8-15.

Listing 8-15. SendToSocket Native Helper Function

```
/**
 * Send data buffer to the socket.
 *
 * @param env JNIEnv interface.
 * @param obj object instance.
 * @param sd socket descriptor.
 * @param buffer data buffer.
 * @param bufferSize buffer size.
 * @return sent size.
 * @throws IOException
 */
static ssize_t SendToSocket(
        JNIEnv* env,
        jobject obj,
        int sd,
        const char* buffer,
        size_t bufferSize)
{
    // Send data buffer to the socket
    LogMessage(env, obj, "Sending to the socket...");
    ssize_t sentSize = send(sd, buffer, bufferSize, 0);
```

```
    // If send is failed
    if (-1 == sentSize)
    {
        // Throw an exception with error number
        ThrowErrnoException(env, "java/io/IOException", errno);
    }
    else
    {
        if (sentSize > 0)
        {
            LogMessage(env, obj, "Sent %d bytes: %s", sentSize, buffer);
        }
        else
        {
            LogMessage(env, obj, "Client disconnected.");
        }
    }

    return sentSize;
}
```

The SendToSocket function uses the send function to send data from the given buffer to the given socket. In case of an error while sending the data, it throws an IOException. Now all necessary helper functions are ready to implement the TCP server flow.

Native TCP Server Method

The nativeStartTcpServer native method is the core of the TCP Echo application. Using the Editor view, append the nativeStartTcpServer native method to the Echo.cpp native module source file, as shown in Listing 8-16.

Listing 8-16. The nativeStartTcpServer Native Method

```
void Java_com_apress_echo_EchoServerActivity_nativeStartTcpServer(
        JNIEnv* env,
        jobject obj,
        jint port)
{
    // Construct a new TCP socket.
    int serverSocket = NewTcpSocket(env, obj);
    if (NULL == env->ExceptionOccurred())
    {
        // Bind socket to a port number
        BindSocketToPort(env, obj, serverSocket, (unsigned short) port);
        if (NULL != env->ExceptionOccurred())
            goto exit;
```

```
        // If random port number is requested
        if (0 == port)
        {
            // Get the port number socket is currently binded
            GetSocketPort(env, obj, serverSocket);
            if (NULL != env->ExceptionOccurred())
                goto exit;
        }

        // Listen on socket with a backlog of 4 pending connections
        ListenOnSocket(env, obj, serverSocket, 4);
        if (NULL != env->ExceptionOccurred())
            goto exit;

        // Accept a client connection on socket
        int clientSocket = AcceptOnSocket(env, obj, serverSocket);
        if (NULL != env->ExceptionOccurred())
            goto exit;

        char buffer[MAX_BUFFER_SIZE];
        ssize_t recvSize;
        ssize_t sentSize;

        // Receive and send back the data
        while (1)
        {
            // Receive from the socket
            recvSize = ReceiveFromSocket(env, obj, clientSocket,
                    buffer, MAX_BUFFER_SIZE);

            if ((0 == recvSize) || (NULL != env->ExceptionOccurred()))
                break;

            // Send to the socket
            sentSize = SendToSocket(env, obj, clientSocket,
                    buffer, (size_t) recvSize);

            if ((0 == sentSize) || (NULL != env->ExceptionOccurred()))
                break;
        }

        // Close the client socket
        close(clientSocket);
    }

exit:
    if (serverSocket > 0)
    {
        close(serverSocket);
    }
}
```

Through the native helper functions that are specified in this section, it opens up a server socket on the port provided through the arguments and waits for incoming connections. When an incoming connection request arrives, it accepts the connection, starts receiving data on client socket, and echoes back the bytes to the client.

Echo Client Activity Layout

Using the Project Explorer view, expand the res directory for resources. Expand the layout subdirectory, and create a new layout file called activity_echo_client.xml. Using the Editor view, replace its content as shown in Listing 8-17.

Listing 8-17. Content of res/layout/activity_echo_client.xml File

```
<LinearLayout xmlns:android="http://schemas.android.com/apk/res/android"
    xmlns:tools="http://schemas.android.com/tools"
    android:layout_width="match_parent"
    android:layout_height="match_parent"
    android:orientation="vertical" >

    <EditText
        android:id="@+id/ip_edit"
        android:layout_width="match_parent"
        android:layout_height="wrap_content"
        android:hint="@string/ip_edit" >

        <requestFocus />

    </EditText>

    <EditText
        android:id="@+id/port_edit"
        android:layout_width="match_parent"
        android:layout_height="wrap_content"
        android:hint="@string/port_edit"
        android:inputType="number" />

    <EditText
        android:id="@+id/message_edit"
        android:layout_width="match_parent"
        android:layout_height="wrap_content"
        android:hint="@string/message_edit" />

    <Button
        android:id="@+id/start_button"
        android:layout_width="wrap_content"
        android:layout_height="wrap_content"
        android:text="@string/start_client_button" />
```

```
<ScrollView
    android:id="@+id/log_scroll"
    android:layout_width="match_parent"
    android:layout_height="0dip"
    android:layout_weight="1.0" >

    <TextView
        android:id="@+id/log_view"
        android:layout_width="match_parent"
        android:layout_height="wrap_content" />
</ScrollView>

</LinearLayout>
```

The Echo client provides a simple user interface to obtain the remote IP address, port number, and the message payload from the user, and also to present the status updates from the native TCP client while it is running.

Echo Client Activity

Using the Project Explorer view, create a new class file called `EchoClientActivity.java` under the src directory. Using the Editor view, populate its content as shown in Listing 8-18.

Listing 8-18. Content of EchoClientActivity.java File

```java
package com.apress.echo;

import android.os.Bundle;
import android.widget.EditText;

/**
 * Echo client.
 *
 * @author Onur Cinar
 */
public class EchoClientActivity extends AbstractEchoActivity {
    /** IP address. */
    private EditText ipEdit;

    /** Message edit. */
    private EditText messageEdit;

    /**
     * Constructor.
     */
    public EchoClientActivity() {
        super(R.layout.activity_echo_client);
    }
```

```java
public void onCreate(Bundle savedInstanceState) {
    super.onCreate(savedInstanceState);

    ipEdit = (EditText) findViewById(R.id.ip_edit);
    messageEdit = (EditText) findViewById(R.id.message_edit);
}

protected void onStartButtonClicked() {
    String ip = ipEdit.getText().toString();
    Integer port = getPort();
    String message = messageEdit.getText().toString();

    if ((0 != ip.length()) && (port != null)
        && (0 != message.length())) {
        ClientTask clientTask = new ClientTask(ip, port, message);
        clientTask.start();
    }
}

/**
 * Starts the TCP client with the given server IP address and
 * port number, and sends the given message.
 *
 * @param ip
 *            IP address.
 * @param port
 *            port number.
 * @param message
 *            message text.
 * @throws Exception
 */
private native void nativeStartTcpClient(String ip, int port,
        String message) throws Exception;

/**
 * Client task.
 */
private class ClientTask extends AbstractEchoTask {
    /** IP address to connect. */
    private final String ip;

    /** Port number. */
    private final int port;

    /** Message text to send. */
    private final String message;

    /**
     * Constructor.
     *
     * @param ip
     *                IP address to connect.
```

```
 * @param port
 *             port number to connect.
 * @param message
 *             message text to send.
 */
public ClientTask(String ip, int port, String message) {
    this.ip = ip;
    this.port = port;
    this.message = message;
}

protected void onBackground() {
    logMessage("Starting client.");

    try {
        nativeStartTcpClient(ip, port, message);
    } catch (Throwable e) {
        logMessage(e.getMessage());
    }

    logMessage("Client terminated.");
}
}
}
```

The EchoClientActivity acquires the necessary parameters from the user and starts the nativeStartTcpClient function, native TCP client implementation, within a separate thread.

Implementing the Native TCP Client

Using the Project Explorer, select the EchoClientActivity, and then choose "Generate C and C++ Header File" from the External Tools menu to generate the native header files. Using the Project Explorer, open the Echo.cpp source file in the editor. Go the top of the source file, and insert the include statement shown in Listing 8-19.

Listing 8-19. Including the EchoClientActivity Header File

```
#include "com_apress_echo_EchoClientActivity.h"
```

The header file contains the function declaration of the nativeStartTcpClient function. Prior to implementing this function, a helper function for the connecting to an address needs to be defined.

Connect to Address: connect

Connecting a socket to a server socket by providing the protocol address is achieved through the connect function.

```
int connect(int socketDescriptor, const struct sockaddr *address,
     socklen_t addressLength);
```

The connect function requires the following arguments to be provided in order to accept a pending incoming connection:

- The socket descriptor specifies the socket instance that the application wants to connect to a protocol address.

- The address specifies the protocol address that the socket will connect.

- The address length specifies the length of the address structure provided.

If the connection attempt is successful, the connect function returns zero; otherwise, it returns -1 and the errno global variable is set to the appropriate error. Using the Editor view, append the ConnectToAddress helper function to the Echo.cpp native module source file, as shown in Listing 8-20.

Listing 8-20. ConnectToAddress Native Helper Function

```
/**
 * Connects to given IP address and given port.
 *
 * @param env JNIEnv interface.
 * @param obj object instance.
 * @param sd socket descriptor.
 * @param ip IP address.
 * @param port port number.
 * @throws IOException
 */
static void ConnectToAddress(
        JNIEnv* env,
        jobject obj,
        int sd,
        const char* ip,
        unsigned short port)
{
    // Connecting to given IP address and given port
    LogMessage(env, obj, "Connecting to %s:%uh...", ip, port);

    struct sockaddr_in address;

    memset(&address, 0, sizeof(address));
    address.sin_family = PF_INET;

    // Convert IP address string to Internet address
    if (0 == inet_aton(ip, &(address.sin_addr)))
    {
        // Throw an exception with error number
        ThrowErrnoException(env, "java/io/IOException", errno);
    }
    else
    {
        // Convert port to network byte order
        address.sin_port = htons(port);
```

```
        // Connect to address
        if (-1 == connect(sd, (const sockaddr*) &address,
            sizeof(address)))
        {
            // Throw an exception with error number
            ThrowErrnoException(env, "java/io/IOException", errno);
        }
        else
        {
            LogMessage(env, obj, "Connected.");
        }
    }
}
```

Upon connecting the socket to a protocol address, the POSIX Socket API functions can be used to exchange data between the application and the server.

Native TCP Client Method

The nativeStartTcpClient native method is the client piece of the TCP Echo application. Using the Editor view, append the nativeStartTcpClient native method to the Echo.cpp native module source file, as shown in Listing 8-21.

Listing 8-21. The nativeStartTcpClient Native Method

```
void Java_com_apress_echo_EchoClientActivity_nativeStartTcpClient(
        JNIEnv* env,
        jobject obj,
        jstring ip,
        jint port,
        jstring message)
{
    // Construct a new TCP socket.
    int clientSocket = NewTcpSocket(env, obj);
    if (NULL == env->ExceptionOccurred())
    {
        // Get IP address as C string
        const char* ipAddress = env->GetStringUTFChars(ip, NULL);
        if (NULL == ipAddress)
            goto exit;

        // Connect to IP address and port
        ConnectToAddress(env, obj, clientSocket, ipAddress,
                (unsigned short) port);

        // Release the IP address
        env->ReleaseStringUTFChars(ip, ipAddress);

        // If connection was successful
        if (NULL != env->ExceptionOccurred())
            goto exit;
```

```
    // Get message as C string
    const char* messageText = env->GetStringUTFChars(message, NULL);
    if (NULL == messageText)
        goto exit;

    // Get the message size
    jsize messageSize = env->GetStringUTFLength(message);

    // Send message to socket
    SendToSocket(env, obj, clientSocket, messageText, messageSize);

    // Release the message text
    env->ReleaseStringUTFChars(message, messageText);

    // If send was not successful
    if (NULL != env->ExceptionOccurred())
        goto exit;

    char buffer[MAX_BUFFER_SIZE];

    // Receive from the socket
    ReceiveFromSocket(env, obj, clientSocket, buffer,
            MAX_BUFFER_SIZE);
    }

exit:
    if (clientSocket > -1)
    {
        close(clientSocket);
    }
}
```

Through the native helper functions that are specified in this section, it opens up a socket and connects it to the IP address and the port number provided through the arguments. When the connection is established, it sends the provided message text through the socket, switches to receiving mode, and displays the data received back from the socket. If everything is successful, the same data should be echoed back from the TCP Echo server. Prior to executing the application, the Echo TCP client and the server activities need to be added to the Android Manifest file.

Updating the Android Manifest

Using the Project Explorer view, open the AndroidManifest.xml in the editor, and replace its content as shown in Listing 8-22.

Listing 8-22. AndroidManifest.xml File

```
<manifest xmlns:android="http://schemas.android.com/apk/res/android"
    package="com.apress.echo"
    android:versionCode="1"
    android:versionName="1.0" >
```

```
<uses-sdk
    android:minSdkVersion="8"
    android:targetSdkVersion="15" />

<uses-permission android:name="android.permission.INTERNET" />

<application
    android:icon="@drawable/ic_launcher"
    android:label="@string/app_name"
    android:theme="@style/AppTheme" >
    <activity
        android:name=".EchoServerActivity"
        android:label="@string/title_activity_echo_server"
        android:launchMode="singleTop" >
        <intent-filter>
            <action android:name="android.intent.action.MAIN" />

            <category
                android:name="android.intent.category.LAUNCHER" />
        </intent-filter>
    </activity>
    <activity
        android:name=".EchoClientActivity"
        android:label="@string/title_activity_echo_client"
        android:launchMode="singleTop" >
        <intent-filter>
            <action android:name="android.intent.action.MAIN" />

            <category
                android:name="android.intent.category.LAUNCHER" />
        </intent-filter>
    </activity>
</application>

</manifest>
```

Rebuild the Android project to reflect the changes. The example application is now ready to be tested.

Running the TCP Sockets Example

In order to test the TCP Echo application, you will need two Android Emulator instances. As described in Chapter XX, create a new Android Emulator instance with the exact same settings. Start the EchoClientActivity and the EchoServerActivity on two separate Android Emulator instances using the Eclipse IDE.

Configuring the Echo TCP Server

The EchoServerActivity will provide a simple user interface, as shown in Figure 8-1, allowing you to specify the port number that the TCP server will be accepting connections on.

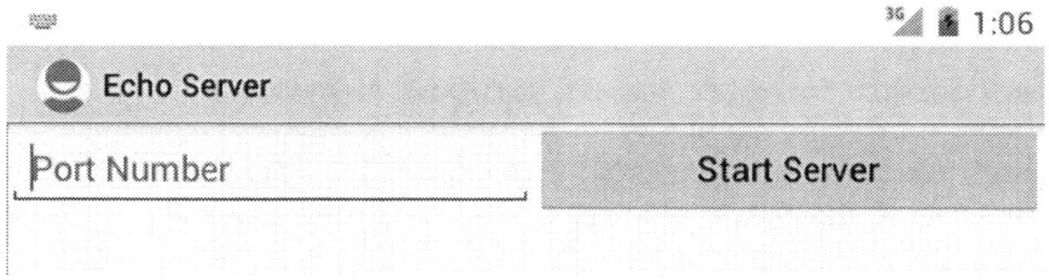

Figure 8-1. Echo TCP server user interface

- Set the Port Number to 0. This will request a random port assignment from the bind function.

- Click the Start Server button to start the Echo TCP server.

Upon starting the TCP server, the bind function will assign the first available port number to the server socket, and this port number will be reported on the screen, as shown in Figure 8-2.

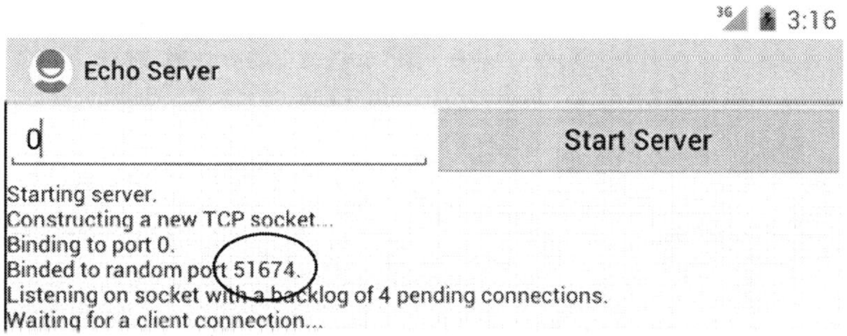

Figure 8-2. Echo TCP server binded to a random port number

Take a note of this port number because you will need it in order to have the Echo TCP Client to connect to the TCP Server.

Interconnecting Emulators for TCP

As both the Echo TCP Client and the TCP Server are running on two separate Android Emulator instances, they cannot directly establish a connection among them. Android Emulators run in a sandboxed environment as a virtual device on a virtual network. Applications running on the Android Emulator can only communicate with the machine hosting the Android Emulator process. The TCP port number should be bridged through the host machine in order to enable the TCP Client and the TCP Server to communicate. This can be achieved through the port forwarding functionality that is provided by the Android Debug Bridge (adb).

Open a command prompt or a Terminal window based on your operating system, as shown in Listing 8-23, and issue the following command by substituting the <port number> with the port number that you have noted earlier, and the <emulator name> with the device name of the Android Emulator instance.

Listing 8-23. Port Forwarding Through adb

```
adb -s <emulator-name> forward tcp:<port number> tcp:<port number>
```

This will map the `<port number>` on the Android Emulator to the `<port number>` on the host machine. Any incoming connections to the `<port number>` on the host machine will get forward to the `<port number>` on Android Emulator through the adb. Port forwarding is a runtime setting, and it will be cleared once the Android Emulator stops.

> **Note** If you are using a firewall application, make sure that the port number is open for incoming connections.

Configuring the Echo TCP Client

The `EchoClientActivity` will provide a simple user interface, as shown in Figure 8-3, allowing you to specify the IP address, the port number of the TCP server to be connected, and the message to be transmitted.

Figure 8-3. Echo TCP client user interface

Follow these steps to start the TCP echo client application:

1. Set the IP Address to `10.0.2.2`. This is the static IP address that can be used to communicate with the host machine from the Android Emulator.

2. Set the Port Number to the port number you noted earlier.

3. Set the Message to test, or any other string that you would like to send to the server.

4. Click the Start Client button to start the Echo TCP client.

Upon clicking the Start Client button, the Echo TCP client will connect to the Echo TCP server that is running on the other Android Emulator instance, and it will send the message payload. Both the client and the server activities will display the socket events and the message transmitted, as shown in Figure 8-4.

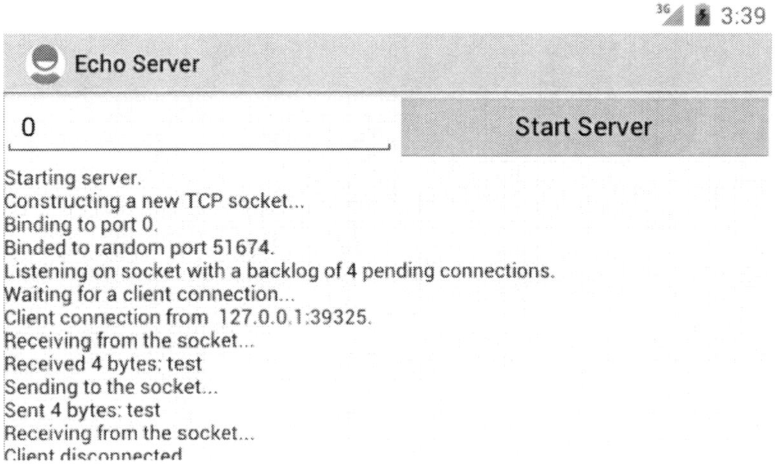

Figure 8-4. Echo TCP client exchanging messages

Connection-oriented protocols like TCP provides an error-free communication channel to the applications requiring a reliable medium of communication in order to properly function. This is achieved at the expense of maintaining an open connection. Certain applications can still perform without having to maintain a connection channel, such as the media applications. The POSIX Socket API also provides support for connectionless communication in the native layer.

Summary

In this chapter, you explored the POSIX Socket APIs that are provided through the Bionic library for connection-oriented communication. You learned about both client and server modes using the TCP protocol. The next two chapters of the book continue the discussion of POSIX Socket APIs. The next chapter will start exploring the POSIX Socket APIs for connectionless communication.

## Chapter 9

POSIX Socket API:
Connectionless Communication

In the previous chapter, you started exploring the POSIX Socket APIs by going through an example of a connection-oriented communication application using the TCP protocol. In this chapter, you will learn how to establish a connectionless communication between the Android application and a remote end-point. Connectionless communication through UDP sockets provides a lightweight communication medium tailed for real-time applications that can work with unordered and lost data packets. This type of connection does not maintain an open connection. Packets get sent to the target protocol address as needed. Since there is no connection in place, packets may get lost or get out of order during transition. The protocol does not provide any service to handle such situations. Throughout this chapter you will continue to modify the example Echo application to include both UDP server and client native implementations.

Adding Native UDP Server Method to Echo Server Activity

In order to experiment with the UDP-based Echo server, the EchoServerActivity needs to be modified to include a new native method, as shown in Listing 9-1.

Listing 9-1. The nativeStartUdpServer Method Added

```
public class EchoServerActivity extends AbstractEchoActivity {
    ...

    /**
     * Starts the UDP server on the given port.
     *
     * @param port
     *              port number.
```

```
     * @throws Exception
     */
    private native void nativeStartUdpServer(int port) throws Exception;

    /**
     * Server task.
     */
    private class ServerTask extends AbstractEchoTask {
        ...

        protected void onBackground() {
            logMessage("Starting server.");

            try {
                nativeStartUdpServer(port);
            } catch (Exception e) {
                logMessage(e.getMessage());
            }

            logMessage("Server terminated.");
        }
    }
}
```

This method now needs to be implemented in the Echo.cpp native source file.

Implementing the Native UDP Server

Using the Project Explorer, select the EchoServerActivity, and then choose "Generate C and C++ Header File" from the External Tools menu to update the generated the native header files.

New UDP Socket: socket

The same socket function can be used to create a socket using the UDP protocol. This is achieved by instructing the function to create a datagram socket instead of a stream socket. In order to make it possible for you to experiment with both types of connections simultaneously, instead of modifying the existing native helper function, a new native function will be defined to create the UDP sockets. Using the Editor view, append the NewUdpSocket helper function to the Echo.cpp native module source file, as shown in Listing 9-2.

Listing 9-2. NewUdpSocket Native Helper Function

```
/**
 * Constructs a new UDP socket.
 *
 * @param env JNIEnv interface.
 * @param obj object instance.
 * @return socket descriptor.
 * @throws IOException
 */
```

```
static int NewUdpSocket(JNIEnv* env, jobject obj)
{
    // Construct socket
    LogMessage(env, obj, "Constructing a new UDP socket...");
    int udpSocket = socket(PF_INET, SOCK_DGRAM, 0);

    // Check if socket is properly constructed
    if (-1 == udpSocket)
    {
        // Throw an exception with error number
        ThrowErrnoException(env, "java/io/IOException", errno);
    }

    return udpSocket;
}
```

The NewUdpSocket is a simple function that creates a new datagram socket and returns the socket descriptor. In case of an error while creating the socket, the socket function returns -1 and sets the errno global variable to the error code. The NewUdpSocket function throws an IOException with an error message mapped to that error code. Once the socket is created, it can be used to send and receive datagrams.

Receive Datagram from Socket: recvfrom

Receiving data from a UDP socket is achieved through the recvfrom function instead of the recv function that you used earlier.

```
ssize_t recvfrom(int socketDescriptor, void* buffer, size_t bufferlength,
        int flags, struct sockaddr* address, socklen_t* addressLength);
```

Like the recv function, the recvfrom function is also a blocking function. If there is no data that can be received from the given socket, it puts the calling process into suspended state until data becomes available. The recvfrom function requires the following arguments to be provided in order to accept a pending incoming connection:

- *Socket descriptor* specifies the socket instance that the application wants to receive data from.

- *Buffer pointer* to a memory address that will be filled with the data received from the socket.

- *Buffer length* specifies the size of the buffer. The recv function will only fill the buffer up to this size and return.

- *Flags* specify additional flags for receiving.

- *Address pointer* provides an address structure that gets filled with the protocol address of the client sending the packet. If this information is not needed by the application, it can be set to NULL.

- *Address length pointer* provides memory space for the size of the protocol address of the client to be filled in. If this information is not needed, it can be set to NULL.

If the recvfrom function is successful, it returns the number of bytes received from the socket; otherwise, it returns -1 and the errno global variable is set to the appropriate error. Using the Editor view, append the ReceiveDatagramFromSocket helper function to the Echo.cpp native module source file, as shown Listing 9-3.

Listing 9-3. ReceiveDatagramFromSocket Native Helper Function

```
/**
 * Block and receive datagram from the socket into
 * the buffer, and populate the client address.
 *
 * @param env JNIEnv interface.
 * @param obj object instance.
 * @param sd socket descriptor.
 * @param address client address.
 * @param buffer data buffer.
 * @param bufferSize buffer size.
 * @return receive size.
 * @throws IOException
 */
static ssize_t ReceiveDatagramFromSocket(
        JNIEnv* env,
        jobject obj,
        int sd,
        struct sockaddr_in* address,
        char* buffer,
        size_t bufferSize)
{
    socklen_t addressLength = sizeof(struct sockaddr_in);

    // Receive datagram from socket
    LogMessage(env, obj, "Receiving from the socket...");
    ssize_t recvSize = recvfrom(sd, buffer, bufferSize, 0,
            (struct sockaddr*) address,
            &addressLength);

    // If receive is failed
    if (-1 == recvSize)
    {
        // Throw an exception with error number
        ThrowErrnoException(env, "java/io/IOException", errno);
    }
    else
    {
        // Log address
        LogAddress(env, obj, "Received from", address);

        // NULL terminate the buffer to make it a string
        buffer[recvSize] = NULL;
```

```
    // If data is received
    if (recvSize > 0)
    {
        LogMessage(env, obj, "Received %d bytes: %s",
                recvSize, buffer);
    }
  }

  return recvSize;
}
```

The ReceiveDatagramFromSocket function relies on the recvfrom function to receive a datagram from the given socket into the provided data buffer. In case of an error, it throws an IOException with the appropriate error message. Sending a datagram is also done in a similar way.

Send Datagram to Socket: sendto

Like the recvfrom function, sending data to a UDP socket is achieved through the sendto function instead of the send function.

```
ssize_t sendto(int socketDescriptor, const void* buffer,
        size_t bufferSize, int flags, const struct sockaddr* address,
        socklen_t addressLength);
```

Like the send function, the sendto function is also a blocking function. If the socket is busy sending data, it puts the calling process into suspended state until the socket becomes available for transmitting the data. The sendto function requires the following arguments to be provided in order to accept a pending incoming connection:

- *Socket descriptor* specifies the socket instance that the application wants to send data to.

- *Buffer pointer* to a memory address that will be sent through the given socket.

- *Buffer length* specifies the size of the buffer. The sendto function will only transmit the buffer up to this size and return.

- *Flags* specify additional flags for sending.

- *Address* specifies the protocol address for the target server.

- *Address length* is the size of the protocol address structure that is passed to the function.

If the sending operation is successful, the send function returns the number of bytes transmitted; otherwise, it returns -1 and the errno global variable is set to the appropriate error. Using the Editor view, append the SendDatagramToSocket helper function to the Echo.cpp native module source file, as shown in Listing 9-4.

Listing 9-4. SendDatagramToSocket Native Helper Function

```
/**
 * Sends datagram to the given address using the given socket.
 *
 * @param env JNIEnv interface.
 * @param obj object instance.
 * @param sd socket descriptor.
 * @param address remote address.
 * @param buffer data buffer.
 * @param bufferSize buffer size.
 * @return sent size.
 * @throws IOException
 */
static ssize_t SendDatagramToSocket(
        JNIEnv* env,
        jobject obj,
        int sd,
        const struct sockaddr_in* address,
        const char* buffer,
        size_t bufferSize)
{
    // Send data buffer to the socket
    LogAddress(env, obj, "Sending to", address);
    ssize_t sentSize = sendto(sd, buffer, bufferSize, 0,
            (const sockaddr*) address,
            sizeof(struct sockaddr_in));

    // If send is failed
    if (-1 == sentSize)
    {
        // Throw an exception with error number
        ThrowErrnoException(env, "java/io/IOException", errno);
    }
    else if (sentSize > 0)
    {
        LogMessage(env, obj, "Sent %d bytes: %s", sentSize, buffer);
    }

    return sentSize;
}
```

The SendDatagramToSocket function relies on the sendto function to send the given data buffer as a datagram through the given socket. Upon implementing these helper functions, you are now ready to implement the UDP Server function.

Native UDP Server Method

The nativeStartUdpServer uses these methods to provide UDP-based Echo server. Using the Editor view, append the nativeStartUdpServer helper function to the Echo.cpp native module source file, as shown in Listing 9-5.

Listing 9-5. The nativeStartUdpServer Native Method

```
void Java_com_apress_echo_EchoServerActivity_nativeStartUdpServer(
        JNIEnv* env,
        jobject obj,
        jint port)
{
    // Construct a new UDP socket.
    int serverSocket = NewUdpSocket(env, obj);
    if (NULL == env->ExceptionOccurred())
    {
        // Bind socket to a port number
        BindSocketToPort(env, obj, serverSocket, (unsigned short) port);
        if (NULL != env->ExceptionOccurred())
            goto exit;

        // If random port number is requested
        if (0 == port)
        {
            // Get the port number socket is currently binded
            GetSocketPort(env, obj, serverSocket);
            if (NULL != env->ExceptionOccurred())
                goto exit;
        }

        // Client address
        struct sockaddr_in address;
        memset(&address, 0, sizeof(address));

        char buffer[MAX_BUFFER_SIZE];
        ssize_t recvSize;
        ssize_t sentSize;

        // Receive from the socket
        recvSize = ReceiveDatagramFromSocket(env, obj, serverSocket,
                &address, buffer, MAX_BUFFER_SIZE);

        if ((0 == recvSize) || (NULL != env->ExceptionOccurred()))
            goto exit;

        // Send to the socket
        sentSize = SendDatagramToSocket(env, obj, serverSocket,
                &address, buffer, (size_t) recvSize);
    }
```

```
exit:
    if (serverSocket > 0)
    {
        close(serverSocket);
    }
}
```

As the UDP-based server is connectionless, it does not use neither of `listen` or accept functions.

Adding Native UDP Client Method to Echo Client Activity

In order to experiment with the UDP-based Echo client, the `EchoClientActivity` needs to be modified to include a new native method, as shown in Listing 9-6.

Listing 9-6. The nativeStartUdpClient Method Added

```
public class EchoClientActivity extends AbstractEchoActivity {
    ...

    /**
     * Starts the UDP client with the given server IP address
     * and port number.
     *
     * @param ip
     *              IP address.
     * @param port
     *              port number.
     * @param message
     *              message text.
     * @throws Exception
     */
    private native void nativeStartUdpClient(String ip, int port,
                                             String message)
            throws Exception;

    /**
     * Client task.
     */
    private class ClientTask extends AbstractEchoTask {
        ...

        protected void onBackground() {
            logMessage("Starting client.");

            try {
                nativeStartUdpClient(ip, port, message);
            } catch (Throwable e) {
                logMessage(e.getMessage());
            }
```

```
        logMessage("Client terminated.");
      }
    }
}
```

After adding the native method declaration to the ClientTask, compile the application project to generate the class files. You will now implement the native implementation for this function.

Implementing the Native UDP Client

Using the Project Explorer, select the EchoClientActivity, and then choose "Generate C and C++ Header File" from the external tools menu to update the generated the native header files.

Native UDP Client Method

Using the Editor view, append the nativeStartUdpClient helper function to the Echo.cpp native module source file, as shown in Listing 9-7.

Listing 9-7. The nativeStartUdpClient Native Method

```
void Java_com_apress_echo_EchoClientActivity_nativeStartUdpClient(
        JNIEnv* env,
        jobject obj,
        jstring ip,
        jint port,
        jstring message)
{
    // Construct a new UDP socket.
    int clientSocket = NewUdpSocket(env, obj);
    if (NULL == env->ExceptionOccurred())
    {
        struct sockaddr_in address;

        memset(&address, 0, sizeof(address));
        address.sin_family = PF_INET;

        // Get IP address as C string
        const char* ipAddress = env->GetStringUTFChars(ip, NULL);
        if (NULL == ipAddress)
            goto exit;

        // Convert IP address string to Internet address
        int result = inet_aton(ipAddress, &(address.sin_addr));

        // Release the IP address
        env->ReleaseStringUTFChars(ip, ipAddress);

        // If conversion is failed
```

```
        if (0 == result)
        {
            // Throw an exception with error number
            ThrowErrnoException(env, "java/io/IOException", errno);
            goto exit;
        }

        // Convert port to network byte order
        address.sin_port = htons(port);

        // Get message as C string
        const char* messageText = env->GetStringUTFChars(message, NULL);
        if (NULL == messageText)
            goto exit;

        // Get the message size
        jsize messageSize = env->GetStringUTFLength(message);

        // Send message to socket
        SendDatagramToSocket(env, obj, clientSocket, &address,
                messageText, messageSize);

        // Release the message text
        env->ReleaseStringUTFChars(message, messageText);

        // If send was not successful
        if (NULL != env->ExceptionOccurred())
            goto exit;

        char buffer[MAX_BUFFER_SIZE];

        // Clear address
        memset(&address, 0, sizeof(address));

        // Receive from the socket
        ReceiveDatagramFromSocket(env, obj, clientSocket, &address,
                buffer, MAX_BUFFER_SIZE);
    }

exit:
    if (clientSocket > 0)
    {
        close(clientSocket);
    }
}
```

The nativeStartUdpServer function starts by creating a new UDP socket. Later it sends the given message text as a datagram to the given IP address and the port number. Upon sending the datagram, it starts waiting for receiving the response datagram.

Running the UDP Sockets Example

The Echo UDP server and the client can be tested using the same way as the Echo TCP server and client. Run both the server and the client on two different Android Emulator instances. Start the Echo UDP server with port number set to zero. Once the UDP server is started, note the assigned port number.

Interconnecting the Emulators for UDP

In order set up port forwarding for UDP ports, you need to use the Android Emulator console.

1. First find out the console port number for the Android Emulator instance by looking at its window title; note the four digit number displayed on its title bar, such as 5556.

2. Using your favorite telnet client, connect to localhost and the port number that you noted in the previous step.

3. Issuing the following command on the Android Emulator console by substituting the <port number> with the port number that the Echo UDP Server to setup UDP port redirection:

   ```
   redir add udp:<port number>:<port number>
   ```

> **Note**   If you are using a firewall application, make sure that the port number is opened through the firewall in order to receive the incoming packets.

This will map the UDP port <port number> on the Android Emulator to the UDP port <port number> on the host machine. Any incoming connections to the <port number> on the host machine will get forward to the <port number> on Android Emulator. Port forwarding is a runtime setting, and it will be cleared once the Android Emulator stops.

Starting the Echo UDP Client

Configure the Echo UDP client with the same set of parameters that are provided for the Echo TCP client, and click the Start Client button. Upon clicking the Start Client button, the Echo TCP client will send the message payload. Both the client and the server activities will display the socket events and the message transmitted, as shown in Figure 9-1.

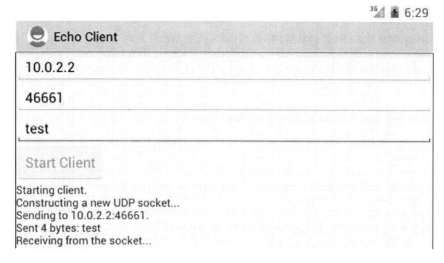

Figure 9-1. Echo UDP client exchanging messages

Summary

In this chapter, you explored the POSIX Socket APIs for connectionless communication. You saw both client and server modes using the UDP protocols. By building on the top of the core concepts that were presented in this and the previous chapter, you can virtually implement any networking protocol to communicate from the native space with various services on the network. The next chapter will demonstrate how the POSIX Socket APIs can be used to establish a communication channel locally on the device between two applications.

10

POSIX Socket API: Local Communication

In the previous two chapters, you explored the POSIX Socket API as it pertains to communication with remote parties. The POSIX Socket API can also be used to establish a communication channel locally on the device between two applications, or between the native and Java layers. In this chapter, you will continue to build on top of the Echo example application. The local socket communication example will demonstrate the following:

- Local socket server implementation in the native layer.

- Local client implementation in the Java layer.

- Establishing a local socket communication between two applications.

Echo Local Activity Layout

Using the Project Explorer view, expand the res directory for resources. Expand the layout subdirectory, and create a new layout file called activity_echo_local.xml. Using the Editor view, replace its content as shown in Listing 10-1.

Listing 10-1. Content of res/layout/activity_echo_local.xml File

```
<LinearLayout xmlns:android="http://schemas.android.com/apk/res/android"
    xmlns:tools="http://schemas.android.com/tools"
    android:layout_width="match_parent"
    android:layout_height="match_parent"
    android:orientation="vertical" >
```

```
<EditText
    android:id="@+id/port_edit"
    android:layout_width="match_parent"
    android:layout_height="wrap_content"
    android:hint="@string/local_port_edit" >

    <requestFocus />

</EditText>

<EditText
    android:id="@+id/message_edit"
    android:layout_width="match_parent"
    android:layout_height="wrap_content"
    android:hint="@string/message_edit" />

<Button
    android:id="@+id/start_button"
    android:layout_width="wrap_content"
    android:layout_height="wrap_content"
    android:text="@string/start_client_button" />

<ScrollView
    android:id="@+id/log_scroll"
    android:layout_width="match_parent"
    android:layout_height="0dip"
    android:layout_weight="1.0" >

    <TextView
        android:id="@+id/log_view"
        android:layout_width="match_parent"
        android:layout_height="wrap_content" />
</ScrollView>

</LinearLayout>
```

The Echo Local provides a simple user interface to obtain the port name to bind the local socket, the message to send, and also to present the status updates from the native local socket server and the client while they are running.

Echo Local Activity

As described earlier, using the Project Explorer view, create a new class file called LocalSocketActivity.java under the src directory. Using the Editor view, populate its content as shown in Listing 10-2.

Listing 10-2. LocalSocketActivity.java File

```java
package com.apress.echo;

import java.io.File;
import java.io.InputStream;
import java.io.OutputStream;
import java.nio.charset.Charset;

import android.net.LocalSocket;
import android.net.LocalSocketAddress;
import android.os.Bundle;
import android.widget.EditText;

/**
 * Echo local socket server and client.
 *
 * @author Onur Cinar
 */
public class LocalEchoActivity extends AbstractEchoActivity {
    /** Message edit. */
    private EditText messageEdit;

    /**
     * Constructor.
     */
    public LocalEchoActivity() {
        super(R.layout.activity_local_echo);
    }

    public void onCreate(Bundle savedInstanceState) {
        super.onCreate(savedInstanceState);

        messageEdit = (EditText) findViewById(R.id.message_edit);
    }

    protected void onStartButtonClicked() {
        String name = portEdit.getText().toString();
        String message = messageEdit.getText().toString();

        if ((name.length() > 0) && (message.length() > 0)) {
            String socketName;

            // If it is a filesystem socket, prepend the
            // application files directory
            if (isFilesystemSocket(name)) {
                File file = new File(getFilesDir(), name);
                socketName = file.getAbsolutePath();
            } else {
                socketName = name;
            }
```

```java
            ServerTask serverTask = new ServerTask(socketName);
            serverTask.start();

            ClientTask clientTask = new ClientTask(socketName, message);
            clientTask.start();
        }
    }

    /**
     * Check if name is a filesystem socket.
     *
     * @param name
     *              socket name.
     * @return filesystem socket.
     */
    private boolean isFilesystemSocket(String name) {
        return name.startsWith("/");
    }

    /**
     * Starts the Local UNIX socket server binded to given name.
     *
     * @param name
     *              socket name.
     * @throws Exception
     */
    private native void nativeStartLocalServer(String name)
            throws Exception;

    /**
     * Starts the local UNIX socket client.
     *
     * @param port
     *              port number.
     * @param message
     *              message text.
     * @throws Exception
     */
    private void startLocalClient(String name, String message)
        throws Exception {
        // Construct a local socket
        LocalSocket clientSocket = new LocalSocket();
        try {
            // Set the socket namespace
            LocalSocketAddress.Namespace namespace;
            if (isFilesystemSocket(name)) {
                namespace = LocalSocketAddress.Namespace.FILESYSTEM;
            } else {
                namespace = LocalSocketAddress.Namespace.ABSTRACT;
            }
```

```java
            // Construct local socket address
            LocalSocketAddress address = new LocalSocketAddress(
                    name, namespace);

            // Connect to local socket
            logMessage("Connecting to " + name);
            clientSocket.connect(address);
            logMessage("Connected.");
            // Get message as bytes
            byte[] messageBytes = message.getBytes();

            // Send message bytes to the socket
            logMessage("Sending to the socket...");
            OutputStream outputStream = clientSocket.getOutputStream();
            outputStream.write(messageBytes);
            logMessage(String.format("Sent %d bytes: %s",
                    messageBytes.length, message));

            // Receive the message back from the socket
            logMessage("Receiving from the socket...");
            InputStream inputStream = clientSocket.getInputStream();
            int readSize = inputStream.read(messageBytes);

            String receivedMessage = new String(messageBytes,
                    0, readSize);
            logMessage(String.format("Received %d bytes: %s",
                    readSize, receivedMessage));

            // Close streams
            outputStream.close();
            inputStream.close();

        } finally {
            // Close the local socket
            clientSocket.close();
        }
    }

    /**
     * Server task.
     */
    private class ServerTask extends AbstractEchoTask {
        /** Socket name. */
        private final String name;

        /**
         * Constructor.
         *
         * @param name
         *            socket name.
```

```
     */
    public ServerTask(String name) {
        this.name = name;
    }

    protected void onBackground() {
        logMessage("Starting server.");

        try {
            nativeStartLocalServer(name);
        } catch (Exception e) {
            logMessage(e.getMessage());
        }

        logMessage("Server terminated.");
    }
}

/**
 * Client task.
 */
private class ClientTask extends Thread {
    /** Socket name. */
    private final String name;

    /** Message text to send. */
    private final String message;

    /**
     * Constructor.
     *
     * @parma name socket name.
     * @param message
     *              message text to send.
     */
    public ClientTask(String name, String message) {
        this.name = name;
        this.message = message;
    }

    public void run() {
        logMessage("Starting client.");

        try {
            startLocalClient(name, message);
        } catch (Exception e) {
            logMessage(e.getMessage());
        }

        logMessage("Client terminated.");
    }
}
}
```

The `LocalEchoActivity` activity the local socket port, and the test message from the UI, and creates two background tasks. The first task runs the native `nativeStartLocalServer` method which creates a local server socket and waits for connections. The second task runs the `startLocalClient` Java method which creates a local socket client using the Java based socket API to communicate with the local socket server. As with the other examples, upon connecting to the server socket, the client sends the test message and waits for the server to echo the test message back.

Implementing the Native Local Socket Server

Using the Project Explorer, select the `LocalSocketActivty`, and then choose "Generate C and C++ Header File" from the External Tools menu to generate the native header files. Using the Project Explorer, expand the `jni` subdirectory, and open the `Echo.cpp` source file in the editor. Go the top of the source file, and insert the include statement shown in Listing 10-3.

Listing 10-3. Including the LocalSocketActivity Header File

```
#include "com_apress_echo_LocalEchoActivity.h"
```

The header file contains the `nativeStartLocalServer` native method declaration. Set of helper functions needs to be implemented first, in order to facilitate the implementation of this native method.

New Local Socket: socket

The same `socket` function can be used to create a local socket. This is achieved by instructing the function to create the socket in the `PF LOCAL` protocol family. In order to make it possible for you to experiment with all types of connections simultaneously, instead of modifying the existing native helper function, a new native function will be defined to create the local sockets. Using the Editor view, append the `NewLocalSocket` helper function to the `Echo.cpp` native module source file as shown in Listing 10-4.

Listing 10-4. NewLocalSocket Native Helper Function

```
/**
 * Constructs a new Local UNIX socket.
 *
 * @param env JNIEnv interface.
 * @param obj object instance.
 * @return socket descriptor.
 * @throws IOException
 */
static int NewLocalSocket(JNIEnv* env, jobject obj)
{
    // Construct socket
    LogMessage(env, obj, "Constructing a new Local UNIX socket...");
    int localSocket = socket(PF_LOCAL, SOCK_STREAM, 0);
```

```
    // Check if socket is properly constructed
    if (-1 == localSocket)
    {
        // Throw an exception with error number
        ThrowErrnoException(env, "java/io/IOException", errno);
    }

    return localSocket;
}
```

The local socket family supports both stream- and datagram-based socket protocols. For this example, you will be using the stream-based protocol.

Bind Local Socket to Name: bind

Same as the TCP and UDP sockets, once they are created, the local socket exists in a socket family space without having a protocol address assigned to it. The same bind function can be used to bind the local socket to a name that can be used by the clients to connect. The protocol address for the local sockets is specified through the sockaddr_un structure, as shown in Listing 10-5.

Listing 10-5. The sockaddr_un Address Structure

```
struct sockaddr_un {
    sa_family_t sun_family;
    char sun_path[UNIX_PATH_MAX];
};
```

The local socket protocol addresses consists of only a name. It does not have an IP address or a port number. Local socket names can be created under two different namespaces:

- *Abstract namespace* is maintained within the local socket communication protocol module. The socket name gets prefixed by a NULL character for binding the socket name.

- *Filesystem namespace* is maintained through the file system as a special socket file. The socket name gets directly passed to the sockaddr_un structure for binding the socket name to the socket.

Using the Editor view, append the BindLocalSocketToName helper function to the Echo.cpp native module source file, as shown in Listing 10-6.

Listing 10-6. BindLocalSocketToName Native Helper Function

```
/**
 * Binds a local UNIX socket to a name.
 *
 * @param env JNIEnv interface.
 * @param obj object instance.
 * @param sd socket descriptor.
 * @param name socket name.
 * @throws IOException
 */
```

```
static void BindLocalSocketToName(
        JNIEnv* env,
        jobject obj,
        int sd,
        const char* name)
{
    struct sockaddr_un address;

    // Name length
    const size_t nameLength = strlen(name);

    // Path length is initiall equal to name length
    size_t pathLength = nameLength;

    // If name is not starting with a slash it is
    // in the abstract namespace
    bool abstractNamespace = ('/' != name[0]);

    // Abstract namespace requires having the first
    // byte of the path to be the zero byte, update
    // the path length to include the zero byte
    if (abstractNamespace)
    {
        pathLength++;
    }

    // Check the path length
    if (pathLength > sizeof(address.sun_path))
    {
        // Ihrow an exception with error number
        ThrowException(env, "java/io/IOException", "Name is too big.");
    }
    else
    {
        // Clear the address bytes
        memset(&address, 0, sizeof(address));
        address.sun_family = PF_LOCAL;

        // Socket path
        char* sunPath = address.sun_path;

        // First byte must be zero to use the abstract namespace
        if (abstractNamespace)
        {
            *sunPath++ = NULL;
        }

        // Append the local name
        strcpy(sunPath, name);

        // Address length
        socklen_t addressLength =
```

```
                    (offsetof(struct sockaddr_un, sun_path))
                    + pathLength;

        // Unlink if the socket name is already binded
        unlink(address.sun_path);

        // Bind socket
        LogMessage(env, obj, "Binding to local name %s%s.",
                (abstractNamespace) ? "(null)" : "",
                name);

        if (-1 == bind(sd, (struct sockaddr*) &address, addressLength))
        {
            // Throw an exception with error number
            ThrowErrnoException(env, "java/io/IOException", errno);
        }
    }
}
```

The BindLocalSocketToName native function binds the given local socket to the given local socket name. It checks if local socket name starts with a slash character to identify whether the abstract or file system namespace to be used. Once the local socket is binded to a local socket name, the application can start waiting and accepting incoming local connections.

Accept on Local Socket: accept

The same accept function is also used to accept incoming connections to the local socket, the only difference being the client protocol address that is returned by the accept function will be a socketaddr_un type. Using the Editor view, append the AcceptOnLocalSocket helper function to the Echo.cpp native module source file, as shown in Listing 10-7.

Listing 10-7. AcceptOnLocalSocket Native Helper Function

```
/**
 * Blocks and waits for incoming client connections on the
 * given socket.
 *
 * @param env JNIEnv interface.
 * @param obj object instance.
 * @param sd socket descriptor.
 * @return client socket.
 * @throws IOException
 */
static int AcceptOnLocalSocket(
        JNIEnv* env,
        jobject obj,
        int sd)
{
    // Blocks and waits for an incoming client connection
    // and accepts it
```

```
        LogMessage(env, obj, "Waiting for a client connection...");
        int clientSocket = accept(sd, NULL, NULL);

        // If client socket is not valid
        if (-1 == clientSocket)
        {
            // Throw an exception with error number
            ThrowErrnoException(env, "java/io/IOException", errno);
        }

        return clientSocket;
}
```

Native Local Socket Server

The nativeStartLocalServer native method is very similar to the nativeStartTcpServer native method, the only difference being that it is using a local socket instead of a TCP socket. Using the Editor view, append the nativeStartLocalServer helper function to the Echo.cpp native module source file, as shown in Listing 10-8.

Listing 10-8. The nativeStartLocalServer Native Method

```
void Java_com_apress_echo_LocalEchoActivity_nativeStartLocalServer(
        JNIEnv* env,
        jobject obj,
        jstring name)
{
    // Construct a new local UNIX socket.
    int serverSocket = NewLocalSocket(env, obj);
    if (NULL == env->ExceptionOccurred())
    {
        // Get name as C string
        const char* nameText = env->GetStringUTFChars(name, NULL);
        if (NULL == nameText)
            goto exit;

        // Bind socket to a port number
        BindLocalSocketToName(env, obj, serverSocket, nameText);

        // Release the name text
        env->ReleaseStringUTFChars(name, nameText);

        // If bind is failed
        if (NULL != env->ExceptionOccurred())
            goto exit;

        // Listen on socket with a backlog of 4 pending connections
        ListenOnSocket(env, obj, serverSocket, 4);
        if (NULL != env->ExceptionOccurred())
            goto exit;
```

```
        // Accept a client connection on socket
        int clientSocket = AcceptOnLocalSocket(env, obj, serverSocket);
        if (NULL != env->ExceptionOccurred())
            goto exit;

        char buffer[MAX_BUFFER_SIZE];
        ssize_t recvSize;
        ssize_t sentSize;

        // Receive and send back the data
        while (1)
        {
            // Receive from the socket
            recvSize = ReceiveFromSocket(env, obj, clientSocket,
                    buffer, MAX_BUFFER_SIZE);

            if ((0 == recvSize) || (NULL != env->ExceptionOccurred()))
                break;

            // Send to the socket
            sentSize = SendToSocket(env, obj, clientSocket,
                    buffer, (size_t) recvSize);

            if ((0 == sentSize) || (NULL != env->ExceptionOccurred()))
                break;
        }

        // Close the client socket
        close(clientSocket);
    }

exit:
    if (serverSocket > 0)
    {
        close(serverSocket);
    }
}
```

The nativeStartLocalServer native method relies on the helper functions that you have defined earlier. It create a local socket and binds it to the given name. It starts waiting for local connections and simply echoes back the received bytes. Both the server and client parts of the local socket communication application is now implemented.

Adding Local Echo Activity to Manifest

The Echo local activity needs to be added to the Android Manifest file in order to be used. Using the Project Explorer view, open up the AndroidManifest.xml in editor, and modify its content as shown in Listing 10-9.

Listing 10-9. Local Echo Activity Added to AndroidManifest.xml File

```
<manifest xmlns:android="http://schemas.android.com/apk/res/android"
    package="com.apress.echo"
    android:versionCode="1"
    android:versionName="1.0" >

        <activity
            android:name=".LocalEchoActivity"
            android:label="@string/title_activity_local_echo" >
            <intent-filter>
                <action android:name="android.intent.action.MAIN" />

                <category
                    android:name="android.intent.category.LAUNCHER" />
            </intent-filter>
        </activity>

</manifest>
```

Running the Local Sockets Example

Since both the server and the client portions of the local socket example are part of the same activity, it can be tested on a single Android Emulator instance by following these steps.

1. Start the local socket activity on the Android Emulator.

2. Set the Socket Name to /file to create the local socket in the filesystem namespace.

3. Set the Message to the text that will be transmitted.

4. Click the Start button to start both the client and the server.

The socket events and the messages will be displayed as shown in Figure 10-1.

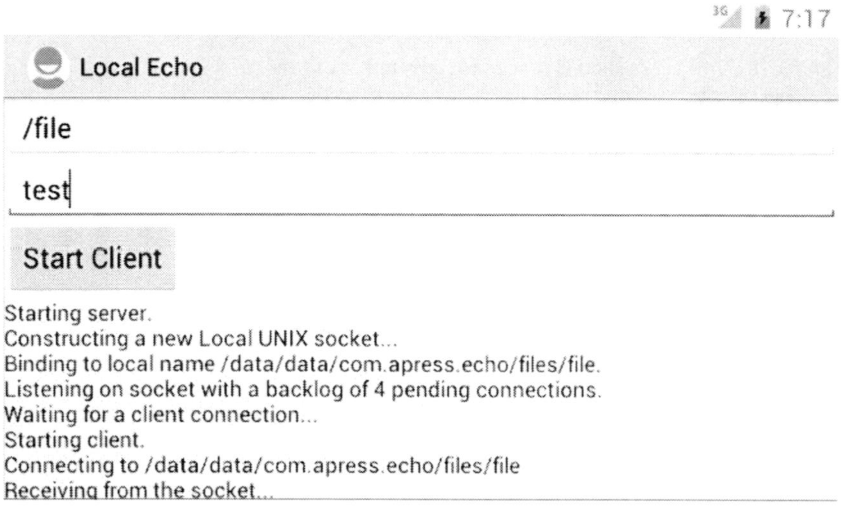

Figure 10-1. Local echo client and server exchanging messages

Asynchronous I/O

As mentioned, most of the socket APIs are blocking function calls. These functions suspend the calling process until a certain condition is met, such as data becoming available on the socket for the read operation. The asynchronous I/O support for the sockets is provided through the select function. Unlike the other socket APIs that can operate on only one socket descriptor at any given time, the select function can take more than one socket descriptor and monitor their states simultaneously. The function blocks until either a monitored event occurs or the specified timeout is reached.

To use the select function, the sys/select.h header file should be included first.

```
#include <sys/select.h>
```

The select function requires the following arguments to be provided:

```
int select(int nfds, fd_set* readfds, fd_set* writefds,
        fd_set* exceptfds, struct timeval* timeout);
```

- The nfds specifies the highest numbered descriptor plus one. The select function will monitor descriptors including to this number.

- The readfds set lists the descriptors that will be monitored for readability.

- The writefs set lists the descriptors that will be monitored for writability.

- The exceptfds set lists the descriptors that will be monitored for any type of error.

- The timeout specifies the maximum interval to block the current process for the selection to complete. If this is not necessary, it can be set to NULL.

If the selection is successful, the select function returns the number of ready descriptors; otherwise -1 is returned and the `errno` is set to the error.

The lists of descriptors are provided to the `select` function through the `fd_set` structure.

```
struct fd_set readfds;
```

In order to manipulate the list of descriptors, the following set of macros are provided:

- FD_ZERO macro takes a pointer to the `fd_set` structure and clears it.

- FD_SET macro takes a pointer to the `fd_set` structure and adds a descriptor to the set.

- FD_CLR macro takes a pointer to the `fd_set` structure and removes a descriptor from the set.

- FD_ISSET macro can be used after the selection completes to check if a descriptor is part of the set that the select function returned.

Summary

In this chapter, you explored the POSIX Socket APIs pertaining to local socket communication on the same device. This chapter briefly introduced the asynchronous I/O capabilities for the POSIX Socket API. Throughout the last three chapters (including this one), you learned the fundamental concepts and the APIs that are offered by Bionic to develop networking applications in the native layer. With this information, any networking protocol can easily be implemented on the native layer.

## Chapter 11

C++ Support

In the previous chapters you explored the functionality that is offered by the Bionic C standard library. Bionic provides frequently needed basic constructs and a common abstract interface to interact with the functionality provided through the operating system and the hardware. Compared to the Java framework, the extent of generic constructs that are offered by Bionic is fairly minimal. In addition to the standard C library, the C++ ISO standard specifies an additional standard library for the C++ programming language, known as the C++ standard library. This library provides several generic containers, strings, streams, and everyday utility functions. Through the building bricks that it provides, the C++ standard library simplifies the native development by allowing the developers to focus on the actual application logic rather than developing the constructs that are necessary to implement the logic. This takes C++ development to a higher level of productivity and promotes code reuse.

In this chapter you will start exploring the C++ runtime support that is provided through the Android platform and the Android NDK. This chapter will emphasize the following key topics:

- Different available C++ runtimes
- Availability of exception and RTTI support
- Overview of C++ standard library concepts
- Thread safety of C++ runtime
- C++ runtime debug mode

Supported C++ Runtimes

The Android platform comes with a very minimal C++ runtime support library, called the system runtime. This runtime does not provide any of the following features:

- C++ standard library
- Exceptions support
- RTTI support

Android NDK provides additional C++ runtime libraries to compliment the system runtime in order to compensate a subset of these missing features. Comparison between the available C++ runtimes is shown in Table 11-1.

Table 11-1. Comparison of Supported C++ Runtimes

C++ Runtime	C++ Exceptions Support	C++ RTTI Support	C++ Standard Library
System	No	No	No
GAbi++	No	Yes	No
STLport	No	Yes	Yes
GNU STL	Yes	Yes	Yes

GAbi++ C++ Runtime

The GAbi++ C++ runtime is an experimental, minimalistic runtime that provides RTTI support on the top of the same set of features provided by the system runtime. It is available as both static and shared libraries.

STLport C++ Runtime

STLport is an open-source, multiplatform C++ standard library implementation. It provides a complete set of C++ standard library headers and support for RTTI. At the time of this writing, STLport C++ runtime support in Android NDK is based on STLport version 5.2.0. STLport is available as both static and shared libraries. It is provided under a royalty-free license for use in both commercial and open-source projects.

GNU STL C++ Runtime

The GNU Standard C++ Library, also known as libstdc++-v3, is the most complete standard C++ runtime available through Android NDK. It is an ongoing open-source project to implement ISO standard C++ library.

Both the C++ exceptions and C++ RTTI are supported through the GNU standard C++ runtime. If the native code does require any of these features, it should be explicitly mentioned through the build system variables as described in the C++ exceptions and C++ RTTI sections in this chapter.

The GNU Standard C++ Library is available as both static and shared libraries through the Android NDK. Different from the other components of the Android NDK components, it is distributed under the GNU General Public License version 3, with the addition of the GCC Runtime Library Exception.

Specifying the C++ Runtime

The Android NDK build system variable APP_STL can be used to specify which C++ runtime library should be used by the native Android project. The APP_STL variable is an application-scope variable that can be only defined in the Application.mk build file in the jni sub-directory, as shown in Listing 11-1.

Listing 11-1. Content of jni/Application.mk File Selecting the C++ Runtime

```
APP_ABI := armeabi armeabi-v7a
...
APP_STL := system
```

The APP_STL variable can take a single value, the name of the C++ runtime to use. At the time of this writing, the following values are supported by the APP_STL variable:

- system: Default minimal system C++ runtime. If APP_STL is not set, the system runtime gets used by default.
- gabi++_static: GAbi++ runtime as a static library.
- gabi++_shared: GAbi++ runtime as a shared library.
- stlport_static: STLport runtime as static library.
- stlport_shared: STLport runtime as shared library.
- gnustl_static: GNU STL runtime as static library.
- gnustl_shared: GNU STL runtime as shared library.

Static vs. Shared Runtimes

For all supported C++ runtimes except the system runtime, both static and shared libraries are provided. Application developers can choose to either statically or dynamically link the preferred C++ runtime with their native modules.

- Static library is only supported if the project contains a single native module.
- Shared library is recommended if the project contains more than one native module.

When the C++ runtime is used in shared library form, the application should explicitly load the necessary shared library before loading any native module that depends on it. As shown in Listing 11-2, you should load the libraries in reverse dependency order.

Listing 11-2. Explicitly Loading C++ Runtime Shared Library

```
static {
    System.loadLibrary("strport_shared");
    System.loadLibrary("module1");
    System.loadLibrary("module2");
}
```

This will load the stlport_shared shared library before loading the native modules, so that the C++ runtime is available while loading the modules that are linked to it. Otherwise, the loading of native modules will fail.

C++ Exception Support

An *exception* is a mechanism to transfer control to a specific function, called an *exception handler*, when an exceptional circumstance, such as an error, occurs in a wrapped block of code. Android NDK provides support for C++ exceptions through the GNU STL C++ runtime. In order to use C++ exception with your native module, you need to first specify GNU STL in Application.mk, like so:

```
APP_STL := gnustl_shared
```

For compatibility and performance reasons, C++ exception support is disabled by default. The C++ exception support can be enabled for a single native module using the LOCAL_CPP_FEATURES build system variable in the Android.mk build file, as shown in Listing 11-3.

Listing 11-3. Content of Android.mk Build File Enabling C++ Exceptions

```
LOCAL_MODULE := module
...
LOCAL_CPP_FEATURES += exceptions
...
include $(BUILD_SHARED_LIBRARY)
```

The C++ exception support can be enabled for all native modules through the APP_CPPFLAGS build system variable in the Application.mk build file, as shown in Listing 11-4.

Listing 11-4. Content of Application.mk Build File Enabling C++ Exceptions

```
APP_STL := gnustl_shared
APP_CPPFLAGS += -fexceptions
```

This enables C++ exception support on all native modules that are part of the application. C++ RTTI support can also be enabled in a similar way.

C++ RTTI Support

Run-Time Type Information (RTTI) is a mechanism that exposes object type information during runtime. It is primarily used for performing safe typecasts. The dynamic_cast and typeid operators and the type_info class are part of the RTTI. Android NDK provides support for RTTI through GAbi++, STLport, or GNU STL C++ runtimes. In order to use RTTI with your native module, you need to first specify the proper C++ runtime in Application.mk, like so:

```
APP_STL := gnustl_shared
```

For compatibility and performance reasons, C++ exception support is disabled by default. The C++ exception support can be enabled for a single native module using the LOCAL_CPP_FEATURES build system variable in the Android.mk build file, as shown in Listing 11-5.

Listing 11-5. Content of Android.mk Build File Enabling RTTI Support

```
LOCAL_MODULE := module
...
LOCAL_CPP_FEATURES += rtti
...
include $(BUILD_SHARED_LIBRARY)
```

The C++ exception support can be enabled for all native modules through the `APP_CPPFLAGS` build system variable in the `Application.mk` build file, as shown Listing 11-6.

Listing 11-6. Content of Application.mk Build File Enabling RTTI Support

```
APP_STL := gnustl_shared
APP_CPPFLAGS += -frtti
```

This enables C++ RTTI support for all native modules that are part of the application.

C++ Standard Library Primer

As the C++ standard library specification is rather large, this section will only provide a brief overview of the functionality that is provided. More information can be found at the respective C++ runtime documentation:

- STLport documentation at www.stlport.org/doc/
- GNU STL documentation at http://gcc.gnu.org/onlinedocs/libstdc++/

Containers

A *container* is an object that stores other objects and provides methods for accessing and manipulating its elements. Containers own the elements within, and the lifetime of an element cannot exceed the lifetime of the container.

Sequence

A *sequence* is a variable-sized container whose elements are in a linear order. The following sequence containers are supported by the C++ standard library:

- vector supports random access to its elements. It provides constant time insertion and removal of elements at the end, and linear time insertion and removal of elements at other positions.
- deque is similar to a vector, with the addition of constant time insertion of removal of elements at the beginning of the sequence. This makes deque the candidate as the base of queue implementations.
- list is a doubly linked list. It supports both forward and backward traversal of the sequence.
- slist is a singly linked list. It supports only forward traversal of the sequence.

Associative Container

An *associative container* is a variable-sized container that supports efficient retrieval of elements through keys. Each element in an associative container must have a key. There are two main types of associative containers: sorted associative container and hashed associative container.

Sorted Associative Container

A *sorted associative container* stores the keys in a case-insensitive ascending order. It guarantees that the complexity of most operations is never worse than logarithmic. The following sorted associative containers are supported by the C++ standard library:

- `set` is a sorted simple associative container. All of its elements are sorted, and no two elements are the same.

- `map` is a sorted unique associative container. It associates elements with keys. No two elements are the same.

- `multiset` is a sorted, simple, and multiple associative container. All of its elements are sorted, and duplicate elements are supported.

- `multimap` is a sorted, multiple container. It associated elements with keys. There is no limit on the number elements with the same key.

Hashed Associative Container

A *hashed associative container* is implemented based on a hash table. It does not store the elements in any meaningful order. A hashed associative container is much faster than a sorted associative container. It guarantees that the worst case complexity of most operations is linear in the size of the container, average case complexity being constant time. This makes the hashed associative container a perfect match when quick lookup of elements are needed. In contrast to sorted associative containers, hashed associative containers do not store the elements and the keys in any meaningful order. The following hashed associative containers are supported by the standard C++ library:

- `hashed_set` is a hashed simple associative container. It does not allow duplicate elements. It is the best match when you would like to quickly check if an element is in a set.

- `hash_map` is a hashed pair associative container. It associates elements with keys and provides quick lookup of elements through these keys. Neither the elements nor the keys are sorted in any meaningful order.

- `hash_multiset` is a hashed, simple, and multiple associative container. It allows duplicate elements to be present in the container. As with other hashed associative containers, it provides a fast lookup of elements through the provided keys.

- `hash_multimap` is a hashed, pair, and multiple associative container. It associates elements with keys and provides quick lookup. It allows duplicate elements with the same key to be present in the container.

Adaptors

Container adaptors are used to provide specialized container types based on the existing generic containers. They achieve this by restricting the set of container functionality for the specialized type. The following containers are provided through the adaptors:

- stack is a last in, first out (LIFO) data structure. It is implemented on top of a deque container by restricting its functionality through the adaptors.

- queue is a first in, first out (FIFO) data structure. It is also implemented on top of deque container by restricting its functionality through adaptors.

String

String is also a container type. It is represented as a sequence of characters. Besides the usual methods that are available to a sequence, the string class also provides additional methods for standard string operations, such as concatenation and search. Through the provided methods, the string values can be converted to and from ordinary C strings.

Iterators

Iterators allow iterating over a range of objects or a container. They are the generalization of pointers, but they are implemented as regular classes. It is a key component of C++ standard library, since iterators are the interface between containers and the algorithms. Five base iterators are provided by the C++ standard library based on the level of access and the type of the operation that will be performed:

- *Input iterator* is used to refer to an element for reading its value.

- *Output iterator* is used to modify the value of the object at the current location.

- *Forward iterator* can be used in multiple algorithms as it corresponds to the usual notion of a linear sequence of values, and it does not dictate either input or output operation.

- *Bidirectional iterator* can be used to traverse the given range of elements both in forward and backward directions.

- *Random access iterator* provides all of the operations of ordinary C pointer arithmetic. It provides constant-time methods for traversing the elements in arbitrary-sized steps.

Derivatives of these iterators are also provided through the adaptors, such as the *reverse iterator* and the *front insert iterator*.

Algorithms

The C++ standard library also provides an extensive set of everyday functions to operate on a range of elements, such as collections. Algorithms provide functions for searching, replacing, copying, and extracting boundaries of elements in a given range of elements. They rely on iterators as the interface to traverse through the containers.

Thread Safety of C++ Runtime

All C++ runtime implementations are thread safe in the sense that simultaneous read access to shared containers is safe; however, the application is responsible for ensuring mutual exclusion if threads are both reading from and writing to shared containers.

C++ Runtime Debug Mode

The C++ runtimes are optimized for performance, so they perform little or no error checking. GNU STL and STLport C++ runtimes provide a debug mode to make it easier to detect incorrect use of the C++ standard library and obscure bugs in application code. The debug mode replaces the unsafe standard containers and iterators with semantically equivalent but safe containers and iterators. The following debugging facilities are provided:

- *Safe iterators* track the container to which the iterator is attached. They perform runtime checking of the iterator's validity and ownership. Errors such as dereferencing an iterator that points to a container that has been destructed are detected immediately in debug mode.

- *Algorithm preconditions* attempt to validate the input parameters to detect errors immediately. Preconditions are validated using any additional information that is available at runtime, such as the position of an iterator within a container.

GNU STL Debug Mode

GNU STL C++ runtime allows the debug mode to be enabled either for a specific portion of the code or for the entire application.

Using Individual GNU STL Debugging Containers

In order to only enable debug mode for a specific portion of the code, GNU STL provides debug mode-enabled counterparts for most containers in the __gnu_debug namespace instead of the std namespace. These debugging containers can be included by prefixing the header file name with the debug sub-directory, as shown in Listing 11-7.

Listing 11-7. Enabling GNU STL Debug Mode in a Portion of the Code

```
// Including debugging vector container
#include <debug/vector>
...
__gnu_debug::vector v;
```

Using the individual GNU STL debugging containers requires code modification, which is not preferable in most cases. GNU STL debug mode can also be enabled during compile-time without modifying the source code.

Enabling GNU STL Debug Mode

The debug mode is controlled through the _GLIBCXX_DEBUG preprocessor symbol. This symbol can be defined either through APP_CFLAGS build system variable for all native modules in the project or through LOCAL_CFLAGS build system variable for a specific native module, as shown in Listing 11-8.

Listing 11-8. Enabling GNU STL Debug Mode for the Module

```
LOCAL_MODULE := module
...
LOCAL_CFLAGS += -D_GLIBCXX_DEBUG
...
include $(BUILD_SHARED_LIBRARY)
```

The native module needs to be recompiled upon enabling or disabling the debug mode.

STLport Debug Mode

The debug mode is controlled through the _STLP_DEBUG preprocessor symbol. This symbol can be defined either through the APP_CFLAGS build system variable for all native modules in the project, or through LOCAL_CFLAGS build system variable for a specific native module, as shown in Listing 11-9.

Listing 11-9. Enabling STLport Debug Mode for Module

```
LOCAL_MODULE := module
...
LOCAL_CFLAGS += -D_STLP_DEBUG
...
include $(BUILD_SHARED_LIBRARY)
```

The native module needs to be recompiled upon enabling or disabling the debug mode.

Redirecting Debug Mode Messages to Android Logs

By default, the error messages get displayed on the standard error output. STLport allows you to override the default behavior by redirecting the error messages to a user-defined function. In order to do so, follow these steps.

1. Modify the Android.mk build file to define the _STLP_DEBUG_MESSAGE preprocessor macro, as shown in Listing 11-10.

    Listing 11-10. Enabling User-Defined Debug Message Output Function

    ```
    LOCAL_MODULE := module
    ...
    LOCAL_CFLAGS += -D_STLP_DEBUG
    LOCAL_CFLAGS += -D_STLP_DEBUG_MESSAGE
    LOCAL_LDLIBS += -llog
    ...
    include $(BUILD_SHARED_LIBRARY)
    ```

2. Implement the __stl_debug_message global function to redirect the error messages to Android logs, as shown in Listing 11-11.

Listing 11-11. Implementation of __stl_debug_message Function

```
#include <stdarg.h>
#include <android/log.h>
...
void __stl_debug_message(const char* format_str, ...)
{
    va_list ap;

    va_start(ap, format_str);
    __android_log_vprint(ANDROID_LOG_FATAL, "STLport", format_str, ap);
    va_end(ap);
}
```

Upon making this change, any STL debug message will get directed to the Android logs with the tag STLport and the log level FATAL, and can be monitored through the logcat.

Summary

In this chapter you started exploring the C++ runtime support that is provided through the Android platform and the Android NDK. Different C++ runtimes that are supported by the Android NDK were compared in terms of the functionality that they offer, such C++ exception support and C++ RTTI support. As the C++ standard library is rather large and complex, the thread safety and the debug mode of C++ runtime was presented in this chapter to facilitate the troubleshooting pertaining to invalid use of C++ components in native applications. In the following chapters, you will be seeing examples of the C++ standard library functions in action.

Chapter 12

Native Graphics API

Needless to say, games and multimedia applications benefit from the Android NDK the most. These applications rely on native code for performance-critical operations. Having the capability to render graphics directly to the display from within the native layer is a highly crucial for such applications. This chapter will explore the following set of native graphics APIs that are provided through the Android NDK:

- JNI Graphics API (aka Bitmap API)
- OpenGL ES 1.x and 2.0
- Native Window API

Throughout this chapter, you will be building an AVI video player application that will be used as a test bed to demonstrate rendering of video frames through the various native graphics APIs that are available.

Availability of Native Graphics API

Not all native graphics API are available for all versions of the Android operating system. These APIs are introduced over time, and they are applicable to only a subset of Android versions. The availability of native graphics API is shown in Table 12-1.

Table 12-1. *Availability of Native Graphics API*

Native Graphics API	Android Version	API Level
JNI Graphics API	2.2 and later	8 and later
OpenGL ES 1.x	1.6 and later	4 and later
OpenGL ES 2.0	2.0 and later	5 and later
Native Window	2.3 and later	9 and later

Before going into the details of displaying graphics in native code, you will be creating a simple AVI video player application.

Creating an AVI Video Player

The AVI video player application will act as a test bed. Throughout this chapter you will be expanding this test application to experiment with the different native graphics APIs that are available in native space. The example application will provide the following:

- An Android application project with native code support.
- A Statically linked AVI library, with basic functions exposed to the Java layer and tied with activity lifecycle.
- A simple GUI to specify the name of the AVI video file and the type of native graphics API to use for playing.

Playing AVI video files requires parsing of AVI files. Although the AVI container format is not too complicated, for the sake of simplicity, a third party AVI library called AVILib will be used to handle the AVI files.

Make AVILib a NDK Import Module

The AVILib library comes as part of a larger open source project called Transcode. Follow these steps to make AVILib available as a NDK import module.

1. Using your favorite browser, navigate to `http://tcforge.berlios.de/`.

2. At the time of this writing, the latest version of Transcode is 1.1.5. Follow the Download link for `transcode-1.1.5.tar.bz2` source archive file.

3. Open up a Terminal window if you are using Mac OS or Linux, or Cygwin if you are using Windows.

4. Change the current directory to Android NDK import modules directory by issuing the following on the command line:

   `cd $ANDROID_NDK_HOME/sources`

5. The transcode source archive file comes as a BZip2 compressed TAR archive. By replacing `<Download Location>` with the actual directory name that you have downloaded `transcode-1.1.5.tar.bz2` into, issue the following command to extract the compressed archive file:

   `tar jxvf <Download Location>/transcode-1.1.5.tar.bz2`

6. Change the current directory to the `avilib` subdirectory of Transcode by issuing the following:

   `cd transcode-1.1.5/avilib`

7. Open the platform.h header file in Eclipse. As shown in Listing 12-1, add the bold lines around the include statement for the config.h header file.

Listing 12-1. Modified Content of AVILib platform.h Header File

```
#ifndef PLATFORM_H
#define PLATFORM_H

#ifdef HAVE_CONFIG_H
#include "config.h"
#endif

#ifdef OS_DARWIN
#include <sys/uio.h>
#endif
```

You are making this change because the AVILib will be compiled through the Android NDK build system, not with the Makefile that came with Transcode project.

8. The Android NDK build system requires the import module described in its own Android.mk file. Using Eclipse, create a new Android.mk in the current directory, with the content shown in Listing 12-2.

Listing 12-2. Android.mk Build File for AVILib Import Module

```
LOCAL_PATH := $(call my-dir)

#
# Transcode AVILib
#

# Source files
MY_AVILIB_SRC_FILES := avilib.c platform_posix.c

# Include path to export
MY_AVILIB_C_INCLUDES := $(LOCAL_PATH)

#
# AVILib static
#
include $(CLEAR_VARS)

# Module name
LOCAL_MODULE := avilib_static

# Source files
LOCAL_SRC_FILES := $(MY_AVILIB_SRC_FILES)

# Include path to export
LOCAL_EXPORT_C_INCLUDES := $(MY_AVILIB_C_INCLUDES)
```

```
# Build a static library
include $(BUILD_STATIC_LIBRARY)

#
# AVILib shared
#
include $(CLEAR_VARS)

# Module name
LOCAL_MODULE := avilib_shared

# Source files
LOCAL_SRC_FILES := $(MY_AVILIB_SRC_FILES)

# Include path to export
LOCAL_EXPORT_C_INCLUDES := $(MY_AVILIB_C_INCLUDES)

# Build a shared library
include $(BUILD_SHARED_LIBRARY)
```

This build script defines both a static and shared import module for the AVILib library.

The AVILib library is now ready. In the next section, you will start implementing the AVI Player example project that will use the AVILib library to play AVI-formatted video files.

Create the AVI Player Android Application

As described earlier in the book, launch the New Android Application Project dialog in Eclipse, and follow these steps.

1. Set Application Name to AVI Player.

2. Set Project Name to AVI Player.

3. Set Package Name to com.apress.aviplayer.

4. Click the Next button to accept the default values for all other settings.

5. Click the Next button to accept the default launcher icon.

6. Uncheck the Create Activity and click the Finish button to create the empty AVI Player project.

7. In order to add native support, using the Project Explorer, launch the Add Android Native Support wizard through the Android Tools context menu.

8. Set Library Name to AVIPlayer.

9. Click the Finish button to add native support to the AVI Player project.

Create the AVI Player Main Activity

The main activity will provide a simple GUI to enable you to specify the name of the AVI video file and the type of native graphics API to use for rendering. Using Eclipse, choose **New ➤ Other** from the top menu bar, expand Android, select the Android Activity, and click Next to launch the New Android Activity dialog. Then follow these steps.

1. Select the Blank Activity template.

2. Click the Next button to proceed.

3. Set Activity Name to MainActivity.

4. Click the Finish button to accept the default settings and to create the new activity.

5. Using the Project Explorer, open the AndroidManifest.xml manifest file, and replace its content with code in the Listing 12-3.

   Listing 12-3. Content of AndroidManifest.xml File

```
<manifest xmlns:android="http://schemas.android.com/apk/res/android"
    package="com.apress.aviplayer"
    android:versionCode="1"
    android:versionName="1.0" >

    <uses-sdk
        android:minSdkVersion="8"
        android:targetSdkVersion="15" />

    <application
        android:icon="@drawable/ic_launcher"
        android:label="@string/app_name"
        android:theme="@style/AppTheme" >
        <activity
            android:name=".MainActivity"
            android:label="@string/main_activity_title" >
            <intent-filter>
                <action android:name="android.intent.action.MAIN" />

                <category
                        android:name="android.intent.category.LAUNCHER" />
            </intent-filter>
        </activity>
    </application>
</manifest>
```

6. Using the Project Explorer, expand the res directory for resources. From the values subdirectory, open the strings.xml string resources file. Replace its content with the code in Listing 12-4.

Listing 12-4. Content of res/values/strings.xml Resource File

```
<resources>
    <string name="app_name">AVI Player</string>
    <string name="main_activity_title">MainActivity</string>
    <string name="file_name_hint">AVI Video File Name</string>
    <string name="file_name_text">galleon.avi</string>
    <string name="play_button">Play</string>
    <string name="hello_world">Hello world!</string>
    <string name="menu_settings">Settings</string>
    <string name="error_alert_title">Error Occurred</string>
</resources>
```

7. The main activity provides a very simple GUI, with a text field for specifying the AVI file and a radio group to choose the native graphics API to use. Using the Project Explorer, expand the layout subdirectory under the res directory. Open the activity_main.xml layout file and replace its content with Listing 12-5.

Listing 12-5. Content of res/layout/activity_main.xml Layout File

```
<LinearLayout xmlns:android="http://schemas.android.com/apk/res/android"
    xmlns:tools="http://schemas.android.com/tools"
    android:layout_width="match_parent"
    android:layout_height="match_parent"
    android:orientation="vertical" >

    <EditText
        android:id="@+id/file_name_edit"
        android:layout_width="match_parent"
        android:layout_height="wrap_content"
        android:ems="10"
        android:hint="@string/file_name_hint"
        android:text="@string/file_name_text" >

        <requestFocus />
    </EditText>

    <RadioGroup
        android:id="@+id/player_radio_group"
        android:layout_width="wrap_content"
        android:layout_height="wrap_content" >

    </RadioGroup>

    <Button
        android:id="@+id/play_button"
        android:layout_width="wrap_content"
        android:layout_height="wrap_content"
        android:text="@string/play_button" />

</LinearLayout>
```

8. And lastly, you need to implement the activity itself. Using the Project
    Explorer, open the `MainActivity.java` source file and replace its content with
    the code in Listing 12-6.

Listing 12-6. Content of MainActivity.java Source File

```java
package com.apress.aviplayer;

import java.io.File;

import android.app.Activity;
import android.content.Intent;
import android.os.Bundle;
import android.os.Environment;
import android.view.View;
import android.view.View.OnClickListener;
import android.widget.Button;
import android.widget.EditText;
import android.widget.RadioGroup;

/**
 * Main activity.
 *
 * @author Onur Cinar
 */
public class MainActivity extends Activity implements OnClickListener {
    /** AVI file name edit. */
    private EditText fileNameEdit;

    /** Player type radio group. */
    private RadioGroup playerRadioGroup;

    /** Play button. */
    private Button playButton;

    /**
     * On create.
     *
     * @param savedInstanceState saved state.
     */
    public void onCreate(Bundle savedInstanceState) {
        super.onCreate(savedInstanceState);
        setContentView(R.layout.activity_main);

        fileNameEdit = (EditText) findViewById(R.id.file_name_edit);
        playerRadioGroup = (RadioGroup) findViewById(
                R.id.player_radio_group);

        playButton = (Button) findViewById(R.id.play_button);
        playButton.setOnClickListener(this);
    }
```

```java
/**
 * On click event handler.
 *
 * @param view view instance.
 */
public void onClick(View view) {
    switch (view.getId()) {
    case R.id.play_button:
        onPlayButtonClick();
        break;
    }
}

/**
 * On play button click event handler.
 */
private void onPlayButtonClick() {
    Intent intent;

    // Get the checked radio button id
    int radioId = playerRadioGroup.getCheckedRadioButtonId();

    // Choose the activity based on id
    switch (radioId) {

     // You will be adding cases here later in this chapter
    default:
        throw new UnsupportedOperationException(
                "radioId=" + radioId);
    }

    // Under the external storage
    File file = new File(Environment.getExternalStorageDirectory(),
            fileNameEdit.getText().toString());

    // Put AVI file name as extra
    intent.putExtra(AbstractPlayerActivity.EXTRA_FILE_NAME,
            file.getAbsolutePath());

    // Start the player activity
    startActivity(intent);
}
}
```

Creating the Abstract Player Activity

While experimenting with different native graphics APIs, a large percentage of the AVI player code will be the same across all these implementations, such as opening and closing the AVI file. The abstract player activity will provide the common code, leaving only the rendering piece to the actual player implementations that are extending it. Follow these steps to implement the abstract player activity.

1. Using the Project Explorer, expand the `src` directory.

2. Right-click on the `com.apress.aviplayer` package.

3. Choose **New ➤ Class** from the context menu to launch the New Java Class dialog.

4. Set Name to `AbstractPlayerActivity`.

5. Click the Finish button to create the new class.

6. Replace the content of `AbstractPlayerActivity.java` source file with the Listing 12-7.

Listing 12-7. Content of AbstractPlayerActivity.java Source File

```java
package com.apress.aviplayer;

import java.io.IOException;

import android.app.Activity;
import android.app.AlertDialog;

/**
 * Player activity.
 *
 * @author Onur Cinar
 */
public abstract class AbstractPlayerActivity extends Activity {
    /** AVI file name extra. */
    public static final String EXTRA_FILE_NAME =
            "com.apress.aviplayer.EXTRA_FILE_NAME";

    /** AVI video file descriptor. */
    protected long avi = 0;

    /**
     * On start.
     */
    protected void onStart() {
        super.onStart();

        // Open the AVI file
        try {
            avi = open(getFileName());
        } catch (IOException e) {
            new AlertDialog.Builder(this)
                    .setTitle(R.string.error_alert_title)
                    .setMessage(e.getMessage())
                    .show();
        }
    }
```

```java
/**
 * On stop.
 */
protected void onStop() {
    super.onStop();

    // If the AVI video is open
    if (0 != avi) {
        // Close the file descriptor
        close(avi);
        avi = 0;
    }
}

/**
 * Gets the AVI video file name.
 *
 * @return file name.
 */
protected String getFileName() {
    return getIntent().getExtras().getString(EXTRA_FILE_NAME);
}

/**
 * Opens the given AVI file and returns a file descriptor.
 *
 * @param fileName file name.
 * @return file descriptor.
 * @throws IOException
 */
protected native static long open(String fileName)
        throws IOException;

/**
 * Get the video width.
 *
 * @param avi file descriptor.
 * @return video width.
 */
protected native static int getWidth(long avi);

/**
 * Get the video height.
 *
 * @param avi file descriptor.
 * @return video height.
 */
protected native static int getHeight(long avi);

/**
 * Gets the frame rate.
 *
```

```
 * @param avi file descriptor.
 * @return frame rate.
 */
protected native static double getFrameRate(long avi);

/**
 * Closes the given AVI file based on given file descriptor.
 *
 * @param avi file descriptor.
 */
protected native static void close(long avi);

static {
    System.loadLibrary("AVIPlayer");
}
}
```

The AbstractPlayerActivity also contains a set of native methods to process AVI video files. These methods need to be implemented in the native space.

7. Choose **Project ➤ Build Project** from the top menu bar to compile the Java source code. This will allow you to use the javah tool to generate the necessary header files for implementing the native portion of AbstractPlayerActivity.

8. Using the Project Explorer, select the AbstractPlayerActivity.

9. Choose **Run ➤ External Tools ➤ Generate C and C++ Header File** from the top menu bar to invoke the javah tool for AbstractPlayerActivity class.

10. Under the jni subdirectory of the project, the com_apress_aviplayer_ AbstractPlayerActivity.h header file will be generated by the javah tool, with the content shown in Listing 12-8.

Listing 12-8. *Content of com_apress_aviplayer_AbstractPlayerActivity.h*

```
/* DO NOT EDIT THIS FILE - it is machine generated */
#include <jni.h>
/* Header for class com_apress_aviplayer_AbstractPlayerActivity */

#ifndef _Included_com_apress_aviplayer_AbstractPlayerActivity
#define _Included_com_apress_aviplayer_AbstractPlayerActivity
#ifdef __cplusplus
extern "C" {
#endif

...

/*
 * Class:      com_apress_aviplayer_AbstractPlayerActivity
 * Method:     open
```

```
 * Signature: (Ljava/lang/String;)J
 */
JNIEXPORT jlong JNICALL Java_com_apress_aviplayer_AbstractPlayerActivity_open
  (JNIEnv *, jclass, jstring);

/*
 * Class:      com_apress_aviplayer_AbstractPlayerActivity
 * Method:     getWidth
 * Signature: (J)I
 */
JNIEXPORT jint JNICALL Java_com_apress_aviplayer_AbstractPlayerActivity_
getWidth
  (JNIEnv *, jclass, jlong);

/*
 * Class:      com_apress_aviplayer_AbstractPlayerActivity
 * Method:     getHeight
 * Signature: (J)I
 */
JNIEXPORT jint JNICALL Java_com_apress_aviplayer_AbstractPlayerActivity_
getHeight
  (JNIEnv *, jclass, jlong);

/*
 * Class:      com_apress_aviplayer_AbstractPlayerActivity
 * Method:     getFrameRate
 * Signature: (J)D
 */
JNIEXPORT jdouble JNICALL Java_com_apress_aviplayer_AbstractPlayerActivity_
getFrameRate
  (JNIEnv *, jclass, jlong);

/*
 * Class:      com_apress_aviplayer_AbstractPlayerActivity
 * Method:     close
 * Signature: (J)V
 */
JNIEXPORT void JNICALL Java_com_apress_aviplayer_AbstractPlayerActivity_
close
  (JNIEnv *, jclass, jlong);

#ifdef __cplusplus
}
#endif
#endif
```

11. In order to implement these native functions, a new C++ source file is needed. Right-click on the jni directory, and choose **New ➤ Source File** from the context menu.

12. Set the Source File to com_apress_aviplayer_AbstractPlayerActivity.cpp.

13. Click the Finish button to create a new C++ source file.

14. The native portion of abstract player activity provides functions to parse the given AVI video file by using the API provided through AVILib third party library. Using the Eclipse, replace the content of com_apress_aviplayer_ AbstractPlayerActivity.cpp source file with Listing 12-9.

Listing 12-9. Content of com_apress_aviplayer_AbstractPlayerActivity.cpp

```
extern "C" {
#include <avilib.h>
}

#include "Common.h"
#include "com_apress_aviplayer_AbstractPlayerActivity.h"

jlong Java_com_apress_aviplayer_AbstractPlayerActivity_open(
        JNIEnv* env,
        jclass clazz,
        jstring fileName)
{
    avi_t* avi = 0;

    // Get the file name as a C string
    const char* cFileName = env->GetStringUTFChars(fileName, 0);
    if (0 == cFileName)
    {
        goto exit;
    }

    // Open the AVI file
    avi = AVI_open_input_file(cFileName, 1);

    // Release the file name
    env->ReleaseStringUTFChars(fileName, cFileName);

    // If AVI file cannot be opened throw an exception
    if (0 == avi)
    {
        ThrowException(env, "java/io/IOException", AVI_strerror());
    }

exit:
    return (jlong) avi;
}

jint Java_com_apress_aviplayer_AbstractPlayerActivity_getWidth(
        JNIEnv* env,
        jclass clazz,
        jlong avi)
```

```
{
    return AVI_video_width((avi_t*) avi);
}

jint Java_com_apress_aviplayer_AbstractPlayerActivity_getHeight(
        JNIEnv* env,
        jclass clazz,
        jlong avi)
{
    return AVI_video_height((avi_t*) avi);
}

jdouble Java_com_apress_aviplayer_AbstractPlayerActivity_getFrameRate(
        JNIEnv* env,
        jclass clazz,
        jlong avi)
{
    return AVI_frame_rate((avi_t*) avi);
}

void Java_com_apress_aviplayer_AbstractPlayerActivity_close(
        JNIEnv* env,
        jclass clazz,
        jlong avi)
{
    AVI_close((avi_t*) avi);
}
```

15. The native portion of abstract player activity will share some common code between the player implementations. This common code will be provided through the Common.h and Common.cpp source files. Right-click on jni directory, and choose **New ➤ Header File** from the context menu.

16. Set the Header File to Common.h.

17. Click the Finish button to create the new header file.

18. Replace the content of new header file with Listing 12-10.

Listing 12-10. Content of the Common.h header File

```
#pragma once

#include <jni.h>

/**
 * Throws a new exception using the given exception class
 * and exception message.
 *
 * @param env JNIEnv interface.
 * @param className class name.
 * @param message exception message.
 */
```

```
void ThrowException(
        JNIEnv* env,
        const char* className,
        const char* message);
```

19. Right-click the jni directory, and choose **New ➤ Source File** from the context menu.

20. Set the Source File to Common.cpp.

21. Click the Finish button to create the new C++ source file.

22. Replace the content of the new source file with the code in Listing 12-11.

Listing 12-11. Content the of Common.cpp Source File

```cpp
#include "Common.h"

void ThrowException(
        JNIEnv* env,
        const char* className,
        const char* message)
{
    // Get the exception class
    jclass clazz = env->FindClass(className);

    // If exception class is found
    if (0 != clazz)
    {
        // Throw exception
        env->ThrowNew(clazz, message);

        // Release local class reference
        env->DeleteLocalRef(clazz);
    }
}
```

23. The build file for the native project should now be updated to include the new source files, as well as to statically linking with the AVILib third party module. Open the Android.mk file from the jni subdirectory and replace its content with the code in Listing 12-12.

Listing 12-12. Content of the Android.mk Build File

```makefile
LOCAL_PATH := $(call my-dir)

include $(CLEAR_VARS)

LOCAL_MODULE    := AVIPlayer
LOCAL_SRC_FILES := \
    Common.cpp \
    com_apress_aviplayer_AbstractPlayerActivity.cpp
```

```
# Use AVILib static library
LOCAL_STATIC_LIBRARIES += avilib_static

include $(BUILD_SHARED_LIBRARY)

# Import AVILib library module
$(call import-module, transcode-1.1.5/avilib)
```

24. Although you have not yet implemented the rendering functionality for AVI
    video playback, build and run the example application on the emulator to
    make sure that it is properly implemented before going to the next step.

Rendering using JNI Graphics API

The Android framework provides the android.graphics.Bitmap class for manipulating and using
bitmap pixel buffers from the Java code. Starting from Android 2.2 (API Level 8), Android provides
the JNI Graphics API, enabling the native code to access and manipulate the pixel buffers of
Bitmap objects.

Enabling the JNI Graphics API

Follow these steps to use the JNI Graphics API in your native application.

1. Include the android/bitmap.h header file.

   ```
   #include <android/bitmap.h>
   ```

2. Update the Android.mk build file to dynamically link with jnigraphics library.

   ```
   LOCAL_LDLIBS += -ljnigraphics
   ```

Upon making these changes, the JNI Graphics API is now available to your native application.

Using the JNI Graphics API

The JNI Graphics API provides four native functions for accessing and manipulating the Bitmap
objects.

Retrieving Information about a Bitmap Object

The AndroidBitmap_getInfo function allows native code to retrieve information about a Bitmap
object in terms of its dimensions, as well as its pixel format.

```
int AndroidBitmap_getInfo(JNIEnv* env,
                          jobject bitmap,
                          AndroidBitmapInfo* info);
```

The function takes JNI interface pointer, the Bitmap object reference, and a pointer to a AndroidBitmapInfo structure that will be used to return the information about the given bitmap, as shown in Listing 12-13.

Listing 12-13. The AndroidBitmapInfo Structure Deceleration

```
typedef struct {
    uint32_t    width;
    uint32_t    height;
    uint32_t    stride;
    int32_t     format;
    uint32_t    flags;
} AndroidBitmapInfo;
```

The format field contains information about the pixel format, as shown in Listing 12-14.

Listing 12-14. The AndroidBitmapFormat Enumeration Deceleration

```
enum AndroidBitmapFormat {
    ANDROID_BITMAP_FORMAT_NONE      = 0,
    ANDROID_BITMAP_FORMAT_RGBA_8888 = 1,
    ANDROID_BITMAP_FORMAT_RGB_565   = 4,
    ANDROID_BITMAP_FORMAT_RGBA_4444 = 7,
    ANDROID_BITMAP_FORMAT_A_8       = 8,
};
```

In case of success, the AndroidBitmap_getInfo function returns zero; otherwise, it returns a negative value. The full list of error codes can be found in the android/bitmap.h header file.

Accessing the Native Pixel Buffer

The AndroidBitmap_lockPixels function locks the pixel buffer to ensure that the memory for the pixels will not move. It returns a native pointer to the pixel buffer for the native application access the pixel data and to manipulate it.

```
int AndroidBitmap_lockPixels(JNIEnv* env,
                             jobject jbitmap,
                             void** addrPtr);
```

It takes a JNIEnv interface pointer, the Bitmap object reference, and a pointer to a void pointer to return the address for the native pixel buffer. In case of success, it returns zero; otherwise, it returns a negative value. As with the AndroidBitmap_getInfo, the full list of error codes for the AndroidBitmap_lockPixels function can be found in the android/bitmap.h header file.

Releasing the Native Pixel Buffer

Each call to AndroidBitmap_lockPixels should be balanced by a call to AndroidBitmap_unlockPixels to release the native pixel buffer. The native application should release the native pixel buffer upon finishing the reading or writing to it. Once it is released, the Bitmap object can be used at the Java layer.

```
int AndroidBitmap_unlockPixels(JNIEnv* env,
                                jobject jbitmap);
```

The `AndroidBitmap_unlockPixels` function takes a JNIEnv interface pointer and the Bitmap object reference. In case of success, it returns zero; otherwise, it returns a negative value.

Updating AVI Player with Bitmap Renderer

To update the AVI player, follow these steps.

1. Using Project Explorer, open the `AndroidManifest.xml` manifest file and declare the new activity as shown in Listing 12-15.

   Listing 12-15. New Bitmap Player Activity Declared in the Manifest File

   ```
   <manifest xmlns:android="http://schemas.android.com/apk/res/android"
       package="com.apress.aviplayer"
       android:versionCode="1"
       android:versionName="1.0" >

       ...

       <application
           android:icon="@drawable/ic_launcher"
           android:label="@string/app_name"
           android:theme="@style/AppTheme" >

           ...

           <activity
               android:name=".BitmapPlayerActivity"
               android:label="@string/title_activity_bitmap_player" >
           </activity>

       </application>

   </manifest>
   ```

2. The title of the new Bitmap Player activity, as well as the label for the Bitmap Player radio button, should be added to the string resources. Open the `strings.xml` string resources file, and add the new string resources as shown in Listing 12-16.

   Listing 12-16. Bitmap Player Activity String Resources Appended

   ```
   <resources>

       ...
       <string name="bitmap_player_radio">Bitmap Player</string>
       <string name="title_activity_bitmap_player">Bitmap Player</string>

   </resources>
   ```

3. The Bitmap Player activity requires a single `SurfaceView` widget in order to function. Using the Project Explorer, expand the `res` directory.

4. Right-click the `layout` subdirectory, and choose **New ➤ File** from the context menu.

5. Set File Name to `activity_bitmap_player.xml`.

6. Replace the content of the new layout with the code in Listing 12-17.

Listing 12-17. Content of the activity_bitmap_player.xml Layout File

```
<LinearLayout xmlns:android="http://schemas.android.com/apk/res/android"
    xmlns:tools="http://schemas.android.com/tools"
    android:layout_width="match_parent"
    android:layout_height="match_parent" >

    <SurfaceView
        android:layout_width="match_parent"
        android:layout_height="match_parent"
        android:id="@+id/surface_view" />

</LinearLayout>
```

7. Using the Project Explorer, expand the `src` directory.

8. Right-click on the `com.apress.aviplayer` package, and choose **New ➤ Class** from the context menu.

9. Set Name to `BitmapPlayerActivity`.

10. Click the Finish button to create the new class.

11. Replace its content with the code in Listing 12-18.

Listing 12-18. Content of the BitmapPlayerActivity.java Source File

```
package com.apress.aviplayer;

import java.util.concurrent.atomic.AtomicBoolean;

import android.graphics.Bitmap;
import android.graphics.Canvas;
import android.os.Bundle;
import android.view.SurfaceHolder;
import android.view.SurfaceHolder.Callback;
import android.view.SurfaceView;

/**
 * AVI player through bitmaps.
 *
 * @author Onur Cinar
 */
```

```java
public class BitmapPlayerActivity extends AbstractPlayerActivity {
    /** Is playing. */
    private final AtomicBoolean isPlaying = new AtomicBoolean();

    /** Surface holder. */
    private SurfaceHolder surfaceHolder;

    /**
     * On create.
     *
     * @param savedInstanceState saved state.
     */
    public void onCreate(Bundle savedInstanceState) {
        super.onCreate(savedInstanceState);
        setContentView(R.layout.activity_bitmap_player);

        SurfaceView surfaceView = (SurfaceView)
                findViewById(R.id.surface_view);

        surfaceHolder = surfaceView.getHolder();
        surfaceHolder.addCallback(surfaceHolderCallback);
    }

    /**
     * Surface holder callback listens for surface events.
     */
    private final Callback surfaceHolderCallback = new Callback() {
        public void surfaceChanged(SurfaceHolder holder, int format,
                int width, int height) {
        }

        public void surfaceCreated(SurfaceHolder holder) {
            // Start playing since surface is ready
            isPlaying.set(true);

            // Start renderer on a separate thread
            new Thread(renderer).start();
        }

        public void surfaceDestroyed(SurfaceHolder holder) {
            // Stop playing since surface is destroyed
            isPlaying.set(false);
        }
    };

    /**
     * Renderer runnable renders the video frames from the
     * AVI file to the surface through a bitmap.
     */
    private final Runnable renderer = new Runnable() {
        public void run() {
            // Create a new bitmap to hold the frames
```

```
            Bitmap bitmap = Bitmap.createBitmap(
                    getWidth(avi),
                    getHeight(avi),
                    Bitmap.Config.RGB_565);

            // Calculate the delay using the frame rate
            long frameDelay = (long) (1000 / getFrameRate(avi));

            // Start rendering while playing
            while (isPlaying.get()) {
                // Render the frame to the bitmap
                render(avi, bitmap);

                // Lock canvas
                Canvas canvas = surfaceHolder.lockCanvas();

                // Draw the bitmap to the canvas
                canvas.drawBitmap(bitmap, 0, 0, null);

                // Post the canvas for displaying
                surfaceHolder.unlockCanvasAndPost(canvas);

                // Wait for the next frame
                try {
                    Thread.sleep(frameDelay);
                } catch (InterruptedException e) {
                    break;
                }
            }
        }
    };

    /**
     * Renders the frame from given AVI file descriptor to
     * the given Bitmap.
     *
     * @param avi file descriptor.
     * @param bitmap bitmap instance.
     * @return true if there are more frames, false otherwise.
     */
    private native static boolean render(long avi, Bitmap bitmap);
}
```

The BitmapPlayerActivity handles the rendering of the video frames through a native method called as render.

12. Choose **Project ➤ Build** Project from the top menu bar to compile the Java source code.

13. Using the Project Explorer, select the BitmapPlayerActivity.

14. Choose **Run ➤ External Tools ➤ Generate C and C++ Header File** from the top menu bar to invoke the javah tool for BitmapPlayerActivity class.

15. Under the jni subdirectory of the project, the com_apress_aviplayer_BitmapPlayerActivity.h header file will be generated by the javah tool.

16. Right-click the jni directory, and choose **New ➤ Source File** from the context menu.

17. Set Source File to com_apress_aviplayer_BitmapPlayerActivity.cpp.

18. Click the Finish button to create a new C++ source file.

19. Using the Eclipse, replace the content of the new source file with the code in Listing 12-19.

Listing 12-19. Content of com_apress_aviplayer_BitmapPlayerActivity.cpp

```
extern "C" {
#include <avilib.h>
}

#include <android/bitmap.h>

#include "Common.h"
#include "com_apress_aviplayer_BitmapPlayerActivity.h"

jboolean Java_com_apress_aviplayer_BitmapPlayerActivity_render(
        JNIEnv* env,
        jclass clazz,
        jlong avi,
        jobject bitmap)
{
    jboolean isFrameRead = JNI_FALSE;

    char* frameBuffer = 0;
    long frameSize = 0;
    int keyFrame = 0;

    // Lock bitmap and get the raw bytes
    if (0 > AndroidBitmap_lockPixels(env, bitmap, (void**) &frameBuffer))
    {
        ThrowException(env, "java/io/IOException",
                "Unable to lock pixels.");
        goto exit;
    }

    // Read AVI frame bytes to bitmap
    frameSize = AVI_read_frame((avi_t*) avi, frameBuffer, &keyFrame);
```

```
    // Unlock bitmap
    if (0 > AndroidBitmap_unlockPixels(env, bitmap))
    {
        ThrowException(env, "java/io/IOException",
                "Unable to unlock pixels.");
        goto exit;
    }

    // Check if frame is successfully read
    if (0 < frameSize)
    {
        isFrameRead = JNI_TRUE;
    }

exit:
    return isFrameRead;
}
```

20. The build file Android.mk needs to be modified, as shown in Listing 12-20, to compile the new source file, as well as to dynamically link with the jnigraphics shared library in order to use the JNI Graphics Bitmap API.

Listing 12-20. Build File Modified for Bitmap Player

```
LOCAL_PATH := $(call my-dir)

include $(CLEAR_VARS)

LOCAL_MODULE    := AVIPlayer
LOCAL_SRC_FILES := \
    Common.cpp \
    com_apress_aviplayer_AbstractPlayerActivity.cpp \
    com_apress_aviplayer_BitmapPlayerActivity.cpp

# Use AVILib static library
LOCAL_STATIC_LIBRARIES += avilib_static

# Link with JNI graphics
LOCAL_LDLIBS += -ljnigraphics

include $(BUILD_SHARED_LIBRARY)

# Import AVILib library module
$(call import-module, transcode-1.1.5/avilib)
```

21. The bitmap player activity is now ready. In order to be able to use it, it needs to be added as a radio button to the activity_main.xml layout file, as shown in Listing 12-21.

Listing 12-21. Bitmap Player Radio Button Added to Main Activity Layout

```
<LinearLayout xmlns:android="http://schemas.android.com/apk/res/android"
    xmlns:tools="http://schemas.android.com/tools"
    android:layout_width="match_parent"
    android:layout_height="match_parent"
    android:orientation="vertical" >

    ...

    <RadioGroup
        android:id="@+id/player_radio_group"
        android:layout_width="wrap_content"
        android:layout_height="wrap_content" >

        <RadioButton
            android:id="@+id/bitmap_player_radio"
            android:layout_width="wrap_content"
            android:layout_height="wrap_content"
            android:checked="true"
            android:text="@string/bitmap_player_radio" />

    </RadioGroup>

    ...

</LinearLayout>
```

22. The main activity source code should also be modified, as shown in Listing 12-22, to dispatch the playback request to Bitmap Player activity when it is selected by the user.

Listing 12-22. Bitmap Player Radio Added to Main Activity

```
/**
 * On play button click event handler.
 */
private void onPlayButtonClick() {

    ...

    // Choose the activity based on id
    switch (radioId) {
    case R.id.bitmap_player_radio:
        intent = new Intent(this, BitmapPlayerActivity.class);
        break;

    default:
        throw new UnsupportedOperationException("radioId=" + radioId);
    }

    ...
}
```

Running the AVI Player with Bitmap Renderer

Now the AVI player application is ready with the Bitmap renderer based on JNI graphics API. Follow these steps to test the application on Android emulator.

1. In order to test the AVI video player application, an AVI-formatted video file is needed. For the simplicity of the example, the application is only using AVI format as a container, expecting that the video payload is provided as uncompressed raw frames in RGB565 color-space. Using your favorite browser, download the sample video file from author's web site at `http://zdo.com/galleon.zip`.

2. Extract the galleon.avi AVI video file from the downloaded ZIP archive.

3. Start the Android emulator.

4. Using the ADB, push the AVI video file to the Android emulator's SD card, like so:

    ```
    adb push galleon.avi /sdcard/
    ```

> **Note**   The galleon.avi AVI video file requires at least 74MB of free space on the SD card. If the ADB push for the file fails, makes sure that you have enough space on the target Android device or the Android emulator. Due to the large size of the video file, pushing it to the SD Card can take 30 or more seconds.

5. Start the AVI player application on the Android emulator.

6. Make sure that Bitmap Player radio button is selected, as shown in Figure 12-1.

Figure 12-1. Choosing the Bitmap Player using AVI player GUI

7. Click the Play button to start the playback. The Bitmap Player activity will be invoked, and the AVI video file will be rendered through the JNI Graphics API, as shown in Figure 12-2. You should see the waving white flag on the galleon.

Figure 12-2. The AVI video file is getting rendered through the Bitmap renderer

Rendering Using OpenGL ES

The Android NDK provides OpenGL ES both version 1.x and 2.0 graphics API to the native code. As indicated earlier in this chapter,

- OpenGL ES 1.0 is supported from Android 1.6 and later.
- OpenGL ES 1.1 is supported only on specific devices that have the corresponding GPU.
- OpenGL ES 2.0 is supported on Android 2.0 and later.

Applications should use the `<uses-feature>` tag in the Android manifest file to indicate the preferred version of OpenGL ES version to use.

Using the OpenGL ES API

In order to use the OpenGL ES API, you need to have a `android.opengl.GLSurfaceView` instance on the Java code. The native application can then call the OpenGL ES API functions to render graphics to the `GLSurfaceView`. More information on available OpenGL ES API can be found at the Khronos Groups web site at www.khronos.org/opengles/.

At the time of this writing, the Android emulator does not support OpenGL ES 2.0 hardware emulation. In order to allow you to experiment with the OpenGL ES-based graphics API, the example application will be using the OpenGL ES 1.x.

Enabling OpenGL ES 1.x API

Follow these steps to use the OpenGL ES 1.x in your native application.

1. Include the OpenGL ES 1.x header files.

   ```
   #include <GLES/gl.h>
   #include <GLES/glext.h>
   ```

2. Update the Android.mk build file to dynamically link with GLESv1_CM library.

   ```
   LOCAL_LDLIBS += -lGLESv1_CM
   ```

Upon making these changes, the OpenGL ES 1.x API will now be available to your native application.

Enabling OpenGL ES 2.0 API

Follow these steps to use the OpenGL ES 2.0 in your native application.

1. Include the OpenGL ES 2.0 header files.

   ```
   #include <GLES2/gl2.h>
   #include <GLES2/gl2ext.h>
   ```

2. Update the Android.mk build file to dynamically link with GLESv2 library.

   ```
   LOCAL_LDLIBS += -lGLESv2
   ```

Upon making these changes, the OpenGL ES 2.0 API will now be available to your native application.

Updating AVI Player with OpenGL ES Renderer

Follow these steps.

1. Using Project Explorer, open the AndroidManifest.xml manifest file and declare the new activity, as shown in Listing 12-23.

   Listing 12-23. New OpenGL Player Activity Declared in Manifest File

   ```
   <manifest xmlns:android="http://schemas.android.com/apk/res/android"
       package="com.apress.aviplayer"
       android:versionCode="1"
       android:versionName="1.0" >

       ...
   ```

```
<application
    android:icon="@drawable/ic_launcher"
    android:label="@string/app_name"
    android:theme="@style/AppTheme" >

    ...

    <activity
        android:name=".OpenGLPlayerActivity"
        android:label="@string/title_activity_open_gl_player" >
    </activity>
</application>

</manifest>
```

2. The title of the new OpenGL player activity, as well as the label for the OpenGL player radio button, should be added to the string resources. Open the `strings.xml` string resources file and add the new string resources, as shown in Listing 12-24.

Listing 12-24. OpenGL Player Activity String Resources Appended

```
<resources>

    ...

    <string name="title_activity_open_gl_player">OpenGL Player</string>
    <string name="open_gl_player_radio">OpenGL Player</string>
</resources>
```

3. The Bitmap Player activity requires a single `GLSurfaceView` widget in order to function. Using the Project Explorer, expand the `res` directory.

4. Right-click on the `layout` subdirectory, and choose **New ➤ File** from the context menu.

5. Set File Name to `activity_open_gl_player.xml`.

6. Replace the content of new layout with the code in Listing 12-25.

Listing 12-25. Content of the activity_open_gl_player.xml Layout File

```
<LinearLayout xmlns:android="http://schemas.android.com/apk/res/android"
    xmlns:tools="http://schemas.android.com/tools"
    android:layout_width="match_parent"
    android:layout_height="match_parent" >

    <android.opengl.GLSurfaceView
        android:layout_width="match_parent"
        android:layout_height="match_parent"
        android:id="@+id/gl_surface_view" />

</LinearLayout>
```

7.   Using the Project Explorer, expand the src directory.

8.   Right-click the com.apress.aviplayer package, and choose **New ➤ Class**
     from the context menu.

9.   Set Name to OpenGLPlayerActivity.

10. Click the Finish button to create the new class.

11. Replace its content with the code in Listing 12-26.

Listing 12-26. Content of the OpenGLPlayerActivity.java Source File

```
package com.apress.aviplayer;

import java.util.concurrent.atomic.AtomicBoolean;

import javax.microedition.khronos.egl.EGLConfig;
import javax.microedition.khronos.opengles.GL10;

import android.opengl.GLSurfaceView;
import android.opengl.GLSurfaceView.Renderer;
import android.os.Bundle;

/**
 * AVI player through OpenGL.
 *
 * @author Onur Cinar
 */
public class OpenGLPlayerActivity extends AbstractPlayerActivity {
    /** Is playing. */
    private final AtomicBoolean isPlaying = new AtomicBoolean();

    /** Native renderer. */
    private long instance;

    /** GL surface view instance. */
    private GLSurfaceView glSurfaceView;

    /**
     * On create.
     *
     * @param savedInstanceState saved state.
     */
    public void onCreate(Bundle savedInstanceState) {
        super.onCreate(savedInstanceState);
        setContentView(R.layout.activity_open_gl_player);

        glSurfaceView = (GLSurfaceView)
                findViewById(R.id.gl_surface_view);

        // Set renderer
        glSurfaceView.setRenderer(renderer);
```

```
        // Render frame when requested
        glSurfaceView.setRenderMode(GLSurfaceView.RENDERMODE_WHEN_DIRTY);
    }

    /**
     * On start.
     */
    protected void onStart() {
        super.onStart();

        // Initializes the native renderer
        instance = init(avi);
    }

    /**
     * On resume.
     */
    protected void onResume() {
        super.onResume();

        // GL surface view must be notified when activity is resumed
        glSurfaceView.onResume();
    }

    /**
     * On pause.
     */
    protected void onPause() {
        super.onPause();

        // GL surface view must be notified when activity is paused.
        glSurfaceView.onPause();
    }

    /**
     * On stop.
     */
    protected void onStop() {
        super.onStop();

        // Free the native renderer
        free(instance);
        instance = 0;
    }

    /**
     * Request rendering based on the frame rate.
     */
    private final Runnable player = new Runnable() {
        public void run() {
            // Calculate the delay using the frame rate
            long frameDelay = (long) (1000 / getFrameRate(avi));
```

```java
            // Start rendering while playing
            while (isPlaying.get()) {
                // Request rendering
                glSurfaceView.requestRender();

                // Wait for the next frame
                try {
                    Thread.sleep(frameDelay);
                } catch (InterruptedException e) {
                    break;
                }
            }
        }
    };

    /**
     * OpenGL renderer.
     */
    private final Renderer renderer = new Renderer() {
        public void onDrawFrame(GL10 gl) {
            // Render the next frame
            if (!render(instance, avi))
            {
                isPlaying.set(false);
            }
        }

        public void onSurfaceChanged(GL10 gl, int width, int height) {

        }

        public void onSurfaceCreated(GL10 gl, EGLConfig config) {
            // Initialize the OpenGL surface
            initSurface(instance, avi);

            // Start playing since surface is ready
            isPlaying.set(true);

            // Start player
            new Thread(player).start();
        }
    };

    /**
     * Initializes the native renderer.
     *
     * @param avi file descriptor.
     * @return native instance.
     */
    private native static long init(long avi);
```

```
/**
 * Initializes the OpenGL surface.
 *
 * @param instance native instance.
 */
private native static void initSurface(long instance, long avi);

/**
 * Renders the frame from given AVI file descriptor.
 *
 * @param instance native instance.
 * @param avi file descriptor.
 * @return true if there are more frames, false otherwise.
 */
private native static boolean render(long instance, long avi);

/**
 * Free the native renderer.
 *
 * @param instance native instance.
 */
private native static void free(long instance);
}
```

12. Choose **Project ➤ Build Project** from the top menu bar to compile the Java source code.

13. Using the Project Explorer, select the OpenGLPlayerActivity.

14. Choose **Run ➤ External Tools ➤ Generate C and C++ Header File** from the top menu bar to invoke the javah tool for OpenGLPlayerActivity class.

15. Under the jni subdirectory of the project, the com_apress_aviplayer_ OpenGLPlayerActivity.h header file will be generated by the javah tool.

16. Right-click the jni directory, and choose **New ➤ Source File** from the context menu.

17. Set Source File to com_apress_aviplayer_OpenGLPlayerActivity.cpp.

18. Click the Finish button to create a new C++ source file.

19. Using the Eclipse, replace the content of the new source file with the code in Listing 12-27.

Listing 12-27. Content of com_apress_aviplayer_OpenGLPlayerActivity.cpp

```
extern "C" {
#include <avilib.h>
}

#include <GLES/gl.h>
#include <GLES/glext.h>
```

```cpp
#include <malloc.h>

#include "Common.h"
#include "com_apress_aviplayer_OpenGLPlayerActivity.h"

struct Instance
{
    char* buffer;
    GLuint texture;

    Instance():
        buffer(0),
        texture(0)
    {

    }
};

jlong Java_com_apress_aviplayer_OpenGLPlayerActivity_init(
        JNIEnv* env,
        jclass clazz,
        jlong avi)
{
    Instance* instance = 0;

    long frameSize = AVI_frame_size((avi_t*) avi, 0);
    if (0 >= frameSize)
    {
        ThrowException(env, "java/io/RuntimeException",
                "Unable to get the frame size.");
        goto exit;
    }

    instance = new Instance();
    if (0 == instance)
    {
        ThrowException(env, "java/io/RuntimeException",
                "Unable to allocate instance.");
        goto exit;
    }

    instance->buffer = (char*) malloc(frameSize);
    if (0 == instance->buffer)
    {
        ThrowException(env, "java/io/RuntimeException",
                "Unable to allocate buffer.");
        delete instance;
        instance = 0;
    }
```

```
exit:
    return (jlong) instance;
}

void Java_com_apress_aviplayer_OpenGLPlayerActivity_initSurface(
        JNIEnv* env,
        jclass clazz,
        jlong inst,
        jlong avi)
{
    Instance* instance = (Instance*) inst;

    // Enable textures
    glEnable(GL_TEXTURE_2D);

    // Generate one texture object
    glGenTextures(1, &instance->texture);

    // Bind to generated texture
    glBindTexture(GL_TEXTURE_2D, instance->texture);

    int frameWidth = AVI_video_width((avi_t*) avi);
    int frameHeight = AVI_video_height((avi_t*) avi);

    // Crop the texture rectangle
    GLint rect[] = {0, frameHeight, frameWidth, -frameHeight};
    glTexParameteriv(GL_TEXTURE_2D, GL_TEXTURE_CROP_RECT_OES, rect);

    // Full color
    glColor4f(1.0, 1.0, 1.0, 1.0);

    // Generate an empty texture
    glTexImage2D(GL_TEXTURE_2D,
            0,
            GL_RGB,
            frameWidth,
            frameHeight,
            0,
            GL_RGB,
            GL_UNSIGNED_SHORT_5_6_5,
            0);
}

jboolean Java_com_apress_aviplayer_OpenGLPlayerActivity_render(
        JNIEnv* env,
        jclass clazz,
        jlong inst,
        jlong avi)
{
    Instance* instance = (Instance*) inst;
```

```
    jboolean isFrameRead = JNI_FALSE;
    int keyFrame = 0;

    // Read AVI frame bytes to bitmap
    long frameSize = AVI_read_frame((avi_t*) avi,
            instance->buffer,
            &keyFrame);

    // Check if frame read
    if (0 >= frameSize)
    {
        goto exit;
    }

    // Frame read
    isFrameRead = JNI_TRUE;

    // Update the texture with the new frame
    glTexSubImage2D(GL_TEXTURE_2D,
            0,
            0,
            0,
            AVI_video_width((avi_t*) avi),
            AVI_video_height((avi_t*) avi),
            GL_RGB,
            GL_UNSIGNED_SHORT_5_6_5,
            instance->buffer);

    // Draw texture
    glDrawTexiOES(0, 0, 0,
            AVI_video_width((avi_t*) avi),
            AVI_video_height((avi_t*) avi));

exit:
    return isFrameRead;
}

void Java_com_apress_aviplayer_OpenGLPlayerActivity_free(
        JNIEnv* env,
        jclass clazz,
        jlong inst)
{
    Instance* instance = (Instance*) inst;

    if (0 != instance)
    {
        free(instance->buffer);
        delete instance;
    }
}
```

20. The build file `Android.mk` needs to be modified, as shown in Listing 12-28, to compile the new source file, as well as to dynamically link with the `GLESv1_CM` shared library in order to use the OpenGL ES API from native space.

Listing 12-28. Build File Modified for OpenGL Player

```
LOCAL_PATH := $(call my-dir)

include $(CLEAR_VARS)

LOCAL_MODULE    := AVIPlayer
LOCAL_SRC_FILES := \
    Common.cpp \
    com_apress_aviplayer_AbstractPlayerActivity.cpp \
    com_apress_aviplayer_BitmapPlayerActivity.cpp \
    com_apress_aviplayer_OpenGLPlayerActivity.cpp

# Use AVILib static library
LOCAL_STATIC_LIBRARIES += avilib_static

...

# Enable GL ext prototypes
LOCAL_CFLAGS += -DGL_GLEXT_PROTOTYPES

# Link with OpenGL ES
LOCAL_LDLIBS += -lGLESv1_CM

include $(BUILD_SHARED_LIBRARY)

...
```

21. The Bitmap Player activity is now ready. In order to be able to use it, it needs to be added as a radio button to the `activity_main.xml` layout file, as shown in Listing 12-29.

Listing 12-29. OpenGL Player Radio Button Added to the Main Layout

```
<LinearLayout xmlns:android="http://schemas.android.com/apk/res/android"
    xmlns:tools="http://schemas.android.com/tools"
    android:layout_width="match_parent"
    android:layout_height="match_parent"
    android:orientation="vertical" >

    ...

    <RadioGroup
        android:id="@+id/player_radio_group"
        android:layout_width="wrap_content"
        android:layout_height="wrap_content" >
```

```
<RadioButton
    android:id="@+id/bitmap_player_radio"
    android:layout_width="wrap_content"
    android:layout_height="wrap_content"
    android:checked="true"
    android:text="@string/bitmap_player_radio" />

<RadioButton
    android:id="@+id/open_gl_player_radio"
    android:layout_width="wrap_content"
    android:layout_height="wrap_content"
    android:text="@string/open_gl_player_radio" />

</RadioGroup>

...

</LinearLayout>
```

22. The main activity source code should also be modified, as shown in Listing 12-30, to dispatch the playback request to the Bitmap Player activity when it is selected by the user.

Listing 12-30. OpenGL Player Radio Button Added to Main Activity

```
/**
 * On play button click event handler.
 */
private void onPlayButtonClick() {

    ...

    // Choose the activity based on id
    switch (radioId) {
    case R.id.bitmap_player_radio:
        intent = new Intent(this, BitmapPlayerActivity.class);
        break;

    case R.id.open_gl_player_radio:
        intent = new Intent(this, OpenGLPlayerActivity.class);
        break;

    default:
        throw new UnsupportedOperationException("radioId=" + radioId);
    }

    ...
}
```

23.   The AVI player application is now ready with the OpenGL ES renderer. Follow the same steps in JNI Graphics API section of this chapter to run the example application on the Android emulator.

Rendering Using Native Window API

Starting from Android API level 9, the Android NDK provides an API to enable the native code to directly access and manipulate the pixel buffer of the native window. This API is known as the native windows API. In this section, you will learn how to use this API to do rendering from the native code directly without involving any Java based API.

Enabling the Native Window API

Follow these steps to use the Native Window API in your native application.

1.   Include the native window header files.

```
#include <android/native_window.h>
#include <android/native_window_jni.h>
```

2.   Update the Android.mk build file to dynamically link with android library.

```
LOCAL_LDLIBS += -landroid
```

Upon making these changes, the native window API will now be available to your native application.

Using the Native Window API

The native window API provides four native functions for accessing and manipulating the Bitmap objects.

Retrieving Native Window from a Surface Object

The ANativeWindow_fromSurface function retrieves the native window from the given Surface object.

```
ANativeWindow* ANativeWindow_fromSurface(JNIEnv* env,
                                         jobject surface);
```

It takes a JNIEnv interface pointer and a Surface object reference and returns a pointer to the native window instance. The ANativeWindow_fromSurface function also acquires a reference on the returned native window instance, and it needs to be released through the ANativeWindow_release function to prevent memory leaks.

Acquiring a Reference on a Native Window Instance

In order to prevent the native window instance from being deleted, the native code can acquire a reference to it using the ANativeWindow_acquire function.

```
void ANativeWindow_acquire(ANativeWindow* window);
```

Every call to ANativeWindow_acquire function should be balanced by a call to ANativeWindow_release function.

Releasing the Native Window Reference

As mentioned earlier, to prevent memory leaks, each native window reference should be released using the ANativeWindow_release function.

```
void ANativeWindow_release(ANativeWindow* window);
```

The ANativeWindow_release function takes a pointer to the native window instance.

Retrieving Native Window Information

The native window API provides a set of functions for the native code to obtain information regarding the native window such as the dimensions and the pixel format.

- The ANativeWindow_getWidth function can be used to obtain the width of the native window.

- The ANativeWindow_getHeight function can be used to obtain the height of the native window.

- The ANativeWindow_getFormat function can be used to obtain the pixel format of the native window.

Setting the Native Window Buffer Geometry

The dimensions and the pixel format of the native window should match the image data that will be rendered. If the image data dimensions or the pixel format is different, the ANativeWindow_setBuffersGeometry function can be used to reconfigure the native window buffer. The buffer will then get automatically scaled to match the native window.

```
int32_t ANativeWindow_setBuffersGeometry(ANativeWindow* window,
                                         int32_t width,
                                         int32_t height,
                                         int32_t format);
```

The function takes a pointer to the previously acquired native window instance, the new width, the new height, and the new pixel format for the native window buffer. In case of success, it returns zero. For all parameters, if zero is supplied, then the parameter value will be reverted to the native window buffer's base.

Accessing the Native Window Buffer

The ANativeWindow_lock function is used to lock the native window buffer and to obtain a pointer to the raw pixel buffer. Native code can then use this pointer to access and manipulate the pixel buffer.

```
int32_t ANativeWindow_lock(ANativeWindow* window,
                           ANativeWindow_Buffer* outBuffer,
                           ARect* inOutDirtyBounds);
```

The function takes a pointer to the previously acquired native window instance, a pointer to a ANativeWindow_Buffer structure, and an optional pointer to a ARect structure. As shown in Listing 12-31, the ANativeWindow_Buffer structure, in addition to the information about the native window, provides access to native pixel buffer through the bits fields.

Listing 12-31. The ANativeWindow_Buffer Structure Declaration

```
typedef struct ANativeWindow_Buffer {
    // The number of pixels that are show horizontally.
    int32_t width;

    // The number of pixels that are shown vertically.
    int32_t height;

    // The number of *pixels* that a line in the buffer takes in
    // memory.  This may be >= width.
    int32_t stride;

    // The format of the buffer.  One of WINDOW_FORMAT_*
    int32_t format;

    // The actual bits.
    void* bits;

    // Do not touch.
    uint32_t reserved[6];
} ANativeWindow_Buffer;
```

In case of success the ANativeWindow_lock function returns zero.

Releasing the Native Window Buffer

Once the native code is done, it should unlock and post the native window buffer back using the ANativeWindow_unlockAndPost function.

```
int32_t ANativeWindow_unlockAndPost(ANativeWindow* window);
```

The function takes a pointer to the native window instance that is locked. In case of success, it returns zero. You will now update the AVI Player test application with the native window renderer to experiment with these functions.

Updating AVI Player with Native Window Renderer

Follow these steps.

1. Using Project Explorer, open AndroidManifest.xml manifest file and declare the new activity as shown on Listing 12-32.

    Listing 12-32. New Native Window Player Declared in Manifest File

    ```
    <manifest xmlns:android="http://schemas.android.com/apk/res/android"
        package="com.apress.aviplayer"
        android:versionCode="1"
        android:versionName="1.0" >

        ...

        <application
            android:icon="@drawable/ic_launcher"
            android:label="@string/app_name"
            android:theme="@style/AppTheme" >

            ...

            <activity
                android:name=".OpenGLPlayerActivity"
                android:label="@string/title_activity_open_gl_player" >
            </activity>
            <activity
                android:name=".NativeWindowPlayerActivity"
                android:label="@string/title_activity_native_window_player" >
            </activity>
        </application>

    </manifest>
    ```

2. The title of the new Bitmap Player activity, as well as the label for the Bitmap Player radio button should be added to the string resources. Open the strings.xml string resources file and add the new string resources, as shown in Listing 12-33.

    Listing 12-33. Native Window Player Activity String Resources Appended

    ```
    <resources>

        ...

        <string name="title_activity_native_window_player"
                >Native Window Player</string>
        <string name="native_window_player_radio"
                >Native Window Player</string>

    </resources>
    ```

3. The Bitmap Player activity requires a single `SurfaceView` widget in order to function. Using the Project Explorer, expand the `res` directory.

4. Right-click the `layout` subdirectory, and choose **New ➤ File** from the context menu.

5. Set File Name to `activity_native_window_player.xml`.

6. Replace the content of new layout with the code in Listing 12-34.

Listing 12-34. Content of activity_native_window_player.xml Layout File

```xml
<LinearLayout xmlns:android="http://schemas.android.com/apk/res/android"
    xmlns:tools="http://schemas.android.com/tools"
    android:layout_width="match_parent"
    android:layout_height="match_parent" >

    <SurfaceView
        android:layout_width="match_parent"
        android:layout_height="match_parent"
        android:id="@+id/surface_view" />

</LinearLayout>
```

7. Using the Project Explorer, expand the `src` directory.

8. Right-click the `com.apress.aviplayer` package, and choose **New ➤ Class** from the context menu.

9. Set Name to `NativeWindowPlayerActivity`.

10. Click the Finish button to create the new class.

11. Replace its content with the code in Listing 12-35.

Listing 12-35. Content of NativeWindowPlayerActivity.java Source File

```java
package com.apress.aviplayer;

import java.util.concurrent.atomic.AtomicBoolean;

import android.os.Bundle;
import android.view.Surface;
import android.view.SurfaceHolder;
import android.view.SurfaceHolder.Callback;
import android.view.SurfaceView;

/**
 * AVI player through native window.
 *
 * @author Onur Cinar
 */
```

```java
public class NativeWindowPlayerActivity extends AbstractPlayerActivity {
    /** Is playing. */
    private final AtomicBoolean isPlaying = new AtomicBoolean();

    /** Surface holder. */
    private SurfaceHolder surfaceHolder;

    /**
     * On create.
     *
     * @param savedInstanceState saved state.
     */
    public void onCreate(Bundle savedInstanceState) {
        super.onCreate(savedInstanceState);
        setContentView(R.layout.activity_bitmap_player);

        SurfaceView surfaceView = (SurfaceView)
                findViewById(R.id.surface_view);

        surfaceHolder = surfaceView.getHolder();
        surfaceHolder.addCallback(surfaceHolderCallback);
    }

    /**
     * Surface holder callback listens for surface events.
     */
    private final Callback surfaceHolderCallback = new Callback() {
        public void surfaceChanged(SurfaceHolder holder, int format,
                int width,
                int height) {
        }

        public void surfaceCreated(SurfaceHolder holder) {
            // Start playing since surface is ready
            isPlaying.set(true);

            // Start renderer on a separate thread
            new Thread(renderer).start();
        }

        public void surfaceDestroyed(SurfaceHolder holder) {
            // Stop playing since surface is destroyed
            isPlaying.set(false);
        }
    };

    /**
     * Renderer runnable renders the video frames from the
     * AVI file to the surface through a bitmap.
     */
```

```
            private final Runnable renderer = new Runnable() {
                public void run() {
                    // Get the surface instance
                    Surface surface = surfaceHolder.getSurface();

                    // Initialize the native window
                    init(avi, surface);

                    // Calculate the delay using the frame rate
                    long frameDelay = (long) (1000 / getFrameRate(avi));

                    // Start rendering while playing
                    while (isPlaying.get()) {
                        // Render the frame to the surface
                        render(avi, surface);

                        // Wait for the next frame
                        try {
                            Thread.sleep(frameDelay);
                        } catch (InterruptedException e) {
                            break;
                        }
                    }
                }
            };

            /**
             * Initializes the native window.
             *
             * @param avi file descriptor.
             * @param surface surface instance.
             */
            private native static void init(long avi, Surface surface);

            /**
             * Renders the frame from given AVI file descriptor to
             * the given Surface.
             *
             * @param avi file descriptor.
             * @param surface surface instance.
             * @return true if there are more frames, false otherwise.
             */
            private native static boolean render(long avi, Surface surface);
        }
```

12. Choose **Project ➤ Build Project** from the top menu bar to compile the Java
     source code.

13. Using the Project Explorer, select the NativeWindowPlayerActivity.

14. Choose **Run ➤ External Tools ➤ Generate C and C++ Header File** from the
     top menu bar to invoke the javah tool for NativeWindowPlayerActivity class.

15. Under the jni subdirectory of the project, the com_apress_aviplayer_ NativeWindowPlayerActivity.h header file will be generated by the javah tool.

16. Right-click on jni directory, and choose **New ➤ Source File** from the context menu.

17. Set Source File to com_apress_aviplayer_NativeWindowPlayerActivity.cpp.

18. Click the Finish button to create a new C++ source file.

19. Using the Eclipse, replace the content of the new source file with the code in Listing 12-36.

Listing 12-36. Content of com_apress_aviplayer_NativeWindowPlayerActivity.cpp

```
extern "C" {
#include <avilib.h>
}

#include <android/native_window_jni.h>
#include <android/native_window.h>

#include "Common.h"
#include "com_apress_aviplayer_NativeWindowPlayerActivity.h"

void Java_com_apress_aviplayer_NativeWindowPlayerActivity_init(
        JNIEnv* env,
        jclass clazz,
        jlong avi,
        jobject surface)
{
    // Get the native window from the surface
    ANativeWindow* nativeWindow = ANativeWindow_fromSurface(
            env, surface);
    if (0 == nativeWindow)
    {
        ThrowException(env, "java/io/RuntimeException",
                "Unable to get native window from surface.");
        goto exit;
    }

    // Set the buffers geometry to AVI movie frame dimensions
    // If these are different than the window's physical size
    // then the buffer will be scaled to match that size.
    if (0 > ANativeWindow_setBuffersGeometry(nativeWindow,
            AVI_video_width((avi_t*) avi),
            AVI_video_height((avi_t*) avi),
            WINDOW_FORMAT_RGB_565))
    {
        ThrowException(env, "java/io/RuntimeException",
                "Unable to set buffers geometry.");
    }
```

```
    // Release the native window
    ANativeWindow_release(nativeWindow);
    nativeWindow = 0;

exit:
    return;
}

jboolean Java_com_apress_aviplayer_NativeWindowPlayerActivity_render(
        JNIEnv* env,
        jclass clazz,
        jlong avi,
        jobject surface)
{
    jboolean isFrameRead = JNI_FALSE;

    long frameSize = 0;
    int keyFrame = 0;

    // Get the native window from the surface
    ANativeWindow* nativeWindow = ANativeWindow_fromSurface(
            env, surface);
    if (0 == nativeWindow)
    {
        ThrowException(env, "java/io/RuntimeException",
                "Unable to get native window from surface.");
        goto exit;
    }

    // Lock the native window and get access to raw buffer
    ANativeWindow_Buffer windowBuffer;
    if (0 > ANativeWindow_lock(nativeWindow, &windowBuffer, 0))
    {
        ThrowException(env, "java/io/RuntimeException",
                "Unable to lock native window.");
        goto release;
    }

    // Read AVI frame bytes to raw buffer
    frameSize = AVI_read_frame((avi_t*) avi,
            (char*) windowBuffer.bits,
            &keyFrame);

    // Check if frame is successfully read
    if (0 < frameSize)
    {
        isFrameRead = JNI_TRUE;
    }
```

```
    // Unlock and post the buffer for displaying
    if (0 > ANativeWindow_unlockAndPost(nativeWindow))
    {
        ThrowException(env, "java/io/RuntimeException",
                "Unable to unlock and post to native window.");
        goto release;
    }

release:
    // Release the native window
    ANativeWindow_release(nativeWindow);
    nativeWindow = 0;

exit:
    return isFrameRead;
}
```

20. The build file Android.mk needs to be modified, as shown in Listing 12-37, to
     compile the new source file, as well as to dynamically link with the android
     shared library in order to use the native window API.

Listing 12-37. Build File Modified for Native Window Player

```
LOCAL_PATH := $(call my-dir)

include $(CLEAR_VARS)

LOCAL_MODULE    := AVIPlayer
LOCAL_SRC_FILES := \
    Common.cpp \
    com_apress_aviplayer_AbstractPlayerActivity.cpp \
    com_apress_aviplayer_BitmapPlayerActivity.cpp \
    com_apress_aviplayer_OpenGLPlayerActivity.cpp \
    com_apress_aviplayer_NativeWindowPlayerActivity.cpp

...

# Link with Android library
LOCAL_LDLIBS += -landroid

include $(BUILD_SHARED_LIBRARY)

...
```

21. The Bitmap Player activity is now ready. In order to be able to use it, it needs
     to be added as a radio button to the activity_main.xml layout file, as shown
     in Listing 12-38.

Listing 12-38. Native Window Player Radio Button Added to the Main Layout

```
<LinearLayout xmlns:android="http://schemas.android.com/apk/res/android"
    xmlns:tools="http://schemas.android.com/tools"
    android:layout_width="match_parent"
    android:layout_height="match_parent"
    android:orientation="vertical" >

    ...

    <RadioGroup
        android:id="@+id/player_radio_group"
        android:layout_width="wrap_content"
        android:layout_height="wrap_content" >

        ...

        <RadioButton
            android:id="@+id/open_gl_player_radio"
            android:layout_width="wrap_content"
            android:layout_height="wrap_content"
            android:text="@string/open_gl_player_radio" />

        <RadioButton
            android:id="@+id/native_window_player_radio"
            android:layout_width="wrap_content"
            android:layout_height="wrap_content"
            android:text="@string/native_window_player_radio" />

    </RadioGroup>

    ...

</LinearLayout>
```

22. The main activity source code should also be modified, as shown in Listing
     12-39, to dispatch the playback request to Bitmap Player activity when it is
     selected by the user.

Listing 12-39. Native Window Player Radio Button Added to Main Activity

```
/**
 * On play button click event handler.
 */
private void onPlayButtonClick() {

    ...

    // Choose the activity based on id
    switch (radioId) {
```

```
    case R.id.bitmap_player_radio:
        intent = new Intent(this, BitmapPlayerActivity.class);
        break;

    case R.id.open_gl_player_radio:
        intent = new Intent(this, OpenGLPlayerActivity.class);
        break;

    case R.id.native_window_player_radio:
        intent = new Intent(this, NativeWindowPlayerActivity.class);
        break;

    default:
        throw new UnsupportedOperationException("radioId=" + radioId);
    }

    ...
}
```

23. The AVI player application is now ready with the native window renderer.
     Follow the same steps given in "JNI Graphics API" section of this chapter to
     run the example application on the Android emulator.

EGL Graphics Library

Starting from API Level 9, the Android NDK also comes with support from EGL graphics library,
enabling the native applications to manage OpenGL ES surfaces. More information on EGL can be
found at Khronos Group's web site at www.khronos.org/egl.

In order to enable EGL graphics library, follow these steps.

1. Include the EGL header files.

    ```
    #include <EGL/egl.h>
    #include <EGL/eglext.h>
    ```

2. Update the Android.mk build file to dynamically link with EGL library.

    ```
    LOCAL_LDLIBS += -lEGL
    ```

Upon making these changes, the EGL graphics library will now be available to your native
application. You can use the EGL graphics library API functions to list supported EGL configurations,
allocate and release OpenGL ES surfaces, and swap/flip surfaces for display.

Summary

This chapter explored the different native graphics APIs that are available to native applications. In
order to help you better understand these graphics native APIs, an AVI video player application was
built throughout this chapter.

## Chapter 13

Native Sound API

In the previous chapter, you explored the multiple flavors of the native graphics APIs that are provided by the Android platform. Starting from Android OS version 2.3, API Level 9, the Android platform also provides a native sound API, enabling the native code to play and record audio without invoking any method at Java layer. Android native sound support is based on the OpenSL ES 1.0.1 standard from Khronos Group. OpenSL ES is the short form of the *Open Sound Library for Embedded Systems*. This chapter will briefly demonstrate the OpenSL ES native sound API pertaining to Android platform.

Using the OpenSL ES API

As the OpenSL ES specification is large, this chapter will only cover the pieces that pertain to the Android platform. More information on OpenSL ES can be found at `$ANDROID_NDK_HOME/docs/opensles/OpenSL_ES_Specification_1.0.1.pdf`.

1. The OpenSL ES API is exposed through a set of header files. The main header file that needs to be included is the `SLES/OpenSLES.h`.

    ```
    #include <SLES/OpenSLES.h>
    ```

2. In order to use the Android extensions, the `SLES/OpenSLES_Android.h` header file should also be included in the source file.

    ```
    #include <SLES/OpenSLES_Android.h>
    ```

3. The OpenSL ES native sound API also requires having a library linked dynamically with the native module. This is achieved by adding the following line to the `Android.mk` build script:

    ```
    LOCAL_LDLIBS += -lOpenSLES
    ```

The Android platform is committed to binary compatibility for applications that are using OpenSL ES. By simply linking with this shared library, the same application is expected to work seamlessly on the feature versions of the platform.

Compatibility with the OpenSL ES Standard

Although it is based on the OpenSL ES 1.0.1 specification, the Android native sound API is not a conforming implementation of any OpenSL ES profile. The Android-specific portions of this implementation are exposed through the Android Extensions API. More information about the Android Extensions can be found in Android NDK documentation at $ANDROID_NDK_HOME/docs/opensles/index.html.

Audio Permissions

In terms of permissions, using the native sound API is not any different from using the Java-based sound API. The application is expected to request the proper permissions, through the uses-permission tag, in its manifest file.

- android.permission.RECORD_AUDIO is needed to create an audio recorder.

- android.permission.MODIFY_AUDIO_SETTINGS is needed to change audio settings and also to use effects.

Creating the WAVE Audio Player

The WAVE audio player application will act as a test bed to demonstrate the OpenSL ES-based native audio playback on the Android platform. The example application will provide the following:

- The Android application project with native code support.

- A statically linked WAVE library to parse WAVE audio files in native code.

- OpenSL ES-based WAVE audio file playback support.

- A simple GUI to specify the WAVE file from the SD card for playback.

Playing WAVE audio files requires parsing of WAVE files. Although WAVE format is not very complex, for the sake of simplicity, a third party WAVE library will be used to handle the WAVE files.

> **Note**   Full source code of this example application can be downloaded from the publisher's web site at www.apress.com.

Make WAVELib a NDK Import Module

The AVILib library that you used in Chapter 10 also comes with WAVE audio file support through the WAVELib. Follow these steps to make WAVELib available as a NDK import module.

1. Open up a Terminal window if you are using Mac OS or Linux; otherwise Cygwin if you are using Windows.

2. Change the current directory to Android NDK import module directory for AVILib (that you installed in Chapter 10) by issuing the following command:

   ```
   cd $ANDROID_NDK_HOME/sources/transcode-1.1.5/avilib
   ```

3. Open up the Android.mk build script in Eclipse. Append the import module description for both static and shared WAVELib library as shown in Listing 13-1.

   Listing 13-1. Android.mk Build File with WAVELib Import Module Changes

   ```
   LOCAL_PATH := $(call my-dir)

   ...

   #
   # Transcode WAVLib
   #

   # Source files
   MY_WAVLIB_SRC_FILES := wavlib.c platform_posix.c

   # Include path to export
   MY_WAVLIB_C_INCLUDES := $(LOCAL_PATH)

   #
   # WAVLib static
   #
   include $(CLEAR_VARS)

   # Module name
   LOCAL_MODULE := wavlib_static

   # Source files
   LOCAL_SRC_FILES := $(MY_WAVLIB_SRC_FILES)

   # Include path to export
   LOCAL_EXPORT_C_INCLUDES := $(MY_WAVLIB_C_INCLUDES)

   # Build a static library
   include $(BUILD_STATIC_LIBRARY)
   ```

```
#
# WAVLib shared
#
include $(CLEAR_VARS)

# Module name
LOCAL_MODULE := wavlib_shared

# Source files
LOCAL_SRC_FILES := $(MY_WAVLIB_SRC_FILES)

# Include path to export
LOCAL_EXPORT_C_INCLUDES := $(MY_WAVLIB_C_INCLUDES)

# Build a shared library
include $(BUILD_SHARED_LIBRARY)
```

Upon making these changes, WAVELib is now available as both a static and a shared library for native modules. The WAVELib is now ready to be used in the example WAVE player application.

Create the WAVE Player Android Application

In order to create the WAVE player application, launch the New Android Application Project dialog and follow these steps.

1. Set Application Name to WAV Player.

2. Set Project Name to WAV Player.

3. Set Package Name to com.apress.wavplayer.

4. Click the Next button to accept the default values on the current and following wizard pages.

5. Once the Android application project is created, using the Project Explorer, launch the Add Android Native Support wizard through the Android Tools context menu.

6. Set Library Name to WAVPlayer.

7. Click the Finish button to add native support to the new project.

Creating the WAVE Player Main Activity

The main activity will provide a simple GUI to specify the WAVE audio file to play from the SD card. Follow these steps to implement the main activity.

1. Using the Project Explorer, expand the res directory for the resources. Populate the string resources by opening the string.xml file from the values sub-directory, and replace its content as shown in Listing 13-2.

Listing 13-2. Content of res/values/string.xml String Resources File

```
<resources>
    <string name="app_name">WAV Player</string>
    <string name="menu_settings">Settings</string>
    <string name="title_activity_main">MainActivity</string>
    <string name="file_name_hint">WAV file</string>
    <string name="play_button">Play</string>
    <string name="error_alert_title">Error Occurred</string>
    <string name="file_name">8k16bitpcm.wav</string>
</resources>
```

2. The main activity provides a simple GUI with a text field to specify the WAVE audio file name, and a Play button to start the playback using OpenSL ES with native code. Using the Project Explorer, expand the `layout` sub-directory from `res` resource directory. Open the `activity_main.xml` layout file, and replace its content as shown in Listing 13-3.

Listing 13-3. Content of res/layout/activity_main.xml Layout File

```
<LinearLayout xmlns:android="http://schemas.android.com/apk/res/android"
    xmlns:tools="http://schemas.android.com/tools"
    android:id="@+id/LinearLayout1"
    android:layout_width="match_parent"
    android:layout_height="match_parent"
    android:orientation="vertical" >

    <EditText
        android:id="@+id/fileNameEdit"
        android:layout_width="match_parent"
        android:layout_height="wrap_content"
        android:ems="10"
        android:hint="@string/file_name_hint"
        android:text="@string/file_name" >

        <requestFocus />
    </EditText>

    <Button
        android:id="@+id/playButton"
        android:layout_width="wrap_content"
        android:layout_height="wrap_content"
        android:text="@string/play_button" />

</LinearLayout>
```

3.   Now you will implement the main activity. The main activity starts an asynchronous play task to start the playback of the specified WAVE audio file through the play native method that you will be implementing later in this chapter using the OpenSL ES. Using the Project Explorer, open up the MainActivity.java source file, and replace its content as shown in Listing 13-4.

Listing 13-4. Content of MainActivity.java Source File

```java
package com.apress.wavplayer;

import java.io.File;
import java.io.IOException;

import android.app.Activity;
import android.app.AlertDialog;
import android.os.AsyncTask;
import android.os.Bundle;
import android.os.Environment;
import android.view.View;
import android.view.View.OnClickListener;
import android.widget.Button;
import android.widget.EditText;

/**
 * WAVE player main activity.
 *
 * @author Onur Cinar
 */
public class MainActivity extends Activity implements OnClickListener {
    /** File name edit text. */
    private EditText fileNameEdit;

    /**
     * On create.
     *
     * @param savedInstanceState
     *              saved state.
     */
    public void onCreate(Bundle savedInstanceState) {
        super.onCreate(savedInstanceState);
        setContentView(R.layout.activity_main);

        fileNameEdit = (EditText) findViewById(R.id.fileNameEdit);
        Button playButton = (Button) findViewById(R.id.playButton);
        playButton.setOnClickListener(this);
    }
```

```java
/**
 * On click.
 *
 * @param view
 *            view instance.
 */
public void onClick(View view) {
    switch (view.getId()) {
    case R.id.playButton:
        onPlayButtonClick();
    }
}

/**
 * On play button click.
 */
private void onPlayButtonClick() {
    // Under the external storage
    File file = new File(Environment.getExternalStorageDirectory(),
            fileNameEdit.getText().toString());

    // Start player
    PlayTask playTask = new PlayTask();
    playTask.execute(file.getAbsolutePath());
}

/**
 * Play task.
 */
private class PlayTask extends AsyncTask<String, Void, Exception> {
    /**
     * Background task.
     *
     * @param file
     *            WAVE file.
     */
    protected Exception doInBackground(String... file) {
        Exception result = null;

        try {
            // Play the WAVE file
            play(file[0]);
        } catch (IOException ex) {
            result = ex;
        }

        return result;
    }
```

```
        /**
         * Post execute.
         *
         * @param ex
         *              exception instance.
         */
        protected void onPostExecute(Exception ex) {
            // Show error message if playing failed
            if (ex != null) {
                new AlertDialog.Builder(MainActivity.this)
                        .setTitle(R.string.error_alert_title)
                        .setMessage(ex.getMessage()).show();
            }
        }
    }

    /**
     * Plays the given WAVE file using native sound API.
     *
     * @param fileName
     *              file name.
     * @throws IOException
     */
    private native void play(String fileName) throws IOException;

    static {
        System.loadLibrary("WAVPlayer");
    }
}
```

The Java portion of the WAVE player application is now ready. You will now start implementing the native Play button to play the specified WAVE audio file using the OpenSL ES library.

Implementing WAVE Audio Playback

Prior starting to implement the native portion of the WAVE audio player application, build the Java portion of the application and make sure that it compiles. Follow these steps to implement the playback functionality.

1. Using the Project Explorer, select the MainActivity.java source file and Choose **Run ➤ External Tools ➤ Generate C and C++ header file** from the top menu bar to generate the com_apress_wavplayer_MainActivity.h header file declaring the native method.

2. The Android.mk build script for the project needs to be modified to statically link with the wavelib_static library for WAVE file format support and dynamically link with the OpenSLES library to use OpenSL ES native sound API. Open up the build script in Eclipse, and replace its content as shown in Listing 13-5.

Listing 13-5. Content of jni/Android.mk Build Script

```
LOCAL_PATH := $(call my-dir)

include $(CLEAR_VARS)

LOCAL_MODULE     := WAVPlayer
LOCAL_SRC_FILES := WAVPlayer.cpp

# Use WAVLib static library
LOCAL_STATIC_LIBRARIES += wavlib_static

# Link with OpenSL ES
LOCAL_LDLIBS += -lOpenSLES

include $(BUILD_SHARED_LIBRARY)

# Import WAVLib library module
$(call import-module, transcode-1.1.5/avilib)
```

3. Open up the WAVPlayer.cpp native source file in Eclipse. Start by including the necessary header files to use both OpenSL ES API and also the WAVLib API, as shown in Listing 13-6.

Listing 13-6. Headers Files Included in jni/WAVPlayer.cpp Source File

```
#include "com_apress_wavplayer_MainActivity.h"

#include <SLES/OpenSLES.h>
#include <SLES/OpenSLES_Android.h>

extern "C" {
#include <wavlib.h>
}

static const char* JAVA_LANG_IOEXCEPTION = "java/lang/IOException";
static const char* JAVA_LANG_OUTOFMEMORYERROR =
        "java/lang/OutOfMemoryError";

#define ARRAY_LEN(a) (sizeof(a) / sizeof(a[0]))
```

4. The OpenSL ES native sound API is designed to operate in asynchronous way. Throughout the playback, a specified callback function will get invoked by the OpenSL ES engine to provide the audio data. This function will need access to the player context in order to render its functionality. The PlayerContext structure will be used to feed the player context into that callback function when it gets registered. The PlayerContext structure holds OpenSL ES and WAVLib constructs, and also the audio buffer. Append the PlayerContext to WAVPlayer.cpp source file as shown in Listing 13-7.

Listing 13-7. PlayerContext Structure to Hold the Native Context

```
/**
 * Player context.
 */
struct PlayerContext
{
    SLObjectItf engineObject;
    SLEngineItf engineEngine;
    SLObjectItf outputMixObject;
    SLObjectItf audioPlayerObject;
    SLAndroidSimpleBufferQueueItf audioPlayerBufferQueue;
    SLPlayItf audioPlayerPlay;
    WAV wav;

    unsigned char* buffer;
    size_t bufferSize;

    PlayerContext()
    : engineObject(0)
    , engineEngine(0)
    , outputMixObject(0)
    , audioPlayerBufferQueue(0)
    , audioPlayerPlay(0)
    , wav(0)
    , bufferSize(0)
    {}
};
```

5. The `ThrowException` is a helper function to easily throw exceptions to Java layer when an error occurs in the native code. Append this function to the source file as shown in Listing 13-8.

Listing 13-8. ThrowException Helper Function

```
/**
 * Throw exception with given class and message.
 *
 * @param env JNIEnv interface.
 * @param className class name.
 * @param message exception message.
 */
static void ThrowException(
        JNIEnv* env,
        const char* className,
        const char* message)
{
    // Get the exception class
    jclass clazz = env->FindClass(className);
```

```
        // If exception class is found
        if (0 != clazz)
        {
            // Throw exception
            env->ThrowNew(clazz, message);

            // Release local class reference
            env->DeleteLocalRef(clazz);
        }
    }
}
```

6. The OpenWaveFile function opens the given WAVE audio file, and CloseWaveFile releases the file once it is no longer needed. If an error occurs, both of these functions throws an IOException to inform the Java application, and the error gets displayed in an alert dialog to inform the user. Append these functions to the source file as shown in Listing 13-9.

Listing 13-9. The WAVLib Helper Functions to Open and Close WAVE Files

```
/**
 * Open the given WAVE file.
 *
 * @param env JNIEnv interface.
 * @param fileName file name.
 * @return WAV file.
 * @throws IOException
 */
static WAV OpenWaveFile(
        JNIEnv* env,
        jstring fileName)
{
    WAVError error = WAV_SUCCESS;
    WAV wav = 0;

    // Get the file name as a C string
    const char* cFileName = env->GetStringUTFChars(fileName, 0);
    if (0 == cFileName)
        goto exit;

    // Open the WAVE file
    wav = wav_open(cFileName, WAV_READ, &error);

    // Release the file name
    env->ReleaseStringUTFChars(fileName, cFileName);

    // Check error
    if (0 == wav)
```

```
        {
            ThrowException(env,
                    JAVA_LANG_IOEXCEPTION,
                    wav_strerror(error));
        }
    exit:
        return wav;
    }

    /**
     * Close the given WAVE file.
     *
     * @param wav WAV file.
     * @throws IOException
     */
    static void CloseWaveFile(
            WAV wav)
    {
        if (0 != wav)
        {
            wav_close(wav);
        }
    }
```

7. The OpenSL ES function calls can fail due to many different issues. Each OpenSL ES function call returns a result code in SLresult type. OpenSL ES does not provide any function to translate these result codes to human readable messages. The ResultToString helper function fills this gap. It takes a result code and returns the corresponding error message. Append the ResultToString function as shown in Listing 13-10.

Listing 13-10. ResultToString Helper Function to Translate Result Code

```
/**
 * Convert OpenSL ES result to string.
 *
 * @param result result code.
 * @return result string.
 */
static const char* ResultToString(SLresult result)
{
    const char* str = 0;

    switch (result)
    {
    case SL_RESULT_SUCCESS:
        str = "Success";
        break;
```

```
case SL_RESULT_PRECONDITIONS_VIOLATED:
    str = "Preconditions violated";
    break;

case SL_RESULT_PARAMETER_INVALID:
    str = "Parameter invalid";
    break;

case SL_RESULT_MEMORY_FAILURE:
    str = "Memory failure";
    break;

case SL_RESULT_RESOURCE_ERROR:
    str = "Resource error";
    break;

case SL_RESULT_RESOURCE_LOST:
    str = "Resource lost";
    break;

case SL_RESULT_IO_ERROR:
    str = "IO error";
    break;

case SL_RESULT_BUFFER_INSUFFICIENT:
    str = "Buffer insufficient";
    break;

case SL_RESULT_CONTENT_CORRUPTED:
    str = "Success";
    break;

case SL_RESULT_CONTENT_UNSUPPORTED:
    str = "Content unsupported";
    break;

case SL_RESULT_CONTENT_NOT_FOUND:
    str = "Content not found";
    break;

case SL_RESULT_PERMISSION_DENIED:
    str = "Permission denied";
    break;

case SL_RESULT_FEATURE_UNSUPPORTED:
    str = "Feature unsupported";
    break;

case SL_RESULT_INTERNAL_ERROR:
    str = "Internal error";
    break;
```

```
        case SL_RESULT_UNKNOWN_ERROR:
            str = "Unknown error";
            break;

        case SL_RESULT_OPERATION_ABORTED:
            str = "Operation aborted";
            break;

        case SL_RESULT_CONTROL_LOST:
            str = "Control lost";
            break;

        default:
            str = "Unknown code";
    }

    return str;
}
```

8. The CheckError helper function throws an IOException if the result code
   indicates an error. It relies on ResultToString function to translate the result
   code to a message. Append the CheckError function as shown in Listing 13-11.

   Listing 13-11. CheckError Function to Throw an Exception in Case of Error

```
/**
 * Checks if the result is an error, and throws
 * and IOException with the error message.
 *
 * @param env JNIEnv interface.
 * @param result result code.
 * @return error occurred.
 * @throws IOException
 */
static bool CheckError(
        JNIEnv* env,
        SLresult result)
{
    bool isError = false;

    // If an error occurred
    if (SL_RESULT_SUCCESS != result)
    {
        // Throw IOException
        ThrowException(env,
                JAVA_LANG_IOEXCEPTION,
                ResultToString(result));
```

```
            isError = true;
    }

    return isError;
}
```

9. Although the OpenSL ES API is C based, it adopts an object-oriented
   approach. Every construct of OpenSL ES is built on the top of two main
   constructs: object and interface. An object is an abstract set of resources
   assigned for well-defined tasks. An interface is an abstract set of related
   features that an object can provide. An object may expose one or more
   interfaces. Objects can be created through either the engine object or
   through the object interface. Every OpenSL ES application starts by first
   creating an engine object in order to access the rest of the API. The engine
   is created through the slCreateEngine API. The CreateEngine helper function
   relies on that function to create an engine object and throws an IOException
   if it fails. Append the CreateEngine function to the source code as shown in
   Listing 13-12.

Listing 13-12. CreateEngine Function to Create the Engine Object

```
/**
 * Creates an OpenGL ES engine.
 *
 * @param env JNIEnv interface.
 * @param engineObject object to hold engine. [OUT]
 * @throws IOException
 */
static void CreateEngine(
        JNIEnv* env,
        SLObjectItf& engineObject)
{
    // OpenSL ES for Android is designed to be thread-safe,
    // so this option request will be ignored, but it will
    // make the source code portable to other platforms.
    SLEngineOption engineOptions[] = {
        { (SLuint32) SL_ENGINEOPTION_THREADSAFE,
          (SLuint32) SL_BOOLEAN_TRUE }
    };

    // Create the OpenSL ES engine object
    SLresult result = slCreateEngine(
            &engineObject,
            ARRAY_LEN(engineOptions),
            engineOptions,
            0, // no interfaces
            0, // no interfaces
            0); // no required
```

```
    // Check error
    CheckError(env, result);
}
```

10. Once the object is created, it is in unrealized state where the object is alive but has not allocated any resources. It needs to be realized first to become usable. This is achieved through the `Realize` method that is exposed by the Object Interface. The `RealizeObject` helper function realizes the objects and throws an `IOException` if it fails. Append the function to the source file as shown in Listing 13-13.

Listing 13-13. RealizeObject Function to Realize Object Instances

```
/**
 * Realize the given object. Objects needs to be
 * realized before using them.
 *
 * @param env JNIEnv interface.
 * @param object object instance.
 * @throws IOException
 */
static void RealizeObject(
        JNIEnv* env,
        SLObjectItf object)
{
    // Realize the engine object
    SLresult result = (*object)->Realize(
            object,
            SL_BOOLEAN_FALSE); // No async, blocking call

    // Check error
    CheckError(env, result);
}
```

11. Once the object is no longer needed, it needs to be destroyed in order to release the allocated resources. This is achieved through the `Destroy` method that is exposed by the Object Interface. Append the `DestroyObject` function to the source code as shown in Listing 13-14.

Listing 13-14. DestroyObject Function to Destroy Unused Objects

```
/**
 * Destroys the given object instance.
 *
 * @param object object instance. [IN/OUT]
 */
```

```
static void DestroyObject(SLObjectItf& object)
{
    if (0 != object)
        (*object)->Destroy(object);

    object = 0;
}
```

12. Each object can expose one or more interfaces. These interfaces can be obtained through the GetInterface method that is exposed by the Object Interface. The GetEngineInterface helper function gets the Engine Interface from the given Engine Object. Append the function to the source file as shown in Listing 13-15.

Listing 13-15. GetEngineInterface Function to Obtain Engine Interface

```
/**
 * Gets the engine interface from the given engine object
 * in order to create other objects from the engine.
 *
 * @param env JNIEnv interface.
 * @param engineObject engine object.
 * @param engineEngine engine interface. [OUT]
 * @throws IOException
 */
static void GetEngineInterface(
        JNIEnv* env,
        SLObjectItf& engineObject,
        SLEngineItf& engineEngine)
{
    // Get the engine interface
    SLresult result = (*engineObject)->GetInterface(
            engineObject,
            SL_IID_ENGINE,
            &engineEngine);

    // Check error
    CheckError(env, result);
}
```

13. The CreateOutputMix function creates an Output Mixer object by invoking the CreateOutputMix method of the Engine Interface with a set of parameters. Append the CreateOutputMix function to the source file as shown in Listing 13-16.

Listing 13-16. CreateOutputMix Function to Create an Output Mixer

```
/**
 * Creates and output mix object.
 *
 * @param env JNIEnv interface.
```

```
 * @param engineEngine engine engine.
 * @param outputMixObject object to hold the output mix. [OUT]
 * @throws IOException
 */
static void CreateOutputMix(
        JNIEnv* env,
        SLEngineItf engineEngine,
        SLObjectItf& outputMixObject)
{
    // Create output mix object
    SLresult result = (*engineEngine)->CreateOutputMix(
            engineEngine,
            &outputMixObject,
            0, // no interfaces
            0, // no interfaces
            0); // no required

    // Check error
    CheckError(env, result);
}
```

14. The InitPlayerBuffer helper function creates a byte buffer to hold the audio data chunks, and the FreePlayerBuffers handles releasing of this buffer once it is no longer needed. The InitPlayerBuffer function consults to WAVE audio file header to come up with the appropriate buffer size based on the input file. Append these functions to the source code as shown in Listing 13-17.

Listing 13-17. InitPlayerBuffer and FreePlayerBuffer Helper Functions

```
/**
 * Free the player buffer.
 *
 * @param buffers buffer instance. [OUT]
 */
static void FreePlayerBuffer(unsigned char*& buffers)
{
    if (0 != buffers)
    {
        delete buffers;
        buffers = 0;
    }
}

/**
 * Initializes the player buffer.
 *
 * @param env JNIEnv interface.
 * @param wav WAVE file.
 * @param buffers buffer instance. [OUT]
 * @param bufferSize buffer size. [OUT]
 */
```

```
static void InitPlayerBuffer(
        JNIEnv* env,
        WAV wav,
        unsigned char*& buffer,
        size_t& bufferSize)
{
    // Calculate the buffer size
    bufferSize = wav_get_channels(wav) * wav_get_rate(wav)
                * wav_get_bits(wav);

    // Initialize buffer
    buffer = new unsigned char[bufferSize];
    if (0 == buffer)
    {
        ThrowException(env,
                JAVA_LANG_OUTOFMEMORYERROR,
                "buffer");
    }
}
```

15. In order to play the WAVE audio file through OpenSL ES, an audio player with a buffer queue will be used. The CreateBufferQueueAudioPlayer function creates an Android simple buffer queue with a single buffer slot as the audio source. For better quality, you may choose to have more buffers slots as appropriate. The function consults the WAVE audio file header to define the parameters for the PCM playback. The output of the audio player gets set to the Output Mixer. Append the function as shown in Listing 13-18.

Listing 13-18. CreateBufferQueueAudioPlayer Function

```
/**
 * Creates buffer queue audio player.
 *
 * @param wav WAVE file.
 * @param engineEngine engine interface.
 * @param outputMixObject output mix.
 * @param audioPlayerObject audio player. [OUT]
 * @throws IOException
 */
static void CreateBufferQueueAudioPlayer(
        WAV wav,
        SLEngineItf engineEngine,
        SLObjectItf outputMixObject,
        SLObjectItf& audioPlayerObject)
{
    // Android simple buffer queue locator for the data source
    SLDataLocator_AndroidSimpleBufferQueue dataSourceLocator = {
        SL_DATALOCATOR_ANDROIDSIMPLEBUFFERQUEUE, // locator type
        1                                        // buffer count
    };
```

```
                    // PCM data source format
                    SLDataFormat_PCM dataSourceFormat = {
                        SL_DATAFORMAT_PCM,       // format type
                        wav_get_channels(wav),   // channel count
                        wav_get_rate(wav) * 1000, // samples per second in millihertz
                        wav_get_bits(wav),       // bits per sample
                        wav_get_bits(wav),       // container size
                        SL_SPEAKER_FRONT_CENTER, // channel mask
                        SL_BYTEORDER_LITTLEENDIAN // endianness
                    };

                    // Data source is a simple buffer queue with PCM format
                    SLDataSource dataSource = {
                        &dataSourceLocator, // data locator
                        &dataSourceFormat   // data format
                    };

                    // Output mix locator for data sink
                    SLDataLocator_OutputMix dataSinkLocator = {
                        SL_DATALOCATOR_OUTPUTMIX, // locator type
                        outputMixObject           // output mix
                    };

                    // Data sink is an output mix
                    SLDataSink dataSink = {
                        &dataSinkLocator, // locator
                        0                 // format
                    };

                    // Interfaces that are requested
                    SLInterfaceID interfaceIds[] = {
                        SL_IID_BUFFERQUEUE
                    };

                    // Required interfaces. If the required interfaces
                    // are not available the request will fail
                    SLboolean requiredInterfaces[] = {
                        SL_BOOLEAN_TRUE // for SL_IID_BUFFERQUEUE
                    };

                    // Create audio player object
                    SLresult result = (*engineEngine)->CreateAudioPlayer(
                            engineEngine,
                            &audioPlayerObject,
                            &dataSource,
                            &dataSink,
                            ARRAY_LEN(interfaceIds),
                            interfaceIds,
                            requiredInterfaces);
                }
```

16. The buffer is managed through the Buffer Queue Interface. Through this interface, buffers can be queued for playback, and a callback can be registered to receive a notification once the queued buffer is fully consumed by the audio player. Append the function to the source file as shown in Listing 13-19.

Listing 13-19. GetAudioPlayerBufferQueueInterface Function

```
/**
 * Gets the audio player buffer queue interface.
 *
 * @param env JNIEnv interface.
 * @param audioPlayerObject audio player object instance.
 * @param audioPlayerBufferQueue audio player buffer queue. [OUT]
 * @throws IOException
 */
static void GetAudioPlayerBufferQueueInterface(
        JNIEnv* env,
        SLObjectItf audioPlayerObject,
        SLAndroidSimpleBufferQueueItf& audioPlayerBufferQueue)
{
    // Get the buffer queue interface
    SLresult result = (*audioPlayerObject)->GetInterface(
            audioPlayerObject,
            SL_IID_BUFFERQUEUE,
            &audioPlayerBufferQueue);

    // Check error
    CheckError(env, result);
}
```

17. The DestroyContext function will be used to release the OpenSL ES resources and the buffer once the player is terminated. Append the function as shown in Listing 13-20.

Listing 13-20. DestroyContext Function to Release Player Context

```
/**
 * Destroy the player context.
 *
 * @param ctx player context.
 */
static void DestroyContext(PlayerContext*& ctx)
{
    // Destroy audio player object
    DestroyObject(ctx->audioPlayerObject);

    // Free the player buffer
    FreePlayerBuffer(ctx->buffer);
```

```
    // Destroy output mix object
    DestroyObject(ctx->outputMixObject);

    // Destroy the engine instance
    DestroyObject(ctx->engineObject);

    // Close the WAVE file
    CloseWaveFile(ctx->wav);

    // Free context
    delete ctx;
    ctx = 0;
}
```

18. The `PlayerCallback` gets invoked by the OpenSL ES audio player object once the player finished playing the previously queued buffer. In this callback, the application simply reads and queues the next audio data chunk for playback. The `DestroyContext` function gets invoked to release the resources if the end of the WAVE audio file is reached. Append the function to the source code as shown in Listing 13-21.

Listing 13-21. PlayerCallback Function

```
/**
 * Gets called when a buffer finishes playing.
 *
 * @param audioPlayerBufferQueue audio player buffer queue.
 * @param context player context.
 */
static void PlayerCallback(
        SLAndroidSimpleBufferQueueItf audioPlayerBufferQueue,
        void* context)
{
    // Get the player context
    PlayerContext* ctx = (PlayerContext*) context;

    // Read data
    ssize_t readSize = wav_read_data(
            ctx->wav,
            ctx->buffer,
            ctx->bufferSize);

    // If data is read
    if (0 < readSize)
    {
        (*audioPlayerBufferQueue)->Enqueue(
                audioPlayerBufferQueue,
                ctx->buffer,
                readSize);
    }
```

```
        else
        {
            DestroyContext(ctx);
        }
    }
```

19. The PlayerCallback gets registered via the RegisterCallback function that is exposed through the Buffer Queue Interface. During the registration, a context pointer can be provided so that the callback function receives this context pointer once it is invoked by the audio player. Append the source code as shown in Listing 13-22.

Listing 13-22. RegisterPlayerCallback Function

```
/**
 * Registers the player callback.
 *
 * @param env JNIEnv interface.
 * @param audioPlayerBufferQueue audio player buffer queue.
 * @param ctx player context.
 * @throws IOException
 */
static void RegisterPlayerCallback(
        JNIEnv* env,
        SLAndroidSimpleBufferQueueItf audioPlayerBufferQueue,
        PlayerContext* ctx)
{
    // Register the player callback
    SLresult result = (*audioPlayerBufferQueue)->RegisterCallback(
            audioPlayerBufferQueue,
            PlayerCallback,
            ctx); // player context

    // Check error
    CheckError(env, result);
}
```

20. The Play Interface is used to interact with the audio player. The GetAudioPlayerPlayInterface helper function gets the Play Interface from the given Audio Player Object, as shown in Listing 13-23.

Listing 13-23. GetAudioPlayerPlayInterface Function

```
/**
 * Gets the audio player play interface.
 *
 * @param env JNIEnv interface.
 * @param audioPlayerObject audio player object instance.
 * @param audioPlayerPlay play interface. [OUT]
 * @throws IOException
 */
```

```
        static void GetAudioPlayerPlayInterface(
                JNIEnv* env,
                SLObjectItf audioPlayerObject,
                SLPlayItf& audioPlayerPlay)
    {
        // Get the play interface
        SLresult result = (*audioPlayerObject)->GetInterface(
                audioPlayerObject,
                SL_IID_PLAY,
                &audioPlayerPlay);

        // Check error
        CheckError(env, result);
    }
```

21. The audio player can be started via the SetPlayState method that is exposed
    through the Play Interface. Once it is set to playing state, the audio player
    starts waiting for buffers to be queued. The SetAudioPlayerStatePlaying
    function sets the audio player state to playing, as shown in Listing 13-24.

    Listing 13-24. SetAudioPlayerStatePlaying Function

```
    /**
     * Sets the audio player state playing.
     *
     * @param env JNIEnv interface.
     * @param audioPlayerPlay play interface.
     * @throws IOException
     */
    static void SetAudioPlayerStatePlaying(
            JNIEnv* env,
            SLPlayItf audioPlayerPlay)
    {
        // Set audio player state to playing
        SLresult result = (*audioPlayerPlay)->SetPlayState(
                audioPlayerPlay,
                SL_PLAYSTATE_PLAYING);

        // Check error
        CheckError(env, result);
    }
```

22. Now all the functions are ready. The play native method implements the
    player flow by relying on the helper functions that you have implemented
    earlier, as shown in Listing 13-25.

Listing 13-25. Play Native Method Implementing the Player Logic

```
void Java_com_apress_wavplayer_MainActivity_play(
        JNIEnv* env,
        jobject obj,
        jstring fileName)
{
    PlayerContext* ctx = new PlayerContext();

    // Open the WAVE file
    ctx->wav = OpenWaveFile(env, fileName);
    if (0 != env->ExceptionOccurred())
        goto exit;

    // Create OpenSL ES engine
    CreateEngine(env, ctx->engineObject);
    if (0 != env->ExceptionOccurred())
        goto exit;

    // Realize the engine object
    RealizeObject(env, ctx->engineObject);
    if (0 != env->ExceptionOccurred())
        goto exit;

    // Get the engine interface
    GetEngineInterface(
            env,
            ctx->engineObject,
            ctx->engineEngine);
    if (0 != env->ExceptionOccurred())
        goto exit;

    // Create output mix object
    CreateOutputMix(
            env,
            ctx->engineEngine,
            ctx->outputMixObject);
    if (0 != env->ExceptionOccurred())
        goto exit;

    // Realize output mix object
    RealizeObject(env, ctx->outputMixObject);
    if (0 != env->ExceptionOccurred())
        goto exit;

    // Initialize buffer
    InitPlayerBuffer(
            env,
            ctx->wav,
            ctx->buffer,
```

```
        ctx->bufferSize);
if (0 != env->ExceptionOccurred())
    goto exit;

// Create the buffer queue audio player object
CreateBufferQueueAudioPlayer(
        ctx->wav,
        ctx->engineEngine,
        ctx->outputMixObject,
        ctx->audioPlayerObject);
if (0 != env->ExceptionOccurred())
    goto exit;

// Realize audio player object
RealizeObject(env, ctx->audioPlayerObject);
if (0 != env->ExceptionOccurred())
    goto exit;

// Get audio player buffer queue interface
GetAudioPlayerBufferQueueInterface(
        env,
        ctx->audioPlayerObject,
        ctx->audioPlayerBufferQueue);
if (0 != env->ExceptionOccurred())
    goto exit;

// Registers the player callback
RegisterPlayerCallback(
        env,
        ctx->audioPlayerBufferQueue,
        ctx);
if (0 != env->ExceptionOccurred())
    goto exit;

// Get audio player play interface
GetAudioPlayerPlayInterface(
        env,
        ctx->audioPlayerObject,
        ctx->audioPlayerPlay);
if (0 != env->ExceptionOccurred())
    goto exit;

// Set the audio player state playing
SetAudioPlayerStatePlaying(env, ctx->audioPlayerPlay);
if (0 != env->ExceptionOccurred())
    goto exit;

// Enqueue the first buffer to start
PlayerCallback(ctx->audioPlayerBufferQueue, ctx);
```

```
exit:
    // Destroy if exception occurred
    if (0 != env->ExceptionOccurred())
        DestroyContext(ctx);
}
```

Upon building the application again with the native module implemented, you are now ready to experiment with the example application.

Running the WAVE Audio Player

In order to experiment with the OpenSL ES-based WAVE player, follow these steps to run the application.

1. Prior running the application, a sample WAVE audio file is needed. Through your web browser, download the 8000 Hz 16bit PCM sample WAVE audio file from www.nch.com.au/acm/8k16bitpcm.wav.

2. Using ADB, push the WAVE audio file to the SD card of the target device or the emulator by invoking the following command:

   ```
   adb push 8k16bitpcm.wav /sdcard/
   ```

3. You can now start the application.

4. Upon starting the application, the simple GUI will be displayed as shown in Figure 13-1.

Figure 13-1. WAVE player simple user interface

5. Click the Play button to start the player. The WAVE audio file will start playing.

Summary

In this chapter you explored the OpenSL ES native sound API that is exposed by the Android platform for native code. By using this API, native code can play and record audio without the need to communicate with the Java layer. Having such capabilities greatly improves the performance of multimedia applications.

Chapter 14

Profiling and NEON Optimization

In the previous chapters, you learned how to develop native applications on the Android platform. You explored the native APIs that are provided by both the Android platform and the Linux operating system. The following key topics will be covered on this last chapter:

  ▣ Profiling the native Android applications to identify performance bottlenecks using the GNU Profiler.

  ▣ Optimizing native applications using ARM NEON technology through compiler intrinsics.

  ▣ Enabling automatic vectorization support in the compiler to seamlessly boost the performance of native applications without changing the source code.

GNU Profiler for Measuring Performance

The GNU Profiler, also known as the gprof application, is a UNIX-based profiling tool. Through instrumentation and sampling, gprof can gather and report the absolute execution time spent in each function. The instrumentation is done through the GNU C/C++ compiler when the –pg option is supplied during compile time. Upon executing the application, the sampling data is automatically stored in the gmon.out data file, which can be processed later with the gprof tool to produce the profiling reports. Android NDK does come with the gprof tool; however, the GNU C/++ compiler toolchain that comes with the Android NDK lacks the implementation of __gnu_mcount_nc function that is necessary for timing the functions. In order to use the gprof tool with the Android NDK native projects, you will be using an open source project called Android NDK Profiler. More information about the Android NDK Profiler open source project can be found on its official site at http://code.google.com/p/android-ndk-profiler/.

Installing the Android NDK Profiler

Follow these steps to install the Android NDK Profiler native module.

1. Via your browser, go to https://github.com/cinar/android-ndk-profiler/zipball/
master to download the Android NDK Profiler native module as a ZIP
archive file.

2. Extract the content of the ZIP archive into the NDK native modules
subdirectory ANDROID_NDK_HOME/sources directory. Rename the extracted
directory cinar-android-ndk-profiler-9cdf13 to android-ndk-profiler.

The Android NDK Profiler is now ready as a native module that can be used by any Android NDK
native project. You will now learn how to enable the Android NDK Profiler for the native projects.

Enabling the Android NDK Profiler

The Android NDK Profiler should be enabled during compile time to collect profiling data. In order to
enable the Android NDK Profiler for a native Android project, follow these steps.

1. The Android.mk build script needs to be updated to statically link with the
andprof library that you installed earlier. Update your Android.mk file as
shown in Listing 14-1.

Listing 14-1. Enabling Android NDK Profiler in Android.mk Build Script

```
LOCAL_PATH := $(call my-dir)

include $(CLEAR_VARS)

LOCAL_MODULE := module

...

# Android NDK Profiler enabled
MY_ANDROID_NDK_PROFILER_ENABLED := true

# If Android NDK Profiler is enabled
ifeq ($(MY_ANDROID_NDK_PROFILER_ENABLED),true)

# Show message
$(info GNU Profiler is enabled)

# Enable the monitor functions
LOCAL_CFLAGS += -DMY_ANDROID_NDK_PROFILER_ENABLED

# Use Android NDK Profiler static library
LOCAL_STATIC_LIBRARIES += andprof
endif
```

```
...

include $(BUILD_SHARED_LIBRARY)

...

# If Android NDK Profiler is enabled
ifeq ($(MY_ANDROID_NDK_PROFILER_ENABLED),true)
# Import Android NDK Profiler library module
$(call import-module, android-ndk-profiler/jni)
endif
```

2. Upon making these changes, you can enable and disable profiling by setting
    the MY_ANDROID_NDK_PROFILER_ENABLED build system variable to true
    or false.

3. As the native code runs within a shared library, the profiling lifecycle should
    be manually managed. The Android NDK Profiler provides functions to start
    and stop collecting profiling data. These functions are declared in the prof.h
    header file, which should be included first to use these functions, as shown
    in Listing 14-2.

    Listing 14-2. Including the Android NDK Profiler Header File

```
#ifdef MY_ANDROID_NDK_PROFILER_ENABLED
#include <prof.h>
#endif
```

4. In order to start collecting profiling data, the monstartup function should be
    invoked. The monstartup function takes the name of the shared library and
    starts collecting profiling data. Depending on your application's lifecycle, as
    shown in Listing 14-3, invoke the monstartup function at the point you want
    to start collecting profiling data.

    Listing 14-3. Invoking the monstartup Function to Start Collecting Data

```
#ifdef MY_ANDROID_NDK_PROFILER_ENABLED
    // Start collecting the samples
    monstartup("libModule.so");
#endif
```

5. You can stop collecting profiling data by invoking the moncleanup function,
    as shown in Listing 14-4. Upon invoking this function, the collected profiling
    data gets saved to the SD card under the file name gmon.out.

Listing 14-4. Invoking the moncleanup Function to Stop Collecting Data

```
#ifdef MY_ANDROID_NDK_PROFILER_ENABLED
    // Store the collected data
    moncleanup();
#endif
```

> **Note**   Make sure that your application has the proper permission to write to the SD card prior profiling your application.

Analyzing gmon.out using GNU Profiler

The gmon.out profiling data file that is generated through the Android NDK Profiler can be processed through the GNU Profiler gprof tool. The tool generates a human-readable report based on provided profiling data file. Follow these steps to process the gmon.out file.

1. Pull the gmon.out profiling data file from the SD card using adb.

    ```
    adb pull /sdcard/gmon.out
    ```

2. The GNU Profiler requires the debug symbols as well as the profiling data file in order to generate a report. Invoke the arm-linux-androideabi-gprof. exe application with the debug version of the shared library and the gmon.out profiling data file.

    ```
    %ANDROID_NDK_HOME%\toolchains\arm-linux-androideabi-4.4.3\prebuilt\windows\bin\arm-linux-androideabi-gprof.exe obj\local\armeabi-v7a\libModule.so gmon.out
    ```

3. Substitute the application path with the proper location of the arm-linux-androideabi-gprof application based on your host platform. Substitute the armeabi-v7a with the proper architecture that you are profiling on.

4. The GNU Profiler will analyze the profiling data file and produce a report, as shown in Listing 14-5. The generated report has two sections, a flat profile and a call graph. Both sections contain a tabulated representation of the profiling data; a description of each measurement is also provided in the report.

    Listing 14-5. GNU Profiler Report File

    ```
    Flat profile:

    Each sample counts as 0.01 seconds.
      %   cumulative   self              self     total
     time   seconds   seconds    calls  ms/call  ms/call  name
    ```

```
99.53      2.12     2.12      361     5.87     5.87  func2
 0.47      2.13     0.01                             func1
```

...

                    Call graph (explanation follows)

granularity: each sample hit covers 2 byte(s) for 0.47% of 2.13 seconds

```
index % time   self  children    called     name
                                                 <spontaneous>
[1]     99.5   0.00     2.12                 func1 [1]
               2.12     0.00    361/361          func2 [2]
-------------------------------------------------
```

You can repeat these steps to monitor the performance of the application while implementing new functionality or optimizing the application. In the next section, you will be using the GNU Profiler while optimizing a native function through ARM NEON intrinsics.

Optimization using ARM NEON Intrinsics

In this section, you will be reusing the Bitmap renderer-based AVI Player example application that you implemented in Chapter 12. You will be expanding the example application by implementing a brightness filter in pure C code. Later in this section, you will be reimplementing the same brightness filter function using ARM NEON intrinsics to optimize its performance. You will be comparing both implementations using the GNU Profiler, as described earlier in this chapter.

Overview of ARM NEON Technology

The implementation of *single instruction, multiple data (SIMD)* technology in ARM processors is called NEON. SIMD enables data level parallelism by performing the same operation on multiple data points. SIMD technology can accelerate the performance of native applications by enabling single instruction vector operations. Multimedia applications benefit from the SIMD technology the most as they perform the same operations on a large set of data, such as video frames or audio chunks. NEON technology is available on most ARM Cortex-A series processors.

In the NEON technology, the data is organized into 64-bit D registers or 128-bit Q registers. These registers can hold 8-, 16-, 32-, and 64-bit wide data vectors, as shown in Figure 14-1.

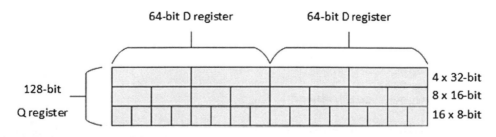

Figure 14-1. NEON registers and data types

NEON technology also provides a set of instructions to perform operations on these data vectors. More information on NEON technology as well as the supported instructions can be found in ARM's "Introducing NEON Development Article" at `http://infocenter.arm.com/help/index.jsp?topic=/com.arm.doc.dht0002a/ch01s04s03.html`.

Adding a Brightness Filter to AVI Player

Follow these steps to add the brightness filter.

1. Using the Project Explorer, create a new C/C++ header file under the `jni` subdirectory.

2. Name the C/C++ header file as `BrightnessFilter.h` and update its content with the code in Listing 14-6.

   Listing 14-6. Content of BrightnessFilter.h Header File

   ```
   #pragma once

   /**
    * Extract the interleaved components. RGB565 color
    * space has a total of 16-bits with 5-bits red,
    * 6-bits green, and 5-bits blue.
    */
   void brightnessFilter(
           unsigned short* pixels,
           long count,
           unsigned char brightness);
   ```

3. Create a new C/C++ source file with the name `BrightnessFilter.cpp` and update its content as shown in Listing 14-7. The `brightnessFilter` function simply dispatches the call to `genericBrightnessFilter` function, which is your plain C brightness filter implementation. It takes an array of 16-bit pixels formatted using RGB656 color space. It decomposes the color components into three 8-bit values and increments them based on the given brightness value. It adjusts each value based on its range and combines them together into a 16-bit pixel in RGB565 color-space.

   Listing 14-7. Content of BrightnessFilter.cpp Source File

   ```
   #include "BrightnessFilter.h"

   static void genericBrightnessFilter(
           unsigned short* pixels,
           long count,
           unsigned char brightness)
   {
       const unsigned char MAX_RB = 0xF8;
       const unsigned char MAX_G = 0xFC;
   ```

```
        unsigned short r, g, b;

        for (long i = 0; i < count; i++)
        {
            // Decompose colors
            r = (pixels[i] >> 8) & MAX_RB;
            g = (pixels[i] >> 3) & MAX_G;
            b = (pixels[i] << 3) & MAX_RB;

            // Brightness increment
            r += brightness;
            g += brightness;
            b += brightness;

            // Make sure that components are in range
            r = (r > MAX_RB) ? MAX_RB : r;
            g = (g > MAX_G) ? MAX_G : g;
            b = (b > MAX_RB) ? MAX_RB : b;

            // Set pixel
            pixels[i] = (r << 8);
            pixels[i] |= (g << 3);
            pixels[i] |= (b >> 3);
        }
    }

    void brightnessFilter(
            unsigned short* pixels,
            long count,
            unsigned char brightness)
    {
        genericBrightnessFilter(pixels, count, brightness);
    }
```

4. The Brightness Filter needs to be invoked for each AVI video frame
    prior to rendering. In order to do so, open the com_apress_aviplayer_
    BitmapPlayerActivity.cpp source file.

5. Add the BrightnessFilter.h header file to the list of includes, as shown in
    Listing 14-8.

Listing 14-8. Adding the BrightnessFilter.h Header File to BitmapRenderer

```
extern "C" {
#include <avilib.h>
}

#include <android/bitmap.h>
```

```
#include "BrightnessFilter.h"
#include "Common.h"
#include "com_apress_aviplayer_BitmapPlayerActivity.h"
```

...

6. Update the `renderer` function to invoke the `brightnessFilter` function for every frame, as shown in Listing 14-9.

Listing 14-9. Invoking brightnessFilter Function for Each Frame

```
jboolean Java_com_apress_aviplayer_BitmapPlayerActivity_render(
        JNIEnv* env,
        jclass clazz,
        jlong avi,
        jobject bitmap)
{
    ...

    // Read AVI frame bytes to bitmap
    frameSize = AVI_read_frame((avi_t*) avi, frameBuffer, &keyFrame);

    // Apply the brigthness filter
    brightnessFilter((unsigned short*) frameBuffer, frameSize/2, 1);

    ...
}
```

7. Add the `BrightnessFilter.cpp` source file the `Android.mk` build script, as shown in Listing 14-10.

Listing 14-10. Adding BrightnessFilter.cpp Source File to Android.mk

```
LOCAL_PATH := $(call my-dir)

include $(CLEAR_VARS)

LOCAL_MODULE    := AVIPlayer
LOCAL_SRC_FILES := \
    Common.cpp \
    com_apress_aviplayer_AbstractPlayerActivity.cpp \
    com_apress_aviplayer_BitmapPlayerActivity.cpp

LOCAL_SRC_FILES += BrightnessFilter.cpp

# Use AVILib static library
LOCAL_STATIC_LIBRARIES += avilib_static
```

8. Now the Brightness Filter is integrated into the AVI Player application. Prior starting the application, you will need to enable the GNU Profiler.

Enabling the Android NDK Profiler for AVI Player

As explained earlier in this chapter, the GNU Profiler needs to be enabled during compile time in order to collect profiling data. Follow these steps to enable the GNU Profiler for the Bitmap renderer AVI Player.

1. Update the Android.mk build script to enable the GNU Profiler.

2. Using the Project Explorer, expand the jni subdirectory, and open the com_apress_aviplayer_AbstractPlayerActivity.cpp source file.

3. Update the code to invoke the Android NDK Profiler functions, as shown in Listing 14-11. The profiling will start as soon as the AVI open gets called and finalizes when the AVI file gets closed. This provides the profiling data during the AVI processing.

Listing 14-11. Invoking Profiler Functions from AbstractPlayerActivity

```
extern "C" {
#include <avilib.h>
}

#ifdef MY_ANDROID_NDK_PROFILER_ENABLED
#include <prof.h>
#endif

...

jlong Java_com_apress_aviplayer_AbstractPlayerActivity_open(
        JNIEnv* env,
        jclass clazz,
        jstring fileName)
{
    avi_t* avi = 0;

#ifdef MY_ANDROID_NDK_PROFILER_ENABLED
    // Start collecting the samples
    monstartup("libAVIPlayer.so");
#endif

    ...
}

...

void Java_com_apress_aviplayer_AbstractPlayerActivity_close(
        JNIEnv* env,
        jclass clazz,
        jlong avi)
{
    AVI_close((avi_t*) avi);
```

```
#ifdef MY_ANDROID_NDK_PROFILER_ENABLED
    // Store the collected data
    moncleanup();
#endif
}
```

4. For the Android NDK Profiler to store the profiling data file on the SD card, the proper permission needs to be added to the manifest file. Using Project Explorer, open up the AndroidManifest.xml and modify it as shown in Listing 14-12.

Listing 14-12. Adding Writing Permission to External Storage

```
<manifest xmlns:android="http://schemas.android.com/apk/res/android"
    package="com.apress.aviplayer"
    android:versionCode="1"
    android:versionName="1.0" >

    ...

    <uses-permission
        android:name="android.permission.WRITE_EXTERNAL_STORAGE"/>

    ...

</manifest>
```

The GNU Profiler is now enabled for the AVI Player project. You can now start the application to collect profiling data.

Profiling the AVI Player

Follow these steps to profile the Bitmap renderer AVI Player application.

1. Start the application an actual Android device.

2. Start AVI file playback using the Bitmap renderer.

3. Wait until the AVI playback ends.

4. Click the hard back key on the device.

5. As explained earlier in this chapter, pull the gmon.out profiling data from the device.

6. Using the gprof tool, generate a report, as shown in Listing 14-13.

Listing 14-13. Profiling Report for Generic Brightness Filter

```
Flat profile:

Each sample counts as 0.01 seconds.
  %   cumulative   self              self     total
 time   seconds   seconds    calls  ms/call  ms/call  name
100.00     2.62      2.62      361     7.26     7.26  brightnessFilter(unsigned short*,
long, unsigned char)
```

Based on this report, the brightnessFilter function, which is using the genericBrightnessFilter function, took 7.26 millisecond to process each frame and took 2.62 seconds overall to process all frames.

Optimizing the Brightness Filter using NEON Intrinsics

You will now optimize the genericBirghtnessFilter function using the ARM NEON intrinsics.

1.   Using the Project Explorer, go to the jni subdirectory.

2.   Open up the BrightnessFilter.cpp source file and add the NEON-optimized neonBrightnessFilter function, as shown in Listing 14-14. Compared to the generic brightness filter implementation, the ARM NEON-optimized brightness filter operates on 8 pixels at a time, instead of only processing 1 pixel.

Listing 14-14. Content of Updated BrightnessFilter.cpp Source File

```cpp
#include "BrightnessFilter.h"

#ifdef __ARM_NEON__

#include <cpu-features.h>

#include <arm_neon.h>

static void neonBrightnessFilter(
        unsigned short* pixels,
        long count,
        unsigned char brightness)
{
    const unsigned char MAX_RB = 0xF8;
    const unsigned char MAX_G = 0xFC;

    uint8x8_t maxRb = vmov_n_u8(MAX_RB);
    uint8x8_t maxG = vmov_n_u8(MAX_G);
    uint8x8_t increment = vmov_n_u8(brightness);

    for (long i = 0; i < count; i += 8)
    {
        // Load 8 16-bit pixels
        uint16x8_t rgb = vld1q_u16(&pixels[i]);
```

```
        // r = (pixels[i] >> 8) & MAX_RB;
        uint8x8_t r = vshrn_n_u16(rgb, 8);
        r = vand_u8(r, maxRb);

        // g = (pixels[i] >> 3) & MAX_G;
        uint8x8_t g = vshrn_n_u16(rgb, 3);
        g = vand_u8(g, maxG);

        // b = (pixels[i] << 3) & MAX_RB;
        uint8x8_t b = vmovn_u16(rgb);
        b = vshl_n_u8(b, 3);
        b = vand_u8(b, maxRb);

        // r += brightness;
        r = vadd_u8(r, increment);

        // g += brightness;
        g = vadd_u8(g, increment);

        // b += brightness;
        b = vadd_u8(b, increment);

        // r = (r > MAX_RB) ? MAX_RB : r;
        r = vmin_u8(r, maxRb);

        // g = (g > MAX_G) ? MAX_G : g;
        g = vmin_u8(g, maxG);

        // b = (b > MAX_RB) ? MAX_RB : b;
        b = vmin_u8(b, maxRb);

        // pixels[i] = (r << 8);
        rgb = vshll_n_u8(r, 8);

        // pixels[i] |= (g << 3);
        uint16x8_t g16 = vshll_n_u8(g, 8);
        rgb = vsriq_n_u16(rgb, g16, 5);

        // pixels[i] |= (b >> 3);
        uint16x8_t b16 = vshll_n_u8(b, 8);
        rgb = vsriq_n_u16(rgb, b16, 11);

        // Store 8 16-bit pixels
        vst1q_u16(&pixels[i], rgb);
    }
}

#endif
```

```
static void genericBrightnessFilter(
        unsigned short* pixels,
        long count,
        unsigned char brightness)
```

3. The brightnessFilter function needs to be updated as well in order to
   invoke the NEON-optimized function when applicable. ARM NEON support is
   only available when targeting armeabi-v7a ABI. However, note that not every
   ARM-v7 based device supports NEON instructions. The native applications
   are expected to detect NEON support during runtime on ARM-v7 based
   devices. In order to address this issue, the Android NDK comes with the
   CPU Features native import module. This module allows detection of CPU
   type as well as the features supported by the CPU at runtime. Update the
   brightnessFilter function as shown in Listing 14-15.

> **Note** Not every ARM-v7 based device supports ARM NEON instructions. You should always use the CPU
> Features import module to detect the NEON support during runtime prior calling any NEON optimized function.

Listing 14-15. Updated brightnessFilter Function Calling NEON Optimized Function

```
void brightnessFilter(
        unsigned short* pixels,
        long count,
        unsigned char brightness)
{
#ifdef __ARM_NEON__

    // Get the CPU family
    AndroidCpuFamily cpuFamily = android_getCpuFamily();

    // Get the CPU features
    uint64_t cpuFeatures = android_getCpuFeatures();

    // Use NEON optimized function only on ARM CPUs with NEON support
    if ((ANDROID_CPU_FAMILY_ARM == cpuFamily)
            && ((ANDROID_CPU_ARM_FEATURE_NEON & cpuFeatures) != 0))
    {
        // Invoke the NEON optimized brightness filter
        neonBrightnessFilter(pixels, count, brightness);
    }
    else
```

```
        {
#endif
        // Invoke the generic brightness filter
        genericBrightnessFilter(pixels, count, brightness);
#ifdef __ARM_NEON__
        }
#endif
}
```

4. Open the Android.mk build script and update it as shown in Listing 14-16.
    This allows compiling the proper flavor of the brightnessFilter function
    during compile time. For the ARMv7a target platform, the NEON-enhanced
    version of brightnessFilter will be used. For all other platforms, the generic
    implementation of the brightnessFilter will be used.

Listing 14-16. The NEON Version of brightnessFilter Added to Android.mk

```
LOCAL_PATH := $(call my-dir)

include $(CLEAR_VARS)

LOCAL_MODULE    := AVIPlayer
LOCAL_SRC_FILES := \
    Common.cpp \
    com_apress_aviplayer_AbstractPlayerActivity.cpp \
    com_apress_aviplayer_BitmapPlayerActivity.cpp

# Add NEON optimized version on armeabi-v7a
ifeq ($(TARGET_ARCH_ABI),armeabi-v7a)
    LOCAL_SRC_FILES += BrightnessFilter.cpp.neon
    LOCAL_STATIC_LIBRARIES += cpufeatures
else
    LOCAL_SRC_FILES += BrightnessFilter.cpp
endif

# Use AVILib static library
LOCAL_STATIC_LIBRARIES += avilib_static

# Android NDK Profiler enabled
MY_ANDROID_NDK_PROFILER_ENABLED := true

# If Android NDK Profiler is enabled
ifeq ($(MY_ANDROID_NDK_PROFILER_ENABLED),true)

# Show message
$(info GNU Profiler is enabled)

# Enable the monitor functions
LOCAL_CFLAGS += -DMY_ANDROID_NDK_PROFILER_ENABLED
```

```
# Use Android NDK Profiler static library
LOCAL_STATIC_LIBRARIES += andprof
endif

# Link with JNI graphics
LOCAL_LDLIBS += -ljnigraphics

include $(BUILD_SHARED_LIBRARY)

# Import AVILib library module
$(call import-module, transcode-1.1.5/avilib)

# If Android NDK Profiler is enabled
ifdef MY_ANDROID_NDK_PROFILER_ENABLED
# Import Android NDK Profiler library module
$(call import-module, android-ndk-profiler/jni)
endif

# Add CPU features on armeabi-v7a
ifeq ($(TARGET_ARCH_ABI),armeabi-v7a)
# Import Android CPU features
$(call import-module, android/cpufeatures)
endif
```

> **Note** You may have already noticed the .neon suffix that is appended to the BrightnessFilter.cpp source file. This suffix tells the Android NDK build system that this source file needs to be compiled with ARM NEON support.

5. Create a new file with the name of Application.mk and include the following content:

    ```
    APP_ABI := armeabi-v7a
    ```

6. As you will be profiling the NEON-enhanced brightnessFilter, having armeabi-v7a ABI as the single target platform is better.

7. Repeat the same profiling steps. The report generated by the GNU Profiler will be similar to Listing 14-17.

    Listing 14-17. Profiling Report for NEON-optimized Brightness Filter

    ```
    Flat profile:

    Each sample counts as 0.01 seconds.
      %   cumulative   self              self     total
     time   seconds   seconds    calls  ms/call  ms/call  name
    100.00     0.50      0.50      361     1.39     1.39  brightnessFilter(unsigned short*,
    long, unsigned char)
    ```

Based on this report, the brightnessFilter function, which is using the neonBrightnessFilter function, took 1.39 millisecond to process each frame and took 0.50 seconds overall to process all frames. Compared to the generic implementation, the NEON-optimized function is 5 times faster.

Automatic Vectorization

As you saw in the previous section, using the ARM NEON support can have a great impact on application performance; however, it requires fluency in either the ARM assembly language or NEON intrinsics constructs. NEON is an ARM-specific flavor of SIMD; to support platforms other than ARM, such as Intel or MIPS, you will need to also provide implementations of your optimized functions for other SIMD flavors such as Intel SSE or MIPS MDMX.

Assembly language or intrinsics are not the only ways of benefitting from SIMD support. In most cases, the GNU C/C++ compiler can also automatically optimize your application to benefit from the available SIMD engine without having you write a single line of assembly code or using intrinsics. This process is known as *automatic vectorization*.

Enabling Automatic Vectorization

In order to enable automatic vectorization, follow these steps:

1. Open the Application.mk build script, and make sure that APP_ABI contains armeabi-v7a.

   ```
   APP_ABI := armeabi armeabi-v7a
   ```

2. Open the Android.mk build script, and add the –ftree-vectorize argument to LOCAL_CFLAGS build system variable, as shown in Listing 14-18.

   Listing 14-18. Enabling GNU C/C++ Compiler Automatic Vectorization

   ```
   LOCAL_PATH := $(call my-dir)

   include $(CLEAR_VARS)

   LOCAL_MODULE := module

   ...

   LOCAL_CFLAGS += -ftree-vectorize

   ...

   include $(BUILD_SHARED_LIBRARY)
   ```

3. Make sure that the source files are getting compiled with ARM NEON support, as shown in Listing 14-19.

Listing 14-19. Enabling ARM NEON Support for All Source Files

```
LOCAL_PATH := $(call my-dir)

include $(CLEAR_VARS)

...

# Add ARM NEON support to all source files
ifeq ($(TARGET_ARCH_ABI),armeabi-v7a)
LOCAL_ARM_NEON := true
endif

...

include $(BUILD_SHARED_LIBRARY)
```

Upon making these changes, the GNU C/C++ compiler will try to automatically vectorize the native application to benefit from the ARM NEON support.

The C/C++ language does not provide any mechanism to specify parallelizing behavior. You may have to give GNU C/C++ compiler additional hints about where it is safe to have the code automatically vectorized. For a list of automatically vectorizable loops, please consult the "Auto-vectorization in GCC" documentation at http://gcc.gnu.org/projects/tree-ssa/vectorization.html.

Troubleshooting Automatic Vectorization

When troubleshooting automatic vectorization issues, you can request more verbose output from the GNU C/C++ compiler by adding the –ftree-vectorizer-verbose=2 argument to the LOCAL_CFLAGS build system variable.

```
LOCAL_CFLAGS += -ftree-vectorizer-verbose=2
```

Once this argument is specified, the GNU C/C++ compiler will produce a verbose output, as shown in Listing 14-20, to give you hints on how the compiler is treating each loop in your application.

Listing 14-20. Verbose Output on Automatic Vectorization

```
Cygwin        : Generating dependency file converter script
Compile thumb : Vectorization <= Vectorization.c

jni/Vectorization.c:9: note: not vectorized: complicated access pattern.
jni/Vectorization.c:4: note: vectorized 0 loops in function.

jni/Vectorization.c:28: note: LOOP VECTORIZED.
jni/Vectorization.c:22: note: LOOP VECTORIZED.
jni/Vectorization.c:18: note: vectorized 2 loops in function.
Executable    : Vectorization
Install       : Vectorization => libs/armeabi-v7a/Vectorization
```

Based on the verbose output from the compiler, you can tune the source code to provide proper hints to the compiler about each loop in your application.

Summary

In this chapter, you learned how to profile your native Android applications using the Android NDK Profiler library and the GNU Profiler application. You also explored how to optimize the performance of your native application using the ARM NEON technology.

Index

▓L

Lightning Source UK Ltd.
Milton Keynes UK
UKOW020613111212

203435UK00007B/333/P